Teaching Kids with Learning Difficulties in the Regular Classroom

Ways to Challenge & Motivate Struggling Students to Achieve Proficiency with Required Standards

Revised and Updated Edition

Susan Winebrenner

Edited by Pamela Espeland

free spirit
PUBLISHING®

Library of Congress has cataloged the previous edition as:
Winebrenner, Susan
    Teaching kids with learning difficulties in the regular classroom : ways to challenge and motivate struggling students to achieve proficiency with required standards / Susan Winebrenner ; edited by Pamela Espeland.
        p. cm.
    Includes index.
    ISBN-13: 978-1-57542-207-7
    ISBN-10: 1-57542-207-7
    1. Learning disabled children—Education—United States. 2. Mainstreaming in education—United States. I. Espeland, Pamela II. Title.
LC4705.W56 2005
371.9'46—dc22   2005025103

eBook ISBN: 978-1-57542-697-6

Free Spirit Publishing does not have control over or assume responsibility for author or third-party websites and their content. At the time of this book's publication, all facts and figures cited within are the most current available. All telephone numbers, addresses, and website URLs are accurate and active; all publications, organizations, websites, and other resources exist as described in this book; and all have been verified as of June 2013. If you find an error or believe that a resource listed here is not as described, please contact Free Spirit Publishing. Parents, teachers, and other adults: We strongly urge you to monitor children's use of the Internet.

Interior design by Percolator

10 9 8 7
Printed in the United States of America

Free Spirit Publishing Inc.
Minneapolis, MN
(612) 338-2068
help4kids@freespirit.com
www.freespirit.com

Printed on recycled paper
including 30%
post-consumer waste

As a member of the Green Press Initiative, Free Spirit Publishing is committed to the three Rs: Reduce, Reuse, Recycle. Whenever possible, we print our books on recycled paper containing a minimum of 30% post-consumer waste. At Free Spirit it's our goal to nurture not only children, but nature too!

green press
INITIATIVE

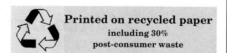

Free Spirit offers competitive pricing.
Contact edsales@freespirit.com for pricing information on multiple quantity purchases.

Dedication

To all of the wonderful educators who have so generously contributed to my bag of tricks over the years, a sincere thank you. To my children, Stacy, Kari, Melinda, and Diana, and my six grandchildren, who always model for me the diversity of learning styles and continuously help me understand the importance of accommodating all types of learners in the classroom. To my beloved uncle, Paul Ginsberg, who throughout his exemplary lifetime, has modeled and explained all I ever needed to understand about respecting individual differences.

And to my husband, Joe, who keeps me calm and sane most of the time.

Acknowledgments

In addition to all of the fine educators acknowledged throughout this book, special thanks go to:

Brenda Goffen, for her patient and expert service as a "special education" consultant;

Lorelei Goldman, for her expertise on helping students with serious behavior problems;

Emmy Bates and Helen Cox, for their networking assistance for the Brain Gym section;

Frank Boulee, for helping me understand the real world of persons with learning disabilities;

Robin Goffen, for her input on students with hearing impairments;

Dr. Patricia Cunningham, for helping me understand her model of teaching reading;

Dr. Kenneth Dunn, for allowing me to use his words: "If students cannot learn the way we teach them, then we must teach them the way they learn";

Dr. Sylvia Rimm, director of the Family Achievement Clinic in Cleveland, Ohio, for helping me understand the similarities between all types of underachievers;

Stephanie Niess, my trusty assistant, who consistently calms my computer and makes it behave as it should;

Keran Hoover, for sharing her deep knowledge of current technology;

Dr. Martin Haberman, for granting me permission to share his work about Star Teachers of Children in Poverty;

Dr. Steve Landfried, for teaching me how to avoid the dangers of enabling;

Dr. Dina Brulles, for enlightening me about English Language Learners;

Edward Ford, for giving me carte blanche to use any of his material from his books to accurately explain his Responsible Thinking Process model to my readers;

Pamela Espeland, my wonderful editor, who taught me how to write; and

Judy Galbraith, founder and president of Free Spirit Publishing; brilliant businesswoman, good friend, and the best marketer in the world! Thank you for all the fabulous opportunities our association has brought to me.

Contents

List of Reproducible Pages

You may download these forms at freespirit.com/teaching-LD-forms. Use the password 2achieve.

Introduction

Has there ever been a more challenging time to be a teacher? From the relentless pressure to make sure that all students score at the proficient level on high-stakes tests, to the rigorous requirements from the legislation known as No Child Left Behind, teachers and principals are being held more accountable than ever before in the history of public education. Some of you remember when the special learning needs of struggling students were met, to a great extent, outside the regular classroom. These days, we have students at every level of performance, from those who do not speak any English to those who may be gifted. And it is perfectly obvious that there are not enough special teachers available to help. How is one teacher supposed to handle it all?

In order to be a successful teacher for students who are struggling to learn, you need to understand that these kids are not necessarily less intelligent or less capable than the successful students. Many are simply *less fortunate* because successful students have enjoyed a match between the way their brain processes information and the skills that are needed to master typical school tasks. By and large, unsuccessful students have not. Although many of these kids have been labeled "learning disabled," a more accurate description is that they are learning *strategy* disabled. Many have never been taught strategies that are compatible with the way they think and learn. Once we teach them the appropriate techniques, their learning problems diminish significantly.

When the right methods are used, it is no longer necessary to water down content or repeat it endlessly. For example, for many years those students who failed to learn to read with a phonics-oriented program were given remedial phonics. The assumption was that everyone had to understand phonics to be able to read. When we taught outlining, we assumed that all kids should learn it the right way. Now that we understand more about how the human brain functions, we know that rather than remediate, we must work to make matches happen between the content to be learned and the learning styles of our students. When the right matches are found, the message we send to struggling students is, "You can be a successful student!"

In addition to the obvious benefits of learning how to expect and get better achievement from students with learning difficulties, there are other advantages to discovering how your students learn and teaching different kids in different ways. Differentiation shows your students that being different is just fine—something to notice and honor rather than something to hide. When kids learn how to stand up for themselves by discovering and using their predominant learning styles in their schoolwork, the incidents of bullying in any form can actually decrease. It's pretty hard to tease or ridicule those who are proud of their individuality.

Another challenge that teachers often face is what to do when the powers that be insist that you follow an adopted program by using every included component, and not use outside materials or strategies in any way. Pressured to prepare all students to meet state standards, we sometimes conclude that there is no time available to teach the way we really want to teach. Most teachers would prefer to teach for understanding, not just coverage. Many teachers have given up many of their favorite topics and activities in favor of more traditional approaches, because those seem to be what is expected. Some teachers are actually grieving the loss of what they perceive as their autonomy in the classroom.

And yet some teachers are finding ways to teach through experiential and meaningful activities that are linked to the expected standards. Many wonderful lesson plans are available from dozens of Web sites. Just take some time to browse and see what you can find so you don't have to always start from scratch when planning new lessons for your students.

I remember hearing a story about a sixth-grade teacher whose kids always moaned that they hated to write. She made a long list of the writing standards expected for the year, tacked copies of the list onto the board, and asked a student to throw a piece of clay so that it would stick to any one of the expected learning outcomes.

The clay chose the standard that said: "The student will write a business letter, using the correct form, content, and punctuation." So the class brainstormed all the reasons people have for writing a business letter. The students could all relate to letters of complaint. The class brainstormed again, this time to make a list of things they wanted to complain about. Many students were angry over the poor quality of the paper tablets sold at the school bookstore. The entire tablet fell apart when they tore off a page or two. The class decided to write a business letter of complaint to the company that made the tablets. The company wrote back and challenged the kids to come up with a better way to make the product. The kids did some research, wrote reports, and presented their ideas to their principal. A formal proposal was sent back to the company.

At the end of the four-week experience, the teacher put the writing standards back on the board and had teams of kids use markers to cross out those that had accidentally been covered during their business-letter experience. More than 20 percent of the standards had been included in this experience, including proper grammar, punctuation, and format, as well as standards associated with public speaking.

The moral of the story is that it is always okay to use real-life, meaningful, relevant experiences to teach required standards. Teachers all over the country continue to teach through activities their students will remember forever, along with the required standards. Classroom simulations such as running a business, raising money for charities and other relief funds, writing newspapers as they would have appeared in a certain historical period, having school elections for a student council and comparing that process to national elections—all these and more teach standards in memorable ways. I truly believe there is no reason to give up on your favorite learning experiences. The only thing you must document is that your students have learned the standards. How that happens is still up to you, most of the time.

Never lose sight of the fact that a crucial 21st-century job survival skill is a positive attitude toward being retrained, which is a lot like going back to school. Every student you are teaching will have to change careers numerous times before he or she retires. People who will be successful at doing this are those who enjoyed their formal schooling days, and therefore look forward to become students again.

In my workshops with teachers, I use the following Differentiation Rationale for Students with Learning Dif-ficulties. I believe that it summarizes the intent of all the strategies in this book.

- All students should experience learning at their own personal challenge level every day.

- High self-esteem, and therefore learning productivity, comes from being successful with tasks the student perceived would be difficult.

- When students feel they have some control over what happens in school, they are more likely to be productive. This feeling of control comes from opportunities to make choices. Teachers can make those available by offering several options about the type of expected task and/or product.

- When learning styles are attended to, and curriculum is challenging and meaningful, students are more likely to choose appropriate behaviors.

- The first place an educator should look for explanations of inappropriate behavior is the curriculum! Is it appropriately challenging? Does it incorporate students' interests wherever possible? Does the student understand why it must be learned? Does it allow access through students' learning style strengths?

- All students must feel they are respected for who they are and what they need in order to be successful learners.

This book presents a wide variety of teaching methods so you can find the right match for every student in your classroom. These practical, easy-to-use strategies, techniques, and activities have been collected from a variety of sources. Actually, that is what makes this book unique! You don't have to do your own research about what works to teach kids how to read, or how to remember their number facts. I've done the research for you, and this book contains the most effective methods I have found for helping students with learning problems become much more successful learners. Simply diagnose the learning weakness a particular student exhibits, find the right chapter in this book, and match the strategies to the student. Significant improvement will take place before your eyes. Using these strategies, you can help bring the learner up to the level of the content rather than lowering expectations for some students.

Throughout this book, there is an emphasis on the belief that high self-esteem can only be achieved through hard work and genuine accomplishments. As author and educator Dr. Sylvia Rimm has said, "The surest path to high self-esteem is to be successful at something one perceived would be difficult." (Yes, I borrowed this idea for my Differentiation Rationale!) Dr. Rimm goes on to say, "Each time we steal a student's struggle, we steal the opportunity for them to build self-confidence. They must learn to do difficult things to feel good about themselves."

There is nothing quite so powerful as our ability to communicate high expectations for success to our students. Over the years, many studies have shown that we get what we expect! For example, the Pygmalion study in the 1960s demonstrated that kids could improve dramatically if their teachers were told they would do extremely well in a given year.* A 1969 report by the President's Committee on Mental Retardation found that some children may function in the retarded range while they are in school for six hours a day, but behave more like normal people once they return home.**

We really don't know for certain how many students we've labeled "slow" or "remedial" over the years have actually been experiencing some type of learning difficulty that can be addressed with the right methods. We don't know if we've properly matched labels to kids or if we have over-labeled. None of that matters, since the strategies in this book will potentially benefit *all* students who find learning difficult.

I do not attempt to match specific strategies to each specific category of special education student. The strategies are generic and are presented as a menu of options for you to use as you empower *all* kids to become successful in your classroom. They are just as effective with students of poverty and with English Language Learners as they are with kids who have been diagnosed with learning disabilities. The best news is that when you find strategies that work with your struggling students, you may observe that they are effective with other kids as well.

You have nothing to lose and everything to gain by trying some of the methods described in this book. You know that your struggling students will continue to struggle if they don't get the help they need. When you find and use strategies that work, teaching and learning become mutually successful experiences.

I promise you that these methods will work for you and your students. They have been used by me and by many other classroom teachers with success. As a staff development specialist, I have presented these concepts to thousands of teachers of all grade levels. The response has been overwhelmingly positive, and many teachers have told me that they wish they had known about these strategies throughout their entire teaching career.

This book will help you become an even better teacher than you already are. All you have to remember is this: *If students are not learning the way you are teaching them, find and use a more appropriate method so you can teach them the way they learn.*

---

* Rosenthal, Robert, and Lenore Jacobson. *Pygmalion in the Classroom: Teacher Expectation and Pupils' Intellectual Development.* Norwalk, CT: Crown House Publishing, 2003.

** The President's Committee on Mental Retardation (PCMR). "The Six-Hour Retarded Child." Washington, DC: U.S. Government Printing Office, 1969.

Here's what you'll find in this book:

- Chapter 1 contains tips for helping all students feel welcome in your classroom, since kids who feel like outsiders are potential candidates for misbehavior and underachievement.

- Chapter 2 presents tried-and-true ways to get all students involved in all learning activities.

- Chapter 3 describes various types of learning difficulties and offers suggestions for intervening with some of those problems.

- Chapter 4 helps you understand and appreciate how to enhance the learning success of your struggling students by matching your teaching to their learning styles.

- Chapter 5 presents state-of-the-art ideas about how learning happens and how teachers can create learning success for all students.

- Chapters 6 through 8 suggest a variety of methods you can use to improve reading and writing success for your struggling students. These methods are compatible with any others you are currently using to teach reading and the language arts.

- Chapters 9 and 10 focus on reading and learning in the other content areas, including science, social studies, and mathematics.

- Chapter 11 describes ways to help your students improve their organizational skills and use effective methods to study what they need to learn.

- Chapter 12 describes several methods that can help you move beyond traditional assessment and get a better picture of what your struggling students are really learning.

- Chapter 13 focuses on behavior issues. Because students with learning problems often seem to have behavior problems, you might be surprised to find this chapter so near the end of the book. In fact, when students' learning styles are attended to and curriculum is appropriately challenging, behavior issues become less worrisome because misbehavior declines!

- Chapter 14 offers suggestions for involving parents as part of the learning team. It describes several ways to reach out to parents—including those who don't seem interested—and make them welcome at school.

Each chapter also includes a Questions and Answers section in which I respond to the questions most frequently asked when I present this content in a workshop format. If you have questions that are not addressed in this book, be sure to write to me so I can respond, either in future editions or by personal communication. Write to me c/o Free Spirit Publishing, 217 Fifth Avenue North, Suite 200, Minneapolis, MN 55401-1299. Send me email at help4kids@freespirit.com, or through the Free Spirit Web site, www.freespirit.com.

Finally, each chapter concludes with a "References and Resources" section that points you toward additional sources of information and materials. These are the best books, articles, videos, organizations, associations, programs, and resources I have found, and I encourage you to seek them out.

The accompanying digital content includes all of the reproducible forms in this book as well as additional content organization charts from my work in the field. You may download the content at freespirit.com/teaching-LD-forms (use the password 2achieve). You can print them out when you need them and customize most for your classroom and students.

I believe that this book can make teaching much more pleasant and effective for you, and learning much more enjoyable and successful for your students with learning difficulties. I'd love to receive any feedback from you that you care to share with me.

Let's get started.

Susan Winebrenner

REFERENCES AND RESOURCES

Good, Thomas L. "Teacher Expectations and Student Perceptions." *Educational Leadership* (February 1987), pp. 415–422.

Olweus Bullying Prevention Program (www.clemson.edu/olweus). A comprehensive, school-wide program designed for use in elementary, middle, or junior high schools. Contact Marlene Snyder, Ph.D., (864) 710-4562.

The President's Committee for People with Intellectual Disabilities (PCPID) (www.acf.hhs.gov). Formerly the President's Committee on Mental Retardation (PCMR). (202) 690-6590.

Rimm, Sylvia. *How to Parent So Children Will Learn.* New York: Crown Books, 1996.

Rosenthal, Robert, and Elisha Bahad. "Pygmalion in the Gymnasium." *Educational Leadership* (September 1985), pp. 87–90.

Rosenthal, Robert, and Lenore Jacobson. *Pygmalion in the Classroom: Teacher Expectation and Pupil's Intellectual Development.* Norwalk, CT: Crown House Publishing, 2003.

CHAPTER 1

Making All Students Welcome in Your Classroom

Do you remember how you felt on the first day of a new school year? Can you recall the questions that were spinning through your brain? *Will the teacher be nice to me? Will the other kids like me? Will anyone want to sit with me at lunch? What if the work is too hard?* If you can relate to those concerns, you can easily understand how most of your students feel as they enter your class.

Students with learning difficulties have the same worries, greatly magnified. Anything you can do to purposefully provide experiences that will help students feel welcome and cared about in your classroom will go a long way toward providing a supportive learning environment for all kids.

Welcoming Activities

Say Hello to Someone Who . . . *

On the first day of class, students should participate in activities that will help them learn about each other. "Say Hello to Someone Who . . . " is an enjoyable way to share and discover interesting information. Afterward, all students will know the names of several other students. Recognition in the halls, other classes, the cafeteria, and on the playground helps to make each student feel like part of a group.

---

* This activity and the handout on page 6 are adapted from *Patterns for Thinking, Patterns for Transfer* by Robin Fogarty and James Bellanca. © 1991 IRI Skylight Publishing, Inc., Palatine, IL. Used with permission.

Give each student a copy of the "Say Hello to Someone Who . . . " handout (page 6). Allow 15 minutes for students to circulate around the room and collect signatures from people who match descriptions on their handout. (*Examples:* If Emilio stayed in town all summer, he's a match and signs his name in that box. If Sarah went on a trip, she signs her name there.) Explain that each student can sign another student's handout only once, and no student can sign his or her own handout. Everyone should try to collect as many signatures as they can. After one student has signed another student's handout, both will say, "Hello, [NAME], glad to meet you!"

Getting to Know You

Whenever you ask students to work in groups, give them time to get to know each other. Here's one good way to do this.

Distribute stick-on nametags. Have students write their name in the center. Then have them write answers to the following questions in each of the four corners (or substitute your own questions):

■ In the top left corner: "Where were you born?"

■ In the top right corner: "What is your favorite food?"

■ In the bottom left corner: "What is your favorite thing to do?"

■ In the bottom right corner: "What is something you are very proud of?"

Say Hello to Someone Who...

Stayed in town all summer	Goes to ball games	Went on a trip
Likes cheeseburgers	Has more than three brothers or sisters	Speaks more than one language
Has been to Disney World	Can kick or throw a ball really far	Is new to our school
Can play a musical instrument	Wears glasses or contact lenses	Likes to read

After students complete their nametags and put them on, have them pair off, interview a partner, then introduce their partner to a group of four or six other students.

```
NEW ORLEANS                    CHEESEBURGERS


              JOSHUA


RIDE MY BIKE            EARNED THE
                       MONEY FOR MY BIKE
```

The Name Game

Have the students sit in a circle. Explain that one student will say his first name, then briefly describe one thing he enjoys doing (*example:* "Bobby. Shooting hoops"). Going around the circle, the next student will repeat what was just said, then add her first name and something she enjoys doing (*example:* "Bobby. Shooting hoops. Maria. Going for bike rides"). The third student will repeat what the first two students said, then add his own information, and so on around the circle.

Make sure the class understands that each student must repeat everything that has been said before adding his or her information. **Tips:** If you know that some kids have memory problems, arrange for them to get their turn early in the game. If you think smaller circles are better, divide the group in two.

Interest Survey

During the first week of school, send home copies of the "Interest Survey" handout (pages 8–9) as a homework assignment. Tell the students that they can ask family members for help in completing their surveys.

When the surveys are in, read them carefully and refer to them often throughout the year. You will find that there are many ways you can use the information from the surveys. *Examples:* Suggest school projects based on the surveys. For kids who seem unmotivated to learn, take a few seconds each day to speak to them about their interests outside of school. This shows that you like them even when they are not being successful in their schoolwork.

Picture This: A Gallery of Ideas

If possible, obtain students' school pictures from last year and make photocopies to use with some of these suggested activities. Or take your own photos; the Polaroid Education Program offers excellent classroom support. See "References and Resources" at the end of this chapter.

- Give each student space on a wall or bulletin board to display anything they want—photographs of themselves, their families, and/or their friends, work they feel proud of, etc. This eliminates the anguish struggling students experience when their work never makes it to the "Our Best Work" display.

- Have students make personalized bookmarks with their photos at the top, then decorate their bookmarks however they choose.

- With parents' permission, make copies of students' photos, add addresses and phone numbers, and create a classroom directory for kids to keep at home.

- Take and display photos of the class in various activities. Make sure that all kids are represented.

People Packages*

The People Packages activity has been successfully used in primary grades to help kids learn to respect and appreciate individual differences.

1. Collect a variety of "nice presents" (*examples:* book, toy, costume jewelry, game) and ordinary objects (*examples:* spoon, paper napkin, sock). Wrap the ordinary objects in beautiful packages and the nice presents in plain brown paper or newspaper and string. The wrapped packages should be different sizes and shapes. Put them in a large carton and bring them to class.

2. Have the students sit in a circle. Spread out the packages in front of them. Ask, "Can you guess which packages have the nicest presents inside?" (Most students will guess the beautifully wrapped packages.)

3. Have students open the packages. Discuss with them how we can't tell what's inside a package by looking at the outside.

4. Call on several students, one at a time, to stand beside you while the other students describe them as if they were packages. The other students should mention hair color, eyes, height, clothing, skin color, etc. Then have the student on display tell the class something interesting about himself or herself that doesn't show. This might be a thought, feeling, experience, pet peeve, personal like or dislike, hobby, interest, or talent.

5. Draw this analogy for the students: "Just as we can't tell what's inside a wrapped package by looking at the outside, we can't tell what's inside a person (thoughts, feelings, personality) from appearance alone."

Repeat the People Packages experience intermittently throughout the year, especially if students engage in name-calling.

---

* Marlene A. Cummings, Fitchburg, Wisconsin, author of "Individual Differences," published by the Anti-Defamation League of B'nai B'rith. Used with permission.

Interest Survey

NAME: _____

1. Do you speak any languages besides English at home? If you do, please tell which languages you can speak and understand.

_____

_____

2. What types of TV programs do you like to watch? Why?

_____

_____

3. Is there a computer at home you are allowed to use? What do you do on the computer?

_____

_____

_____

4. Tell about your favorite games or hobbies.

_____

_____

_____

5. What kinds of movies do you like to see? Why?

_____

_____

_____

6. Tell about a vacation you would like to take.

_____

_____

_____

7. What is your favorite activity or subject at school? Why?

_____

_____

_____

8. What is your least favorite activity or subject at school? Why?

_____

_____

_____

9. What kinds of things have you collected? What do you do with the things you collect?

_____

_____

_____

continued ➡

10. What career(s) do you think might be right for you when you are an adult?

_____

_____

_____

_____

11. What kinds of books do you like?

_____

_____

_____

12. What are your favorite magazines?

_____

_____

_____

13. What parts of the newspaper do you like to look at? If you don't read the newspaper, how do you learn about the news?

_____

_____

_____

14. What is your first choice for what to do when you have free time at home?

_____

_____

_____

15. If you could talk to any person alive today, who would it be? Why? Think of three questions you would ask the person.

_____

_____

_____

_____

_____

_____

_____

16. Imagine that you could invent something to make the world a better place. Describe your invention.

_____

_____

_____

17. What is something you can do really well?

_____

_____

_____

18. Tell me something else about yourself that you would like me to know.

_____

_____

_____

Ready, Set, Go

Sometime during the first week of school, take your students into the gym. Have them form a line facing a wall about 20–30 feet away. They should all be the same distance from the wall. Tell them that when you say GO, they should all run as fast as they can to the wall. Say that as soon as someone reaches the wall, you'll blow a whistle as a signal for everyone to FREEZE where they are.

Give the GO signal. As soon as the first person touches the wall, blow the whistle. Then say, "Now notice where you are standing and where you started from. Walk until you get to the wall." When everyone is at the wall, say, "See—we all started in the same place, and we all ended up in the same place, but we got there at our own pace! We'll do the same with our class work this year. So don't be concerned about anyone's pace but your own."

Walk in Your Own Shoes*

Exchange shoes with one of the students. The more extreme the exchange, the better (examples: high heels for high-tops, large loafers for small sneakers). With the rest of the class as your audience, try to walk around the room in each other's shoes. Feel free to be silly. Discuss why people should wear their own shoes.

Tell the class that each student's job is to make sure that the "shoes" they are asked to wear for each subject "fit" them. Explain that your job as teacher is to see that your students are wearing the right shoes for them. They should only be concerned about the shoes they are wearing themselves—they are not to worry about anybody else's shoes. If their shoes don't feel right for a particular learning activity, they should talk to you.

More Ways to Create a Welcoming Environment

- Greet your students at the door every day by name. For students who are very shy or not working up to grade-level standards, use information from the Interest Survey to speak to them about something in which they are personally interested. This communicates that you like them even if they are not doing well academically.

- Students of all ages love to put personal touches on their classroom to make it their home away from home. *Example:* One teacher writes her room number on a large sheet of tagboard, cuts out the numbers, then cuts each number into a jigsaw pattern. Each student gets one piece of the jigsaw puzzle to illustrate in a way that describes him or her. The pieces are reassembled and displayed on the classroom door.

- Use your students' names in scenarios and examples you give to illustrate different subject areas.

- Avoid using labels to describe your students, especially those with learning difficulties or disabilities. *Example:* Instead of saying, "Will the kids who need help with their reading come to this table?" simply say, "Harold, Jessie, and Sam, we need you to work with Miss Armstrong at this table for a while."

- Work with the school to make sure that the student handbook meets the needs of all students, including new students and those with disabilities. *Examples:* Include maps to the cafeteria, office, school counselor, library, etc. Indicate elevators, ramps, and extra-wide doors that are wheelchair accessible. If your school doesn't publish a student handbook, perhaps this could be a class project.

- Contact parents early in the school year with good news—something positive you have noticed about their child. For students with low academic skills, you might comment on personality traits or certain behaviors that have made a positive contribution to the class. It's much easier to enlist parents' assistance with school-related problems after they have heard something positive from you. All students will feel more welcome in your class when they realize you are looking hard to find their positive qualities.

- Consistently model and teach respect for individual differences and needs. When you offer differentiated learning tasks for students, call attention to the fact that all students do not need the same work, and we honor that because we honor individual differences.

- Identify and honor individual learning styles and personality strengths. (See Chapter 4 for specific strategies and suggestions.) Once you understand your students' learning styles, and once you allow them to demonstrate what they are learning in a manner compatible to their learning style strengths, it's easier to notice them for what they do well.

- Avoid emphasizing competition and individual grades.

- Take every opportunity to show that mistakes are valued for the learning opportunities they present. *Example:* When you notice that someone seems confused, say, "You're confused? Good for you! How exciting. Since confusion comes before learning, we know that learning will happen soon."*

---

* Linda Reynolds, teacher, Elgin, Illinois.

- Help students maintain their dignity and sense of worth at all times. *Example:* When you see someone doing something wrong, ask, "What are you getting ready to do?" instead of "What are you doing?"*

- Avoid words or situations that could be interpreted as put-downs. Some of the things we say in jest are not funny to kids. *Example:* Something as innocent as asking "Let's look around and see who we are waiting for now!" sends a message that it's okay to tease a poky student. It's much better to say, "I'm happy to see so many of you ready to move on the next subject," and hope that poky kids will get the message. It's also helpful to put your hand on a student's shoulder and say, "We're moving on to math now. Please get ready." Private verbal transactions are always better than public reminders.

- At the end of the school year, have your students write letters to kids who will be coming into your classroom next year. Explain that the letters should help the new students understand you, the rules of your classroom, and the special things that make your classroom exciting and wonderful. Collect the letters for distribution at the start of the new school year.

Welcoming English Language Learners (ELLs) into the Classroom

English Language Learners (ELLs), also known as Limited English Proficient Students (LEPs), English as a Second Language (ESL) students, and language-minority children, are a rapidly growing population in many schools. Who would have imagined that one day we'd hear nearly 400 different languages in our classrooms, from Spanish to Hmong, Cantonese, Arabic, Tagalog, Farsi, Lakota, and Urdu?

- Pronounce the student's name; check pronunciation with the student or parent.

- Introduce the student to several classmates, one at a time. Seat the newcomer beside someone he or she has been introduced to. Seat the pair near your desk for a while. Make sure that the student is not left alone during recess and lunch—that someone is keeping him or her company.

- Allow new students a few days for silent observation of the class and its routines. Take some time daily to talk to them, even if you need to enlist the help of another person who knows their language.

- Within a week, expect new students to participate orally in class with the help of their partners, using the Name Card method (pages 14–17). It doesn't even matter if the students actually understand what they are saying. They will still feel more like group members than if you wait until their language is more fluent to expect them to participate.

- Keep a routine to your instruction, and be consistent in how you give directions. Review routines often.

- Label everything in the classroom in English.

- Use picture dictionaries.

- Present new ideas by starting with the concrete and moving to the abstract.

- Use slower speech, occasional pauses, and controlled vocabulary, but do not talk louder or sound condescending. Avoid idioms and figures of speech. Allow extra time for students to process language.

- Avoid yes/no questions. Always have the student show you what he or she knows or understands. Demonstrate a variety of methods students can use to show their understanding of a given topic.

- Let the student know when you do not understand him or her. When there is a communication breakdown, use simple written language in manuscript form to clarify. Suggest that the student draw pictures or symbols to communicate with you until she has better written language in English.

- Structure lessons so that students can demonstrate understanding using various language arts skills (reading, writing, speaking, and/or listening).

- Give assignments one at a time using short steps.

- Re-teach, repeat, and review frequently, making adjustments as needed.

- Be aware of and modify language used in test and assignment directions. ELL students often don't understand terms such as "match items," "identify," "discuss," and "compare."

- Maintain high expectations. Expect students to do quality work, and grade on forward progress. Provide specific praise for things students do correctly.

- Teach, model, and expect all students to accept mistakes their peers make without laughing or teasing.

- Provide adaptations for all assignments regarding the number of examples students must do, the amount of time they should work on a specific task, and the amount of help they can receive while working. ELL students often respond positively to the same strategies we use successfully with visual, tactile, and/or kinesthetic learners.

---

* Rita McNeeley, teacher, Port Huron, Michigan.

- Whenever possible, use graphic organizers with consistent topics. See "The Content Organization Chart" (pages 140–142).

- Provide hands-on materials and manipulatives.

- Structure activities so students can apply their newly acquired understanding.

- Hold the same behavioral expectations for non-English-speaking students as you do for other class members.

- Create opportunities for students to share their native language and customs with the class.

- Don't discourage parents from speaking or reading in their native language at home. For school events you want parents to attend, send notices home in the family's native language, and let parents know if translators and/or childcare will be available.

- Provide different types of assessments at different levels of literacy development to measure growth in understanding.

- Find and use any available technology that will speed up the student's ability to become more comfortable with English.

Many of these suggestions are also helpful for making new students feel welcome in your classroom.

Questions and Answers

"Won't some students, particularly those in the upper grades, think that the welcoming activities are silly or weird?"

Students with learning difficulties often perceive school as impersonal and uncaring. Many students who drop out of school feel alienated from their peers. Welcoming activities like "Say Hello to Someone Who . . ." (page 5) can give students a vital sense of belonging. To make this activity more relevant (and less silly) for adolescents, create your own handout with different information in the boxes. If you need more ideas for use with older kids, brainstorm possibilities with your colleagues.

"What if a particular child's parents don't respond to my attempts to contact them? Some parents seem totally uninterested in their children's school experience, and I feel I may be wasting my time with those parents."

There are many reasons why some parents seem to resist the school's efforts to reach out to them. This problem is discussed in more detail in Chapter 14. Keep in mind that for many parents of students with learning difficulties, most previous contact with the school has been unpleasant. Once parents realize that you are trying to bring out the best in their child, their attitude may change. Be sure to call home weekly with good news about some success their child has experienced in school. The more good news they get, the more likely they are to visit the school when invited. Ask your public librarian or university library to help you find information about programs designed to increase parents' participation in their children's school experience.

REFERENCES AND RESOURCES

CARE: Courtesy and Responsibility Everyday. A program to help students focus on positive and productive behaviors. Contact Dassel Elementary School, P.O. Box 368, Dassel, MN 55325; (320) 286-4100 ext. 1500.

Dinkmeyer, Don, Sr., and Don Dinkmeyer Jr. *Developing Understanding of Self and Others (DUSO)*. Revised edition. Circle Pines, MN: American Guidance Service, 1982. A puppet program to teach tolerance and understanding in grades K–4. Out of print; check local school and university libraries or online bookstores.

everythingESL.net. The Web site of ESL (English as a Second Language) teacher Judie Haynes includes lesson plans, teaching tips, downloads, discussion topics, and resource picks for teachers grades K–12.

Fogarty, Robin, and James Bellanca. *Patterns for Thinking, Patterns for Transfer: A Cooperative Team Approach for Critical and Creative Thinking in the Classroom*. Palatine, IL: IRI Skylight Publishing Inc., 1991.

Friends Who Care. Developed by Easter Seals, this program helps teachers, parents, and young people develop a better understanding of what it means to have a disability. Search for "Friends Who Care" on the Easter Seals Web site (www.easterseals.com).

Moorman, Chick, and Nancy Weber. *Teacher Talk: What It Really Means.* Saginaw, MI: Personal Power Press, 1989. A helpful guide to using teacher talk to manage students and their problems in the classroom.

National Clearinghouse for English Language Acquisition & Language Instruction Educational Programs (NCELA) (www.ncela.gwu.edu). Information and resources for teachers, parents, and community members. Part of the Office of English Language Acquisition, Language Enhancement, and Academic Achievement for Limited English Proficient Students (OELA). 1-800-321-6223.

Teachers of English to Speakers of Other Languages (www.tesol.org). Tips, strategies, and more for grades K–12. An organization devoted to maintaining professional expertise in teaching English language learners.

Getting Everyone Involved in Learning

Because *all* students are capable learners, you as a teacher must demonstrate that *all* students are expected to fully participate in *all* activities. Sometimes you will want to offer options for students to choose from, but everyone should be involved in learning. Students who are allowed to disengage from active participation in your class are less likely to be successful than those who are highly engaged.

Some of our teaching behaviors actually encourage *dis*engagement. When certain students we call on don't respond and we move on to other students, those we leave may assume that we don't see them as capable. They may not realize that our reason for moving on is to save them from embarrassment. Our good intentions send the wrong message.

The Name Card Method*

The Name Card method communicates our expectation that *all* students will be active in class discussions. It gives kids a chance to develop friendships. Plus it eliminates many typical classroom problems:

- No students will ever be able to hide from you again by being uninvolved.

- No students will ever be able to dominate class discussions.

---

* Adapted from "Think-Pair-Share, Thinktrix, Thinklinks, and Weird Facts" by Frank T. Lyman Jr., in *Enhancing Thinking through Cooperative Learning,* edited by Neil Davidson and Toni Worsham. NY: Teachers College Press, 1992. Used with permission.

- Blurting or calling out answers will be dramatically reduced.

- Listening behaviors will be dramatically improved.

- There will be nearly 100 percent participation in all discussions.

- You will not unconsciously engage in ethnic, cultural, or gender bias as you lead discussions.

- Students of all ages and abilities will find this method preferable to traditional hand raising and will be motivated to participate in discussions.

Well-meaning teachers often unintentionally communicate low expectations for some students by always asking them the easier questions, or by letting them off the hook during class discussions. Unfortunately, the message students get when we do not hold them completely accountable is that we do not really believe they can handle the material. The Name Card Method makes certain that we communicate only high expectations that all students will be able to successfully participate in discussions.

Getting Ready

1. Tell your students that there will be no more hand raising during class discussions unless you specifically ask them to raise their hands.

2. Write each student's name on a 3" x 5" card and gather the cards into a deck. **Tips:** Some teachers have kids make their own name cards and decorate them, but I prefer to have some space on each card for jotting down

information about the student. Some junior and senior high school teachers use color-coded cards so there's a specific color for each class period. Some special education teachers with very small groups make double and triple decks, with each student's name appearing several times in the deck. And some primary teachers use tongue depressors rather than cards. This is okay, as long as the names that are called go back into the *same can* from which they are drawn.

3. Group students in discussion buddy pairs and seat them together. Place your most capable students with each other; place high achievers with the more average students; place kids who love to help others with students who struggle the most. In other words, allow *some* disparity in ability but not large gaps. If you have some highly capable students who want to work with kids with learning difficulties, allow them to do so on a limited basis.

   Research on role modeling by Dale Schunk indicates that a great disparity between partners inhibits the struggling student and robs the gifted student of opportunities to experience new learning.* Tell your students that the pairs will be changed on a regular basis so they will not have to work with the same partner indefinitely.

   If your students are in rows, seat the pairs across the aisle from each other. During discussions, they move their chairs together; at other times, they sit in their regular rows. If kids come to a rug or other gathering place for discussions, have them sit beside their discussion buddies. If your students are already in groups, designate pairs within the groups as discussion buddies. Students whose partners are absent should join another pair.

Using the Name Card Method

Explain to your students the reasons you are using the cards. Feel free to adapt and use one or more of the reasons listed on page 14, or come up with your own. Students who are reluctant to use the cards will be more likely to cooperate when they know the reasons.

To get the best results with the Name Card method, start with a discussion that uses open-ended questions, such as a discussion of a book students are reading, a current events discussion, or some challenging questions from any subject matter. Shuffle the cards often during the discussion. When students never know when their card is coming up, attending behaviors are very high. If you place the used cards on the bottom of the deck, kids will

learn that they can mentally go to sleep as soon as their turn is over.

1. Tell the class that you are going to ask a series of questions. Explain that you will call on several students for the answer to each question, so no one should talk or blurt anything until it's their turn.

2. Ask a question. Give the students 10–15 seconds to THINK about their answer. Do not acknowledge any blurting or similar outbursts. Remind students who start to talk prematurely that thinking time is not up yet.

3. Have the students PAIR up with their partners. The first time you do this, describe the signal you will use to call them back to your voice. You may have to practice this with the students until it becomes a habit for them. *Examples:* You might say "Time's up!" and/or clap your hands. As soon as you give the signal, they should stop talking—even in the middle of a sentence or a word—and return their attention to you.

   Have the students discuss possible answers to the question for 30–45 seconds. Tell them to use soft voices. If they want, they can write down their answers. Explain that these notes are for their own use and will not be collected.

   While the students are talking, walk around to monitor that they are all on task. If some students get off task, consider the possibility that you've given them too much time. It's always better if they feel a little concern about needing to finish their discussion before you give the signal.

   You might also use this time to coach a reluctant student to prepare an answer in case his or her card is drawn. (Sometimes you already *know* this will happen, but the students don't know that you know.)

   When the time is up, use the signal you practiced to bring them back to attention. It is now time to SHARE.

4. Call on the student whose name is on the top card in the deck. Don't show the cards to the students, because sometimes (as in the scenario on page 17) you may want to manipulate the cards for a specific reason. **Tip:** Don't look at the cards before calling on students. In this way, you avoid the possibility of trying to match a question's level of difficulty with your perception of a student's intelligence. When we ask difficult questions of students we consider capable, and easy questions of those we think are not so capable, we communicate low expectations for struggling students.

5. Once you call on a student, stay with that student until you get a response. If you ask the student to call on someone for help, or if you ask the class for someone to help this particular student, you send a low-expectations message. Allow several seconds for the student to collect his thoughts, then expect a response.

---

* Schunk, Dale H. "Peer Models and Children's Behavioral Change." *Review of Educational Research* 52:2 (1987), pp. 149–174.

Tip: Don't repeat a student's response; this encourages lazy listening.

If no response is forthcoming within 10 seconds, invite the student to confer again with his partner and tell him that you will return in a few moments for his answer. (Now the whole class does not have to wait for the student's answer.) You might also allow the student to say, "I need a little more time. Please come back to me." Meanwhile, hold the student's name card in an obvious way so he knows that you will remember to come back to him. It's imperative that you do return within the next minute or so. This lets the student know that you absolutely believe he is capable of responding. If the student still cannot respond, you may coach him by offering a choice between two options, or by giving a clue or hint.

6. Receive three or more responses to the same question without indicating whether the responses are correct. After each response has been given, say "Thank you," put that student's card in the middle of the deck, and call on another student with the same question. When you show that you will receive multiple responses to the same question, students don't stop thinking about the question even after someone else has answered it, because they know their name card might be next and they'll have to come up with a reasonable response as well.

Of course, we would never ask a responder if the idea she is expressing is hers or her partner's. What really matters is that all students are thinking about their answers to every question you ask!

7. Before moving on to the next question, and for the benefit of students who enjoy sharing their deep wealth of knowledge, ask, "Does anyone have anything to add that has not already been said?" Students with something to add should raise their hands.

Explain that the ticket to being able to add to the discussion is to listen well to everyone else's contribution. If a student repeats something said earlier, you will simply say, "That's already been said." Students should be aware that you will not call on that student again during this discussion unless his or her card comes up. Tell the class that you don't need any help noting who has repeated information. In other words, you don't want to hear a loud chorus of "That's a repeat!" each time it happens.

Remember to use the Name Card method when reviewing for assessments. It will amaze you how much more students will remember for those tests because they have been paying much closer attention to the lessons and discussions.

Only very rarely do teachers tell me their students resist the Name Card method. If that happens with your students, try these ideas:

■ Be sure that you have taken the time to assign partners and to let the partners work together during discussions. If you use the method without the partners, students' anxiety levels rise dramatically. Not much clear thinking goes on when anxiety is high.

■ Be sure to explain the reasons you're using the cards. When students understand your goals, they are more likely to comply. You can use the list on page 14.

■ If all else fails, tell your students you are taking a graduate class and must do this for an assignment. Ask them to please try it out with you for two weeks so you can complete your assignment and get your grade. At the end of the two weeks, have a discussion with them about the reasons for use and their experience with the experiment. Most students, by virtue of their positive experience with the method, will agree that it's okay for you to keep using it.

Variations on Think-Pair-Share

As you lead your students through the THINK and PAIR steps of the Name Card method, you can also help them practice the following thinking categories of Dr. Frank Lyman's Thinktrix model, which is described in more detail in Chapter 5.*

■ *Recall:* Students simply remember what they have learned.

■ *Similarity:* Students find ways in which ideas, people, or events are similar.

■ *Difference:* Students find ways in which ideas, people, or events are different.

■ *Cause-Effect:* Students demonstrate that they understand the relationships between causes and effects of events, behaviors, ideas, etc.

■ *Idea to Example:* Students give specific examples of ideas being discussed.

■ *Example to Idea:* Students draw conclusions, make summaries, explore themes, explain rules, etc. to show that they get the big ideas.

■ *Evaluation:* Students give their opinion concerning the value of something: good or bad, right or wrong,

---

* Adapted from "Think-Pair-Share, Thinktrix, Thinklinks, and Weird Facts" by Frank T. Lyman Jr., in *Enhancing Thinking through Cooperative Learning*, edited by Neil Davidson and Toni Worsham. NY: Teachers College Press, 1992. Used with permission of Frank T. Lyman Jr., teacher educator and originator of the Think, Pair, Share method as well as Thinktrix, Principle-Based Coaching Wheels, and the Problem-Solving Flow Chart.

significant or insignificant. This usually involves analyzing for cause and effect.

Students can vary the time they spend as they PAIR by:

- taking turns teaching each other what the teacher has just taught
- explaining their own thinking about the concepts being learned to their partner
- identifying the type of thinking being called for by the questions
- writing about what they have learned as a pair
- reading aloud certain passages to each other to gather information or answer questions
- reviewing information for upcoming assessments.

Finally, students can vary the ways in which they SHARE by:

- speaking
- reading
- acting out their ideas
- finding connections between old and new ideas
- indicating their judgments of material they are learning.

Scenario: Sean

Sean was a very pleasant young man but a reluctant learner. Whenever he was put on the spot, he blushed noticeably. He was extremely nervous the first time I used the Name Card method to review the state capitals, which all fifth graders in our district were required to know. When I called his name, he just sat there silently, daring me to do something about it. I asked if I could speak to him after class.

"Sean," I said, once everyone else had left the room, "I don't think you like this Name Card method."

Sean replied sarcastically, "What was your first clue?"

"Well," I said, "I can see that you're upset, and I want to reassure you that my goal in using the cards is not to make anyone uncomfortable. Perhaps you are worried about too many things, like when your card is coming up and what state I will ask you about."

"Yeah," he replied. "Isn't everybody worried about the same things?"

"Well," I said, "they may be worried, but it certainly isn't affecting them the way it's affecting you. So let's try to make this less stressful for you. Tomorrow, when your card comes up, I'll ask you to name the capital of South Dakota."

Sean paused for a few seconds, looked at me suspiciously, and asked, "How do you know you'll ask me that?"

"Trust me," I replied. "I just know. But there's one rule that goes with this arrangement. You can't tell anyone else at school about it."

"Why not?" he asked.

"Because this is a special private arrangement between you and me, and no one else needs to know," I stated simply.

For nine consecutive days, on his way out to recess, Sean made it his business to toss something into the trash can near my desk. As he walked by, I softly said the name of his state for the following day. On the tenth day, he looked as if he was going to leave without getting the prompt.

"Sean," I called from the desk, "didn't you forget something here?"

"Oh," he said, smiling sheepishly, "I don't need that anymore."

And he didn't!

Imagine the outcome if I had thought, *Oh, poor Sean, he blushes and he's embarrassed, so I guess I'll leave him alone.* Excusing him from participation would have indicated my agreement with him that he was unable to participate. Insisting on his participation—with the appropriate support system—sent him a clear message: "You *can* participate. You *will* participate. This is something you can do."

Cooperative Learning

Cooperative learning can dramatically improve learning outcomes for students who are struggling in school. Cooperative learning is quite different from traditional group work and is actually designed to eliminate most of the problems that kids experience before someone teaches them how to work together. Students with learning difficulties do much better in classrooms where cooperative learning is used regularly, because it becomes acceptable for kids to help each other learn.

How to Integrate Students with Learning Difficulties into Cooperative Learning Groups

In classrooms where competition is the expectation, there is little or no incentive for students to help struggling students learn. In classrooms where cooperative learning is valued, every student's chances for success are enhanced. When students who struggle to learn are placed in cooperative groups, we must create conditions so their presence is not resented. If other students perceive that struggling students will lower the outcomes for everyone, resistance and resentment are predictable. Following are suggestions for integrating students with learning difficulties into cooperative learning groups.

Group Gifted Students Together

Group your three or four most capable students into their own group and give them an extension of the regular task. When gifted students are in mixed-abilities cooperative learning groups with struggling students, the gifted kids tend to take over and get bossy, since they fear that if they don't take charge the group product or outcome will not meet their high standards. When gifted students are not in the regular groups, other kids have the chance to show off their talents.

Avoid Group Grades

Instead, set up the assessment so that all students earn credit for their own contribution, in addition to a bonus for the group product. When everyone in the group achieves a certain level of learning, everyone gets a bonus. *Example:* Add five points to each person's actual score.

It is perfectly acceptable to enter into special agreements with struggling students so their presence does not create a hardship for other students in their group. At the beginning of a cooperative learning activity, ask those students to set their own goals regarding what they expect to achieve. If they reach their goals—even if they are less than what you expect from the rest of the group—they can still contribute to the group's bonus.

Assign Group Roles

Give students with special learning needs a job or role that allows them to demonstrate their learning strengths. *Example:* Some students may be highly creative or good at assembling things. Try putting them in the leadership role in a group activity that relies on spatial, visual, mechanical thinking, such as working with tangrams puzzles. Traditionally, linguistically gifted kids do very poorly at a tangram-type task, while struggling students can suddenly show how capable they are because they are often exceptionally good at tasks that require visual-spatial ability.

Create and Use Home Groups*

Home groups give all kids an anchor group to belong to. A home group is the group the student sits with for a few minutes each day at the beginning of class. Students move from their home groups to their work groups for cooperative learning activities and tasks or for more independent learning activities. They return to their home groups at the end of class to make sure that each group member understands the homework and remembers to take it home.

A home group might be made up of students who live in the same neighborhood, so group members can take homework to absent students. If attendance is a problem at your school, you might offer a group incentive, such as points toward a prize, each day that all group members come to school. If group members have each other's telephone numbers (get parents' permission first), they might actually call each other and provide encouragement to come to school so the group can earn its points.

Other ways for home group members to support each other might include:*

- taking attendance
- helping all group members have the school supplies needed for the day
- drilling each other on basic information that must be learned (number facts, spelling, etc.)
- studying together for a test
- brainstorming the "K" in KWPL ("Know," "Want," "Predict," "Learned"; see page 92) to list what is already known about a topic
- brainstorming solutions to class problems in preparation for class meetings (see page 205)
- doing show-and-tell in small groups rather than for the whole class
- collecting homework for absent students and delivering it to them
- checking homework together by comparing answers and reaching consensus, then making corrections in a different-colored pencil or pen
- turning in completed homework. Students receive their own grades plus bonus points if all group members turn in completed homework, and they earn more bonus points if all homework papers meet specific grade criteria.

Use Pair Practice**

Use this technique when you are lecturing or teaching something to the whole class. It's especially effective when kids are working on a thematic unit and you want to find out how much they know about the entire topic, rather than just their small portion of it.

Designate students "Partner A" and "Partner B." After you have lectured about or taught a small portion of information, ask Partner A to re-teach it to Partner B using any method that seems comfortable. Use the Name Card method to check to see how many students understand the concept. If it looks as though most students understand it, teach another small portion, then have Partner B re-teach Partner A.

---

* Adapted from *Cooperation in the Classroom* by David Johnson, Roger Johnson, and Edythe Holubec. Interaction Book Company, 7208 Cornelia Drive, Edina, MN 55435. 7th edition, 1998. Used with permission.

** Adapted from *Tape 9: Biology—Visual Learning Tools (High School)*. The Lesson Collection. Alexandria, VA: ASCD Video, 2000. Used with permission.

More Ways to Get Everyone Involved in Learning

- In one school, each student was required to set one academic goal and one social/behavioral goal at a time and focus on them until they were achieved. The school purchased a button-making machine and made "Yes I Can" buttons for everyone. Kids set goals, talked about their goals, and learned how to congratulate each other when goals were accomplished. The program was most successful when kids set short-term goals for each week or grading period. You might start a yearlong campaign to focus on students' growth through goal setting. As part of your campaign, emphasize positive self-talk. Whenever kids speak negatively about themselves by saying, "I can't do this," other kids (and the teacher) chant, "Yes You Can!" Then the students answer, "Yes I Can!" Talking about this at parent conferences provides a positive note for every conference.

- Teach your students that meaningful success comes from the ability to set and accomplish realistic short-term goals. Remember that kids who perceive themselves as incapable are unlikely to reach lofty goals of getting high grades unless they learn how to reach those goals in small, doable steps. See "Goal Setting" on pages 65–68.

- Create an atmosphere in which making mistakes is always expected, always encouraged as an opportunity for learning, and never the object of ridicule. Regularly tell your students that there is no learning happening if work is always correct. Share personal stories from your own life, especially your childhood, that illustrate how you use mistakes as learning experiences.

- Set up a volunteer peer tutoring location in the classroom where struggling students can meet with students who can help. Never coerce any student into being a peer tutor; ask for volunteers only. Keep in mind that some kids are better tutors if they are still trying to master a concept than if they have already mastered it.

- Model, teach, and reinforce the concept that in your classroom, equal does not mean the same. Explain that everyone has an equal opportunity to learn and move ahead, but they won't always be doing the same things. Emphasize that it is each student's job to make sure that he is learning, not to worry about how other students are learning. In this way, you avoid creating an environment in which students accuse you of being unfair when it appears that all students aren't being treated the same. Instead, you create an environment in which all individuals are greatly respected.

- Involve the whole class in working as a team to integrate students with learning difficulties. Share as much information as you have about how and why learning difficulties manifest themselves, so fact will replace rumor and misinformation. Whenever possible, let your students deal with the challenges that come with integrating kids with learning problems into your class, instead of feeling that you have to do the job alone.

Ticket Out the Door

1. A few minutes before the end of a lesson, ask students to take out a half sheet of paper. Tell them not to write their name on it, but to write "boy" or "girl" at the top and their class period. (This will allow you to see if your students perceive that you are treating boys and girls the same way.) Ask them to write:

   - two things they understand well about today's lesson, and

   - one thing they don't completely understand about the lesson, or a question they would like to have answered.

   Explain that spelling and mechanics aren't important. Tell them that this is their "ticket out the door." They can't leave the classroom unless they give it to you on their way out.

2. Stand at the classroom door and collect the tickets as the students leave.

3. Use the information from the tickets to plan the next day's lesson.

Involvement improves when students know they have to create a written record of what they have learned.

Variation: If students don't leave the room between lessons, you can call these "tickets to the next lesson" and have kids complete them before you go on to the next lesson.

Questions and Answers

"What do I do when kids refuse to answer when their name comes up in the Name Card method?"

This may happen the first few times you try this strategy, as certain students who have convinced some of their teachers that they can't talk or participate try to get you to believe the same thing. Sean's scenario (page 17) describes one way to deal with reluctant or openly resistant students. *Always* allow students to confer with a partner before you call on them; this goes a long way toward reducing anxiety. Call on them early in the process, when they still have answers left on their written list. Give them a particularly supportive partner. In most cases, students become less anxious about the Name Card method as it becomes more familiar to them. In cases of serious emotional problems, consult with the school counselor, psychologist, or social worker for advice on how to ease the student into the process.

"I've had some students who simply won't talk to anyone in the classroom—not to me and not to other students. What can I do about this?"

Observe the students to see if they talk in other classes, on the playground, in the halls, or in the cafeteria. Use the Name Card method (pages 14–17) and hold them accountable for responding. Use the strategies described in Chapter 1 to make sure they know at least one of their classmates by name. Call on them early in discussions so they have responses to share. The longer we allow students to choose not to actively engage in learning, the longer they will hide. There is a small chance that such shy children are experiencing a type of anxiety disorder, so consult counselors or social workers if your attempts don't lead to improvement or if they increase the students' anxiety.

Remember that if you tell the kids the questions before the discussion and give them a few moments to talk to their partners about the questions, their anxiety will be significantly reduced. It also helps when you explain the reasons why you are using the Name Card method.

"Won't gifted kids develop an overinflated opinion of themselves if they are always in their own cooperative learning group?"

Gifted kids often become more humble when their task is appropriately challenging and they realize they can't complete it with ease. Furthermore, the makeup of a gifted cooperative learning group often changes with different subject areas. The most gifted artists are not always the most capable readers, and the most gifted math students don't always shine in reading.

"Won't other students resent special arrangements you make with struggling students to earn credit in the cooperative learning group?"

Other students are more likely to resent it if some students' severe learning difficulties are perceived as a disadvantage for their group. If all mixed-abilities cooperative learning groups have at least one student who needs special arrangements, or if the student who has these special needs is rotated among several groups over time, there should be no resentment.

REFERENCES AND RESOURCES

Cohen, Elizabeth. *Designing Groupwork: Strategies for the Heterogeneous Classroom.* 2nd edition. New York: Teachers College Press, 1994.

Johnson, David, Roger Johnson, and Edythe Holubec. *Cooperation in the Classroom.* 7th edition. Edina, MN: Interaction Book Company, 1998.

Kagan, Spencer. *Cooperative Learning.* San Juan Capistrano, CA: Kagan Cooperative Learning, 1994.

Lyman, Frank T., Jr. "Think-Pair-Share, Thinktrix, Thinklinks, and Weird Facts." In Neil Davidson and Tony Worsham, editors, *Enhancing Thinking through Cooperative Learning.* NY: Teachers College Press, 1992.

Schunk, Dale H. "Peer Models and Children's Behavioral Change." *Review of Educational Research* 52:2 (1987), pp. 149–174.

Strategies for Reading Comprehension: Think-Pair-Share (www.readingquest.org/strat/tps.html). A summary of Dr. Frank Lyman's cooperative discussion strategy.

Tape 9: Biology—Visual Learning Tools (High School). The Lesson Collection. Alexandria, VA: ASCD Video, 2000.

Think-Pair-Share SmartCard (www.kaganonline.com). Describes many variations of Dr. Frank Lyman's Think-Pair-Share part of the Name Card method. Kagan Publishing & Professional Development also offers many materials to help you facilitate cooperative learning using Dr. Spencer Kagan's methods. 1-800-WEE CO-OP (1-800-933-2667).

Understanding Learning Difficulties and Intervening Effectively

There are so many types of learning difficulties that entire books have been devoted to each type. After careful research, I have concluded that it is not the classroom teacher's job to definitively identify the specific category into which a struggling student fits. There is so much crossover between categories that even the experts are not always sure of their diagnoses. Rather, the teacher's job is to gather and apply as many teaching strategies as possible, with the intent of matching those that work best to each student's needs. This book does the *gathering*. The *application* is up to you!

This chapter summarizes characteristics of students with significant learning problems and offers suggestions for intervening with some of those problems. The material can help you to better understand and meet the needs of students in your classroom who are having significant trouble learning, including special education students who spend part or all of each day in regular education classrooms, and students who are not fluent in English. To obtain more detailed information about specific types of learning difficulties, see "References and Resources" at the end of this chapter.

As you work with your struggling students, keep the following points in mind:

■ Huge numbers of children who appear to have learning difficulties are not really learning disabled—they are learning *strategy* disabled. Once they learn to use effective strategies, their disabilities fade away. This leaves us with a small number of students whose brains perceive different messages than their senses.

■ Never forget the important fact that kids with learning difficulties really *cannot* learn in traditional ways. They are *not* choosing to fail. The strategies presented in this book have been proven to help struggling students become more successful learners. Don't worry about using the wrong strategy or technique for the wrong category of student. Don't worry about whether a student has been formally labeled "learning disabled" or "special education." Just use what works and congratulate yourself for trying!

■ Many kids who struggle to learn have average or above-average intelligence. Their learning challenge is unrelated to intelligence. Frustration with learning significantly increases inappropriate behaviors and might make students appear less competent than they really are. Many behavior problems improve significantly when students perceive themselves as being successful in school.

■ Ritalin and similar drugs are intended to be used with kids whose neurological impairments include hyperactivity and/or attention disorders so they can focus better on academic subjects and appropriate social behaviors. However, chemical intervention should occur only after several modifications in curriculum and behavior management have been tried. For some students, the modifications are enough. For those who need chemical intervention, the dosage may be adjusted once compensation behaviors have been learned and have become somewhat automatic.

■ Before you take a stand for or against chemical intervention, talk to adults with ADHD (attention deficit hyperactivity disorder) or ADD (attention deficit disorder without hyperactivity). They are in the best position to describe their life with and without medication. Read *Faking It* by Christopher Lee and Rosemary Jackson, *Making the Words Stand Still* by Donald E. Lyman, and *Driven to Distraction* by Edward M. Hallowell and John J. Ratey for additional insights (see "References and Resources"). These books can increase your empathy for kids with bona fide learning disabilities.

■ Be assertive in asking for assistance from the special education staff and administrators for challenges you face in teaching students with exceptional learning needs. These professionals should provide the support you need so you don't have to significantly reduce the level of attention and services you give to your other students. So-called inclusion programs were not designed to totally sacrifice the needs of regular education children to the needs of special education students.

■ Many of the strategies that help struggling students become more successful are also helpful with other students, including those who are not fluent in English. All of your students—and their parents as well—will appreciate your efforts to improve learning success for everyone.

LD

The term *learning disabled,* or *LD,* refers to individuals who have some neurological impairment that mixes up signals between the senses and the brain.* (Although students with ADD/ADHD may exhibit learning difficulties, these specific categories are considered behavioral disorders rather than learning disabilities. The strategies in this book have been very effective with students with ADD/ADHD.) Students with LD do not exhibit all of the behaviors in any list of characteristics.

By definition, students with LD have average to above-average intelligence, but they experience processing problems when their brain receives stimuli from their senses. There is a significant discrepancy between their ability as measured on an individual IQ test and their school performance as evaluated by their teachers. The disability reflects the area of the brain where processing problems occur. For example, some students misperceive symbolic language but may be highly capable when dealing with concrete representations. Words and numbers do not make logical sense to them when found outside a meaningful, concrete context.

People with LD usually have some learning problems throughout their lives. One does not outgrow LD; one develops coping strategies. For example, many students with LD have developed an "I don't care" attitude to divert attention from their inability to perform school tasks. These kids are often immature, since their LD may also have affected their growth in the areas of physical coordination and emotional development. They may be unable to detect the subtleties that enable people to function capably and appropriately in social situations, and may therefore exhibit socially unacceptable behaviors. Some experience constant stress and tension as a result of their LD, which may cause physical symptoms and further inhibit their capacity to learn.

Types of LD

Having a learning disability is like trying to learn a foreign language. Can you remember how frustrating this was for you? Before you could think fluently in the new language, you were forced to translate back and forth. Kids with LD always have to translate lesson content into a language their brain can process and understand.

There are many different types of LD. Following are descriptions of some types you may observe in students who are struggling in school.

Visual Perceptual Disability

Students with this type of LD perceive letters and numbers in different positions from how they are written, either reversed or rotated. They may confuse left and right, up and down, or back and forth. They may have trouble distinguishing important objects from their backgrounds, and with depth perception and/or judging distances. They often skip words or confuse lines as they read. Students may also have trouble with eye-hand coordination, leading to awkwardness in physical activity.

This condition was formerly called *dyslexia.* More recently, the term *dyslexia* has been broadened to encompass any significant problem in learning to read, including word recognition, decoding, spelling, and other phonological problems as well as comprehension.

A somewhat related condition called *hyperlexia* is found in some children (mostly boys) who appear to have taught

---

* The term "learning differences" is replacing "learning disabilities" in many schools and publications because it is more positive and accepting. "Disabilities" has negative connotations for many people, especially kids who are labeled "learning disabled."

themselves to read sometime between the ages of 18 months and 2 years but are unable to understand what they read. They may exhibit unusual language learning disorders, such as marked impairment in the ability to initiate or sustain conversations and problems in social development. Hyperlexia is often associated with autism.

Auditory Perceptual Disability

Students with this challenge have difficulty distinguishing subtle differences in sounds and may hear something different from what a speaker actually says. This makes it very difficult for them to follow directions, especially if many directions are given at once. They may confuse sounds from several sources and may not be able to block out background noise, giving the impression that they are never paying attention. They may take longer to process the meaning of what they hear, losing their place in discussions because they are still working on understanding something that was said moments earlier. When we call on them, they are lost because they have not been able to keep up with what we are saying, even though our pace is appropriate for the other students. It's more effective to limit the number of directions given.

Language Learning Disability

These students may have trouble communicating their thoughts through speech, or they may be able to speak but can't answer specific questions. Some may have difficulty understanding what others say to them. Part of the problem results from the inability to place information in the correct brain centers and retrieve it when it is needed.

Perceptual Motor Disability

These students may have coordination problems that make them appear clumsy or disoriented in space. Many are unable to do things that are simple for other kids, such as coloring, cutting, and pasting. Their hands may be in constant motion and may get in their way.

Students with fine motor problems have very real trouble writing down their thoughts. They can tell wonderful stories and convey information verbally, but actually experience physical discomfort and great anxiety when asked to write. Keyboarding and voice recognition writing programs are very helpful for these kids.

Hyperactivity

Students who are hyperactive may have difficulty controlling their muscle or motor activity and may be constantly on the move. They may flit from task to task without finishing anything, or they may persevere on one task with

which they have found success, ignoring others they are supposed to do.

Impulsivity

Impulsive students appear to live in a totally random way, succumbing to whatever attracts their attention. These kids are obviously difficult to keep on task and may often act out without thinking first.

Distractibility

Distractible students are unable to differentiate between important and unimportant stimuli. They may be disorganized because they can't follow through on thought processes in an orderly fashion. Their attention is often diverted from the task at hand, making it very difficult for them to complete their assignments.

Abstraction Disability

Abstraction is the ability to figure out the correct general meaning from a particular word or symbol. Students with this challenge have difficulty transferring concrete information to abstract applications. Their short- or long-term memory may be impaired, leading them to forget what they have learned.

Sequencing Disability

Students with this challenge have trouble remembering the correct sequence of letters within words, numerals within numbers, days of the week, months of the year, and the order of events within a situation. Or they may know the sequence but cannot use the concepts out of the sequence.

Memory Disability

Students with memory problems may have trouble with short- or long-term memory and may therefore be unable to remember things they have already learned. For these students, many repetitions may be needed in the learning phase.

How It Feels to Have LD

One of the most poignant descriptions of what it's like to have severe LD is found in the book *Faking It* by Christopher Lee and Rosemary Jackson. Following is a summary of some of the observations Christopher makes about his experiences.*

---

* Summarized from *Faking It: A Look into the Mind of a Creative Learner* by Christopher Lee and Rosemary F. Jackson, pp. 21, 25, 28–29. Portsmouth, NH: Heinemann, 1992. Used with permission.

Christopher was in the second grade before he realized that something was wrong with him. He was pulled out of public school and placed in a school for so-called "special" kids. It didn't take him long to realize that the word "special" did not mean "extraordinary" and, in fact, did not have a positive meaning at all. He soon concluded that "learning disabled" was a cover phrase for "slow and stupid."

He experienced teasing and cruel treatment from his peers and even from well-meaning teachers who constantly admonished him to try harder, revealing their inability to understand that his learning problems were too complex to be solved by more effort. His coping strategy was to hide his inabilities from his teacher, his parents, and his peers—to fake being normal.

Christopher's learning problems affected his ability to see and hear letters correctly and to express his thoughts orally and in writing. Spelling was particularly painful for him because "words never seemed to be spelled the way I heard them and words never looked the same twice." For many years, he assumed that writing and spelling were synonymous, and since he could not spell, he felt he could not write. It was only after encountering a computer with a spell-check program that he realized that writing was connected more to content than to mechanics. In his words: "Spending so much time on trying to teach someone with a learning disability to spell might be detrimental to that person's ability to ever learn to write."

The mechanics of writing were very difficult for him to master. "When I am writing, I see a continuous line. I don't see punctuation . . . and so I don't stop when I read. I don't see where sentences and paragraphs begin or end. I never see any structure when I read and therefore I don't know how to use it when I am writing." His thoughts went faster that he could speak or write them, and he had to stop and start often when trying to express a complete thought. At the same time, he was sidetracked by trying to find out what different words and phrases meant, and he eventually forgot what he wanted to write.

His auditory deficits made it almost impossible for him to attach the correct sound to the letters that represent them, so a phonics approach simply didn't work for him. When the same words were written with a capital letter or a lower-case letter at the beginning, or appeared in different type fonts, he perceived them as different words. His deficits in understanding language made it impossible for him to understand much of what people are saying when they tried to explain things to him, including his own disabilities.

Christopher concluded that labels of deficiency create fewer learning opportunities for kids. In effect, a person's identity becomes attached to the definition of his or her disability.

Another excellent source of information about what it's like to have LD is the work of Dr. Richard LaVoie. His videos, *How Difficult Can This Be?* And *Last One Picked . . . First One Picked On,* are memorable and moving. Either can help people without LD understand those with LD and be more supportive of individuals with any type of learning difficulty. See "References and Resources."

Ways to Intervene with LD

"If students cannot learn the way we teach them, then we must teach them the way they learn." These words from Queens College professor Dr. Kenneth Dunn, coauthor with Dr. Rita Dunn of several books on learning styles, sum up the essence of this book. Whatever methods you are currently using that are not leading to success for certain students should be abandoned and replaced, for those students only, with methods more likely to lead to learning success. Students who are experiencing learning success with the regular teaching methods should continue to use those.

The most helpful outcome from learning what we can about all types of learning difficulties is that it helps us stop focusing on blame and guilt, and start focusing on learning and using the most effective compensation strategies we can find. This book is one source of these strategies. The "References and Resources" section lists many more.

Create Learning Style Compatible Conditions

- Teach to students' learning style strengths. Involve all parts of the brain in all activities; physical movement, visualization, music, rhythm, and emotion all help learning. Have kids act or dance out words and concepts. Whenever practical, turn off some or all lights and play soothing instrumental music in the background. Encourage students to make mental pictures of what they are learning and to study those pictures with their eyes closed. Have them visualize what the subject looks, sounds, and smells like. Repeating visualizations many times improves memory. Use these interventions as your first-choice teaching methods rather than as remediation techniques.

- Keep visual and auditory distractions to a minimum. Since some kids with LD are distracted by their surroundings, it's probably better for them not to be seated beside colorful, stimulating displays. Permit students to work in study carrels or screened-off areas if these arrangements lead to more productivity.

- Allow students to listen to soothing instrumental music on headphones while they work.

- Record lectures, presentations, and text material on audiocassettes, CDs, or DVDs. Make several copies for kids with learning problems to take home. Or contact Recording for the Blind & Dyslexic (RFB&D). This esteemed organization may already have copies available of the texts and literature you need. See "References and Resources."

- Give hyperactive kids frequent opportunities to move. *Examples:* Suggest that they tap their pencil on their sleeve or leg instead of a desk; have them sharpen pencils for a group of kids; use masking tape to draw a border on the floor around their desk and let them move all they want within that area.

- Make learning concrete. Almost all students with LD do extremely well when a learning task is something they can actually get their hands on and when it is connected to something they are interested in or curious about.

- Whenever possible, find alternatives to large-group work. Kids with LD often work better alone or with a partner.

- Find and use available technology assistance. Don't wait until students can do something on their own before allowing them to use helpful technology. *Examples:* Let them use calculators for computation, word processors and spell-check programs for written work, and voice recorders for oral reports.

- Keep in mind that kids with LD work more enthusiastically on projects than on skill work. They learn better if immersed in one topic for several days, as opposed to moving from topic to topic each day. Use the Log of Project Work (page 76) to help them stay on track during project work. At the start of each work period, students enter the date and the task they plan to accomplish that day. Five minutes before project work ends, they record what they actually accomplished. Spillover work is written in the next line as their plan for the next day. As they accomplish each task, a new task is planned and recorded.

- Allow struggling students to take classroom tests in untimed situations. Let them read a test aloud or have someone else read it to them; in many cases, this leads to improved test results.

- Never assume that kids who struggle to learn could do better if they just tried harder.

- Consult chapters 4 and 5 for more strategies and suggestions.

Use Praise Effectively

Many teachers think that praise of any type is helpful for improving student motivation and self-esteem. Yet there is ample proof that in order to be effective, praise must follow these guidelines:

- It must happen almost instantly after the praiseworthy event.

- It must be specific—it must describe the exact act or behavior you want to see more often. *Example:* Instead of saying, "I'm so proud of you, Juan!" say, "You are becoming much more accurate on your timed number facts tests. Good work, Juan!"

- It must be sincere—you must mean it and the student must believe it. You can tell how the act makes you feel. *Example:* "When you were helpful to your friend, I noticed how happy he was."

- It should never be accompanied by a negative statement. *Example:* Avoid saying things like, "Your desk is very neat right now, but I wonder if you can keep it that way."

Tip: Coach your students on how to praise themselves. Perhaps they could respond to a visual signal from you when you observe some praiseworthy behavior. Your signal could be their cue to administer some self-praise.

Improve Students' Attending Behaviors

- Put a large, clear sign on or beside your classroom door so students with space-orientation problems can find the room easily.

- Write daily schedules where all can see them. Check things off as they are completed so students have a sense of progress. Have students use daily assignment notebooks.

- Have students set goals for how much of a task they predict they can do in an allotted time, instead of expecting them to work as long as it takes to complete the entire task. Use the Goal Planning Chart (page 66) and goal-setting strategies (pages 65 and 67) to help students do this.

- Provide students with a Daily Task Checklist (page 26) to keep at their desks. Give them some control over choosing from among several tasks and deciding how much of a task they can do in the allotted time. Whenever they complete an activity, have them indicate their progress on the checklist so they can receive positive reinforcement immediately instead of waiting until the end of a class period or school day. If a student procrastinates consistently despite the checklist,

Daily Task Checklist

NAME: _____

Portion of task for this work period	Check here when portion is done	Check here if you did not complete the portion

set up a behavior-consequence situation. *Example:* "Josie, if you complete the items on your checklist by the time we agreed upon, you can work on a choice activity for ten minutes. If you can't reach your goal, you won't have time for the choice activity."

■ Talk slowly. Some kids with LD, and certainly English Language Learners (ELLs), process speech in slow motion. Give them advance notice (a physical cue, a special word) that you will be asking them a question. Use words sparingly. Keep conversations brief.

■ Be succinct in giving directions, and always model and demonstrate what you want students to do by showing them a concrete example of what the finished product should look like. Never give a string of directions all at once. Instead, give one direction at a time, demonstrate it, and show an example of what the product should look like. Have students repeat the directions before they begin their work. Give positive reinforcement as soon as the first task is completed.

■ Establish eye contact while speaking to students, but don't insist that they maintain it if it makes them uncomfortable.

■ For students who are confused by too much to look at on a page, provide windows cut out of paper or cardboard that expose only portions of the page at a time. These can also be used as line or place markers.

■ Use neon-type highlighters to call students' attention to important sections of handouts. Avoid using red ink to mark errors. This only reinforces incorrect responses in the student's mind.

■ Use humor frequently, but be very careful not to use sarcasm. *Examples:* Include students' names in silly scenarios in the content areas. Have a recording of a laugh track handy to play when things get too serious. Have kids bring in cartoons they think are funny or create new captions for funny pictures. Develop a "Good Humor" bulletin board. Joke with the class on a regular basis and show appreciation for the funny things kids say. Throw smiles for kids to catch and put on their faces instead of frowns.

■ Use game formats to teach vocabulary and skills. Most students can learn significantly more material in a game of quiz-show format than with traditional paper-and-pencil tasks. Create or purchase generic game boards that can be used with various card decks of skill work; students advance playing pieces on the board for each correct response they make. As an alternative to game boards, let students keep each card for which they give a correct response. The student with the most cards at the end of the game is the winner.

■ Expose all of your students to high-quality curriculum and learning experiences. Skill work is more likely to hold kids' interest if it is connected to meaningful content.

■ Never do for your students what they can do for themselves.

■ Consult chapters 4 and 5 for more strategies and suggestions.

Improve Students' Social Skills

As if having trouble learning weren't enough, many struggling students find it very difficult to behave in socially appropriate ways. Because of their learning delays, they appear immature. Their social/interactive skills resemble those of much younger children, so they may seem silly or babyish to those around them. Since children tend to socially reject kids who are different for any reason, students with learning difficulties often find it hard to make and keep friends.

Their hyperactivity and disorganization often make them stand out and become the objects of negative attention. They just don't seem to get it in social situations, constantly missing subtle clues that other kids pick up easily. They may seem unaware of things they say and do that might lead to their being shunned or disliked by other kids. If their hyperactivity is manifested in talking too much, they may be perceived as wanting to dominate conversations. In many groups, it becomes fashionable for these kids to become the targets of teasing.

As teachers, we play a crucial role in how kids are treated by their peers. When we become annoyed, impatient, or angry about a child's irritating behavior, our other students may pick up on our negative feelings and infer that we are giving them implicit permission to denigrate kids who are so different from the norm. If this is the situation in your classroom, you might seek help from specialists who know the learning needs and challenges faced by students with learning difficulties. The goal in *all* classrooms is for *all* kids to be accepted for the sensitive people they are, even if they exhibit some behavior that needs changing. We need to lead the way so all kids can be noticed and appreciated first for their strengths.

■ Find and use programs that teach social/interactive skills, such as those by Arnold Goldstein and Dorothy Rich (see "References and Resources"). Seek assistance from a school counselor, social worker, special education staff person, student teacher, or paraprofessional.

■ Choose a particular social skill that needs improvement and teach it to those students who could most benefit from learning it. See page 199.

- Arrange and use a subtle signal that will indicate to a student when he or she is engaging in inappropriate social behavior. The signal can also prompt the student to recall and use the more appropriate skill that has been taught.

- Teach students to keep track of their own progress. They might use the Awareness Tallies method described in Chapter 13 (see page 197).

- Make sure that all students understand the consequences of inappropriate behavior. Consequences should be applied in an objective fashion, without anger or excessive emotion.

- Expect that anyone who behaves inappropriately will make amends by apologizing directly to the injured party, and that the injured party will accept the apology—unless the inappropriate behavior is repeated over time, in which case apologies are meaningless.

- Teach yourself and your students to ignore inappropriate behavior unless someone's safety (physical or emotional) is in jeopardy. If it is, the preferred response is to state, "I don't like that. I don't like it when you do that. I want you to stop doing that right now." Make it very clear that retaliation is not allowed.

- Consult Chapter 13 for more ideas on how to help students with social problems.

Deal Effectively with Behavior Problems

- Encourage students with LD to learn more about LD. See "Recommended Readings for Students" at the end of this chapter.

- Consistently notice students for their strengths and special abilities.

- Agree upon and use nonverbal signals to indicate approval or disapproval of a student's behavior or times when you want behavior to change. *Examples:* "When I nod at you, this means that you are behaving appropriately. When I look at you and push my glasses further up on my nose, this means that you are not behaving appropriately. When I put my hand on your shoulder, this means that I want you to pay attention to me." Ask first to make sure that a touch is acceptable to the student.

- Demonstrate ways for class members to ignore inappropriate behaviors. Help students develop consistent non-reinforcing responses. *Examples:* Show students how to move away from others who are bothering them, end eye contact, and refuse to respond to taunts or insults.

- Seat students whose behaviors are distracting behind the vision of other kids. Surround them with students who can model appropriate behavior.

- Teach yourself and your students to recognize and immediately reinforce positive behaviors from *all* students, including those who are just learning more appropriate classroom behaviors. *Example:* When a student who usually blurts out remembers to raise his hand before speaking, students around him should acknowledge that behavior by quietly saying, "Good for you for raising your hand!" Avoid an entire class display (such as applause), since this would only call undue attention to the situation.

- Establish and use predictable routines in class activities and in transitions. Give notice if a routine will be changed or interrupted. Unpredictability throws many struggling students off-balance. (This may be one reason they misbehave when a substitute teaches for you.)

- Consult Chapter 13 for more strategies and suggestions.

Being Gifted and Having Learning Challenges at the Same Time

Some students are clearly gifted in some areas and clearly in need of learning assistance in other areas. The gifted education world has labeled these students "twice exceptional." Historically, schools have ignored the gifts and concentrated almost all of the students' time in school on remediating the weaknesses. However, the fairest way to handle this situation is to treat these students as gifted in their areas of strength, and not take time away from those strength areas to make more time for working on their difficulties. When learning in their areas of difficulties, they should be taught the same compensation strategies as any other student who needs them.

The LD might be as simple as not being fluent in English. It is safe to assume that other cultures have the same percentage of gifted students as the United States does among its fluent English speakers. Notice and recognize signs of gifted abilities in students of all cultures, and don't wait to provide appropriate learning challenges for these kids until English fluency is attained. For specific strategies on how to nurture the giftedness in children from other cultures, consult *Reaching New Horizons* by Jaime A. Castellano and Eva Díaz. See "References and Resources."

Many gifted kids with LD are not diagnosed as either gifted *or* learning disabled. Their LD often brings their school performance down into the average range, and it is difficult for teachers to notice the gifted behaviors they may exhibit. The parents of these students may be perceived by educators as dreamers who wish that their perfectly average children could be intellectually gifted. But parents are in the unique position of seeing how precocious their children are at home, where they can express their exceptional learning abilities in ways that are naturally fluent for them.

What alarms many educators (and parents) is that many of the characteristics that describe gifted students are strikingly similar to the characteristics of students with ADD/ADHD. Gifted kids may be restless and physically active when the tasks they are asked to perform do not capture their interest. Their intensity often leads them into confrontations with authority because they need a good reason to conform. Their daydreaming may actually be directed toward the mental contemplation of complex and creative scenarios. They may present different personas in different situations: naughty at school but pleasant at scout meetings, restless at their desks but totally immersed in a book they are reading for pleasure, socially inept with their classmates but charming when talking to adults. If these students are mistakenly identified as having LD, ADD, or ADHD, the danger is that their giftedness will go unnoticed because the deficit label usually takes precedence over other learning exceptionalities.

Some gifted kids do have LD, but most do not. Rather than worrying about the distinction, we should do everything in our power to ensure that *all* students with LD are offered learning style compatible tasks that emphasize hands-on learning. We should make every effort to identify our students' passionate interests and find ways for them to work on them during school time. Gifted behaviors will be observable as students take simple learning tasks and make them more abstract and complex.

Generally speaking, gifted kids who *do* have LD:

- usually show noticeably discrepant scores between the verbal and nonverbal sections of ability tests

- have extremely uneven academic skills that cause them to appear unmotivated to learn and to avoid many school tasks, leading to incomplete assignments

- have auditory and/or visual processing problems that cause them to respond, work, and appear to think very slowly (this leads to great difficulty in explaining or expressing their ideas and feelings; they may talk around a topic and appear unable to get to the point)

- have problems with motor skills as exhibited by clumsiness, poor handwriting, and difficulty completing paper-and-pencil tasks

- may be able to tell lots about what they know but greatly resist writing anything on paper

- have trouble with long- and short-term memory

- lack organizational and study skills and appear messy and disorganized

- exhibit low self-esteem through anger, put-downs, crying, disruptive behaviors, and apathy

- are extremely frustrated with school.

Yet many gifted kids with LD also:

- have scored in the gifted range on ability, achievement, or creativity tests

- have a wide range of knowledge about many topics and can express their knowledge verbally

- have wild and crazy ideas

- express humor in unusual and sometimes bizarre ways

- have fertile imaginations

- have penetrating insights, a superior vocabulary, and sophisticated ideas and opinions.

Scenario: Toni

Toni always had something in her hands: pencils, toys, even gum. Unfortunately, the gum often found its way into her hair, requiring her teachers to be creative in the gum removal department. Her LD resource teacher addressed that problem by giving Toni a round, polished stone to keep her hands occupied, and that helped some.

In third grade, Toni had difficulty getting her thoughts down on paper, and she worked slowly and laboriously on all of her assignments. Her writing was small and cramped, and her sentence structure weak and disorganized. But if you let her tell you a story she had in her mind, that was another matter. She was always coming up with highly creative (if totally impractical) ways to solve classroom problems for other kids. She loved dominating class discussions so much that it seemed her tongue was one of her most hyperactive body parts!

Toni read at a sixth-grade level, but all of her other schoolwork was below third-grade level. Her teacher was very frustrated because he thought that Toni's advanced reading ability was proof that she could do the other work if she only applied herself and tried a little harder. The teacher feared that Toni was manipulating him by pretending not to be able to do the third-grade work.

When Toni's LD was documented, her teacher and I created learning style compatible ways for her to express what she was learning. Although her drawing skills leaned toward the blood-and-gore model, she was able to use these skills in a detailed study of killer sharks. The LD resource teacher located a retired media specialist who became Toni's mentor and helped her to create a narrated slide show.

Classroom accommodations included teaching Toni to use word processing and spell-check support in her written work, allowing her to illustrate her marvelous stories and record them on audiocassette, teaching her research skills in conjunction with the work she was doing with her mentor, and eliminating time pressures for activities and tests. At the beginning of each work period, Toni set a goal for her projected productivity, using the Daily Task Checklist (see page 26).

As Toni became more successful with some school tasks, her attitude and behavior clearly improved. As she realized that others appreciated her for her creative strengths, she became more comfortable accepting help in her areas of weakness.

Intervening with Gifted Students with or without LD

- First, find out what your students know and give them full credit for it.

- Find out what they are passionately interested in outside of school and allow them to work on related projects in school. Many of the standards you are teaching this year could probably be learned in the context of any topic.

- Allow students to express what they know in ways that are compatible with their learning styles. Allow them to be gifted in their areas of strength while accommodating their LD in their areas of weakness.

- Provide alternate learning experiences instead of the regular work, and behavior problems may disappear. You will then have the proof you need that the learning difficulties of these students were really a combination of boredom and frustration.

- Consult my book *Teaching Gifted Kids in the Regular Classroom* for more strategies to keep gifted students highly motivated and productive in school. See "References and Resources."

Other Conditions That Make Learning Difficult

The following sections describe some characteristics of students who have conditions that interfere with their ability to learn. Each list of characteristics is followed by intervention guidelines. Suggestions for intervening with behavior problems are found in Chapter 13, which is entirely devoted to behavior issues.

Behavior Disorders Including Emotional Disturbances (E/BD)

Students with E/BD exhibit some, many, or all of the following characteristics. Some children with these behaviors have been diagnosed with Oppositional Defiant Disorder (ODD).

- They have a history of outbursts of serious misbehavior, tantrums, and general discipline problems, which are evident in many children with E/BD before age three.

- They are restless, anxious, and/or irritable much of the time.

- They may spend much of their school time in the hall or in the office of some person responsible for discipline. They are often truant and may have a history of needing police intervention.

- They have short fuses and may become extremely angry at the slightest frustration or provocation. They act impulsively and appear unable to consider their options before they act.

- They constantly test the limits on everything from class rules to bedtime.

- They defy authority, saying things like "You can't tell me what to do when I'm not at school" or "You can't make me stop." They argue constantly.

- They deliberately annoy people, including both adults and other kids.

- They may be extremely physically aggressive, using force to get objects from others or to do something before it is their turn. They may strike or kick adults. Many are labeled "bullies."

- They may steal or destroy property. Some abuse animals and other children. They may justify taking revenge on others because they believe that the system has abused them.

- They may appear somewhat paranoid, believing that no one likes them or that others are laughing at them. They don't usually want to work in groups, partly because they think the other kids don't want them around. (Unfortunately, these perceptions may be accurate.)

- They may express an inappropriate emotion at the wrong time. *Example:* laughing when someone is hurt.

- They may use terms like "dummy" and "weirdo" to describe themselves. Because their behavior so often interferes with their learning, they do, in fact, develop academic deficiencies.

- Some kids with E/BD are almost invisible. They try to blend into the background and not be noticed. These kids may appear terrified when asked to recite or participate in class.

- Some are unusually sad or depressed. They may develop physical symptoms or irrational fears when in school, a condition sometimes referred to as "school phobia."
- Some suffer from anxiety or panic disorders.
- Some seem unable to learn, even though there is no diagnosed LD.

Autism

Autism is a complex developmental disability that usually appears by age three and significantly impacts an individual's ability to speak and interact socially. The symptoms occur in different degrees in different people. Some have difficulty expressing their needs and coping with change. They may repeat words or gestures in perseverant ways. Sensory integration problems, extreme sensitivity to irritation and pain, a lack of fear, and preference for monologues over dialogues all contribute to the difficulty in treating children with autism. For more information, contact the Autism Society of America. See "References and Resources."

Asperger's Syndrome

A neurobiological disorder, Asperger's Syndrome (also called Asperger's Disorder) is often considered a mild form of autism. Children with Asperger's Syndrome have normal intelligence and language skills and may even have an advanced talent or gifted ability in a particular area. However, they exhibit significant deficiencies in social and communication skills, and they become alarmed and upset with any type of change in their routine. For more information, consult Tony Attwood's book *Asperger's Syndrome*. See "References and Resources."

Intervening with Serious Behavior Problems

Many students whose behavior is described in the preceding sections need interventions beyond what many teachers are equipped to provide. Some of the strategies described in Chapter 13 can be helpful, especially Edward Ford's Responsible Thinking Process. For students with serious behavior problems, other professionals usually need to be involved, so be sure to ask for that help from the special education staff. A comprehensive evaluation is recommended; individual or family counseling is often very helpful. More information is available from the American Academy of Child & Adolescent Psychiatry. See "References and Resources."

Educationally Delayed (ED)

Children who are educationally delayed (ED)—formerly labeled "mentally retarded"—behave and learn at far less sophisticated levels than their age peers. Much of their behavior resembles that of very young children. Although they represent a significant range of abilities and characteristics, their learning difficulties tend to fall into the following categories.

Attention Deficits

Students have trouble paying attention to the task at hand or to the person describing the task. Their attention span may be very short, and their attention may be easily captured by extraneous sounds or movements. They have difficulty remembering what they learn from one day to another. However, once a particular skill is moved into long-term memory, they may be able to remember it quite well.

Academic Deficits

Students learn and perform well below average in typical academic subjects at any age. Most never achieve fluency in abstract and conceptual thinking. They have great difficulty generalizing what they learn in one situation and applying it to another.

Language Deficits

Students may not be able to clearly understand what they are told, and they are unable to express their thoughts clearly. Their speech may sound labored, and their voice quality may be unusual.

Motor Coordination Problems

Students' development of large or gross motor skills like running, skipping, or hopping is delayed. Development of fine motor skills needed for writing, cutting, and other school tasks is much less mature than for their age peers. Many ED students have significant vision and/or hearing problems as well.

Social Problems

In their efforts to get attention, students who are educationally delayed often behave inappropriately and sometimes even aggressively. They may act silly, make funny noises, push, hit, or kick other kids for no apparent reason, and annoy others by excessive displays of affection, such as hugging and kissing. Their behavior is inconsistent, unpredictable, and immature, and since it appears babyish to their peers, these students may not be accepted into the group unless teachers purposefully provide coaching to them and their peers.

Intervening with ED

- Most kids with ED can be taught to greatly improve their social skills. For one approach, see page 199.

- You and the other students may have to concentrate for some time on helping these kids develop appropriate social behaviors. Students with ED need to be told consistently when their behavior is inappropriate. Any student who is the target of unwanted behavior by another child should say directly to that child, "I don't like that. I don't like it when you do that. I want you to stop doing that right now."

- Once these students' social behavior is in the acceptable range, you may pay more attention to their academic growth. It is never appropriate to hold the class back to wait for students with ED to catch up. Rather, adjust the amount of work you give them and the methods they may use to learn. Students with ED need to work on simplified versions of what the rest of the class is doing, and they need more time to complete their work. Break tasks into small component steps and sequence the steps from simplest to most difficult. As with all struggling students, consistently use concrete examples and experiences to teach abstract concepts.

- Students with ED also need to spend time on life skills such as listening, sitting still, following directions, getting in and out of their outer clothing, and so on. You may need to teach some of these basic skills explicitly.

- Ask for student volunteers to serve as learning buddies for students with ED. Be sure to rotate the buddies so many kids share in the responsibility of helping each other learn.

- Teach them how to use the Daily Task Checklist (page 26). If they can't print, have them use stickers to illustrate specific tasks.

Substance Exposed (SE)

Children who were exposed before birth to alcohol or other addictive drugs create significant challenges for classroom teachers. Many experts believe that crack-cocaine-affected children need a minimum of two years in a special class before they are introduced into a regular classroom. The rationale is that without intervention in a separate environment, their problems are likely to last throughout their school career.

Students with SE exhibit some, many, or all of the following characteristics:

- They engage in behaviors that appear hyperactive. They are impulsive and distractible and often abandon tasks before completion. Many appear to be in a constant state of high stimulation.

- Some have an unusual walking gait. Some present facial and head malformations, especially head circumference too small for the body.

- They may resist the basic kinds of nurturing that caring adults wish to give because their nervous systems are already so sensitive and overstimulated that any added stimulation is painful. They may cry a lot because of this.

- Since they are so needy themselves, it may be difficult for them to be aware of or respond to the needs of others.

- They may experience sudden mood swings and have more intense and less predictable outbursts than kids with E/BD.

- Many appear to have no sense of limits. Some may be violent and may attack others with no reason or provocation. They seem unable to learn from experience, and they repeat destructive acts without visible remorse. They appear not to understand or care about the consequences of their behaviors. Some are labeled "asocial," as they appear to actually enjoy their inappropriate behaviors.

- They may possess normal or above-average intelligence despite their serious learning problems.

- They are often unable to learn independently or by imitating the behavior of other kids. They need to be directly taught all academic and social skills.

Intervening with SE

- Most of what works with students with ADHD should also work with kids who have been exposed prenatally to harmful substances. Keep trying until you find something that is effective. (Look back at "Ways to Intervene with LD" on pages 24–28.)

- Many of these children are super-sensitive to stimuli. In teaching and interacting with them, use only one stimulus at a time. *Either* talk to them *or* touch them *or* look at them; don't combine stimuli, and keep in mind that many can't tolerate much touching.

- Remove highly stimulating objects in the classroom from their line of vision.

- Limit choices; kids with SE are easily confused and overstimulated by too many choices.

- Allow adequate space between them and other students. In general, leave enough room for arms and legs to swing without touching anyone else.

- Be prepared to physically restrain them during outbursts. Get permission from parents and administrators in advance. Remove items from the classroom that could be used to hurt others.

- Model or demonstrate exactly what you want them to do in work, play, and showing emotion.

- Teach very directly, one thing at a time, until some progress is made. Teach the way each child learns best and use the same methods consistently.

- Establish and use routines without variation. Transitions from one activity to another must be specifically taught and experienced as having a beginning, a middle, and an end. Always give ample warning before transitions. (*Example:* "In one minute, we will put our books away and stand up for brief exercise.") Always use the same words for each transition, even if you have to read from a script.

- Make a simple list of essential class rules and give copies to each child to keep at her desk. If a child has to leave the room, she should bring along the list of rules.

- Celebrate (in a low-key way) each milestone these students reach. Abandon grade-level expectations in favor of indications of individual progress.

- There should always be more than one adult in your classroom, since these children need so much attention and support.* A major goal is for the child to develop an attachment to an adult. For this to happen, the student/teacher ratio should be lower than in a typical class. Students with SE require a lot of one-on-one attention. If you don't have a full-time aide, work with the student's parent to advocate for one through the special education department.

Other Conditions That Create Special Learning Needs

In addition to LD, E/BD, ED, and SE, there are other conditions that affect learning and create special learning needs. Whenever possible, consult with the teachers who have previously taught these students. As you adapt your teaching for students with special learning needs, you will constantly be seeking more information. Some of the best sources are the national organizations that exist to deliver support services for people whose disabilities present special life challenges. See "References and Resources" for several suggestions.

Physical Disabilities

Students with physical disabilities include those who are in wheelchairs; those with cerebral palsy, muscular dystrophy, and spina bifida; those with epilepsy and other conditions that result in seizures; those with arthritis and congenital malformations; and students with any other condition that affects their mobility.

Students with physical disabilities exhibit some, many, or all of the following characteristics:

- They may have normal to above-average intelligence.

- They may suffer multiple related afflictions, such as vision or speech disorders.

- They may have to miss school regularly for long-term hospital care. If hospital teachers are available, you may be asked to guide them by keeping them aware of what the students would have been learning in school. Ask to be kept informed of the students' medical status and any changes. Hospital stays may also be accompanied by traumatic events, so expect some setbacks when the children return to school.

Intervening with Physical Disabilities

- Don't assume that these students have had the same background experiences as their classmates, since their physical limitations may have prevented them from participating in many activities other kids have shared.

- Seek training in specific interventions for physical problems such as seizures. Ask the special education staff in your district; perhaps they can offer the training or refer you to someone who can.

- Make their learning experiences developmentally appropriate by assessing which skills they possess, then teaching them at levels that cause them to stretch and move ahead.

- Sometimes these kids have become overly dependent on assistance from others. Use goal-setting strategies (see pages 65–68) and behavior contracts (see pages 200–205) as needed.

Hearing Impairment

Students who have been identified with any degree of hearing loss, from mild to profound, are said to be "hearing impaired." If there are kids in your class whose attention to task consistently wavers, you should carefully observe

* Vincent, Lisbeth J., et al. *Born Substance Exposed, Educationally Vulnerable.* Reston, VA: Council for Exceptional Children (CEC), 1991, page 19.

them for indicators that their hearing might be impaired. These include:

- frequent ear and respiratory infections; family history of hearing impairment

- leaning forward, cupping their hands behind their ears, and/or turning their heads to hear better

- asking others to repeat what's been said; moving closer to the sound source

- the appearance that they are not paying attention; frequent daydreaming

- speech, voice, and articulation problems

- a noticeable change in academic performance.

Intervening with Hearing Impairment

- Face the class while teaching. Rather than turning away to write on the board, prepare transparencies in advance and display them on an overhead projector.

- Use lots of demonstrations, exhibits, and hands-on learning experiences.

- Allow students to work away from background noise, since they may have difficulty separating speech from other sounds.

- Permit them to move around the room as necessary to get closer to what they want and need to hear.

- Have them work with buddies who can jot down important points made during class discussions.

- Allow them to use scripts of soundtracks for videos, movies, CD-ROM programs, and so on. Scripts may be available from the production companies on request.

- During class discussions, have kids raise their hands after they are called on so students with hearing impairments can identify the speakers and watch them as they speak.

- Consult an audiologist to learn about technologies that can enhance communication for students with hearing impairments.

- If some kids know and use the manual (finger-spelling) alphabet, have them teach it to several other students so they can communicate with kids who are hearing impaired. If no one in your classroom knows the manual alphabet, someone in your school probably does. Or contact your district office and say that you would like someone to visit your class and teach the manual alphabet. See page 35 for a handout you can give to your students.

- Introduce your class to American Sign Language (ASL). Since this is a real language, not just an alphabet, you probably will want to invite someone who knows ASL to demonstrate it for your class.

Visual Impairment

Students who are visually impaired may rub their eyes a lot, close or cover one eye, hold books close to their eyes, squint or frown frequently, and have significant difficulty reading. Their eyes may itch or burn, they may complain that things are blurry, and they may have frequent headaches. If they have been legally blind from birth, they may lack understanding of abstract concepts such as "color" and "sky."

Intervening with Visual Impairment

- Always face these students when you are speaking.

- Repeat aloud anything you write on the board or an overhead transparency.

- Make sure that all handouts are clear and readable, with dark letters and numbers and adequate white space between words and lines. Use a photocopier to enlarge written material for these students.

- Record your lectures on audiocassette so students can listen to them again later.

- Provide concrete, hands-on learning materials.

- Find and provide recorded versions of teaching materials. Check with libraries and national organizations such as the American Foundation for the Blind (see "References and Resources").

- Seat students with visual impairments next to volunteer buddies who can help them follow along. Rotate buddies at least once a month.

- Contact an optometrists' or ophthalmologists' association for advice on helping students with vision problems, as some doctors have developed very effective methods. *Example:* The Irlen Institute has successfully used color therapy for a condition called *scotopic sensitivity*, which makes print appear as if it is moving around. For some kids, placing a colored transparency over text keeps the print from moving and makes it easier to read and understand. To contact the Irlen Institute, see "References and Resources."

Poverty*

Huge numbers of children who live in poverty have severe achievement deficiencies. With the expectations of No

* Information in this and the following section is adapted from Martin Haberman, *Star Teachers of Children in Poverty.* Indianapolis, IN: Kappa Delta Pi, 1995. Used with permission of the Haberman Educational Foundation (www.habermanfoundation.org).

The Manual Alphabet

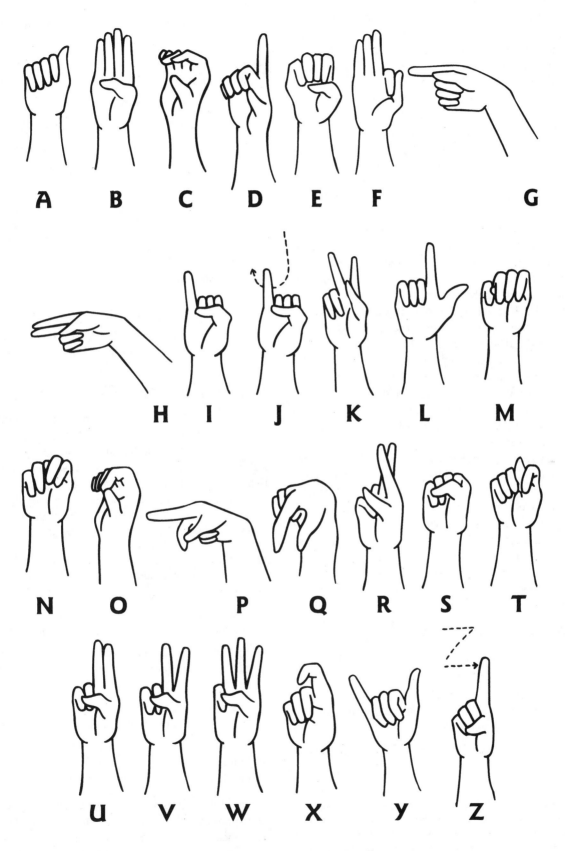

Child Left Behind and tests of state standards, coming from poverty is no excuse for failing to learn.

Dr. Martin Haberman has done an intensive study of this situation and has reported on it in his book *Star Teachers of Children of Poverty*. He claims that for children of poverty, having star teachers is a matter of life or death.

Several recent studies have documented the positive effect that really good teachers have on students. What is even more surprising is evidence that if a child has an ineffective teacher for one year, it will take him or her two years to catch up. If the child has an ineffective teacher for two consecutive years, he or she might never catch up.*

The reason it is important to know this is that many schools have assigned the most difficult students to the newest and most inexperienced teachers. Of course, many new teachers are highly effective, and some veteran teachers are less effective, but the important point here is to match severely underachieving students with the most effective teachers. Early evidence on the effectiveness of this practice is extremely positive.

Further, Dr. Haberman claims that 3,000 students drop out of high school every day. Just do the math and you can imagine what a devastating effect this has on our society and economy. The school dropout syndrome begins in elementary school. Students who are not fluent readers by the end of third grade are at great risk of not completing high school. Share this information with your principal, to help him or her make the most effective teacher/student assignments possible.

So what is it that makes a teacher so effective, especially with children who live with so many disadvantages? Dr. Haberman observes that star teachers truly feel that success in school for *every* child is of enormous importance. They expect that their students will have issues, and they approach those situations proactively. They don't base their success on whether or not they work in a dysfunctional system. They simply take the necessary responsibility to guarantee learning success for all of their students.

What Star Teachers Do**

- Make school a positive place, and make learning as enjoyable and successful as possible.

- Do whatever is possible in school, regardless of the realities of students' homes, families, and neighborhoods. Never blame the victim.

- Connect learning to students' interests and relevant issues.

- Model and teach appreciation of learning for its own sake.

- Convince students that they are welcome in the school and in their classroom.

- Remain gentle while consistently firm; manage well with much flexibility.

- Seek to understand without judging.

- Own up to their mistakes and try to fix them.

- Carefully choose homework and assign it sparingly.

- Base student evaluation at least partly on student effort and progress.

- Acknowledge their students' interest in a problem-solving, real-life application approach to learning the curriculum; use whatever methods are effective in building learning success.

- Maintain positive ongoing contact with all parents and caregivers.

- Use behavior management techniques that teach children to take responsibility for their own behavior; avoid arbitrary discipline or punishment measures.

Successful Schools

In 2004, the Prichard Committee for Academic Excellence in Kentucky released a study of top-scoring elementary schools in that state whose students included large numbers of children in poverty. These successful schools reported fewer than 15 points difference in achievement levels between majority and minority populations and between low-income and middle-income students. The schools shared the following characteristics:

- The faculty does not make an issue of students who live in poverty. Disadvantaged and advantaged students are treated in fundamentally similar ways.

- The relationships among adults in the school are caring and respectful. Decisions are collaborative.

- All staff work hard to meet their students' needs in nutrition, transportation, and other areas with enthusiasm and without complaint.

- There is careful recruitment, hiring, and placement of teachers and staff. Staff assignments are based solely on students' needs.

- There is evidence of personal willingness to work with and believe in all students.

Dr. Haberman's work, the Prichard study, and other research proves that a school program can make a positive difference in achievement, even in the presence of other factors that might work against the attainment of proficiency

---

* Sanders, William L., and June C. Rivers. "Cumulative and Residual Effects of Teachers on Future Student Academic Achievement." Knoxville, TN: University of Tennessee Value-Added Research and Assessment Center, November 1996.

** I have summarized this list from my own reading of Dr. Haberman's book *Star Teachers of Children in Poverty,* which contains information on this topic in much more detail.

levels for some students. Combining high expectations for all students with appropriate intervention strategies for students who need them can dramatically affect students' perception of their own learning abilities and positively impact their achievement.

Working as a Team with Special Education Teachers

There are many good reasons to bring students with specific learning or functional disabilities into the regular classroom. We provide them with higher expectations for doing age- and grade-appropriate work, and more positive role models for behavior and learning. We prepare the so-called normal kids to live and work beside them and perceive them as regular people and in a positive light. Since almost all people with disabilities have parents without disabilities, we may assume that the future parents of people with disabilities are the children we are teaching today! Based on their school experience of seeing the benefits of integrating functionally challenged people into regular classrooms, they will be able to provide high expectations for their own children to actualize their learning potential.

Regular education and special education teachers must work together to create environments that promote optimum learning conditions. The degree to which the cooperative relationship exists may be the key to the learning success of students with significant learning challenges. When special education programs changed so that most of a child's education would take place in the regular classroom, it was with the understanding that the special education staff would serve as active advisors to the regular classroom teachers. Since students who formerly spent lots of time in the special education classroom are now spending most of their school time in your classroom because it is considered the least restrictive environment, you are probably in need of help. If you are a regular classroom teacher with special education students who interact regularly with and get support from special education teachers, the inclusion program is working the way it was supposed to work. If your support from the special education staff is minimal, you have the right to ask for and receive assistance. So do not hesitate to ask—and ask again, and continue asking until you get the assistance you need.

In the best of situations, the special education staff and the regular classroom teacher work as teammates. The specialists are available to help *all* students who need help, not just those who have been identified as special education students. Everyone benefits from the integration of former special education students into the classroom, particularly if adequate help for teachers and students is available from specialists on staff.

Many schools have created teams of specialists to act as resources for regular classroom teachers. Originally formed to reduce the number of kids who were being referred for separate special education classes, these teams may also be used to prevent learning or behavior problems from becoming unmanageable in the regular classroom. Called Teacher Assistance Teams (TATs) or Learning Resource Teachers (LRTs), they are on call by regular classroom teachers and administrators to go into the classroom, observe those students with learning or behavior difficulties, and assist the teacher with specific intervention strategies. Team members continue to provide support until the target student and the regular classroom teacher are able to manage the time spent in the regular classroom independently.

Plan with special education teachers to locate and bring into your school staff development programs that enable teachers to appreciate diversity that goes beyond multiculturalism. If you bring guest speakers into your classroom throughout the year, make sure that some of them are people with learning difficulties and other disabilities who have succeeded in life.

Questions and Answers

"How can I teach kids with such exceptional educational needs? I've never had any special education training."

It may help you to know that many labeled special education students don't actually belong in the categories in which they have placed. Some gifted kids have been misdiagnosed as delayed learners because they wouldn't do their work! The learning needs of many diagnosed students are closer to those of kids in regular education classrooms. Most kids with exceptional learning needs benefit from the chance to learn with students who have a wider range of abilities than those found in special education settings.

Programs in which students with special needs spend most of their time in regular classrooms were designed under the assumption that special education staff would work as partners with regular education teachers to provide appropriate assistance. If you're not receiving the help you need, ask for it, and keep asking until you get results.

Invite someone from the special education staff to observe the dynamics of the situation in your classroom vis-à-vis a particular student and make specific intervention suggestions. Also ask that person to help you monitor the success of those changes. If you need more help, invite the principal to come in and make the same kinds of observations. Ask her to locate additional services that might be available for you, perhaps from a county or state special education agency. Beyond that, ask the principal how a change can be made to the student's Individual Education Plan (IEP) to get help from a paraprofessional who would work with you in your classroom. Also ask for input on how to access other appropriate support services.

According to the Individuals with Disabilities Education Act (IDEA), all children who are eligible for special education services have the right to a free, appropriate public education in the least restrictive educational environment. For some kids with profound exceptional learning needs, the least restrictive environment may not be in the regular classroom. If you use several of the strategies described in this book with a particular student and see no improvement, document your intervention attempts and ask the appropriate administrator for a reevaluation of that student's placement in your class.

"Isn't it better for special education kids to spend most of their time in programs with teachers who have the right kind of training?"

It's better for *some* students to spend most of their school time in special education classrooms . . . but very few. Inclusion practices resulted in part from the *over*-identification of students for special educational services. We need to be careful not to recommend a student for out-of-classroom placement until we have consistently used appropriate intervention strategies.

"I'm confused. So many of these kids have opposite needs. How am I supposed to know the right thing to do on the spur of the moment?"

Remember, it's not necessary for you to match the correct intervention to each individual student's needs. Refer to the general suggestions on pages 21–22 first; many of them are effective with students in several categories of learning needs. Use whatever works!

"If we make all of these accommodations for struggling students, won't it hurt them when they get into the real world? Isn't there a time when they should learn basic skills without the aid of technology or extra help? Where will they find adult environments in which such deference is paid to their special needs?"

There are many colleges that have special programs for students with learning difficulties. There are programs that provide lifetime coaching for people who need a little extra support to get to work and complete the tasks there. As teachers, we need only be concerned that these students leave school feeling confident that they can learn and that they are worthwhile members of learning communities. When they feel that way, they are much more likely to make their way successfully in the real world.

"Won't kids who need a learning buddy become targets for teasing?"

So many learning activities today happen in pairs or groups that learning buddies are just an extension of that condition in many classrooms. Avoid negative labeling and approach this in a low-key fashion. There are often many students in each class who enjoy helping other kids learn, and they make good learning buddies. Make sure the rest of the class understands that having a learning buddy is simply another way in which individual differences are recognized and accommodated in your classroom, and that it does not imply any deficiency.

"Is it legal and/or ethical to test some students in untimed situations? My testing manuals are very specific about sticking to time limits."

When giving a standardized test, you definitely should stick to the time limits for all of your students. But it might be useful—and enlightening—to find out what your struggling students actually can do. Before you send in their answer sheets, make photocopies and mark the places where they ended. Send in the original answer sheets with those from the rest of the class. A week or two later, have the students complete as much of the test as they can without timing it. Score this version manually. Do *not* send it to the testing company, and do not use the results to compare the target students' performance against that of others in the same class or at the same grade level. Simply use the results to document what the students can do in untimed test situations, and use the data to document their actual strengths and weaknesses.

REFERENCES AND RESOURCES

A.D.D.—From A to Z: Understanding the Diagnosis and Treatment of Attention Deficit Disorder in Children and Adults (www.drhallowell.com/store). A video version of a lecture by Dr. Edward M. Hallowell, a leading authority on the subject of Attention Deficit Disorder. See The Hallowell Center below. (978) 287-0810.

A.D.D. WareHouse (addwarehouse.com). Offers the most comprehensive catalog I have found of materials for and about children with attention deficits and other learning problems. Many are designed to be used by kids themselves. 1-800-233-9273.

Alexander Graham Bell Association for the Deaf and Hard of Hearing (www.agbell.org). Resources for persons with hearing disabilities. (202) 337-5220 (TDD available).

American Academy of Child & Adolescent Psychiatry (www.aacap.org). Information about the understanding and treatment of developmental, behavioral, and mental disorders that affect children and adolescents. (202) 966-7300.

American Association on Intellectual and Developmental Disabilities (www.aaidd.org). Help for families with persons who have mental retardation, including Down syndrome. 202-387-1968

American Foundation for the Blind (www.afb.org). Information, help, and advocacy for those living with vision loss, their families, and friends. 1-800-AFB-LINE (1-800-232-5463).

Armstrong, Thomas. *The Myth of the A.D.D. Child: 50 Ways to Improve Your Child's Behavior and Attention Span Without Drugs, Labels, or Coercion.* New York: Penguin/Plume, 1997. A must-read for educators as well as parents, to help avoid premature decisions to medicate kids with ADD/ADHD.

Attention Deficit Disorder Association (ADDA) (www.add.org). Materials and services to help people with attention deficit disorders. 1-800-939-1019.

Attwood, Tony. *Asperger's Syndrome: A Guide for Parents and Professionals.* London: Jessica Kingsley Publishers, 1997.

Autism Society (www.autism-society.org). Information, support, and advocacy for individuals within the autism spectrum and their families. 1-800-3AUTISM (1-800-328-8476).

Banks, Carmelita B. "Harmonizing Student-Teacher Interaction: A Case for Learning Styles." *Synthesis* 2:2 (1991). Springfield, IL: Illinois State Board of Education.

Baum, Susan M., and Steve V. Owen. *To Be Gifted and Learning Disabled: Strategies for Helping Bright Students with LD, ADHD, and More.* Mansfield Center, CT: Creative Learning Press, 2004.

Birely, Marlene. *Crossover Children: A Sourcebook for Helping the Learning Disabled/Gifted Child.* Reston, VA: The Council for Exceptional Children, 1995.

Birth Defect Research for Children (www.birthdefects.org). Information and support services for children born with birth defects and their families. (407) 895-0802.

Brain Gym International (www.braingym.org). Help for kinesthetic learners. The Brain Gym program has been used successfully by parents and teachers to significantly improve learning attitudes and achievement through nonacademic means. It works on the assumption that people with learning difficulties have immature nerve networks in the brain that can be significantly improved through certain forms of exercise. Teachers have found that if they precede each learning activity with two to three minutes of exercise, kids are more able to focus on the actual lesson. Students may stand beside their chairs to do the exercises. *Two sample exercises:* Cross Crawl: Have students march in place while touching the right hand to the left knee and the left hand to the right knee. Lazy 8's: Draw an infinity sign (∞) on a chart. Have students draw it in unison several times by starting in the middle of the figure and moving down and to the left, up and to the right, back to the middle, down and to the right, up and back down to the left center, just like drawing an 8 lying on its side. Visit the Web site to find certified Brain Gym instructors and classes in your area. Brain Gym books and learning materials by Paul E. Dennison and Gail E. Dennison are also available. Organization: 1-800-356-2109. Store: 1-888-388-9898.

Castellano, Jaime A., and Eva Díaz. *Reaching New Horizons: Gifted and Talented Education for Culturally and Linguistically Diverse Students.* Upper Saddle River, NJ: Allyn & Bacon, 2001. A comprehensive overview of the interface between bilingual/multicultural/ESL education.

The Center for Speech and Language Disorders (www.csld.org). This nonprofit organization offers family-centered services for children with language disorders. The Web site has a list of frequently asked questions, resource materials (books, audios, and videos) available for purchase, and an e-newsletter sign-up. (630) 652-0200.

Children and Adults with Attention-Deficit/Hyperactivity Disorder (CHADD) (www.chadd.org). Information and support for parents and teachers of children with ADD. 1-800-233-4050.

Coalition of Essential Schools (www.essentialschools.org). Founded by Dr. Theodore R. Sizer, this organization supports a network of schools that share a set of common principles based on research and practice that are used to guide whole-school reform efforts in the areas of school design, classroom practice, leadership, and community connections. (401) 426-9638.

Cooper, Carolyn, Mary Ann Lingg, Angelo Puricelli, and George Yard. *Dissimilar Learners.* St. Louis, MO: Pegasus Publications, Ltd., 1995.

Council for Exceptional Children (CEC) (www.cec.sped.org). Services, articles, and resources for helping young people with all types of learning difficulties. 1-888-232-7733.

Delpit, Lisa. *Other People's Children: Cultural Conflict in the Classroom.* New York: The New Press, 1995. Shows teachers how to make school a productive learning experience for children in poverty and children of color by sending consistently high expectations that students will become proficient with grade level standards.

Dowdy, Carol, et al. *Attention-Deficit Hyperactivity Disorder in the Classroom: A Practical Guide for Teachers.* Austin, TX: PRO-ED, 1997.

Educating Peter (www.films.com). This 1992 Academy Award–winning documentary follows a child with Down syndrome who is mainstreamed into a public school. It vividly captures Peter's achievements as he makes a place for himself among his peers. *Graduating Peter* (2001) highlights Peter's experiences in sixth grade, eighth grade, and high school and his progress toward building a meaningful life for himself. Both are HBO productions. 1-800-322-8755.

The Efficacy Institute (www.efficacy.org). Founded by Dr. Jeff Howard, the Efficacy Institute offers training and services for measurable improvement in academic performance and character development. Students learn that "smart is something you can *get*" and success depends on the level and quality of one's effort. Adults are taught never to give any indication that they are judging students' abilities, even when young people confront difficulty, but to model excitement and determination about figuring out what the problem is. (781) 547-6060.

Eisenberg, Nancy, and Pamela H. Esser. *Teach and Reach Students with ADD.* Houston, TX: Multigrowth Resources, 1994.

ERIC Education Resources Information Center (www.eric.ed.gov). This online information center offers many articles on teaching students with a wide variety of learning disabilities. I especially recommend the following ERIC digests:

- "ADHD and Children Who Are Gifted" by James T. Webb and Diane Latimer. ERIC # ED358673; ERIC Digest #522 (1993).

- "Collaboration Between General and Special Education Teachers" by Suzanne Ripley. ERIC # ED409317 (1997).

- "Dual Exceptionalities" by Colleen Willard-Holt. ERIC # ED430344; ERIC Digest E574 (1999).

- "Gifted but Learning Disabled: A Puzzling Paradox" by Susan Baum. ERIC # ED321484; ERIC Digest E479 (1990).

- "Integrating Students with Severe Disabilities." ERIC # ED321501; ERIC Digest E468 (1990).

- "Meeting the Needs of Gifted and Talented Minority Language Students" by Linda M. Cohen. ERIC # ED321485; ERIC Digest E480 (1988).

Note: ERIC Digests were formerly available through the ERIC Clearinghouse system. When that system was eliminated in 2003, most of the content at the former ERIC sites found new homes. As of this writing, www.eric.ed.gov is the new ERIC. Search by title to find the digests listed above.

Goldstein, Arnold, et al. The Skillstreaming Series (www.researchpress.com). Books, skill cards, CD-ROMs, and videos help kids learn appropriate social/interactive skills and make good behavior choices. The series includes *Skillstreaming in Early Childhood, Skillstreaming the Elementary School Child,* and *Skillstreaming the Adolescent.* 1-800-519-2707.

The Haberman Educational Foundation (www.haberman foundation.org). This not-for-profit organization works to teach and implement research-based models for identifying educators who serve students at risk and in poverty. (713) 667-6185.

Haberman, Martin. *Star Teachers of Children in Poverty.* Indianapolis, IN: Kappa Delta Pi, 1995. Available from www.kdp.org; 1-800-284-3167.
—*Star Teachers: The Ideology and Best Practice of Effective Teachers of Diverse Children and Youth in Poverty.* Houston: Haberman Educational Foundation, 2005. Available from www.habermanfoundation.org; (713) 667-6185.

The Hallowell Center (www.drhallowell.com). Founded by Dr. Edward M. Hallowell, a psychologist and leading national expert in ADD, the Hallowell Center helps people with ADD lead happier, more productive lives. Dr. Hallowell also manages a national system of life coaches who help people with ADD get through life one day at a time. (978) 287-0810.

Hallowell, Edward M. *ADD from A to Z: Understanding the Diagnosis and Treatment of Attention Deficit Disorder in Children and Adults.* New York: Pantheon Books, 1994. A comprehensive guide to understanding and intervening with persons with ADD.

Hallowell, Edward M., and John J. Ratey. *Delivered from Distraction: Getting the Most Out of Life with Attention Deficit Disorder.* The follow-up to Hallowell and Ratey's Driven to Distraction is an up-to-date guide to living a successful life with ADD. New York: Ballantine Books, 2005.
—*Driven to Distraction: Recognizing and Coping with Attention Deficit Disorder from Childhood Through Adulthood.* New York: Simon & Schuster, 1995. This practical and useful book is considered a classic in the field.

Harwell, Joan M. *Complete Learning Disabilities Handbook: Ready-to-Use Strategies & Activities for Teaching Students with Learning Disabilities.* New 2nd Edition. San Francisco, CA: Jossey-Bass, 2002.

Hennigh, Kathleen. *Understanding Dyslexia: A Professional's Guide.* Westminster, CA: Teacher Created Materials, 1995.

Hopfenberg, Wendy S., Henry M. Levin, and Associates. *The Accelerated Schools Resource Guide.* San Francisco: Jossey Bass Publishers, 1993. Describes the Accelerated Schools program and provides information on how to contact schools that are using it.

Hot Topics Series. Phi Delta Kappa International (www.pdkintl.org). Hot Topics volumes are compilations of research articles and professional opinion on pressing issues in education. Available at the time of this book's publication: *Assessing Inclusion: Strategies for Success* (2000). 1-800-766-1156.

How Difficult Can This Be? The F.A.T. City Workshop: Understanding Learning Disabilities (www.shoppbs.org). Hosted by Dr. Richard LaVoie, seen on PBS, this documentary program looks at the world through the eyes of a learning-disabled child. A must-see for all teachers—great for staff meetings. Also available: *Last One Picked . . . First One Picked On,* hosted by Dr. LaVoie, addresses the social problems kids with LD often face. 1-800-531-4727.

International Dyslexia Association (www.interdys.org). An international organization dedicated to the study and treatment of dyslexia. Formerly the Orton Dyslexia Society. (410) 296-0232.

Irlen Institute (www.irlen.com). Diagnostic testing and help for children and adults with perceptual reading and learning problems, available in certified testing centers nationwide. For some children, the use of colored overlays or lenses for their glasses (the Irlen method) dramatically improves their learning success. 1-800-55-IRLEN (1-800-554-7536).

Kannapel, Patricia, and Stephen K. Clements with Diane Taylor and Terry Hibpshman. "Inside the Black Box of High-Performing, High-Poverty Schools." A report from the Prichard Committee for Academic Excellence, Lexington, Kentucky (February 2005). This fascinating study documents the characteristics that are found in low-income, high-poverty schools, suggesting that learning success can be accomplished regardless of adverse social and economic conditions. Available as a PDF file on the Prichard Committee Web site (www.prichardcommittee .org). (859) 233-9849.

Kravetz, Marybeth, and Imy F. Wax. *The K&W Guide to Colleges for Students with Learning Disabilities or Attention Deficit Disorder: A Resource Book for Students, Parents, and Professionals.* 6th edition (check for the latest). Burlington, MA: The Princeton Review, 2003.

Lawton, Millicent. "Co-Teaching: Are Two Heads Better than One?" Harvard Education Letter (March/April 1999). Available online at the *Harvard Education Letter* Web site (www.edletter.org).

LDOnline (www.ldonline.org). This comprehensive Web site is the first one I go to when I need information about students with learning challenges.

Leadership and Learning Center (www.leadandlearn .com). Chairman and founder Dr. Douglas Reeves identifies five factors present in schools with performance at or above the 90th percentile in which 90+ percent of the students come from combined minorities and 90+ percent of the students are on free and reduced lunch. They are: strong emphasis on achievement, focus on essential curricular areas, frequent assessments with multiple chances for students to show improvement, writing across the curriculum, and use of consistent rubrics across all classes for assessment. Call for more information and a list of schools that qualify. 1-866-399-6019.

Learning Ally (www.learningally.org). This organization makes available taped recordings of most textbooks and some literature used in schools throughout the United States. Their fees are nominal. 1-800-221-4792

Lee, Christopher, and Rosemary F. Jackson. *Faking It: A Look into the Mind of a Creative Learner.* Portsmouth, NH: Heinemann, 1992.

Levine, Mel. *A Mind at a Time.* New York: Simon and Schuster, 2002. Explains how parents and teachers can encourage children's learning strengths and bypass their learning weaknesses.

Lyman, Donald E. *Making the Words Stand Still.* Boston: Houghton Mifflin, 1986. Writing from his own experience, Lyman describes the anguish that kids with LD feel as they try to learn, then describes his own unique teaching methods.

March of Dimes Birth Defects Foundation (www. marchofdimes.com). Materials to support the development and education of children born with birth defects. (914) 997-4488.

McMurchie, Susan. *Understanding My Learning Differences.* Verona, WI: IEP Resources/Attainment Company, 2003. Twenty-three lesson plans help students with LD become more aware of their learning differences and develop coping and self-help skills. 1-800-327-4269.

Morsink, Catherine Voelker. *Teaching Special Needs Students in Regular Classrooms.* Boston: Little, Brown and Co., 1984.

Nation's Challenge: A Guide for Educators of Children Affected by Alcohol and Other Drugs, parts 1 and 2 (store.samhsa .gov). In two videotapes from a 1995 Department of Education teleconference, panels of experts (educators, administrators, doctors, social workers) discuss ways to discover the uniqueness of substance-exposed children and unlock their potential. Available from SAMHSA's National Clearinghouse for Alcohol & Drug Information (NCADI).

Parker, Harvey C. *The ADD Hyperactivity Handbook for Schools: Effective Strategies for Identifying and Teaching ADD Students in Elementary and Secondary Schools.* Plantation, FL: Specialty Press, 1992.

The President's Committee for People with Intellectual Disabilities (PCPID) (www.acf.hhs.gov). Formerly the President's Committee on Mental Retardation (PCMR). (202) 690-6590.

Reif, Sandra F. *How to Reach and Teach Children with ADD/ ADHD.* San Francisco, CA: Jossey-Bass, 2005.

Rich, Dorothy. *MegaSkills: Building Children's Achievement for the Information Age*. New and expanded edition. Boston: Houghton Mifflin, 1998. How to teach children the basic skills needed to be competent in life, including confidence, motivation, effort, responsibility, perseverance, focus, and common sense.

ricklavoie.com (www.ricklavoie.com). The Web site of Dr. Richard Lavoie, a nationally recognized expert on learning disabilities and host of the *How Difficult Can This Be?* and *Last One Picked . . . First One Picked On* videos (see above). His books, videos, articles, and workshops are fabulous resources for anyone who lives and works with students with learning difficulties. He really understands these kids, and he helps parents and teachers do the same.

Ross, Jerilyn. *Triumph Over Fear: A Book of Hope and Help for People with Anxiety, Panic Attacks, and Phobia*. New York: Bantam, 1995.

Sanders, William L., and June C. Rivers. "Cumulative and Residual Effects of Teachers on Future Student Academic Achievement." Knoxville, TN: University of Tennessee Value-Added Research and Assessment Center, November 1996. Available to download at www.heartland.org.

Stainback, Susan, and William Stainback. *Integration of Students with Severe Handicaps into Regular Schools*. Reston, VA: Council for Exceptional Children (CEC), 1985.

Suskind, Ron. *A Hope in the Unseen: An American Odyssey from the Inner City to the Ivy League*. New York: Broadway Books, 1998. Based on a Pulitzer Prize–winning true story about how one teen from the inner city of Washington, D.C., was able to move out of the cycle of poverty toward a college education, with the help of several people from inside and outside his neighborhood.

Vail, Priscilla. *Smart Kids with School Problems (Gifted/LD): Things to Know and Ways to Help*. New York: Plume/NAL Dutton, 1989.

Vincent, Lisbeth J., et al. *Born Substance Exposed, Educationally Vulnerable*. Reston, VA: Council for Exceptional Children (CEC), 1991.

Waller, Mary Bellis. *Crack-Affected Children: A Teacher's Guide*. Newbury Park, CA: Corwin Press, 1993.

Williams, Donna. *Somebody, Somewhere*. New York: Times Books, 1994. A first-person account of autism.

Winebrenner, Susan with Dina Brulles. *Teaching Gifted Kids in Today's Classroom: Strategies and Techniques Every Teacher Can Use*. Minneapolis: Free Spirit Publishing, 2012.

RECOMMENDED READINGS FOR STUDENTS

Fisher, Gary, and Rhoda Cummings. *The Survival Guide for Kids with LD (Learning Differences)*. Minneapolis: Free Spirit Publishing, 2002. Explains LD in terms kids ages 8 and up can understand, describes the different kinds of LD, and discusses LD programs. Includes resources for parents and teachers.

Gordon, Michael. *I Would If I Could: A Teenager's Guide to ADHD/Hyperactivity*. Syracuse, NY: GSI Press, 1992.

Hayes, Marnell. *The Tuned-In, Turned-On Book about Learning Problems*. Novato, CA: Academic Therapy Publications, 1994. Written directly to adolescents with LD, this book helps kids identify and capitalize on their individual learning styles.

Janover, Caroline. *Josh: A Boy with Dyslexia*. Burlington, VT: Waterfront Books, 1988. Young readers go into the mind and heart of a fifth grader with LD. Includes questions and answers about dyslexia and LD. For ages 8–12.
—*Zipper: The Kid with ADHD*. Bethesda, MD: Woodbine House, 1997.

Levine, Mel. *Keeping a Head in School: A Student's Book About Learning Abilities and Learning Disorders*. Cambridge, MA: Educators Publishing Service, 1991. Helps students develop and use effective strategies for getting better results with schoolwork.

Moss, Deborah. *Shelley the Hyperactive Turtle*. Bethesda, MD: Woodbine House, 1989. For ages 4–9.
—*Lee, The Rabbit with Epilepsy*. Bethesda, MD: Woodbine House, 1989. For ages 4–9.

Quinn, Patricia O., and Judith M. Stern. *Putting On the Brakes: Young People's Guide to Understanding Attention Deficit Hyperactivity Disorder*. Revised edition. New York: Magination Press, 2001. Written for kids by a pediatrician and a special education teacher, this book clearly explains ADHD and offers practical suggestions for coping with the problems it presents. For ages 8–13.
—*The "Putting on the Brakes" Activity Book for Young People with ADHD*. New York: Magination Press, 1993. Pictures, puzzles, questionnaires, and games teach kids how to get organized, follow directions, study effectively, and more.

Taylor, John F. *The Survival Guide for Kids with ADHD*. Minneapolis: Free Spirit Publishing, 2013. Helps kids diagnosed with ADD or ADHD succeed in school, get along better at home, and form healthy and enjoyable relationships with peers. Includes a special message for parents. For ages 8–12.

Matching Your Teaching to Your Students' Learning Styles

The term *learning styles* refers to the way the brain perceives and processes what it needs to learn. The students we teach best are those whose learning styles match the teaching style with which we are most comfortable. Sometimes we underestimate the learning capabilities of students who don't learn the right way. In fact, there is no right way. The only way for each student is the one that works!

This chapter will help you to understand and appreciate how you can enhance the learning success of your struggling students by matching your teaching to their learning styles. You'll discover that many of the differences you have with your students are not personality conflicts but rather are clashes between your preferred teaching style and their preferred learning styles. You'll see how certain easy-to-make modifications in the learning environment and the way you teach will allow students with learning difficulties to improve their learning productivity. Of course, as your students become more successful, your attitudes and satisfaction about your teaching effectiveness will improve as well.

Scenario: Eric

Eric was a fourth grader for whom school had not been a pleasant experience. Since his reputation preceded him, teachers dreaded hearing that they were getting Eric for the upcoming school year.

Eric was constantly moving—touching other students or fidgeting with a toy or some other inappropriate object. He was never in his seat. He jumped up often to sharpen his pencil (although he never seemed to use it), and he made funny noises while he worked—somewhere between a squeak and a snort. He always had something in his mouth, preferably gum or candy. If the teacher took that away from him, in went a pencil, sleeve, or shoestring.

Eric's cumulative records folder showed a pattern established early in kindergarten. Most of the parent-teacher conferences his parents attended were filled with teacher observations of Eric's inability to meet expected behavior and productivity guidelines. As each year progressed, teachers became less tolerant of Eric's behavior and more insistent that he be evaluated by a doctor and put on some kind of medication.

Eric's fourth-grade teacher attended one of my workshops on learning styles. Once there, she was quickly able to identify that Eric was a tactile-kinesthetic learner. After hearing more about that particular learning style, she returned to the classroom and provided the following interventions:

- She moved Eric's desk to a place where his movements would be least likely to attract the attention of the other students.

- She used masking tape to define a perimeter around Eric's desk measuring roughly a foot and a half in each direction. Then she told Eric that he could move as much as he wanted to, as long as he stayed within that space.

- She began allowing Eric to do his work in his favorite position of balancing on one knee on his chair and leaning over his desk, rather than requiring him to sit up straight.

- She gave Eric permission to chew gum in class, since chewing helped him to work off excess energy. However, he couldn't leave the classroom with the gum in his mouth. He was required to wrap it up and throw it away in a designated lined wastebasket.

- Since Eric needed to tap a pencil as another way to release excess energy, his teacher showed him the simple trick of tapping his pencil on his sleeve, arm, shirt, pant leg, or other soft surface instead of his desk or chair. Now Eric could tap without disturbing his classmates.

Working together, Eric's teacher and I adapted as many learning tasks as possible into a tactile-kinesthetic format. This enabled Eric to learn by touching and moving and to express what he learned with products that were easier for a tactile-kinesthetic learner to create. Examples included:

- having him record his work in chart form with pictures and drawings

- always letting him see the end of a task before starting to work

- teaching basic skills through jingles, chants, and movement

- letting him act out events in literature and other subjects

- teaching him how to purposefully relax before beginning school tasks

- letting him listen to soothing music through headphones as he worked

- giving him a soft ball to hold and squeeze.

These accommodations drastically cut down on Eric's distracting behavior. Because his basic learning style needs were being met, his mind was free to concentrate on learning.* Eric understood that as long as he followed his teacher's guidelines for appropriate behavior during work times, the choice about whether to move, chew, or lean was his. When he didn't follow the guidelines, the choice was taken away from him for a day or two until he could make another plan to follow the guidelines.

Understanding Learning Styles

The human brain is a complex and fascinating organism about which little was known until about the past 15 years. It is composed of three main parts: the cerebrum, the cerebellum, and the brain stem. Only the cerebrum—the newest part—is capable of learning academic material. The next oldest part, the cerebellum, is in charge of our emotions; the oldest part, the brain stem, is our survival center. When we experience stress, our brain stem functions take over the other two parts of the brain and order us to fight or flee. When students are asked to engage in a learning task that conflicts with the way they learn, they feel stressed. Their brain stem sends the message, "Put up a fight or get out of here!"

According to brain researcher Leslie Hart, curriculum must be brain-compatible or it cannot be learned.** Since different kids' brains function and learn differently, it stands to reason that we must teach them differently. To make new learning happen, we must connect it to a pattern the brain already knows and recognizes. When we do this, the brain perceives the new learning in a language it can easily understand. Equally important, the learning environment must be comfortable. When the body is in distress, the brain stem focuses on the discomfort and no learning takes place.

Drs. Marie Carbo, Rita Dunn, and Kenneth Dunn have described three styles of learning: *auditory, visual,* and *tactile-kinesthetic.****

- Auditory people learn by listening.

- Visual people learn by seeing. They must get a picture in their brain in order to understand what they need to learn.

- Tactile-kinesthetic people learn by touching and moving.

Auditory learners are logical, analytical, sequential thinkers. They are comfortable with typical school tasks including analyzing sounds and numbers, following directions in order, and just doing the right thing. Since their learning needs are usually met in the classroom, they are considered good students. Auditory learners are perfectly comfortable in rooms that are quiet, well-lit, and equipped with desks for each student. For these kids, typical classroom

---

* Students with ADD or ADHD (neither of which Eric was identified as having) will probably need a combination of medication and classroom intervention to achieve positive results. However, the medication should not cause students to behave like zombies. They should be sufficiently in control of themselves to learn and attend in an environment that takes advantage of their learning style strengths. Neither the medication nor the teacher should be expected to solve the problem alone.

** Hart, Leslie. *Human Brain and Human Learning.* Kent, WA: Books for Educators, 1998.

*** Information on learning styles presented in this chapter, and the "Analytical or Global?" learning styles inventory on page 46, are adapted from *Teaching Students to Read Through Their Individual Learning Styles* by Marie Carbo, Rita Dunn, and Kenneth Dunn. Englewood Cliffs, NJ: Allyn & Bacon, 1986. Used with permission of Marie Carbo, executive director, National Reading Styles Institute, Syosset, NY.

arrangements work very well and actually enhance their productivity.

Visual and tactile-kinesthetic learners are global thinkers. They are not good with logical, analytical, sequential tasks until they can see the big picture. They can learn to think logically, analytically, and sequentially, but they must do it by working backwards from the whole to the parts. They must learn new material in a meaningful context. Their thought patterns tend to be random; classroom discussions lead them onto divergent thinking pathways, and they make creative and unusual associations with the subject at hand. When we call on them, they may say something that seems totally irrelevant to the topic. However, if we stop and ask them to explain their statement, they can usually help us to see how they made a particular connection.

Visual and tactile-kinesthetic learners are actually distracted by environments that are quiet, brightly lit, and equipped with standard furniture. In order for their brains to concentrate, they need an environment with much less light, background sound, and comfy furniture or permission to work on the floor! So the very rules we usually apply to all children actually work against the productivity conditions that global learners need.

It will come as no surprise to anyone that visual learners have become the largest group in any heterogeneous classroom. Before the general use of computers and video games, this was probably not the case, but it is definitely an issue all teachers must deal with now. The kids we used to call the "good kids" because they would actually listen to and follow our directions are gone forever. The good news is the good kids are still in our classes—they just aren't auditory learners anymore! They are strongly visual, and we must accommodate that preference in all of our teaching.

One way to understand the significance of these learning style differences is by considering the conflicts we have with people we live with. You can do this by taking the simple learning styles inventory on page 46. Write your initials beside those characteristics that describe you, and the initials of your S.O. (Significant Other) beside those characteristics that describe him or her. For purposes of this test, your S.O. might be your spouse or partner, another adult you know well and have occasional conflicts with, a child so different from you that you're sure they switched infants at the hospital, or a family member with whom you often clash.

As you review your responses, you'll probably notice many glaring differences between you and your S.O. Especially in the case of a spouse or partner, we tend to seek out people who compensate for our weaknesses. For example, my husband and I differ in many ways. I'm very auditory and I love words. I talk a lot and enjoy getting new information by listening to others talk. I'm sociable

and like meeting new people. I plan ahead because I'm afraid that if I wait too long I won't get the arrangements I want. I analyze things to death, always asking myself if there's one more aspect I should consider before making a decision. Even after a decision is made, I keep rehashing it, wondering if a different decision would have been better. I can't accept anything at face value; instead, I'm always looking for proof. Plus I'm helpless when it comes to assembling things unless the directions are very clear.

So when I was looking for a mate, the qualities I don't possess were the ones that appealed to me. I was attracted to someone who is very visual, who can easily draw pictures and diagrams, and who doesn't say much unless he's sure of what he wants to say. He strongly resists planning ahead, preferring to go with the flow. He can assemble and fix things when he feels like it, but he balks at following anyone else's timetable for his projects. His decisions are intuitive, and once they are made, he lets them go and doesn't try to second-guess himself. Clearly, we are more different than alike.

When two people notice in each other certain qualities they wish they had, an intense, irresistible attraction can develop—and it's called love! What's ironic is that once we commit to spending our lives together enjoying each other's strengths, those same qualities slowly but surely become irritating. Instead of appreciating the differences that initially drew us together, we expend enormous amounts of time, energy, and emotion trying to make the other person better (in other words, more like us!).

As you can see from the inventory, our thinking and learning styles predict certain preferences in our environmental conditions. These environmental preferences are so innate that we can exert very little conscious control over them. Many disagreements between S.O.s are caused by conflicts in environmental preferences.

It shouldn't surprise you to learn that conflicts with your students can be minimized by adjusting their learning environment. Once the environment is more compatible with your students' learning styles, their ability to learn improves automatically and dramatically. Your ultimate goal is to provide a brain-compatible environment for *all* students.

Learning Styles and the Hierarchy of Needs

Another way to understand the importance of accommodating learning styles is through psychologist Abraham Maslow's famous Hierarchy of Needs.* Maslow taught that needs on the lower levels must be met before needs on

---

* Hierarchy of Needs from *Motivation and Personality,* 3rd edition, by Abraham H. Maslow. New York: HarperCollins Publishers, 1987. Reprinted by permission of HarperCollins Publishers, Inc.

ANALYTICAL OR GLOBAL?

When it comes to . . .	Analytical thinkers tend to prefer . . .	Global thinkers tend to prefer . . .
1. Sound	Silence for concentrating	Some sound for concentrating
2. Light	Bright light for reading/studying	Very low light for reading/studying
3. Room temperature	Turning thermostat warmer; wearing heavy clothing	Turning thermostat cooler; wearing lightweight clothing (even in winter)
4. Furniture	Studying at a desk and chair	Studying on a bed or floor
5. Mobility	Sitting still for long periods of time	Moving around constantly
6. Time of day	Learning in the morning; going to bed early	Learning later in the day; staying up late (a night owl)
7. Eating	Eating breakfast and regular meals	Skipping breakfast; snacking while learning
8. Learning	Working alone or under the direction of one other person; being self-directed, independent	Working in a group or peer learning; discovering answers rather than being told
9. Tasks	Working on one job at a time until done; being somewhat compulsive	Starting more jobs than they complete; procrastinating
10. Planning	Making lists for everything; planning far ahead; putting tasks on a calendar; avoiding risk-taking	Doing things when they feel like it; not planning ahead, but going with the flow; experimenting; trying things out
11. Deciding	Taking a long time to make decisions; second-guessing decisions	Being spontaneous in making decisions; doing what feels right
12. Time	Punctuality; wearing watches with large numbers	Running late; wearing fashion watches with few or no numbers, but they match one's outfit
13. Neatness	Neat, well-organized appearance; outfits that go together	Disorganized appearance; clothes may not match or may be very colorful
14. Perceiving	Seeing things as they are at the moment; noticing details	Seeing things as they might be; perceiving the whole; ignoring details
15. Assembling	Following directions step-by-step; starting over if they get stuck	Studying a picture of how something will look when complete, then assembling it their way
16. Thinking	Logically, analytically, sequentially; seeing cause-and-effect; perceiving differences; figuring out things step-by-step; understanding symbolic codes	Intuitively and randomly; seeing similarities and connections; working backwards from whole to parts, from concrete to symbolic
17. Learning	Sequential tasks and concrete, logical steps	Learning through open-ended tasks; creating new ideas; learning through simile and metaphor
18. Remembering	Remembering what has been spoken	Remembering images of what has been seen and experienced
19. Taking tests	Predictable test formats (multiple choice, true-false, essay)	Opportunities to express themselves in ways other than writing

SELF-ACTUALIZATION NEEDS
To develop our talents and be true to our goals; to realize our potential; to have peak experiences

SELF-ESTEEM AND COMPETENCE NEEDS
To achieve; to gain approval and recognition from others for our achievements; to be able to trust in our own abilities

BELONGING AND LOVE NEEDS
To love and be loved; to have relationships and be accepted; to know that we are a valued member of a group

SAFETY NEEDS
To feel safe, secure, and out of danger; to feel confident that we will not be harmed either physically or psychologically

PHYSIOLOGICAL NEEDS
To have the food, water, clothing, shelter, sleep, exercise, and comfort we need to survive

Abraham Maslow's Hierarchy of Needs

the higher levels can be addressed. In other words, when we overlook the physiological needs of students who are struggling to learn, we actually contribute to their learning problems.

We already know some of this intuitively. For example, we would never try to teach a new skill to an infant who was desperately hungry or overdue for a diaper change. Babies learn when their physiological needs are met.

Working up the pyramid, we find that other needs can be assigned to certain age groups. Kids in the elementary grades learn when their physiological *and* safety needs are met. Adolescents learn when their physiological, safety, *and* belonging needs are met. Adults learn when their physiological, safety, belonging, *and* self-esteem needs are met. To read a book, take a workshop, enroll

in a continuing education course, or pursue an advanced degree, one must be confident enough in one's own abilities and achievements to take risks. Self-actualization needs are met once all of the needs below them in the pyramid have been satisfied. Maslow taught that very few people ever reach this level.

He further taught that no matter what level we are currently functioning on, all of our energy and attention will immediately be drawn to any lower level for which we perceive an unmet need. For example, suppose that you are engrossed in this book (self-esteem and competence level) when you suddenly smell smoke. You will drop the book and refocus your attention on the safety level until you discover the source of the smoke and do what you must to feel safe again.

With this in mind, consider the typical classroom. There are certainly some tactile-kinesthetic students in every room. If we insist that they sit still while we lecture and they do their tasks, sooner or later their physiological need to move will take precedence over any other need. The longer we ignore it, the more stress they will feel and the less they will learn. Many students we label "hyperactive" are tactile-kinesthetic learners whose hyperactive behaviors can be diminished if their learning tasks allow them to move while learning.*

Learning Styles and School Success

All babies are born with their tactile-kinesthetic learning style predominant. Parents naturally acknowledge the fact that babies learn by doing—by getting into everything, touching everything, pulling things apart and knocking them down. Although we might prefer that children learn by letting us tell them things, we understand that a tidy house and a small child simply can't coexist.

Imagine how inappropriate it would be to sit a toddler in a high chair and say, "Today Mommy is going to show you the kitchen. I want you to watch and listen as I describe it, but I don't want you to touch anything." If we restricted young children from touching, feeling, moving, dancing, and jumping, we know we would impair their ability to learn.

Success at most school tasks requires children to make the transition from tactile-kinesthetic to auditory-analytical. The brain of one gender is ready to make that transition at about age six, while the brain of the other gender might not be ready for that transition until as late as eight or nine years old. Guess which gender is more likely to be ready at age six? Girls! Guess which gender has many persons who have probably not made the thinking transition required for understanding early reading skills? Boys! Guess which gender significantly overpopulates special education and remedial reading programs? Boys again!

Are boys really less capable than girls? Are visual-kinesthetic learners less intelligent than auditory learners? Or are many unsuccessful students simply being taught in a manner incompatible with their basic thinking and learning style? By the time some boys are ready to succeed with typical school tasks, their self-esteem is so badly damaged that they may be emotionally incapable of perceiving themselves as successful students—and they may never catch up.

Since most school tasks require listening, following step-by-step directions, or analyzing the sounds in words,

auditory-analytical learners are far more likely to be successful than global (visual and/or tactile-kinesthetic) learners, unless the appropriate modifications are made for the global kids. The following lists of preferences can be used to design successful learning activities for both kinds of global students. The overlap in the lists is due to the fact that their learning preferences may be similar at times and somewhat different at other times.

Remember that global learners prefer a learning environment with some sound, low light, and opportunities for movement. They tend to study in a relaxed posture, they like to eat or chew when concentrating, and they usually must see or hear the whole before learning the parts.

Students who are generally successful with academic learning are probably auditory-analytical, or they enjoy a combination of styles that allows them to learn just about anything with ease. Since this book is about helping students with learning difficulties, I will not spend time discussing that group.

What Visual Learners Prefer

When the first edition of this book was published in 1996, best estimates were that in a typical class about 35 percent of learners were visual. In 2005, that has zoomed to 65 percent or more. I'm certain you know the reason: Television, video and computer games, and learning software with lots of action and sound. What are the chances these influences will go away anytime soon? You know the answer to that as well: None! Regardless of how well logical, analytic, and sequential tasks worked for earlier generations of students, the predominant learning style now is visual, with a significant amount of kinesthetic thrown in for good measure. And that's just the way it is.

In general, visual learners prefer:

- pictures rather than words

- viewing rather than reading (videos, demonstrations, and examples work well for them)

- being shown an example of what the finished product should look like rather than hearing an explanation of the task

- reading the end of a book or story first to see if it's worth the effort to read the whole thing

- stories with excitement, humor, and adventure

- visualizing scenes, characters, and actions as they read about them

- learning phonics, skills, and vocabulary in context after hearing or reading the selection

- finding visual cues in texts (charts, graphs, photographs)

---

* Marie Carbo, Rita Dunn, and Kenneth Dunn.

- graphic organizers (mapping, illustrating in chart form what they learn)

- writing down what they need to learn (but they may never need to look at their notes again)

- writing in many media (different colors and textures, shaving cream, finger paints, etc.)

- using artistic means to express what they learn

- drawing or doodling while listening

- opportunities to write out words during spelling bees and games

- being shown the correct version of what they have gotten wrong (never circle or highlight their errors)

- visual order in their workplace (visual learners are often quite neat and well-organized; however, some can work in a mess and find things right where they left them).

What Tactile-Kinesthetic Learners Prefer

Between 15 and 30 percent of the students in your class are probably tactile-kinesthetic learners. They prefer:

- receiving concrete examples at the beginning of a learning experience

- hands-on activities (*examples:* building the volcano or the simple electrical circuit instead of reading about it or watching a video or film)

- moving while learning; acting out words and phrases; touching everything within reach

- learning academic tasks after doing some physical activity (one teacher took her students on a run around the building each morning before beginning regular instruction, which dramatically improved their learning; for some tactile-kinesthetic learners, their reading fluency increases if they rotate their arm in a circular motion while reading)

- stories with lots of action, adventure, and excitement

- reading the end of a book or story first to see if it's worth the effort to read the whole thing

- creative dramatics and Readers' Theater (see page 101); acting out stories and events

- learning by doing; trying out rather than learning about

- using manipulatives whenever possible

- fidgeting or chewing while thinking (**tip:** to greatly reduce the amount of moving around, let them hold and squeeze a small rubber ball such as a Kush ball)

- writing in many media (sand, salt, shaving cream, or pudding; with their fingers on each other's backs; etc.)

- word processing instead of handwriting

- figuring out math problems with finger multiplication and Fingermath (see pages 151 and 153–154), number lines, and other number manipulation systems

- not having to listen to long lectures, lessons, or conversations

- learning the shapes of spelling words, not just the letters (they also prefer action words over nouns)

- displaying what they know in chart form with actual pictures or objects rather than telling about it

- learning and creating raps, rhythms, rhymes, and jingles

- speaking as little as possible; being terse and succinct

- expressing their feelings physically

- developing their own system of organization instead of using one designed for analytical thinkers.

*Electroboards**

Although there are many commercially manufactured learning tools available, they may be out of reach for teachers with limited budgets. Electroboards are a less expensive way to provide hands-on learning for kids who need it, without requiring unlimited batteries.

Tactile-kinesthetic learners are delighted by electroboards because their hands can keep moving while they are learning the required information or concepts. This simple tool can be used for many types of learning tasks. For best results, make several electroboards with different circuit patterns so students must do the work instead of doing the pattern.

You'll need the following materials for each electroboard:

- two pieces of heavy tagboard, each measuring 7" x 5", laminated

- multipurpose copper foil shielding tape or other durable metal strips, such as heavy-duty aluminum foil folded four times

- circuit continuity tester with battery and penlight (available from hardware stores); cut tip to 1/2"

- paper punch

- masking tape

- heavy-duty stapler

- permanent marker.

---

* Ann Potter, teacher, Elgin, Illinois.

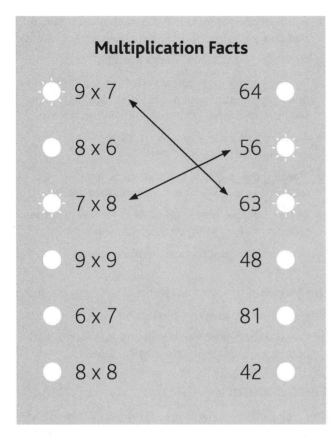

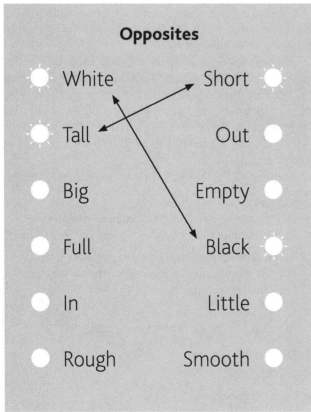

Arrows indicate circuits on the back of the electroboards. Circuits link items on the front of the boards. The light only lights up if these matches are touched.

1. Punch six holes in a vertical row down each long side of a piece of tagboard. This is the front of the board.

2. Place the front piece over the back piece and trace the holes.

3. To the back piece, apply one strip of foil between two hole tracings, making sure to completely cover the holes.

4. Apply masking tape along the foil strip, leaving only the traced holes exposed. Test the connection with the continuity tester.

5. Apply more foil strips and masking tape to connect the other holes in the same manner, two at a time. Test each connection as you go. Make sure that masking tape covers the foil to avoid unwanted circuit connections.

6. Staple the front and back pieces together, being careful to precisely align the holes.

7. Use permanent marker to write your items to match the circuits on the front of the board. Use nail polish remover if you need to change the board.

Once you make an electroboard, you can use many different kinds of task cards in it. *Examples:*

■ number facts

■ vocabulary words and meanings

■ states/countries with capitals

■ presidents and contributions

■ periodic elements and symbols

■ homonyms and synonyms

■ synonyms and antonyms.

The Three Magic Rules

The key to letting kids do whatever they need to better concentrate on their learning tasks is to offer *any* options to *all* students as long as they follow the Three Magic Rules. Explain to your students that anyone who chooses to do their work away from the direct instruction area, or anyone who chooses to chew or eat, tap or move around, must follow the Three Magic Rules:

1. Don't bother anyone else.

2. Don't call attention to yourself.

3. Work on your learning tasks for the entire period.

Explain to your students that as long as they honor all three of these conditions, they can make their own choices. If they fail to follow any of the conditions, you will choose for them for that day. They can try again on the next day to enjoy their choices by meeting the required conditions for acceptable behavior. **Tip:** For students with serious concentration problems, try focusing only on rule #1 for a week or two. Then add the others one at a time, expecting the students to keep following the rules they have already learned.

Since you have not limited access to what your students would consider privileges by including some students and excluding others, there is no resentment toward those who choose certain options. So you can let kids who need to listen to music use headphones, and kids who need to sit on the floor to do so as long as they stay visible, and kids who need less light to sit in a section of the room where the lights are turned off. Those who need to eat snacks before lunch because they consistently skip breakfast can do so, and kids who don't want to eat don't have to. You can send a message home to parents telling them which snacks are acceptable and which are not. **Tip:** It may be a good idea to explain to your principal why you are making these allowances before he or she finds out during a visit to your classroom!

Caution: When testing time comes, you should try to keep allowing kids to enjoy the same learning style accommodations they have on non-testing days. If kids are allowed to work on the floor, they might take their test on the floor. If kids are allowed to listen to soothing music as they work, they should have the same option while they take tests. Without these accommodations, stress increases, and brains do not function at their best in high-stress situations.

Teaching Students About Learning Styles

Early repeated failure to learn can be devastating. Once students are convinced that they are incapable of learning, their expectations of failure often become a self-fulfilling prophecy. The most effective way to convince struggling students that they can learn is to show them by teaching *to* their learning style strengths.

We also need to teach them *about* their own learning styles. This empowers kids to act intelligently when learning seems difficult for them. When they realize that their inability to learn is not their fault, they no longer feel guilty and stupid. Instead, they stop and think, "The method I've been using to learn this is not working for me. I need to try another method that matches my learning style strengths. When I find the right way to work on this problem, it will be a lot easier for me."

Scenario: Mrs. Potter's Classroom*

Teacher Ann Potter uses a highly effective method to teach students about their own learning styles. First, she introduces them to environmental preferences like those listed in "What Kind of Learner Are You?/What's Your Learning Style?" on pages 52–53. She explains that different people have different preferences when it comes to their learning environment, and that they learn more effectively when conditions are right for them. Then she has them experiment with light levels, room temperature, body posture, and so on to determine which conditions best enable them to concentrate and get their work done.

For example, her students spend several days exploring various sound conditions. Specific areas in the classroom are set aside for silence, soft talking, and listening to recordings of soothing music or environmental sounds. At the end of the third class period on sound conditions, Mrs. Potter tapes several sheets of paper together to form a chart, draws a long line (continuum) from one end to the other, labels the left end "Total Silence" and the right end "Listening to Recordings," and posts it along a wall. She asks her students to line up in front of the continuum according to where they perceive they can best concentrate, and then she writes their names on the chart.

Something amazing happened one October to demonstrate that Mrs. Potter's students were understanding and appreciating differences in learning style preferences. She had assigned a sustained silent reading period. One of her students, a boy named Jason, had trouble finding his book in his desk and was late getting to the rug. After looking for a place on the floor with a pillow on which to rest his head, he carefully settled in and opened his book. Slowly he became aware that someone nearby was mumbling. Jason was a student who preferred total silence while he worked. But instead of getting upset, he looked around to see who was mumbling. It was a girl named Linda. Jason glanced up at the continuum chart and located her name. Then he said to her, "Oh, Linda, I see that you're auditory. You subvocalize when you read. I like to read in silence. But you were here first, so I guess I'll move." And he did!

Teaching Your Students About Their Learning Styles

Use "What Kind of Learner Are You?/What's Your Learning Style?" (pages 52–53) to help your students learn about and understand their own learning style strengths and weaknesses.** When students appreciate that differences between them are often explained by learning style needs and differences, they become much more tolerant of each other. Once your students have developed the vocabulary and understanding of learning styles, they will appreciate everything you do to accommodate those differences.

---

* Ann Potter, teacher, Elgin, Illinois.

** Please copy these two pages as a two-sided handout. It will be easier for kids to manage, and you'll save paper besides.

What Kind of Learner Are You?

Did You Know?

When you have trouble learning, that doesn't mean you're not smart. It means that you haven't tried using your learning style—the way that's best for your brain.

There are two main types of learning styles: **analytical** and **global**.

Analytical learners learn by listening. They learn best when teachers tell them what they need to learn. If you are an auditory learner, you are usually comfortable with tasks that ask you to figure things out, that require logical thinking, or that are presented in order from easier to harder.

Global learners learn by seeing or doing. They learn best when information is presented with pictures, diagrams, videos, and other visuals. Some global learners enjoy learning actively instead of writing down what they learn. They like to see the whole unit or chapter before learning the parts.

Both types of learners are smart. Neither is smarter or better than the other. Both can have learning problems when they try to learn something new in a way that isn't comfortable for their brain.

The other side of this handout is a chart that describes things that analytical and global learners tend to prefer (like best). When you read the chart, which things sound more like you? Do you think you're an analytical learner or a global learner? Can you find statements that describe you in both columns? Draw a circle around the statements that best describe the way you are most of the time. Then come back to this page and read the next section.

What Does It Mean?

If you're an analytical learner, you are probably successful in school. Not because you're smarter than other kids, but because most school tasks are comfortable for your learning style.

If you're a global learner (either visual or tactile-kinesthetic), you may have trouble with some school subjects. Not because you're less smart than other kids, but because most school tasks are not as comfortable for your learning style. **Tip:** You can ask your teachers to help you learn by giving you visual aids or graphic organizers, which will make it much easier for you to remember what you are supposed to know. You can also ask to learn things using music or rhythm. For example, maybe you can sing rhymes or jump rope while memorizing number facts.

If your style is described almost equally in both columns, it means that you can learn in many different ways. That's a good thing. It makes learning easier for you, no matter what style your teachers choose to use.

continued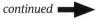

What's Your Learning Style?

When it comes to . . .	Analytical learners tend to prefer . . .	Global learners tend to prefer . . .
1. Sound	Quiet in order to concentrate	Radio or TV as background noise
2. Light	Bright light; no shadows	Low light
3. Room temperature	Warmer	Cooler
4. Study space	Desk and chair	Cushions or floor
5. Movement	Sitting still for long time periods	Lots of movement; rarely sits down completely
6. Alert time of day	Going to bed early and getting up early	Staying up late (night owl); has trouble getting up in the morning
7. Eating	Three meals a day—wants breakfast	Skipping breakfast; eating late at night; chewing on things
8. Time	Wearing a watch; is always on time	Not wearing a watch; is rarely on time (and often late)
9. Neatness	Being neat and well-organized	Being messy; has trouble finding things
10. Planning	Making and following lists	No lists; just doing what feels right
11. Learning	Finishing one task at a time	Jumping around from task to task
12. Group work	Working and learning on their own	Working with others
13. Processing information	Sequential information, in logical steps	Focusing on the whole rather than details
14. Rules/directions	Complete teacher explanations	Clear examples to understand teacher's expectations
15. Studying	Remembering facts	Meaningful contexts
16. Phonics	Sounding out words	Learning whole words better than words in syllables
17. Reading	Lots of reading	High-interest reading: mystery, adventure, etc.
18. Sequence	Arranging ideas in his or her head	Manipulating ideas and information hands-on
19. Skill work	Figuring things out independently	Getting help while learning
20. Recall	Many facts and figures	High-interest words or phrases

And there will be significantly fewer behavior problems when students' learning styles are accommodated.

Imagine walking over to the desk of a kinesthetic kid who constantly drums on his desktop with a pencil or his fingers. If your student knows nothing about learning styles, you might say something ineffective: "How many times have I told you to stop doing that?" Instead, because he *does* know about learning styles, you can say something highly effective: "Dmitri, when you make that noise on your desk, it really bothers the auditory learners in here, including me. So, if you want to continue your drumming, please tap on your arm or leg so you can enjoy the physical activity without infringing on the rights of other learners." End of power struggle!

Gum chewing can be handled the same way. The reason gum chewing is rarely allowed in school is because kids stash their used gum in yucky places, which they do because they don't want to get caught with the evidence. But what if you allow gum chewing in your classroom for students who follow certain rules? In my class, kids could chew gum if and only if:

- the piece was no bigger than a stick of Dentyne
- they did not chew fruit-flavored gum (I hated the smell)
- they deposited used gum in only one wastebasket— a plastic-lined vessel beside my desk
- they always left their gum in the wastebasket when leaving the room.

Anyone who wanted to chew gum in my classroom did. And you can probably guess what happened. During the first few days, everyone chewed gum. By the fourth day, the only kids chewing gum were those who needed it. And the ones who didn't need it had absolutely no problem with the fact that other kids were chewing it.

Learning Styles and Multiple Intelligences

Once we create a comfortable learning environment for our students, our next step is to apply the learning styles approach to curriculum and learning activities. Dr. Howard Gardner has developed a theory of multiple intelligences that describes eight ways in which people learn and solve problems.* His theory represents a unique phi-

losophy about how kids learn, how teachers should teach, and how schools can be effective for everyone.

Most students tend to be strong in one or two intelligences. However, some can become adept at several intelligences, so our goal as teachers is to expose all of our students to many types of learning activities. Authors including Thomas Armstrong, Carolyn Chapman, and David Lazear have translated Gardner's model for practical use in the classroom; see "References and Resources" at the end of this chapter. The following tips and suggestions draw on their ideas.

On page 55, you'll find a handout summarizing the eight intelligences.** Make copies for your students and/or display it in the classroom so kids can refer to this information as they work and learn.

Linguistic Intelligence

Linguistically talented people understand and use language easily. They think logically, analytically, and sequentially, and their work shows it. They enjoy reading and writing, memorizing information (especially trivia), talking, and building their vocabularies (they are great spellers). They may be excellent storytellers.

There is no real secret to teaching students with this learning strength, since school loves them and they love school. They do well at typical school tasks in which talking and listening lead to successful learning outcomes.

Logical-Mathematical Intelligence

Logical-mathematical people use numbers and math concepts with ease. They understand cause-and-effect, enjoy abstract reasoning, and are often drawn to the sciences. They are fascinated by how things work, and they love games, riddles, and computers. They recognize patterns and often find unusual ways to solve problems, even though they may not be able to show their work or explain how they arrived at their solutions. A lot of good thinking goes on in their heads.

Tips: Teach math from concrete to abstract. Tie abstractions to real-life scenarios. Use computer-assisted learning, mnemonics, and visual and graphic organizers.

Visual-Spatial Intelligence

Visual-spatial people understand the relationships of figures and images in different spatial fields. They can easily represent artistically what they perceive visually. They are very skilled at taking things apart and reassembling them. They may draw or doodle every chance they get, often creating multidimensional drawings. They love puzzles,

---

* Howard Gardner's landmark work *Frames of Mind: The Theory of Multiple Intelligences,* Tenth Anniversary Edition (New York: Basic Books, 1993) describes seven intelligences. Dr. Gardner added an eighth intelligence (Naturalist) in 1995. At the time of this book's publication, Gardner and his team are speculating that there might be a ninth intelligence (Existential). He calls this the "intelligence of big questions." Whatever new intelligences might be added in the future, all will fit into one or more of the categories discussed in this book: auditory, visual, and tactile-kinesthetic.

** Used with permission from Howard Gardner, *Frames of Mind.* New York: Basic Books, 1993.

Eight Intelligences

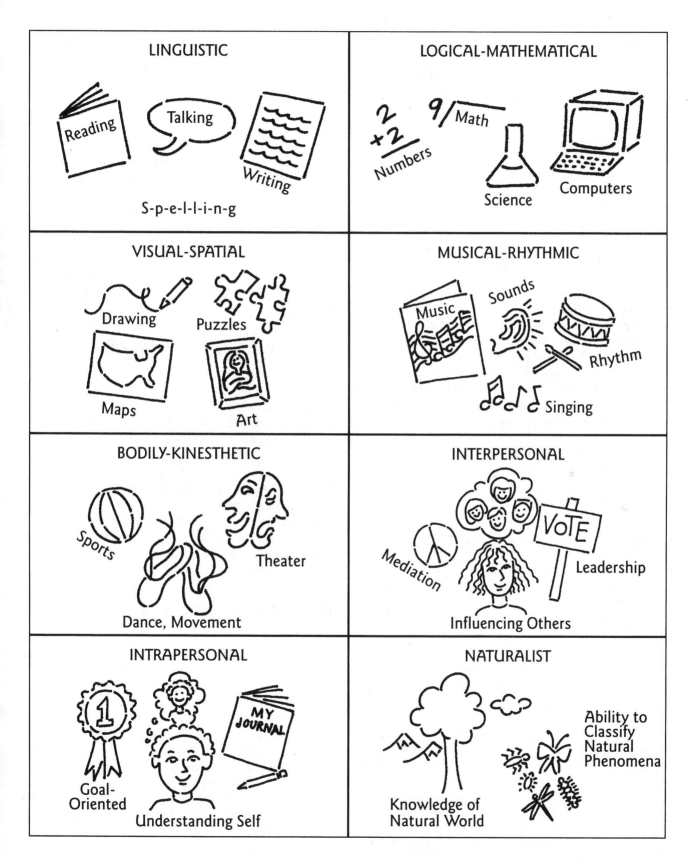

especially the 3-D type, and may be very good at board games such as chess. They excel at Tangrams. They have a keen sense of direction and enjoy maps. Students with strengths in this area have the most potential to be successful in the emerging technologies.

Tips: Show videos, films, or other visual representations of what you want these students to learn. Use visual and graphic organizers and color-coded systems. Illustrate what you are saying on an overhead or chalkboard. Ask students to visualize what they are trying to learn. Have students build models (with LEGOs and other materials) to demonstrate what they know. Create a colorful environment by hanging posters, illustrations, and charts around the classroom. When teaching science, use hands-on materials and field trips, either real or virtual.

Musical-Rhythmic Intelligence

Budding musicians understand music theory and play musical instruments with gusto, sometimes without the benefit of formal instruction. They innately hear tone and pitch; they have a highly developed sense of rhythm, which they may tap out at all hours with any kind of stick, from a drumstick to a pencil. They love to sing and may hum while they work. They notice environmental noises and sounds more keenly than others. They may be able to improvise songs or new arrangements for existing pieces of music.

Tips: Use music and rhythm to teach. Let students use music and rhythm (dances, songs, raps) to demonstrate what they have learned. When teaching history, let them approach a specific period or era by studying its music.

Bodily-Kinesthetic Intelligence

In cultures that value competitive sports, this may be the most acceptable form of intelligence. Bodily-kinesthetic people can move their bodies through space with grace, strength, and ease. They enjoy training the body to do its physical best. They need frequent opportunities to move, and they usually love games where movement is involved. They are very adept at manipulating objects and often excel at crafts. They can accurately mimic others' gestures or mannerisms. They learn academics best when they can feel or experience what needs to be learned. Having to sit still for long periods of time is very uncomfortable for them.

Tips: Use dramatics, pantomime, and Readers' Theater (see page 101). Create several learning centers around the room and allow students to move among them. Set lessons to music or have students learn them as raps or rhymes. (*Example:* If they can chant the song "B-I-N-G-O," they can learn the names of countries or states, the sounds of letters, the parts of government, or just about anything by creating new lyrics to fit the melody.) Encourage them

to use their bodies as reference points while learning. (*Example:* "Imagine that your head is Wisconsin and your left foot is Florida.") Have available large walk-on floor or playground maps, electroboards (pages 49–50), clay and papier-mâché (for making models to demonstrate related concepts), and other learning materials that invite them to get physical.

Interpersonal Intelligence

People with this type of intelligence are our present and future leaders. They can work well with others and lead them; they easily perceive and respond to others' moods and feelings. Unfortunately, this intelligence is not always used in positive ways. Gang leaders have strengths in this area.

Tips: Use cooperative learning and give students leadership roles. Offer a variety of learning tasks and allow them to create unique solutions to problems. These students thrive in simulations and make great peer tutors and mediators.

Intrapersonal Intelligence

People with this type of intelligence understand themselves much better than others may understand them. They are highly motivated to be true to their goals and are not overly concerned about what other people will think of them. They learn well when they can connect what they need to learn to some personal memory.

Tips: Give them opportunities to write in their journals about their favorite topic—themselves! Let them work independently; they tend to resist cooperative learning. Allow them to set and accomplish their own goals and bring their out-of-school interests into the curriculum. These students work best when they can choose their own topics or projects.

Naturalist Intelligence

People with a strong naturalist intelligence have an outstanding knowledge of things that exist in the natural world, such as plants and animals, and an ability to intuit how things fit into categories (even if the items are outside of nature). Naturalists like to fish, garden, cook, and carefully observe whatever catches their interest.

Tips: Naturalists love to work with real plants and animals. Let students learn botany by growing plants in the classroom or school grounds. Encourage them to garden at home. Because they are good observers, have them record their observations of the class pets (hamsters, fish, etc.). They would prefer to build or draw an ecosystem rather than read about it and discuss it, so make this type of option available.

Teaching to Multiple Intelligences

The best way to teach to the multiple intelligences is by establishing several permanent learning centers in the classroom—if possible, one for each intelligence. Get into the habit of designing learning tasks to fit several categories. *Example:* If you want kids to learn about the parts of speech, you might offer the following tasks at the various learning centers:

- *Linguistic learning center:* Reading and writing tasks.

- *Logical-mathematical learning center:* Students count the number of nouns, verbs, adverbs, etc., on a page of a story.

- *Visual-spatial learning center:* Students draw cartoons with the parts of speech highlighted in the talk balloons. Or they draw pictures of how different parts of speech are used.

- *Musical-rhythmic intelligence learning center:* Students write new lyrics to familiar songs, noting parts of speech with different-colored markers.

- *Bodily-kinesthetic learning center:* Students build sentences with cards of different colors and shapes, with each color and shape representing a particular part of speech. (*Examples:* Blue rectangles = nouns; yellow squares = verbs; green triangles = adjectives; orange circles = adverbs.) You might also teach subjects and predicates in this way.

- *Interpersonal intelligence learning center:* Students form pairs or groups to work on cooperative learning tasks about the parts of speech.

- *Intrapersonal intelligence learning center:* Students choose from any task at any center to work on independently—or they make up their own task.

- *Naturalist intelligence learning center:* Students create taxonomies of various types of objects by assigning the objects to categories. *Example:* Collect leaves on a walk around the building and create categories based on various attributes of the leaves. Students can note the parts of speech for these activities.

Schools across the United States are implementing multiple intelligences theories and practices, some with remarkable success. At the New City School, an inner-city school in St. Louis, Missouri, attention to multiple intelligences positively affected both the students and the teachers. Discipline referrals dropped dramatically, since kids who enjoy learning don't need to cause trouble.

Learning styles and multiple intelligences theories are complementary. Teaching strategies and techniques developed to meet the needs of specific learning styles can also be used to enhance specific intelligences (and vice versa).

Learning Styles	Multiple Intelligences
Auditory	Linguistic Logical-Mathematical Interpersonal Intrapersonal Naturalist
Visual	Visual-Spatial Logical-Mathematical Intrapersonal Naturalist
Tactile-Kinesthetic	Bodily-Kinesthetic Visual-Spatial Musical-Rhythmic Naturalist

I believe that we as teachers don't have to choose between these two approaches. Instead, let's combine them and use the best of each—whatever works for our students.

Teaching to Complement Learning Styles

- When you want to remember what's most important in helping global thinkers to become successful learners, use the acronym WHOLISTIC: Whole to parts; Hands-on learning; Organize information visually; Learning styles focus; Immerse the senses; Seek patterns and connections; Technology assistance; Integrate skills into context; Concrete to abstract. On page 58, you'll find a set of WHOLISTIC bookmarks. Make several copies, place back-to-back for added strength, laminate, cut apart, and use. Place them in your manuals, notebooks, and other teaching materials. Use WHOLISTIC as a checklist to plan learning experiences, to identify what might be missing when global thinkers are struggling to learn, and to remind yourself of what to do differently when your students are not learning successfully.

- Never conduct an entire lesson in any one modality. If you spend most of the class time lecturing and explaining, this clearly favors students with linguistic learning strengths. If the entire lesson is hands-on learning, linguistic learners will be uncomfortable. However, it is not necessary to include all learning styles in every lesson. Use a variety of approaches over

Whole to parts
Hands-on learning
Organize information visually
Learning styles focus
Immerse the senses
Seek patterns and connections
Technology assistance
Integrate skills into context
Concrete to abstract

Copyright © 2006, 1996
Susan Winebrenner

Whole to parts
Hands-on learning
Organize information visually
Learning styles focus
Immerse the senses
Seek patterns and connections
Technology assistance
Integrate skills into context
Concrete to abstract

Copyright © 2006, 1996
Susan Winebrenner

Whole to parts
Hands-on learning
Organize information visually
Learning styles focus
Immerse the senses
Seek patterns and connections
Technology assistance
Integrate skills into context
Concrete to abstract

Copyright © 2006, 1996
Susan Winebrenner

Whole to parts
Hands-on learning
Organize information visually
Learning styles focus
Immerse the senses
Seek patterns and connections
Technology assistance
Integrate skills into context
Concrete to abstract

Copyright © 2006, 1996
Susan Winebrenner

Whole to parts
Hands-on learning
Organize information visually
Learning styles focus
Immerse the senses
Seek patterns and connections
Technology assistance
Integrate skills into context
Concrete to abstract

Copyright © 2006, 1996
Susan Winebrenner

Whole to parts
Hands-on learning
Organize information visually
Learning styles focus
Immerse the senses
Seek patterns and connections
Technology assistance
Integrate skills into context
Concrete to abstract

Copyright © 2006, 1996
Susan Winebrenner

several lessons, and focus on methods that global learners favor during re-teaching times.

- Incorporate visuals into every lesson. For example, you might talk for 10–15 minutes, then show a film or video for another block of time. Showing parts of films or videos is fine if you don't want to use them in their entirety. Check to see what types of visual aids are available from publishers of textbooks and teaching support materials. Use charts and overhead transparencies whenever you can.

- Play appropriate background music while kids are working. For many students, learning is enhanced when certain types of music play softly in the background. Particularly effective are Pachelbel's Canon in D and the largo (slow) movements of concertos by Handel, Bach, Telemann, and Corelli. Some researchers have observed that listening to Mozart appears to improve math competencies. If the music bothers the auditory learners in your classroom, give them a portable music player with headphones and let them listen to a recording of environmental sounds or white noise.

- Provide hands-on experiences as often as possible. Students could build models of what they are studying, play a game that requires some movement, or act out a particular concept. Remember the old but reliable Chinese proverb: "I hear, and I forget; I see and hear, and I may remember; I do, and I understand."

- Offer a good balance between cooperative learning and independent work. Remember that if kids strongly resist cooperative learning but get their work done independently, there is no reason to force them into cooperative groups all the time. Expecting all students to choose to work on at least one cooperative learning task each week is more appropriate than requiring students who work best alone to cooperate to the point of learning style discomfort. For more on cooperative learning, see pages 17–19.

- Regularly give students time to reflect on what has been taught and learned. Some students will choose to record their reflections in a journal, while others would prefer to create a sketch or model. Insisting that all kids write in journals many times each week favors linguistic and visual learners but discriminates against artistic and kinesthetic students.

- Encourage all students to talk about their learning style strengths, and how knowing about those strengths improves their success with school tasks.

- Expect all students to set goals from one grading period to the next. Be sure the goals include the language of learning styles. *Example:* A student might choose a goal of "using graphic organizers to help remember content I should learn" or "using graphic organizers to take notes." Be sure to take time to check students' goals with them at each marking period, and to help them set realistic goals for the next checkpoint. For more information, see Chapter 12, especially pages 184–185.

- Find and use software that motivates students to be successful learners, especially software that provides individualized guidance so students can move ahead on their own personally designed path of achievement. One example is SuccessMaker. See "References and Resources."

- For students who often seem confused, teach exercises that are cross lateral—those designed to stimulate both sides of the brain to communicate with each other and prevent one side from being too dominant, thus opening the learner to more successful intake of learning material. More information and teaching materials are available from Brain Gym International. See "References and Resources."

Questions and Answers

"How can I possibly teach to accommodate all of these styles and intelligences when I have so many students with so many needs?"

The only thing you really *must* do is to constantly ask yourself this question: "If this student is not learning the way I am teaching, what environmental or curricular modifications might enable him or her to learn more effectively?" You are not expected to rearrange your entire classroom, nor is it necessary to diagnose and teach to each individual student's learning style. However, awareness of learning style implications for learning success will make you more aware of the need for certain modifications as specific students indicate that they are not learning successfully. As you offer these modifications, you will observe that other students' learning success is also being affected positively, and you can generalize the effects of the modifications. Some teachers who regularly use learning centers orient them around specific learning style categories and let students find the tasks that allow them to demonstrate best what they are learning.

"Isn't it a bad practice to always teach to students' learning style strengths? Don't we all have to learn to blend and understand stimuli from many different styles? Won't kids be at a disadvantage in the real world if we only teach to their learning style strengths?"

Although our ultimate goal is to teach *all* students to respond to tasks from many types of learning styles, we must begin by teaching to the individual student's learning style strengths. Many struggling students believe that they are incapable of learning. The most powerful evidence to convince them otherwise is success in tasks they formerly couldn't do. They will be at a much greater *advantage* in the real world if they become successful students than if they continue to perceive themselves as poor learners.

"Our school has rules against chewing gum, eating food, or bringing portable music players to class. How can I make appropriate modifications to the learning environment while remaining within these rules?"

I've never claimed to follow all of the rules I was expected to obey as a classroom teacher. (There . . . my secret is out!) Rules are often made in reaction to misconduct. Schools ban gum because of where kids tend to hide it; of course, there's no need to hide it if it's not against the rules to chew it. Food creates grazing grounds for critters; when kids bring nutritious snacks from home, they should be responsible for cleanup. If there's a chance that kids' portable music players might get taken by other students, perhaps you can keep them locked in your desk between uses. When I tell my students that they can only chew gum in my room and must dispose of it only in the plastic-lined wastebasket, kids who follow those rules are allowed to chew; kids who don't follow them lose their chewing privileges for a while. Chewing releases excess energy, especially for tactile-kinesthetic kids; if you simply can't allow it, try letting students tap on a spot that creates no noise (e.g., their arm or leg) or swing their leg into a space through which other students are unlikely to pass. Remember that the reason for offering these options is to improve learning outcomes; if that doesn't happen, there's no need to provide the options any longer. When kids understand this, they usually react in positive ways.

"I'm concerned about how my principal and other adults will react to some of the modifications I've made to accommodate various learning style preferences."

Don't wait for their reactions; be proactive! Explain your reasons for allowing certain liberties *before* you expect a classroom visit. Send newsletters home to parents describing these changes in the context of other teaching decisions. Keep reminding people that your goal is to improve your students' learning, and you will continue to use only those methods that lead to positive outcomes.

"How can I undo the damage I may have done to some kids in the past because I didn't know about learning styles?"

If you are taking the time to read this book, you can assume that you have a generous and friendly attitude toward students. Teachers are not in the practice of purposefully harming young people. We all make teaching decisions based on the information available to us at a given time. As you try some of these techniques with your own students, start passing information about them to

some of your colleagues—particularly the teacher who is being driven to distraction by a student you had last year, for whom you now know what to do differently!

REFERENCES AND RESOURCES

Armstrong, Thomas. *Multiple Intelligences in the Classroom.* Alexandria, VA: ASCD, 1994. A handy guide to using the theory of multiple intelligences in the classroom.

Brain Gym International (www.braingym.org). Help for kinesthetic learners. The Brain Gym program has been used successfully by parents and teachers to significantly improve learning attitudes and achievement through non-academic means. Visit the Web site to find certified Brain Gym instructors and classes in your area. Brain Gym books and learning materials by Paul E. Dennison and Gail E. Dennison are also available. Organization: 1-800-356-2109. Store: 1-888-388-9898.

CAPSOL Styles of Learning (www.stylesoflearning.com). An assessment that measures nine student preferences (auditory, visual, bodily-kinesthetic, individual, group, oral expressive, written expressive, sequential, global), profiling from low to high. Use it in the classroom to identify learning strengths and weaknesses and adjust instruction. Available in two versions: grades 3–9 and grade 10–adult. 1-800-578-6930.

Carbo, Marie, Rita Dunn, and Kenneth Dunn. *Teaching Students to Read Through Their Individual Learning Styles.* Englewood Cliffs, NJ: Allyn & Bacon, 1986. Helps teachers assess and accommodate students' reading styles and teach reading skills in ways that are friendly to tactile-kinesthetic learners.

Chapman, Carolyn. *If the Shoe Fits: How to Develop Multiple Intelligences in the Classroom.* Palatine, IL: IRI Skylight Publishing, 1993.

Dixon, John Philo. *The Spatial Child.* Springfield, IL: Charles C. Thomas, 1983. Dixon explains how some students who have great trouble learning in traditional ways have outstanding spatial abilities that allow them to develop and understand relationships between things in the physical world.

Educating Everybody's Children video series (shop.ascd.org). These videos help teachers use learning styles information to enhance learning for their students. The series includes *Attitudes and Beliefs* and *Capitalizing on Students' Strengths*. 1-800-933-ASCD (1-800-933-2723).

Freed, Jeffrey, and Laurie Parsons. *Right-Brained Children in a Left-Brained World: Unlocking the Potential of Your ADD Child.* New York: Simon and Schuster, 1998. Freed shares his techniques for teaching compensation learning strategies to children who have trouble learning. The strategies work whether or not the child has ADD.

"Gardner Announces the Eighth Intelligence." *Renewal Connection* 3:2 (Fall 1995), pp. 1 and 4.

Gardner, Howard. *Frames of Mind: The Theory of Multiple Intelligences.* 10th Anniversary Edition. New York: Basic Books, 1993.

Hart, Leslie. *Human Brain and Human Learning.* Kent, WA: Books for Educators, 1998. Helps teachers understand how the brain learns and how to create brain-compatible learning conditions in the classroom.

howardgardner.com (www.howardgardner.com). Visit Dr. Gardner's Web site for information about multiple intelligences—current research, findings, papers, books, projects, talks, presentations, and more.

Lazear, David. *Eight Ways of Teaching: The Artistry of Teaching with Multiple Intelligences.* 4th edition. Thousand Oaks, CA: Corwin Press, 2003. Includes Lazear's description of what intelligence-focused lessons look like, and an examination of the process for creating them. Features lessons incorporating all eight intelligences into a single learning experience.
—*Eight Ways of Knowing: Teaching for Multiple Intelligences.* 3rd edition. Thousand Oaks, CA: Corwin Press, 1999. Practical strategies for awakening the full spectrum of intelligences.
—*Pathways of Learning: Teaching Students and Parents About Multiple Intelligences.* Tucson, AZ: Zephyr Press, 2001.

LDOnline (www.ldonline.org). This comprehensive Web site is the first one I go to when I need information about students with learning challenges.

Levine, Mel. *A Mind at a Time.* New York: Simon and Schuster, 2002. Explains how parents and teachers can encourage children's learning strengths and bypass their learning weaknesses.

Maslow, Abraham H. *Motivation and Personality.* 3rd edition. New York: HarperCollins Publishers, 1987.

Multiple Intelligences poster set (www.kaganonline.com). Set includes nine colorful 11" x 17" posters, one for each of the eight intelligences, plus one that shows all eight. Available from Kagan Publishing & Professional Development. 1-800-WEE CO-OP (1-800-933-2667).

Our Other Youth. Jerry Conrath's materials on youth at risk and discouraged learners. Look for the following:
—*Intervention with Secondary Students,* Grades 7–12 (2002).
—*Our Other Youth* (1989).

Salend, Spencer J. *Creating Inclusive Classrooms: Effective and Reflective Practices for All Students.* 5th edition. Upper Saddle River, NJ: Prentice Hall, 2005.

Shake and Learn (www.shakeandlearn.com). Products that use music and movement to teach academic standards. *Shake and Learn: Grammar and Usage, Language Arts, Mathematics,* and *Science* each include a music CD with kinesthetic cues, lesson plans, reproducibles, and extension activities. Also available: *Shake and Learn Mathematics* DVD. From SALT Productions, Inc. 1-800-884-3764.

Silverman, Linda Kreger. *Upside-Down Brilliance: The Visual-Spatial Learner.* Denver, CO: DeLeon Publishers, 2002. New ways of understanding students who think in images rather than words.

Success Design International (www.nlpla.com). Materials to teach adults and children to understand human behavior, learning, and thinking processes, and to learn techniques for attaining positive change in those areas. 1-877-734-6463.

SuccessMaker (www.pearsonschool.com). Scalable digital courseware for grades K–8. Individualizes instruction to the specific needs of each student by automatically presenting instruction at the level at which a student is ready to learn, creating a successful learning experience. Aligns with district, local, and national standards, and is supported by a comprehensive management system. Used in more than 16,000 schools in the United States and 1,500 abroad. Courseware is available in customizable bundles. Program costs vary, depending on the software purchased, the range of grade levels to be covered, and the amount of professional development services requested.

Vitale, Barbara Meister. *Unicorns Are Real: A Right-Brained Approach to Learning.* Torrance, CA: Jalmar Press, 1982. Although not a recent publication, this book is filled with many teaching and learning tips for right-brained, visual, kinesthetic learners.

RECOMMENDED READING FOR STUDENTS

Armstrong, Thomas. *You're Smarter Than You Think: A Kid's Guide to Multiple Intelligences.* Minneapolis: Free Spirit Publishing, 2003. Helps kids ages 8–12 understand Howard Gardner's theory of multiple intelligences, what it means to them, and how to make the most of their own abilities and potential.

Cummings, Rhoda, and Gary Fisher. *The School Survival Guide for Kids with LD* (Learning Differences). Minneapolis: Free Spirit Publishing, 1991. Specific tips and strategies especially for students with LD. For ages 8 and up.
—*The Survival Guide for Teenagers with LD* (Learning Differences). Minneapolis: Free Spirit Publishing, 1993. Helps young people with LD succeed in school and prepare for life as adults. For ages 13 and up.

Teaching So All Students Can Learn

Each day, children come to school hoping to experience successful learning. Learning happens when the brain acquires a program—a fixed sequence of steps that is useful to the learner. For this to occur, the brain must be able to connect new learning to some pattern it already knows.* Kids learn best when they perceive that certain skills or information will help them to better understand something they know or are eager to know more about.

Children are naturally creative thinkers who construct fascinating theories to explain the world around them. While visiting Disney World in Orlando, we watched divers feed the sea life in a huge aquarium. A three-year-old nearby observed, "Look—there's a fireman feeding the fish!" Clearly, the child was trying to understand what she was seeing; she knew that firefighters sometimes wear masks and black suits, and she was applying what was true in one context to another. Her wise dad, instead of correcting her, asked her to explain why she thought the man was a firefighter. The father validated his daughter's thinking ability; she in turn wanted to know more. The stage was set for learning.

We thwart children's capacity to learn when we treat them as passive vessels waiting to be filled with knowledge. We invite low performance when we communicate low expectations for what they can achieve. One reason why kids in remedial education so rarely outgrow their need for remediation is because the curriculum is too easy. Remember the words of Dr. Sylvia Rimm: "The surest path to high self-esteem is to be successful at something one perceived

would be difficult." And also those of Dr. Kenneth Dunn: "If students cannot learn the way we teach them, then we must teach them the way they learn."

The way to help struggling learners meet required standards is to teach that content in the students' preferred learning styles. When we allow struggling students to work on tasks they think are easy or babyish, we communicate our belief that they simply can't do the regular work. This confirms their worst fears—that they were born stupid and even their teachers think they are incapable of learning. The longer they have to wait for successful learning to happen, the deeper and more destructive their fears become.

This chapter describes a variety of teaching strategies and techniques for you to try. All have been proven effective in real classrooms, where they have helped struggling students overcome their fears and free themselves to learn. When we demonstrate that a simple change of method can lead to learning success, students begin to regain the confidence lost over several years of failure.

A Few Words About the Revised IDEA

The IDEA (Individuals with Disabilities Education Act), revised in 2004, contains specific language for ensuring that students with learning disabilities get the help they need to succeed in school. A student with a specific learning disability has a disorder in one or more of the basic psychological processes involved in understanding or in using language, spoken or written, that may manifest

---

* Hart, Leslie. *Human Brain and Human Learning*. Kent, WA: Books for Educators, 1983, page 33 and chapters 3–11.

itself in the imperfect ability to listen, think, speak, read, write, spell, or do mathematical calculations. The legislation expects that there will be an ongoing relationship between the regular classroom teacher and the special education personnel.

I believe that regular education teachers can actually *prevent* certain students from needing to be referred for special education testing if they know how to provide helpful in-class interventions such as those described in this book. For students with Individual Education Plans (IEPs), these strategies can be used during the times the students spend in the special education *and* regular education classrooms.

Before Referring a Student for Special Education Testing

The regular classroom teacher might find that some referrals are unnecessary once appropriate curricular and behavioral interventions have been successfully applied in the classroom.

A highly kinesthetic student who has a lot of trouble sitting still and is up and moving much of the day might respond favorably to being allowed to move back and forth between two desks designated for him in the classroom, so movement is part of his routine. He might calm down and be able to stay on task longer while chewing gum, squeezing a Kush ball, and/or listening to soothing music. He might be more successful at showing what he knows through active learning options, rather than always having to write his thoughts.

Students who are reading significantly below grade level might respond positively to the Carbo Recorded Book method (see pages 88–90) or the Language Experience method (see pages 86–88). Students with spelling problems may greatly improve their spelling outcomes by using the Spelling Styles method (see pages 116–119).

When classroom teachers find and use methods that improve students' academic success in the regular classroom, the need for referral for special education testing can be significantly reduced. As a matter of fact, many school districts provide teacher assistance teams that actually work with classroom teachers to try many strategies before resorting to formal referrals.

After Referring a Student for Special Education Testing

Once a student has been evaluated and has an Individualized Education Plan, the classroom teacher's ongoing efforts to not only follow the recommendations in the IEP but continue to try other strategies that may lead to better learning success can make the IEP implementation more effective.

Of course, any strategies used in the classroom should be brought to the attention of the special education teacher and made part of the IEP written plan when it is revised.

Attribution Theory

Many teachers and parents worry about over-helping kids with learning difficulties. This is a legitimate concern. Above all, we want to make sure we do not create a condition in these kids called "learned helplessness." Students who have learned helplessness exhibit some or all of the following behaviors:

- They are slow to start their work and often don't complete it.
- They act out inappropriately rather than being discovered as not being competent.
- They give up at the first twinge of frustration.
- They use body language (slumping, frowning, sighing) to describe their helpless feelings; they appear tired and depressed.
- They turn in their work facedown at the last possible moment.

As teachers, we can empower all of our students to become more successful learners. One teaching technique uses the psychology of attribution theory to counter learned helplessness. Attribution theory defines to whom or what we attribute our success or failure. Successful learners attribute their success to having exerted enough effort to succeed, and they attribute any failure to inadequate effort on their part. Unsuccessful students expect to fail, since they perceive they lack the ability to succeed. They don't see any connection between effort and results.

Students who believe they will succeed begin a learning task by thinking, "I can do this. If I work hard, I will be able to complete this task." Students who believe they will fail begin by thinking, "I can't do this by myself. I need help. If no one will help me, then it is not my fault that I can't learn this or get this done." They create a self-protecting set of explanations for whatever happens to them, all of which give the control to an external source. When they fail, they tell themselves, "I did a rotten job on that assignment because the teacher never helps me." And *even when they succeed,* they rationalize, "I got a good evaluation on my story because my teacher helped me. Without his help, I could not have done a good job."

When people get too much help over time, the message they receive is that they really need help. They come to believe they are not capable, because if they *were* capable, they wouldn't need all that help. So the irony is that over-helpers are contributing to students' incapacities rather than strengthening their abilities to learn. The more we help them, the more helpless they become!

The way we respond to frustrated students shapes how they handle frustration in the future. When kids become convinced that they can't do things without help, they begin to take pleasure in having things done for them. They may become quite assertive in demanding our help. We reinforce their learned helplessness by giving in, thus enabling the helplessness to continue in what actively becomes a codependent relationship.* They expect constant prompts from us, we oblige, and that only proves they can't succeed without us.

According to Dr. Steven Landfried, who has studied this issue for many years, adults over-help children in many ways. Landfried defines educational enabling as:**

- doing things for students they can learn to do for themselves

- allowing students to choose behaviors that do not lead to productivity

- over-protecting, coddling, rescuing, bailing out, and other behaviors that teach youngsters they will not be held accountable for their choices and behaviors

- practices done in the spirit of helping that foster co-dependency and lower the learner's self-expectations, competencies, and self-esteem.

He describes enabling behaviors and suggests other actions—*true* help—we could choose instead. Both kinds are described in the chart below.

Caution: When dealing with students who have learned to be helpless, it's easy to blame them for their own failures. But until we have taught them the way they learn best, they have no control over whether they succeed or fail. We can avoid learned helplessness by using all the strategies we can find to teach to students' learning style strengths, thus empowering students to be successful with grade-level standards. We need to give kids the right kind of help—the kind that says and demonstrates, "Of course you can do this! We just have to find the method that works best for you, and success will be within your grasp."

Attribution Retraining***

We need to replace struggling students' thoughts of "I can't" with "The strategy I used didn't work, so I will use a different strategy and try again." We need to help them learn to attribute whatever happens to the presence or absence of their own efforts, as well as to the selection and use of effective learning strategies. When they are successful, we need to say, "You did well on that task because you worked hard

---

* Landfried, Steven E. "Educational Enabling: Is 'Helping' Hurting Our Students?" *Middle School Journal,* May 1990, pp. 12–15.

** The definition of educational enabling and the Debilitating Help/Positive Help chart are used with permission of Steven E. Landfried, Caring Accountability Workshops, 21 Albion Street, Edgerton, WI 53534; (608) 531-1716.

*** Shelton, T., A. Anastopoulous, and J. Linden. "An Attribution Training Program with Learning Disabled Children." *Journal of Learning Disabilities* 18:5 (1985), pp. 261–265. Used with permission of Dr. Terri L. Shelton, Associate Professor of Psychiatry and Pediatrics, University of Massachusetts Medical Center.

Debilitating Help That Enables into Helplessness	Positive Help That Facilitates Autonomous Behaviors
Protecting	Setting clear limits
Rescuing from expected outcomes	Imposing agreed-upon consequences
Over-controlling	Letting the person experience his or her own life
Overlooking errors and other problems	Discussing issues and creating solutions
Frequently reminding	Giving clear directions; providing visual examples
Nagging	Letting student set his or her own short-term goals
Speaking for	Waiting for responses; suggesting two alternatives
Making work and assessments easy	Teaching at challenge levels through learning strengths
Giving inflated grades	Using rubrics honestly
Accepting excuses	Making expectations clear; coaching to goals
Inconsistency	Consistency with fairness
Allowing inattentiveness	Holding accountable for paying attention
Allowing inappropriate behaviors	Teaching self-monitoring

and used helpful strategies." Students should be even more specific with their self-assessments. *Example:* "I did well on the spelling test this week because I studied the words in the way that's best for my learning style strength."

Attribution retraining is a simple, effective way to address learned helplessness. It leads students away from negative self-talk and prevents excuses for not learning. Plan to spend six one-hour sessions spread out over three weeks. This could replace the student's formal reading program for that time period.

1. Write or print 16 sentences on paper strips. Ten should be easy for the student, and the other six more challenging. Print an "E" on the back of each easy sentence strip and a "D" on the back of each difficult one. If more sentences are needed, prepare additional sets of 16 following the same criteria.

2. Prepare two sets of cue cards for students to read after they finish reading each sentence. One set (for correct readings) says: "That's right! I tried hard and did a good job!" and "I'm getting to be a pretty good reader!" The other set (for incorrect readings) says: "I didn't get that quite right, but that's okay. We learn through our mistakes" and "I can use a different strategy next time and put forth more effort, and I'll do better."

3. Start the first session by saying, "I'm going to help you learn how to help yourself learn more successfully and enjoy school more. You're going to read some sentences aloud to me. After each sentence, you'll read some statements on a cue card I'll show you."

4. Model correct and incorrect readings of sample sentences. Follow each example by reading an appropriate cue card.

5. Say, "Now I'm going to ask you to read one sentence aloud to me." Show an easy sentence and follow up with an appropriate cue card. Have the student whisper the statements on the cue card before saying them aloud.

6. Repeat with several sentences, following the sequence shown below for Session 1. Coach the student to choose an appropriate cue card after reading each sentence. Whenever the student reads a sentence incorrectly,

model a specific strategy for making corrections. (See chapters 6 and 7 for suggestions.)

7. Use the sequences shown below for the remaining sessions. You may want to have the student prepare his own sentence strips, including both easy and difficult sentences. You might also give the student the option of preparing his own cue cards.

SENTENCE SEQUENCES

E = easy, D = difficult

Session 1: E E E D D D E E D E E E D D E E
Session 2: E E D E E D D D E E E D D E E E
Session 3: E E D D D E E E D D E E D E E E
Session 4: E E E D D D E E D E E E D D E E
Session 5: E E D E E D D D E E E D D E E E
Session 6: E E D D D E E E D D E E D E E E

Goal Setting

I believe that the most significant difference between students who are successful in school and those who are not is the ability to set and accomplish realistic short-term goals. Students who are unsuccessful either don't set goals or they aim for lofty goals that are beyond their reach. It's extremely important to teach *all* students that success is not measured by grades or by semester or school year outcomes. Rather, success hinges on setting and reaching goals. When that happens regularly, success comes naturally.

1. Give each struggling student a copy of the "Goal Planning Chart" handout (page 66) with the "Subject Area/Task" column filled in.

2. At the beginning of each work period, ask the students to set a personal goal for how much work they expect to accomplish within the allotted time. (Limit their time period to five minutes less than what the rest of the class will have, since you will need to talk to these kids before the other students require your attention.) *For this method to work, students must set their own goals.*

GOAL PLANNING CHART

Subject Area/Task	Monday	Tuesday	Wednesday	Thursday	Friday
Journal Writing	3/10	3/10	3/10	4/10	4/10
Math	2/15	2/15	3/15	3/15	4/15
Science	1/10	1/10	2/10	2/10	2/10

 # Goal Planning Chart

NAME: _____

Each day, predict how much you can do in the time you have.

Subject Area/Task	Monday	Tuesday	Wednesday	Thursday	Friday

3. Have the students write their goals as ratios—predicted work to amount of time—on their charts. *Example:* 3 sentences in 10 minutes = 3/10.

4. At the end of the designated time period, return to each student and quickly correct his or her work.

If the goal has been met, ask the following questions:

- "What was your goal?"

- "Did you accomplish your goal?"

- "Who is responsible for your success in accomplishing your goal?" It may take patience and prodding, but the student must respond, "I am responsible for my success in accomplishing my goal."

- "How does it feel to be successful?" Again, you may have to prompt the student to say, "It feels good to be successful."

- "How can you congratulate yourself or give yourself some recognition for a job well done?" Offer suggestions if necessary. Remember that students who are used to low achievement tend to credit their success to luck or to the people who helped them.

If the goal has not been met, ask the following questions:

- "What was your goal?"

- "Did you accomplish your goal?"

- "Who is responsible for the fact that you did not reach your goal?" The student will probably blame some external source, such as another student who talked to him, or the fact that the teacher was unavailable for help. Don't ask how it feels to not accomplish the goal. Instead, prompt until the student can say, "I am responsible for not reaching my goal."

- "What plan can you make for tomorrow to prevent the same problem from happening again?" Have the student write her plan on the Goal Planning Chart.

Tips: Never punish students who don't reach their goals. The best way to get kids on track is to help them learn to set realistic goals and feel satisfaction from reaching them. The inability to earn positive feedback (from themselves and from you) is all the punishment they need.

If you must grade students' work under this arrangement, I recommend the following:

- a C for reaching a goal that is well below the work you expect from the rest of the class

- a B for when the goal gets into the grade-level range

- an A only for exceptional work. (When we give students high grades for work they know is below expected outcomes for their age peers, they conclude that we think they are not capable of improving.)

Finally, have students work on *one* area or subject at a time until progress is apparent and success feels comfortable to them. If you add other areas or subjects too quickly, students may develop a fear of success. ("Adults always expect more of you if you show them what you can do. I guess I should stop working so hard.")

Scenario: Kirsten

Kirsten was a sweet eight-year-old who was prone to crying huge tears only seconds after a task was assigned. Looking up at me, she would moan softly, "I don't know what to do. I didn't hear the directions. Where should I start? Help me!" She easily became discouraged and overwhelmed.

She and I began sitting together for a minute at the beginning of each task, planning her goal in terms of how much she could complete in the allotted time period. Once, when the task was to write a short descriptive paragraph, Kirsten seemed paralyzed and unable to begin.

"We are going to work on this for twenty minutes today," I said. "I'd like you to tell me how many good sentences you think you can write in fifteen minutes."

She looked at me with soulful eyes and ventured, "Two?"

"So you predict you will be able to write two good sentences in the next fifteen minutes?"

"I think so."

I showed her how to write her goal as a ratio at the top of her paper, with the completed work prediction as the top number and the amount of time as the bottom number—in this case, 2/15. Then I told her, "You may begin now, and I'll be back in fifteen minutes to see how you're doing. Remember, Kirsten, that you will be successful if you can accomplish your goal for this time period."

At the end of 15 minutes, I returned to her and said, "Okay, time's up. Let's take a look at the progress you've made in accomplishing your goal. What was your goal?"

She looked at the ratio she had written at the top of her paper and replied, "Two sentences in fifteen minutes."

"Did you complete your goal?"

She looked at what she had done and said, "Yes, I wrote two sentences."

My third question was, "Well, now, who is responsible for your success?" She looked at me quizzically, since this definition of success—the ability to set and accomplish realistic goals—was a new concept for her.

Finally, she said, "I think you are responsible."

"Why do you think that?"

"Because you let me choose a smaller number of sentences."

"That's true . . . but who actually completed the goal?"

"I guess I did."

"I agree! Now I'd like you to say that to me in a complete sentence. Tell me—who is responsible for your success in reaching the goal you set?"

And after much encouragement and even a little manipulation of her mouth with my hand, Kirsten was able to say, "I am responsible for my success because I reached the goal I set."

Then I asked her, "How does it feel to be successful?" (The purpose of this question is to help students who are caught in a failure cycle to realize that success can feel good. This may seem strange to people who are success-oriented, but we have to understand that kids who perceive themselves as failures actually come to *prefer* failure because it is comfortable and predictable. Success represents change, and we all know how scary change can be!) I talked with Kirsten about how reaching a goal is worth celebrating, and explained that there were several ways she might congratulate herself for achieving success—like getting a big handshake, patting herself on the back, or giving herself a thumbs-up. By the end of our discussion, Kirsten was smiling.

Each day for several weeks, we repeated this procedure in all subjects. Kirsten's goals remained quite small for several class periods until she began to feel more confident, at which point she set her goals slightly higher. Within two months, her goals in most subject areas were near grade-level expectations.

Metacognition*

Metacognition is the monitoring of one's own thinking throughout the learning process. It helps students become more aware of how they think, recognize when they don't understand something, and adjust their thinking accordingly.

I like to tell students, "Metacognition is thinking about your thinking before, during, and after a learning task." It begins when students consider which strategies they might use to accomplish the task. It continues as they choose the most effective strategies and then decide for themselves if the results meet agreed-upon standards. Time spent teaching a variety of strategies pays off as students make strategy selection an integral part of doing their work.

To model metacognition, think out loud as you teach something. Instead of saying, "First we . . . , next we . . . , then we . . . , and finally we . . . ," let students hear what you are thinking as you solve a learning problem. *Example:*

1. Start by saying, "I need to know what the word *eerie* means in this sentence: 'There were eerie sounds coming out of the haunted house.' I have to figure out the meaning of this word, and I want to do it without going to the dictionary.

   "I'll start by figuring out the meaning of the whole sentence. I go to a haunted house that the Lions' Club

in our town sets up each Halloween. I'm remembering the sounds I hear in the haunted house—lots of squeaking and moaning and groaning. Those sounds are supposed to scare me, and they do! So I'm going to guess that *eerie* means 'strange and scary.'

   "Now I'll substitute that meaning for the word in the sentence: 'There were strange and scary sounds coming out of the haunted house.' Does that make sense? Yes, it does. Now I can move on."

2. Invite a few students to make sense of the same word by thinking out loud.

3. Have the class repeat the process privately, whispering their self-talk.

4. Have one student try the same process aloud with a different word.

5. Have several students repeat the process with the same word.

6. Have the class repeat the process privately, whispering their self-talk.

7. Tell the students that you expect them to use this process as they encounter unfamiliar words in reading assignments. Whenever they ask you for the meaning of a word, remind them to think out loud and figure it out for themselves.

Give each student a copy of the "Thinking About What I Do" handout (page 69).** Tell the class, "Each time you need to monitor your thinking or behavior, picture yourself sitting on your own shoulder. Close your eyes and visualize your task from beginning to end. Visualize yourself completing the task successfully, one step at a time. As you work, keep asking yourself the questions on the checklist." Students may tally their responses in the checkboxes so this handout can be used for several checkpoints during a particular activity.

Providing a Meaningful and Challenging Curriculum

Deciding What to Teach

Before No Child Left Behind, we could reassure ourselves that when we had done the best we could do, if some kids chose not to do their work, then they were choosing to fail and would have to experience the consequences of their choice. Educators no longer have that luxury. We are responsible for the learning success of *all* of our students—no excuses, no rationalizations. The success of students,

---

* Meichenbaum, D. *Cognitive-Behavior Modification: An Integrative Approach.* New York: Plenum Press, 1977. Used with permission.

** Adapted from "Self-Monitoring Checklist" by Anita DeBoer, consultant in education. Used with permission.

Thinking About What I Do

NAME: _____

What am I supposed to do?

_____

_____

_____

_____

What is my plan for doing it today?

_____

_____

_____

_____

✓ Have I closed my eyes to visualize the task I'm supposed to do? ☐ YES ☐ NO

✓ Have I visualized myself doing the task successfully? ☐ YES ☐ NO

Ask yourself this question several times during your work period:

How well am I doing?

Check your progress with questions like these:

✓ Am I drifting off and losing my attention? ☐ YES ☐ NO

✓ Am I noticing what is really important and ignoring what is not important? ☐ YES ☐ NO

✓ Have I worked as long as my goal said I would? ☐ YES ☐ NO

✓ Do I need a short break now? ☐ YES ☐ NO

If I accomplish my goal, how will I reward myself?

_____

_____

_____

If I don't accomplish my goal this time, what is my plan for the next time I try?

_____

_____

_____

teachers, and entire schools is being measured by how well students perform on high-stakes tests based mostly on state standards.

Part of the No Child Left Behind legislation was prompted by complaints from U.S. employers that high school graduates were not prepared to enter the workforce. In 1991, the U.S. Secretary of Labor appointed a special commission to learn how schools were preparing young people for work. The Secretary's Commission on Achieving Necessary Skills (SCANS) talked with business owners, public employers, managers, union officials, and workers. Their findings were published in a report titled "What Work Requires of Schools: A SCANS Report for America 2000." The report describes a set of competencies and foundation skills that all American high school students must develop in order to enjoy a productive, full, and satisfying life. In summary, all students need to acquire:*

- *basic skills* including typical core school subjects (reading, writing, arithmetic, listening, speaking)

- *thinking skills* including creative thinking, problem-solving, decision-making, and reasoning

- *personal qualities* including self-esteem, responsibility, punctuality, integrity, and the ability to grow in the job

- *interpersonal skills* including teamwork and leadership

- *skills for managing resources* such as time, money, materials, and people

- *skills for acquiring, organizing, communicating, and processing information* in order to interpret and understand what is needed to do one's job well

- *skills for selecting and applying technology* in order to select equipment and tools and apply available technology to one's work

- *skills for understanding social, organizational, and technological systems* in order to monitor and correct performance and understand how to use and/or improve the systems.

This list could probably match any school district's expected standards list and might serve as an assessment rubric against which to measure which parts of a curriculum are truly essential.

It really doesn't matter how much you *teach* your students. What matters is how much they remember and can demonstrate on assessments and on the job. When considering the standards assigned to a particular grade level, we have to make some choices about which standards to focus on and which to cover more lightly.

When we teach students who have trouble learning, our first impulse is to keep it simple and focus on the basics. Many of these kids have had very little exposure to learning activities that include higher-level thinking. Yet many students with learning problems have a streak of creativity inside them, and many respond positively to the same kinds of activities we have historically used mostly for gifted kids.

So whenever possible, give *all* of your students activities that provide experience in metacognition—thinking about their thinking. These skills can be generalized to all types of learning and testing situations. Think back on what you remember from your own schooling. Your most memorable learning probably happened at a level that demanded real thinking, not rote memorization.

Thinktrix: A Critical Thinking Model**

Thinktrix is a thinking typology developed by Dr. Frank Lyman, who also created the Think-Pair-Share component of the Name Card method (see pages 14–17). Over time, teach your students the seven categories of thinking. Spend time during each class discussion using the vocabulary of thinking and helping kids explain how they know they are experiencing certain categories. Each category has its own symbol, so students can eventually respond to the symbols without having to hear or speak the category names.

When you use this model of stimulating thinking, along with the Name Card method, you communicate high expectations to all students and demonstrate your belief that struggling students can be successful with higher-level thinking activities.

 Recall. Students simply remember what they have learned and talk about it. *Example:* "Tell the sequence of events in this story."

 Similarity. Students compare objects or phenomena to see what attributes they have in common. *Example:* "How are the causes of colds and the flu similar?"

 Difference. Students compare things to notice how they are different. *Example:* "How is a triangle different from a parallelogram?"

 Cause-Effect. Students look at how one action leads to or comes from another. *Examples:* "What causes a rainbow to be formed?" "What effects do rainbow sightings have on people?"

* U.S. Department of Labor and the Secretary's Commission on Achieving Necessary Skills (SCANS). "What Work Requires of Schools: A SCANS Report for America 2000." Washington, DC: U.S. Government Printing Office, 1991. Available to download at wdr.doleta.gov/SCANS/whatwork/.

** Adapted from "Think-Pair-Share, Thinktrix, Thinklinks, and Weird Facts" by Frank T. Lyman Jr., in *Enhancing Thinking through Cooperative Learning,* edited by Neil Davidson and Toni Worsham. NY: Teachers College Press, 1992. Used with permission of Frank T. Lyman Jr.

Idea to Example. Students try to find facts, events, or objects to prove that an idea they have is supportable by evidence, or to deepen a concept. *Example:* "What are some examples of bravery in the stories in this unit?"

 Example to Idea. Students find patterns shared by events, sets of facts, or objects. *Example:* "What conclusions can be drawn from the evidence at the crime scene?"

 Evaluation. Students decide whether events, situations, facts, etc. are right or wrong, truthful or not, significant or not. *Example:* "Study recent Supreme Court decisions and give reasons why you agree or disagree with them."

Scenario: Brandon

When Brandon walked into my fifth-grade class for the voluntary summer school program, he took a seat as far away from the front of the room as possible. He seemed quiet, shy, and reluctant to be there. I was teaching a specific approach to problem-solving for gifted students, and I began the class with a series of brainstorming activities. Almost in spite of himself, Brandon became animated, and by the end of the half-day session he had contributed several unique and interesting ideas.

On the second day of class, he had a little smile on his face, and he chose a seat near where I had stood the day before to chart the brainstorming results. His sense of humor began to show itself, and he displayed a knack for piggybacking wild and crazy ideas onto some of his classmates' contributions. When we broke into smaller groups, he volunteered to lead his group. His shyness had disappeared, and he was an eager and active participant in the day's activities.

On the morning of the third day, he walked into class with his mother beside him. His original shy demeanor had returned. "I had to bring Brandon to school today," his mother explained. "He skipped the first two days of the summer program."

"No, he didn't," I protested. "He was here both days and he has been doing great!"

"Well, now, I'm confused," she responded. "The remedial teacher called me yesterday to report that Brandon hadn't come to school."

After a brief investigation, we solved the mystery. Our state was providing summer programs for only two groups: gifted kids and those with remedial reading problems. Brandon had been signed up for the remedial class and had accidentally wandered into our class for gifted kids. Until we discovered he was remedial, he had behaved as though he was gifted and had fit right in with the other problem-solvers.

I wish I could report that Brandon was allowed to stay with our class, but at that time students could be either remedial or gifted—not both. Brandon's mom took him to the class where the state funding formula required him to stay. However, he usually stopped by for a visit on his way to or from class, and his remedial reading teacher was willing to try some of the techniques I was using with my students.

This experience has kept me humble ever since on the subject of appreciating every student's strengths even while addressing their learning weaknesses. It has also kept me mindful of the fact that a meaningful and challenging curriculum creates better learning outcomes.

Giving Choices

The most potent motivator in any classroom is for students to consistently have meaningful choices. Although we have long included choice in programs for the gifted, we overlook the power it has for all kids.

The easiest choices to give are those that relate to:

- what students will learn (*example:* "You can learn about our moon or the moons that belong to other planets")
- how they will learn (*example:* "You can read about your topic or watch a DVD on the topic")
- how they will express what they have learned (*example:* "You can either write a paragraph or draw a picture and add a caption").

When kids make choices that reflect their learning style strengths, and when teachers accept products other than written papers, we can almost always expect positive results. Kids will do whatever is necessary to learn something they really want to know about.

Presenting Exciting and Relevant Content

When students are presented with exciting and relevant content, much of their resistance to learning disappears. If you can answer "yes" to all or most of the following questions about your teaching, then you can probably assume that your students are motivated to learn:

- Am I able to modify the academic program without compromising appropriately high expectations? Am I teaching challenging content through my students' learning style strengths?
- Is the content likely to intrigue my students? Is it about issues that really matter to them? Have I considered their interests? (See "Interest Survey" on pages 8–9.)

- Is the emphasis on interpretive thinking and in-depth knowledge—on learning fewer things well?

- Am I presenting how-to-learn strategies within the context of meaningful content?

- Can my students see how to apply what they learn to other settings?

Many teachers are engaging students in learning the curriculum within the context of what has been called "problem-based learning." Essentially, a problem is identified, and students work to solve it at the same time as they are learning skills and competencies. *Examples:*

- Eighth graders worked to decide whether their town's main shopping area, which had been closed to vehicular traffic for many years, should be reopened to automobiles, since sales in the stores had been lagging. Students created a survey instrument, worked in teams to interview town residents, explored what other towns with similar problems had done, created a recommendation for the town council to consider, and presented it to the council at a regular meeting.

- Fifth graders spent three consecutive days at an outdoor education program in a natural setting. They observed plants and animals in nature, discussed how pollution affects natural growth, and learned how to survive in the forest.

- High school students adopted a section of a local highway. They researched the costs of cleaning up litter from roads, developed an ad campaign for broadcast on local cable TV, and conducted a monthly clean-up mission on their stretch of road.

- Third graders adopted grandparents from a local senior citizens' facility where people had been complaining of loneliness. They interviewed their grandparents and developed a historical narrative of life in their community over several generations. Then they developed autobiographies their grandparents helped them prepare and rehearse for presentation to a combined meeting of their class and the senior citizens.

- Seventh graders took rubbing impressions from a local cemetery with graves dating back to the 1600s. They constructed a group story about life in those times, including information about diseases that affected people in the past but are no longer a threat today. Then they acted out their story in a presentation at the local historical society. They also made plans to help preserve the cemetery.

Turning Kids On to Learning Through Projects

Scenario: Louisa

Louisa was an eight-year-old with LD. Her hard-working teacher, Mr. Hanover, was frustrated because Louisa wasn't doing any of her class work.

"What does she do?" I asked.

"Absolutely nothing."

"I understand she's not doing any of the assigned work, but if you were to close your eyes and visualize Louisa during the school day, what would you see?"

"I would see her out of her chair, spending the entire day at the snail cage."

At that, my ears perked up. "What does she do at the snail cage?" I asked.

"Not one thing except watch the snails."

"Well, then, let's take advantage of this passion she has for snails!"

We began by having Louisa record in a journal everything she observed the snails do at certain intervals throughout the day. We set up a table for her beside the snail cage, then gave her a cassette player, a cassette with a recorded signal that beeped every five minutes, a spiral notebook, and some pencils. We demonstrated how she should watch the snails until she heard the beep. At that point, she was to write down one thing she had observed over the previous five minutes. If the snails did not move, she was supposed to write, "The snails did not move."

"But I can't write!" Louisa protested.

We reassured her that all she had to do was make a few marks or draw a simple picture. Then she could tell the teacher what she had written.

After several days of coaching, Louisa was faithfully stopping at every tone to record something in her journal. Mr. Hanover scheduled brief conferences with her three times each day: before recess and lunch and near the end of the school day. During each conference, Louisa could read at least one observation aloud. It wasn't long before Louisa volunteered to share some of her observations with the class during journal-sharing time, and her status among her classmates improved significantly.

As Louisa became interested in developing her observation and recording skills, she began asking how to spell certain words. Her journal entries started looking like written text. After a few weeks, Mr. Hanover asked Louisa to write one observation every ten minutes. At the end of each day, she was to select one written observation and illustrate it. Next, she learned how to write a question for each observation. Soon some of her days were spent recording information she found in books and magazines. Within six weeks, Louisa had become the class expert on snails.

Using Project-Based Learning

Project-based learning has the potential to turn on turned-off students. Teachers have discovered that they can teach the same objectives or outcomes to kids who are working on projects that they would have taught through the regular curriculum.

Some teachers worry that struggling students need *more* teacher control, not less. In fact, the best control comes from letting students immerse themselves in what they are learning. Many behavior problems decrease or disappear.

For one week each month in an inner-city school in Pittsburgh, teachers set aside their normal routines and lead groups of students in projects that give them an in-depth look at a topic of their choice. All projects are designed to teach kids the same skills they would get from the regular curriculum. The students work for an entire week without interruption; they don't even change classes. Classroom work is enhanced by library visits and field trips. The resulting projects demonstrate the truth in the following assumptions:

■ All students are capable of higher-level learning with in-depth study of a topic.

■ Basic skills can be taught within the context of meaningful learning and critical thinking.

■ Most students learn best in a community of learners. They also learn how to help each other learn.

Because there is positive status associated with project-based learning, and because all students are receiving a high-quality educational experience, many students who formerly had negative attitudes about school have decided that this type of learning is cool. In addition, they have begun supporting each other as learners instead of disparaging the efforts of those who want to succeed in school.

1. Give each student a copy of the "Project Planner" handout (page 74).

2. Have students identify a topic they might like to explore. **Tip:** If they have trouble coming up with a topic, have them stroll through the stacks of your school or public library and shop the library shelves.

3. Have them list at least four possible subtopics. Explain that a subtopic is a smaller piece of a larger topic and give examples. Once students have listed their subtopics, have them choose one to focus on. Emphasize that this should be something they really want to learn more about.

4. Help students locate and collect sources of information about their subtopic. **Tips:** Use the school library. Ask the librarians at your local public library for assistance. They can gather resources across a wide range of reading abilities and lend them to you for an extended

period of time. Consider inviting parents to help kids search for information.

5. Provide a place for students to store the information they collect. *Examples:* space on a bookshelf; a storage container; a cubby or extra desk.

6. Teach students to look through one source at a time and record important facts, phrases, and sentences on paper or notecards. Insist that they *not* look through several sources simultaneously. Model the use of metacognition (see page 68) to translate paragraphs and long sentences into short phrases. Encourage visual learners to use diagrams, maps, and other visual formats to record information.

7. Help students prepare timelines showing the various parts of their project, including the due date. **Tip:** Global thinkers usually find it easier to prepare a timeline *backwards* from the due date, planning each step from last to first.

8. Have students select a method of expressing what they have learned. See page 75 for lists of products compatible with learning style strengths. Don't expect formal written reports, since most struggling students have negative feelings about writing. If some students want to prepare a written report, let them use a computer (if available). Investigate programs like HyperStudio that allow kids to create polished-looking products. See "References and Resources" at the end of this chapter.

   Other suggestions: Have students create a transparency picture by drawing or copying a picture or photograph onto a blank transparency. They can color and show the transparency to the class while they report what they have written on a notecard. This allows them to share their passionate interests with their peers and gain status because they can give reports like everyone else.

9. Have students make their presentations. For projects that take a long time to complete, students can give brief progress reports every two to three weeks about what they have learned in that interval. **Tips:** Set a time limit for presentations so they don't run on forever. If some students need to share more information than the class needs to know, suggest that they meet with you privately to tell you what else they learned from working on their project.

To help kids stay on track during project work, have them keep a daily Log of Project Work (page 76). At the beginning of each work period, they enter the date and the task they plan to accomplish that day. Five minutes before project work ends, they record what they actually accomplished. Spillover work is written in the next line as their plan for the next day. As they accomplish each task, a new task is planned and recorded.

Project Planner

NAME: _____ **DATE:** _____

A Topic I Want to Learn About: _____

Subtopics (list at least 4, then circle the number of the one you choose):

1. _____   6. _____

2. _____   7. _____

3. _____   8. _____

4. _____   9. _____

5. _____   10. _____

Sources of information (list at least 5, and use no more than one encyclopedia):

1. _____   6. _____

2. _____   7. _____

3. _____   8. _____

4. _____   9. _____

5. _____   10. _____

How I will use my learning style strength to learn the material:

_____

_____

How I will share what I've learned with the class in ways that are learning-style friendly:

_____

_____

Variation: The Eight-Section Report*

This simpler version of project-based learning is recommended for beginning researchers or students who are easily frustrated or discouraged.

1. Have students identify a topic they would like to learn more about.

2. Give each student a large sheet of paper (such as newsprint) folded into eight sections.

3. Have students draw or find eight pictures for their topic, arrange them in a logical sequence on the paper, and paste each one in the appropriate section.

4. Have them write two sentences about each picture. Then have them write an introductory sentence and a concluding sentence.

Reports can be left as is or copied onto regular paper. If the sections are not in the correct sequence, they may be cut apart and rearranged before the writing stage. Catalog all reports and store them in the school library.

Products Compatible with Learning Style Strengths**

Whenever students work on projects or other extended learning tasks, have them demonstrate what they learn in brain-compatible ways. See the chart below for possible products. Also check with your technology specialist to see what software programs are available for students to use to create more sophisticated products. Ask about HyperStudio. (See "References and Resources.")

More Teaching Techniques to Try

Background Music

Over the past 20 years, much research has been done to see if background music enhances learning. Conclusive evidence is hard to find, yet we know that global learners can concentrate better when there is soothing music playing in the background.

Test this method with your students: Play soothing music for periods of time when you are not directly teaching and students are working on various tasks. Choose classical music by Bach, Vivaldi, Mozart, Corelli, Haydn, and other composers played slowly; an optimal speed seems to be 60 beats per minute. Or try some New Age instrumental music. Ask your students to notice how the music affects their ability to concentrate and remember what they are learning.

---

* Barb Luring, elementary educator, Cedar Falls, Iowa.

** Adapted from *Writing Units That Challenge*, edited by James Curry and John Samara © 1990 Maine Educators for the Gifted and Talented, Portland, Maine. Used with permission.

Products for Auditory Learners	Products for Visual Learners	Products for Tactile-Kinesthetic Learners
Give a speech or a talk.	Give a transparency presentation.	Create a diorama or a mobile.
Write a song, rap, poem, story, advertisement, or jingle; perform it for the class.	Illustrate songs, raps, or poems.	Create and produce a skit or play.
Hold a panel discussion, round-robin discussion, or debate.	Create a HyperStudio product. See "References and Resources."	Give a demonstration.
Conduct an interview.	Create a video production.	Perform an experiment.
Present a "You-Are-There" simulated interview or description.	Write, illustrate, and design a travel brochure.	Create a game for others to play to learn the same information.
Write an article or editorial for a newspaper.	Make a chart or poster representing a synthesis of information.	Make a three-dimensional map.
Create a newspaper.	Create a diorama or a mobile.	Make and demonstrate a model.

 # Log of Project Work

NAME: _____

Project Topic: _____

Date	Planned Work	Work Actually Completed Today

If most believe that hearing music is helpful but some don't, offer sound-blocking headphones to those who are bothered by it. If only a few of your students favor the music, arrange to have it played through a listening station.

Group Response Methods

When we ask a question and get a response from one student, all this proves is that one student knows the answer. Think back to the last time you led a review for an upcoming test. If you discussed all of the test questions, you probably felt confident that everyone would pass the test—but the distribution of grades didn't change much from the previous test, and there were still some failing grades. Why? Because there was only one person who actually responded to all of the review questions—you!

When you ask "Any questions?" and no one raises a hand, this doesn't mean that everyone understands what you have just taught. Group response methods are a much more reliable way of determining how many students really get what you are teaching.

■ Use the Name Card method (see pages 14–17) to dramatically increase student participation, responsibility, and understanding.

■ Teach nonverbal ways of responding to questions. *Examples:* hand signals (thumbs up for "agree," down for "disagree," sideways for "not sure"); holding up a certain number of fingers to indicate a choice between several alternatives. Instruct students to withhold their responses until you give a "show me" signal (raising your right hand, snapping your fingers, clapping your hands, etc.). At your signal, all students respond simultaneously.

■ Have students write their responses on handheld slates and raise them simultaneously when you give the signal. You can purchase small slates and chalk from school supply companies. Or make your own slates from shiny plastic-coated squares or similar material (available from building supply companies) and provide students with erasable markers.

■ Give each student two 3" x 5" cards—one green, one red. Holding up the green card means "I agree" or "true"; holding up the red card means "I disagree" or "false."

Peer Teaching

Peer teaching opportunities—whether formal or informal—allow students who already understand something to explain it to kids who haven't yet grasped it. Pair Practice is an easy-to-implement peer teaching technique; see pages 17–19. Of course, peer teaching should be limited to volunteers. Highly capable students should not feel obligated to tutor other students.

Some schools have Peer Assistance programs in which students help others with learning difficulties. Assistants are trained in peer tutoring techniques, and both tutors and those being tutored benefit from the experience.

Bringing Technology into the Classroom

Children who watch lots of television and play computer and video games all the time expect to be entertained while they learn. They prefer to learn by viewing; they want color, sound, and visual effects; they anticipate speedy solutions to complex problems because most TV crises are resolved in less than an hour. We can either wait until students once again become interested in traditional ways of learning, or we can train them for a workplace that will expect them to be comfortable and capable with all kinds of technology.

The effective use of technology in the classroom narrows the gap between potential and performance, especially for students who struggle to learn. Some educators have resisted using technology in the classroom, fearing that students will become dependent on the learning aids and unable to learn independently. This attitude makes as much sense as requiring kids with vision problems to take off their glasses in school. Students with learning difficulties can't become more successful learners simply by trying harder. We should be thrilled that so much technology is available, and we should use whatever we can get our hands on!

To continue using computers in schools only to support the acquisition of traditional skills is a waste of time and technology. The current practice is to make computers an integral part of the learning process so students learn *from* them instead of *with* them. Some schools have eliminated computer literacy classes altogether in favor of letting kids use computers to create exciting learning products. Students are illustrating and animating documents, creating multimedia presentations with PowerPoint, becoming filmmakers, and even helping their teachers with hardware and software. Many teachers are delighted to observe former troublemakers and struggling students turning out products that rival those of students considered to have higher ability.

From 1985–1998, Apple Classrooms of Tomorrow (ACOT), a research and development collaboration among public schools, universities, research agencies, and Apple Computer, studied how the routine use of technology by teachers and students might change teaching and learning. Some of ACOT's findings included:

- Students' enthusiasm and motivation to learn increase dramatically when technology is used.

- Student productivity increases in all subject areas, causing teachers to scramble for material to fill up the balance of the year since basic competencies are mastered sooner.

- More spontaneous peer and cooperative learning happens when students are working together on technology-assisted instruction.

- Most struggling writers, even very young children, become more fluent on the keyboard.

- Standardized test results for struggling students who use technology are superior to those of students in control groups who do not.

- High school students who use technology routinely have a higher graduation rate and a higher college participation rate. They receive more honors than other students.

In short: Don't worry about students becoming dependent on technology. Just be glad it's available to make learning more accessible and exciting for everyone.

Your success in using technology depends on how well you can match students' learning needs to the hardware and software available to you. Call on the technology expert in your school or district for advice and assistance. If there is no such person, contact your state department of education and ask to speak to their technology consultant.

When ordering software, try to get it on a trial basis so you can return it if it doesn't work on your classroom computers or doesn't appear to improve learning outcomes. If you don't understand the software, borrow students from the upper grades who are self-proclaimed computer wizards and enlist their help. Don't be surprised if some of those kids have been labeled "poor students" at some point during their schooling. Although they may struggle with typical school tasks, the sky's the limit when they work with computers. There's a lesson in here somewhere.

Remember that kids need to learn how to use technology in the same way they learn everything else: through direct teaching that includes practice in thinking out loud. In the early stages, it's important to provide appropriate coaching so students don't become as frustrated with technology as they have been with more traditional learning methods.

Simple Technologies

Word Processors

Teach keyboarding to all students who have trouble writing, especially those who work slowly and tediously. Find a word processing program appropriate for each age group.

There is absolutely no reason to deprive kids of this valuable technology until their handwriting improves to legibility or fluency. Some teachers have found that writing assignments finished on computers are much better and more polished than anything those students could have produced with pencil and paper. Many kids with negative attitudes toward writing approach the task enthusiastically when they are given access to computers; many say that this makes them feel like real writers. Students eventually began to use word processing in other subject areas as well.

Calculators

Calculators are to math what word processors are to language and writing. For students who are dramatically less fluent in computation skills than their age peers, calculators enable them to progress to more authentic (and interesting) math tasks. When we keep struggling students from real problem-solving while we wait for them to catch up on their fluency in math facts, we help to create an ever-widening gap between them and their grade-level curriculum.

Many standardized tests, including the SAT, now allow students to use calculators. Contrary to what we might expect, students who use calculators regularly do as well or better on standardized tests than those who have been stuck in remedial classes that focus on computation.

Students with LD and/or hearing impairments should have calculators with tape or paper printouts; when they get a wrong answer, they can go back and check their work. Students who are visually impaired need calculators with large keyboards and readouts.

Small Electronics

Make hand-held spellcheckers or dictionaries available. Some include a synthesized speech feature; students can key in unfamiliar words, hear them pronounced, and access their definitions.

Many manufacturers produce a wide variety of inexpensive electronic calendars and/or diaries that can help students organize their chaotic lives. Check availability and pricing at your local office supplies superstore. Franklin Electronic Publishers offers a wide variety of electronic spellcheckers, dictionaries, and organizers. See "References and Resources."

Cassette Players/Recorders

Cassette players can make learning much more pleasant and successful, and their uses are virtually unlimited (*examples:* note-taking; recording lectures for later listening and review; recording reports for presentation; listening to recorded books; playing soothing music while working). Models with variable speed controls allow students to adjust the speed to their own comfort level. Cassette technology is being replaced by compact discs, CD-ROMs, DVDs, and downloads, but programs should continue to be available for some time for schools that use cassette players.

Computer-Assisted Instruction (CAI)

Use computer-assisted instruction to help students learn the basics—reading, spelling, math facts, etc. Some schools have shown impressive gains in standardized test scores for kids who use computers to learn. Companies like Broderbund and Sunburst Technology offer lots of software for this purpose; see "References and Resources." Check with the publishers of the curriculum materials you are using to see if they have companion software. Students with LD benefit from software with auditory and visual cues—warning commands, blinking cursors, beeps, toots, whistles, quacks—that call attention to mistakes and reinforce correct responses.

High-Tech Options

Following are very basic descriptions of technologies currently available. Any attempt to make more specific or detailed recommendations would likely be out of date by the time the ink was dry on this book. Stay in touch with your school's or district's technology person so you always know the latest ways to enhance learning success for your students with learning difficulties. You can also visit the Web sites of organizations that specialize in educational technology. The International Society of Technology in Education's Web site (www.iste.org) is an excellent source of educator resources, advocacy information, and more. From there, you can access numerous other organizations and resources, including companies committed to technology in education. See "References and Resources."

If you have the opportunity to suggest topics for inservice meetings, ask for training on how to use technology resources to help you ease into the classroom of the future.

Text-to-Speech Programs

These programs translate written materials into spoken words. Before too long, there will be affordable computer programs that turn spoken words into text (and almost make keyboarding obsolete!).

CD-ROMs and DVDs

CD-ROMs and DVDs are rapidly replacing cassettes, both audio and video. Each CD-ROM can store roughly the equivalent of 550,000 pages of printed text. The amount and type of material available on CD-ROMs is increasing exponentially and now includes encyclopedias (with text, illustrations, video clips, and audio clips), talking diction-aries, atlases, literature, and much more. Some CD-ROMs allow students to hear a story while watching the book on video—an exciting pre-reading experience.

The Internet and the World Wide Web

In 1996, when the first edition of this book was published, the Internet was just becoming available to schools, homes, and libraries. Now we have entire schools—even entire cities—equipped with wireless technology. Your school probably has Internet access in all classrooms.

One easy-to-use Internet feature is email (electronic mail). Students can communicate with anyone on the Internet, including specialists on any topic they are exploring. Contact your media or technology specialists for further information, or call your state office of education and speak to their technology specialists.

Assistive Technology[*]

One of the most dramatic changes in education in the last ten years is the availability of assistive technology. Any software or hardware that improves learning success for students with learning difficulties falls into this category. Keran Hoover teaches a self-contained class for students with learning difficulties so severe that total inclusion in regular education classes for these kids is unrealistic. She uses assistive technology with her students daily.

I asked Keran whether such assistance interferes with the student's ability to eventually learn more independently. She replied that with some students, the use of such technology is the *only* way they can learn. When this is the case, she believes, some learning is better than no learning! I certainly agree. There are hundreds of colleges in the U.S. that provide ongoing access to assistive technology for students with learning difficulties to allow them to succeed in college level courses.

I also asked Keran how the use of assistive devices affects students at test-taking times. We both believe that students who have had successful experiences learning during the regular school year are better test-takers than kids who have only experienced failure in their classroom lessons.

Following is an annotated list of hardware and software that Keran recommends. Some have downloadable free trials or 30-day trial offers; be sure to ask about those options when contacting the companies. Consult your teaching manuals and component descriptions for adopted text programs.

Co:Writer (www.donjohnston.com). Predicts the words a student will want to use as he or she is typing a document. 1-800-999-4660.

---

[*] Keran Hoover, special day class teacher and member of Special Education Teacher Technology Specialists (SETTS), Rancho Cucamonga, California.

Clicker (www.cricksoft.com/us). A talking word processor that allows students to start writing with a picture, then helps them turn it into text. 1-866-33-CRICK (1-866-332-7425).

Draft:Builder (www.donjohnston.com). Helps kids build final documents from outlines; allows students to see the outline and draft side-by-side. 1-800-999-4660.

Inspiration Software (www.inspiration.com). Inspiration (for older students) and Kidspiration (for younger kids) create graphic organizers from text students enter so they can see what they are thinking. The programs then help students transfer information from the graphic organizers to written documents. 1-800-877-4292.

Math Companion (www.toolsforteachers.com). Allows you to create worksheets when the math text you are using does not provide sufficient practice. 1-800-877-0858.

Reading Plus (www.readingplus.com). Helps students of all ages improve their reading process. Students can change the background color to facilitate clearer vision. Keran Hoover lets her students experiment with this feature, starting with yellow print on a black background. The goal is to find a combination of background and text that appears most clear to the individual reader and doesn't allow the words to move around on the screen. 1-800-READ-PLUS (1-800-732-3758). For more on using colors to improve reading skills, contact the Irlen Institute (www.irlen.com); 1-800-55-IRLEN (1-800-554-7536).

Simon S.I.O. (Sounds It Out) (www.donjohnston.com). Very helpful in teaching phonemic awareness and phonics. The program engages students with an animated personal tutor. 1-800-999-4660.

TestTalker (www.freedomscientific.com). Turns any paper test, worksheet, or other form into a computerized version that can talk. 1-800-444-4443.

WordMaker (www.donjohnston.com). This phonics, phonemic awareness, and spelling program based on the work of Dr. Patricia Cunningham (see chapters 6, 7, and 8 of this book) helps kids remember words they have learned and use them in their writing. 1-800-999-4660.

Write:OutLoud (www.donjohnston.com). Helps younger and older students by saying words as they are being typed, so students can both read and hear what they have written. 1-800-999-4660.

Writer's Companion (www.writerscomp.com). A tutorial that guides students through the entire writing process. 1-866-215-8155.

Summary of Teaching Strategies for Students with Learning Difficulties and Those Emerging into Fluency in English

The remaining chapters in this book address specific content areas (reading, writing, math), assessment, behavior, and parent involvement. Before we move on, it will be helpful to summarize the ten key strategies to use when teaching struggling students to achieve proficiency with required standards. Keep in mind that these strategies are just as effective with students of poverty and English language learners as they are with kids who have been diagnosed with learning disabilities. The strategies are:

1. Actively reduce anxiety levels through attention to learning style strengths and goal-setting instruction.

2. Teach from the whole back to the parts.

3. Enter standards through students' personal interests and include creative thinking activities.

4. Let students listen to soothing music as they work.

5. Use visual strategies throughout, including graphic organizers.

6. Use color cues everywhere, from all content areas to organizational strategies.

7. Allow learning in pairs or groups; use games, games, and more games.

8. Teach new material in meaningful contexts.

9. Combine verbal instruction with visual and kinesthetic cues; always show students an example of the completed activity.

10. Remember that active involvement is preferable to paper-and-pencil activities.

The methods in this book can be used with any content. It may feel as though you don't have enough time to try new methods. But the truth is, you can't afford *not* to try them. One thing is certain: When you keep doing things the way you are currently doing them, you and your students will keep getting the same results. To change the results, you must change the methods. Not for the whole class, and not for your successful students—but for students who are far behind expected standards, you really have no other choice.

Questions and Answers

"How can I find time each day to work one-on-one with struggling students on goal setting?"

Always give those students five minutes less to work on a task than you give the others so you have the last five minutes of the work period to debrief their results. In other words, if the rest of your class has 30 minutes to complete a task, your struggling students will have 25 minutes. Have them use this figure in the ratio on their Goal Planning Chart (see page 60).

"What can I do if the curriculum assigned to me is not very interesting for my students?"

Be creative! Find out from your curriculum guide what skills and competencies your students are expected to learn and demonstrate, then figure out how to teach those skills and competencies in ways that are exciting and meaningful for your students. *Examples:* If students find geography boring, try teaching it through current events. Have students watch a daily news program; use daily newspapers and weekly news magazines as your texts and point out (or have students discover) how different sources report the same stories from slightly different perspectives. Consult teaching journals and other publications for ideas. Contact your state teachers' union office; put out an inquiry on the Internet; bribe colleagues to eat lunch together in your room by bringing chocolates to the meeting, then brainstorm creative teaching ideas together. Seek out and use available software programs.

"Our district has very little technology available. How can I use technology to help my students learn?"

Focus on simple technologies—word processors, calculators, small electronics, etc. (see page 77). If your parent-teacher organization has any money to contribute, suggest that they help expand the school's technology resources. Talk to your media specialist, public librarian, and the technology director at your state office of education for other ideas.

"How can I be sure to teach my students what they really need to know?"

More than 75 percent of what we now know will change by the year 2025; almost 75 percent of the jobs that will be available then have not yet been invented! We simply don't know what specific information or skills will be needed in the future. We do know that people will have to change careers anywhere from three to seven times before they retire, and that many of those career changes will require going back to school for new training. If you can make learning exciting and meaningful for your students, and if you can help them to be more successful learners, you will have taught them what they really need to know: how to learn.

REFERENCES AND RESOURCES

Accelerated Schools PLUS (AS PLUS) (www.accelerated schools.net). Many urban schools with dreary achievement records have adopted this program developed by Professor Henry Levin of Stanford University. Based on the premise that students with learning problems have to learn at a faster rate than that expected of average students, the curriculum focuses on comprehensive enrichment strategies based on problem-solving and interesting, relevant applications of learning rather than on remediation. The goal is to build on the learning strengths of all children. Located at the University of Connecticut, AS PLUS works in partnership with the National Research Center for Gifted Education and Talent Development. Go online for regional contact information.

Allen, Dorothea. *Hands-On Science: 112 Easy-To-Use, High Interest Activities for Grades 4–8.* West Nyack, NY: Center for Applied Research in Education, 1991. Strategies to make science curriculum concrete and realistic.

Apple Classrooms of Tomorrow (ACOT) (imet.csus.edu/imet1/baeza/PDF%20Files/Upload/10yr.pdf). ACOT was a research and development collaboration among public schools, universities, research agencies, and Apple Computer, Inc. Its goal was to study how the routine use of technology by teachers and students might change teaching and learning. The project began in 1985 and concluded in 1998. Go online to read an extensive set of ACOT reports and explore educational products based on ACOT results.

Beecher, Margaret. *Developing the Gifts and Talents of All Students in the Regular Classroom.* Mansfield Center, CT: Creative Learning Press, 1996. A fabulous resource for creating high-quality learning experiences for all of your students. Many reproducible forms help you to enrich everyone's school experience.

Broderbund (www.broderbund.com). Publishers of educational and reference software including Reader Rabbit, Oregon Trail, and the Eyewitness Encyclopedias. 1-800-395-0277.

Clark, Barbara. *Optimizing Learning: The Integrative Education Model in the Classroom.* Columbus, OH: Charles E. Merrill, 1986. Explains how to utilize all of the power of the brain in learning.

Coil, Carolyn. *Becoming an Achiever: A Student Guide.* Beavercreek, OH: Pieces of Learning, 1994.

—*Teaching Tools for the 21st Century.* Revised and updated version with CD. Beavercreek, OH: Pieces of Learning, 2005.

Compu-Teach (www.compu-teach.com). Educational software in the subject areas. 1-800-44-TEACH (1-800-448-3224).

Core Knowledge Foundation (www.coreknowledge.org). Founded by E.D. Hirsch Jr., author of the Cultural Literacy series, the Foundation conducts research on curricula, develops books and other materials for parents and teachers, offers workshops for teachers, and serves as the hub of a network of Core Knowledge schools. The Core Knowledge curriculum assumes that in order to become fully functioning adults, children need to learn a common body of knowledge. Since the Core Knowledge content is quite sophisticated, kids perceive that what they are being taught is important, and they are instinctively more likely to be interested and challenged. 1-800-238-3233.

Curry, James, and John Samara, editors. *Writing Units That Challenge.* Portland, ME: Maine Educators for the Gifted and Talented, 1990.

Delta Education (www.delta-education.com). Inquiry-based, hands-on science and math curricula, supplemental teaching materials, classroom accessories, and reading materials that integrate the language arts with science. 1-800-258-1302.

DeMarco, John. *Peer Helping Skills: A Handbook for Peer Helpers and Peer Tutors.* Edina, MN: Johnson Institute, 1992.

Fairfax Network (FNET) (www.fcps.edu/fairfaxnetwork). Distance learning enrichment programs for grades K–12, staff development, teacher training, and parent programs. Sample titles: *America on the Move, Giant Pandas, She's Got It!* (about women inventors), and *Universal Words.* Past programs are available for purchase on video. 1-800-233-3277.

Flaro, L. *Mending Broken Children: Cognitive Ability Patterning for Success.* Edmonton, Canada: MacNab, 1989.

Franklin Electronic Publishers (www.franklin.com). Electronic learning aids for the classroom including dictionaries, bilingual dictionaries, and organizers. 1-800-BOOKMAN (1-800-266-5626).

Freed, Jeffrey, and Laurie Parsons. *Right-Brained Children in a Left-Brained World: Unlocking the Potential of Your ADD Child.* New York: Simon and Schuster, 1998. Freed shares his techniques for teaching compensation learning strategies to children who have trouble learning. The strategies work whether or not the child has ADD.

Glasgow, Neal A., and Cathy D. Hicks. *What Successful Teachers Do: 91 Research-Based Classroom Strategies for New and Veteran Teachers.* Thousand Oaks, CA: Corwin Press, 2002.

Hart, Leslie. *Human Brain and Human Learning.* Kent, WA: Books for Educators, 1983.

Hirsch, E.D. Cultural Literacy series. Includes *The New First Dictionary of Cultural Literacy: What Your Child Needs to Know.* 3rd Revised & Updated Edition. Boston: Houghton Mifflin, 2004. Hirsch is also the founder of the Core Knowledge Foundation (see above).

HOTS: Higher Order Thinking Skills (www.hots.org). A general thinking skills program for Title I and LD students in grades 4–8 that accelerates learning, test scores, and social confidence. Demo unit available to download. 1-800-999-0153.

HyperStudio (www.hyperstudio.com). A multimedia thinking tool for project-based learning. Includes brainstorming tools, visual organizers, project planners, desktop publishing features, multimedia presentation capabilities, and authoring tools for CD-ROMs and Web site development.

Integrated Thematic Instruction (ITI) (www.kovalik.com). Kids can learn anything if we immerse them in it. Created by Susan Kovalik, ITI is a brain-compatible instructional model that anchors curriculum to a year-long theme and rationale. Visit the Web site for background and resources including books and videos. (253) 815-8800.

International Society for Technology in Education (www.iste.org). An organization committed to "providing leadership and service to improve teaching and learning by advancing the effective use of technology in education." Their Web site is a gateway to much information and many resources. Members have access to publications, events, and professional development opportunities. 1-800-336-5191.

Joyce, Bruce, and Marsha Weil. *Models of Teaching.* 7th edition. Old Tappan, NJ: Prentice-Hall, 1986.

Kovalik, Susan, and Karen Olsen. *Integrated Thematic Instruction.* 3rd edition. Kent, WA: Books for Educators, 1994. How to immerse students in in-depth learning experiences that integrate tasks from many subject areas. See also Integrated Thematic Instruction above.
—*Teachers Make the Difference.* Kent, WA: Books for Educators, 1989.

Landfried, Steven E. "Educational Enabling: Is 'Helping' Hurting Our Students?" *Middle School Journal* (May 1990), pp. 12–15.

LD Resources (www.ldresources.com). Resources for the LD community include articles, commentaries, and lists of tools, schools, organizations, and professionals. Browsable categories include "Technology Issues and Ideas" and "Tools and Technology."

Levine, Mel. *A Mind at a Time*. New York: Simon and Schuster, 2002. Explains how parents and teachers can encourage children's learning strengths and bypass their learning weaknesses.

Macrorie, Ken. *The I-Search Paper*. Portsmouth, NH: Heinemann, 1988.

Marzano, Robert J., Debra J. Pickering, and June E. Pollock. *Classroom Instruction That Works: Research-Based Strategies for Increasing Student Achievement*. Alexandria, VA: ASCD, 2001.

McGinley, William. "Meaningful Curriculum for All: Project-Based Learning." *Educational Leadership* 52:3 (1994).

Meichenbaum, D. *Cognitive-Behavior Modification: An Integrative Approach*. New York: Plenum Press, 1977.

News Currents (www.newscurrents.com). A weekly current-events discussion program written on three levels for grades 3–12. Annual subscription. Available online or on DVD. 1-800-356-2303.

Pathways to School Improvement (www.ncrel.org/sdrs). A project of the North Central Regional Educational Laboratory, Pathways provides access to information educators can use to improve their schools. Online multimedia documents called "Critical Issues" synthesize research on topics including assessment, at-risk students, and technology in education.

Perkins, David. *Smart Schools: From Training Memories to Educating Minds*. New York: Free Press, 1992. A plan to improve the quality of thinking and learning in our schools.

Perry, Collin. "Maverick Principal." *Reader's Digest* (October 1994), pp. 134–138.

Purkey, William, and Paula Stanley. *Invitational Teaching, Learning and Living*. Washington, D.C.: NEA, 1991.

Rose, Colin. *Accelerated Learning for the 21st Century: The Six-Step Plan to Unlock Your Master-Mind*. New York: Dell Publishers, 1998.

Saphier, John, and Robert Gowan. *The Skillful Teacher: Building Your Teaching Skills*. Carlisle, MA: Research for Better Teaching Inc., 1997. A gold mine of strategies to improve teaching and classroom management.

Savoie, J., and A. Hughes. "Problem-Based Learning as Classroom Solution." *Educational Leadership* 52:4 (1994), pp. 54–57. (www.smartkidssoftware.com).

Science Sleuths. This CD-ROM series uses humorous science mysteries to engage students in problem-solving and critical thinking. The mysteries are fictitious but introduce real science concepts and processes.

Shelton, T., A. Anastopoulous, and J. Linden. "An Attribution Training Program with Learning Disabled Children." *Journal of Learning Disabilities* 18:5 (1985), pp. 261–265.

Silver, Harvey F., Richard W. Strong, and Matthew J. Perini. *So Each May Learn: Integrating Learning Styles and Multiple Intelligences*. Alexandria, VA: ASCD, 2000.
—*Tools for Promoting Active, In-Depth Learning*. Second Edition. Ho-Ho-Kus, NJ: Thoughtful Education Press, 2001.

Tom Snyder Productions (www.tomsnyder.com). Multimedia resources to support active learning in science, math, social studies, reading, and language arts. A Scholastic company. 1-800-342-0236.

Stepien, W., and S. Gallagher. "Problem-Based Learning: As Authentic As It Gets." *Educational Leadership* 50:7 (1993), pp. 25–28.

SuccessMaker (www.pearsonschool.com). Scalable digital courseware for grades K–8. Individualizes instruction to the specific needs of each student by automatically presenting instruction at the level at which a student is ready to learn, creating a successful learning experience. Aligns with district, local, and national standards, and is supported by a comprehensive management system. Used in more than 16,000 schools in the U.S. and 1,500 abroad. Courseware is available in customizable bundles. Program costs vary, depending on the software purchased, the range of grade levels to be covered, and the amount of professional development services requested.

Sunburst Technology (www.sunburst.com). The publisher of educational software programs. 1-800-321-7511.

Think-Pair-Share SmartCard (www.kaganonline.com). Describes many variations of Dr. Frank Lyman's Think-Pair-Share part of the Name Card method. Kagan Publishing & Professional Development also offers many materials to help you facilitate cooperative learning using Dr. Spencer Kagan's methods. 1-800-WEE CO-OP (1-800-933-2667).

Tomlinson, Carol Ann. *How to Differentiate in the Mixed-Ability Classroom*. Alexandria, VA: ASCD, 1995.

U.S. Department of Labor and the Secretary's Commission on Achieving Necessary Skills (SCANS). "What Work Requires of Schools: A SCANS Report for America 2000." Washington, DC: U.S. Government Printing Office, 1991. Available to download at wdr.doleta.gov/SCANS/whatwork; 1-877-US-2JOBS (1-877-872-5627).

Wolk, Steve. "Project-Based Learning: Pursuits with a Purpose." *Educational Leadership* 52:4 (1994), pp. 42–45.

Teaching Reading: Stories

Reading is the ability to make meaning from printed words. How does meaning happen? Good readers automatically use strategies to adjust their reading rate to the material and check to see if what they are reading makes sense. Poor readers don't even know that such strategies exist. They think that good readers were born that way.

The ability to derive meaning from text is related to whether the reader can activate prior knowledge about the topic. If we give kids a nonsense passage they can easily decode, no meaning is present. If we give them a passage and they know the words but nothing about the topic, their reading is not meaningful. This leads to a frustrating situation: kids who seem able to read the words but don't get the message.

School success depends on reading ability. The definition of *dyslexia* has been expanded to include any significant problem that interferes with reading fluency and/or comprehension. Reading stories, reading math word problems and explanations of math concepts, and reading in other content areas: All categories of learning demand fluency in reading with excellent comprehension. Any student who is not a fluent reader by third grade is at risk of dropping out of school before high school graduation. Dropping out often leads to lifelong frustration in finding a satisfying career and earning a good income. Fluent reading in the elementary grades is vital to a positive self-concept.

Children learn to read by reading, so all of our efforts to improve student performance should begin with improving reading ability. Many reading programs are very prescriptive and contain multiple layers of activities students are expected to do. The reading program your school has adopted may be exactly right for most of your students. However, you probably still have some kids who have not magically improved in their reading ability. Finding the right method to bring each of your below-level readers closer to fluency and comprehension is essential. Since all students do not respond positively to any one strategy, you may need to try several. When students discover that their reading problems do not stem from their lack of intelligence, but rather from not having found and used the right strategies for them, their self-esteem gets back on track and school feels like a good place to be.

An effective reading program is really a program of literacy development that combines several reading methods. There is no such thing as *one* reading method that works for *all* kids, primarily because of the different learning styles represented in our classrooms.

This chapter and the two that follow suggest a variety of methods you can use to improve reading and writing success for your struggling students. You may apply these methods to selections from texts, anthologies, or literature. Start by finding the subject(s) or skill(s) you are currently teaching and try some of the strategies described for them. For example, if you are teaching vocabulary, try the Vocabulary Attributes Chart (see pages 113–115). When you're ready, add other strategies and methods.

Make sure that your students spend time each day reading literature, reading in the content areas, understanding sound/letter/word relationships, and writing. A reading program that ignores any of these components is incomplete.

Teacher-Directed Reading

1. Select something you know will appeal to reluctant readers. They love adventure, mystery, survival, fantasy, real-life adventure, and humor. Skip all other types of reading or schedule them for later in the year.

2. Read the selection aloud to the struggling readers in your class. Because global thinkers must see the big picture first, their ability to understand a story is

strengthened when they hear it read aloud in its entirety before they begin to read it themselves. Some auditory learners, who love to analyze and predict as they read a story, may object to hearing it before they read. Allow those students to listen to music or headphones during the read-aloud.

3. Have the students listen to a recording of a short section of the piece (see "The Carbo Recorded Book Method," pages 88–90). Or have them read the section aloud to a buddy.

4. Bring the group back together to discuss the meaning of what they have just read.

5. Teach a specific reading skill. Have students work with partners and metacognitively think out loud as they coach each other in how to do the skill. (See pages 68–69.)

6. Teach the vocabulary of the section the students have read, using visual aids such as the Vocabulary Attributes Chart (see pages 113–115). Teaching vocabulary to global thinkers before they read the story is not appropriate, since the context is absent.

7. Create a story map (see pages 97–100) to help kids see how the various elements of the story—plot, setting, characters, etc.—relate to each other and are somewhat predictable. Fill in the map as the story is being read.

8. Repeat steps 1–7 with other selections.

Big Books*

Many publishers produce giant-size versions of books for young readers. These big books make it possible for students to see the text and illustrations simultaneously as you read aloud. Later, kids can read aloud together. Emerging readers especially enjoy anticipating and predicting repeated words or phrases.

1. Before starting to read, show the cover of the book, read the title, and discuss the cover illustration.

2. Have students predict what might happen in the story, based on the cover illustration. Later, they can predict a story by looking at all of the pictures before you (or they) read the text.

3. Read the entire story straight through, using a pointer to indicate each word as you read it. Read in phrases to enhance meaning. Be very enthusiastic in your reading and pointing.

4. Reread the story immediately, asking the students to join in whenever they can.

5. Repeat the story several more times over several days until most of the students are familiar enough with the text to read it on their own.

6. If you have the related small books (regular-size versions of the big book), have students read to each other in groups. Encourage them to check out copies to read to family members at home. Demonstrate how they should point to each word as they read it.

Variations

■ Promote understanding of letter-sound relationships by having students point to all of the words on a page that begin with a particular letter.

■ Have students make a transparency version of the story by illustrating the major events on blank transparencies.

■ Have students make a chart version of the story and work in groups to illustrate the text—one page per group.

■ Have students create a personal version of the story by drawing their own pictures for it.

■ For the benefit of tactile-kinesthetic learners, incorporate drama into the reading experience. Make masks representing the key characters, or name cards for student actors to wear around their necks. The actors perform while the other students read the story aloud.

Predictable Books

Originally used only in preschools and kindergartens but now available for older students as well, predictable books teach readers how to construct meaning from the printed page. The stories contain patterns that enable students to learn how comprehension is made easier when the reader makes continuous predictions. These stories build fluency, teach about rhyming and word families, and create reading enjoyment.

Find any story in which a particular word or phrase is repeated often. *The House That Jack Built, The Three Billy Goats Gruff,* and similar stories lend themselves beautifully to this method. (Ask a librarian or reading specialist to recommend other titles.) Read the story aloud with great expression; stop just before each occurrence of the predictable word or phrase and let the students chant it together. Later, students can learn to recognize the words that represent a repetitive phrase and point them out.

---

* This activity and the variations that follow are adapted from a method used by Theresa Catalina, reading specialist, Port Huron, Michigan. Used with permission.

The Language Experience Method*

Scenario: Jonathan

Jonathan was a third grader who could barely read at pre-primer level. His teacher, Mrs. Taylor, was extremely frustrated because all of her other students were reading at or above third-grade level. Each day, she had to prepare a separate lesson for Jonathan using first-grade materials.

Jonathan was almost ten. He had repeated kindergarten because his teachers thought that he was too immature for first grade; he had repeated first grade because it was obvious that he was not learning to read. Although he was still a non-reader in second grade, that teacher passed him on to Mrs. Taylor, who referred him for staffing by the special education team.

The team leader advised Mrs. Taylor to abandon the basal reader and spend almost all of Jonathan's learning time shoring up his skills in phonics. Since Jonathan was a global learner, and success in phonics requires skill in analytic thinking, this strategy did not work. His attendance became sporadic, and he looked sad and disheveled much of the time.

During our meeting, I taught Jonathan's teacher how to use the Language Experience method. She agreed to a two-week trial period during which she would replace all of her current methods with stories that Jonathan would provide from his own life experiences.

When I returned to the school a few weeks later, I poked my head in the doorway of Mrs. Taylor's classroom. Signaling to get her attention, I whispered, "How's it going?" In response, she yelled, *"Jonathan! She's here! Get the envelope!"*

Jonathan glanced up to recognize me, left his desk with a funny smirk on his face, went to a shelf, and took down a huge manila envelope. In the two weeks since his teacher had started using the Language Experience method, Jonathan had dictated and learned to read three full stories about the beloved animals in his menagerie at home. The manila envelope contained about 20 sentences from three stories, each sentence cut into word pieces fastened together with a paper clip.

Jonathan approached me with the envelope, now smiling broadly. Mrs. Taylor said, "Show Mrs. Winebrenner how you read. Just choose any sentence." Jonathan dug his arm up to the elbow into the envelope, came out with one sentence, and said proudly, "This one."

"Let's go over to the table and you can read it to me there," I suggested. I took the sentence from him, removed the paper clip, and turned all of the word pieces upside down

on the table. After mixing them up in a grand gesture, Jonathan chose one word, looked at it, and correctly read "was."

"Very nice," I said. "Try another." He chose another word and correctly read "his."

More than a little intrigued, I said, "Keep on going until you can tell me what the sentence says." The third word was "birthday," and Jonathan immediately recalled the entire sentence that described the birthday of his pet hamster. He then repeated this performance with several other sentences. It was clear that Jonathan was not just saying words he had memorized, but was actually reading. By the time we were finished, he was grinning from ear to ear.

"What should we do next?" Mrs. Taylor asked.

"Why tamper with success? Just continue with what you've been doing and I'll be back in a couple of weeks."

During the next two weeks, eager third graders nearly drove the teacher crazy trying to be the one to help Jonathan read his stories. By my next visit, Mrs. Taylor had discovered that an upcoming story about dogs in the third-grade reader contained a lot of words that Jonathan had learned. "What would happen," she mused, "if we just brought him into the third-grade group to read this story?" We decided to give it a try.

Jonathan did quite well with the story and clearly enjoyed being able to work with the same material as his classmates. His self-esteem skyrocketed, since he had succeeded at something that was difficult for him. His physical appearance even improved.

One day, while Jonathan was reading one of his stories to me, he stopped suddenly in the middle of a sentence. An incredulous look came over his face and he softly said, "Oh! Now I see!"

"What do you see?" I prompted.

"You know all these words on all these papers in all these stories? They're just someone else's stories written down!" he exclaimed with awe.

Jonathan had unraveled the secret of reading. Until then, he had always thought that what his teachers called "reading" was doing the work. Because he was able to read the stories he had written, he finally understood the thinking-speaking-writing-reading connection that underlies successful reading experiences.

At about this time, the special education team finished their study of Jonathan and concluded that he had severe learning disabilities. They suggested that he be moved to another class led by a teacher with special education training. Mrs. Taylor believed that this was not the correct placement for him. She met with his parents and explained how much progress Jonathan had been making in the regular classroom and how much his success meant to the rest of the class. She asked them to request a resource assistant to work with Jonathan in her classroom. They agreed, and Jonathan was able to spend most of his learning time with the class that had so lovingly nurtured him into becoming a successful reader.

---

* Adapted from Russell G. Stauffer, *The Language Experience Approach to the Teaching of Reading.* New York: HarperCollins, 1980.

Could Jonathan learn to read? Absolutely! His problem had resulted from a mismatch—between the skill-based phonics methods that had been used with him in the first and second grades, and his global learning style, which preferred more holistic methods. As soon as we provided a better match for his learning style, he was able to become successful in reading—even though he had LD.

The Language Experience Philosophy

The Language Experience method can be summed up with three simple affirmations:

If I can think about something, I can talk about it.

If I can talk about something, I can write down my ideas.

If I can write down my ideas, I can read what I have written.

This method is especially useful for children who cannot read well, including those who don't speak English fluently. Obviously, their stories will lack proper syntax and grammar, but the point of this method is *not* to teach correct story construction. Rather, it is to help students understand how the elements that comprise the act of reading relate to each other.

Using the Language Experience Method with One or Two Students

If you have only one or two struggling readers in your classroom, have each student create his or her own story.

1. Ask each student to dictate four to six sentences about a subject that comes from the student's personal life—siblings, pets, a favorite TV show, a proud moment, a memorable experience, etc.

2. Print the sentences *exactly as they are dictated,* errors and all. The Language Experience method teaches students that reading is just thoughts written down, and if you don't use their exact thoughts, you can't lead them to that essential conclusion. Begin each sentence on a new line and space the words evenly, since both the sentences and the words will eventually be cut apart.

3. Have students read their sentences to you, pointing to the words and phrases while saying them aloud. If they get stuck on a word, tell them what it is. **Tip:** If students are unable to remember what they wrote, use fewer sentences. When they can read the sentences in and out of order, perhaps even forwards and backwards, you will know that they are recognizing the words.

4. Cut the sentences apart. Spend several days having students read their sentences in and out of the correct order.

5. When students are able to read the sentences easily, cut them into word pieces. Paperclip the words from each sentence together. Have students choose one sentence at a time. Place all of the words for that sentence face down. Turn over one word at a time for students to read aloud until they can infer the rest of the sentence. Then have them arrange the words in the correct order and read the sentence again. When all of the sentences have been assembled, have the students read the entire story. **Tip:** If students turn over the words themselves, they will be more kinesthetically involved in the reading experience.

6. As students get to the point of easily recognizing the words out of context, have them create word files using notecards and recipe boxes. Throughout the learning process, they can continue to add words to their word files. You can use these words to teach letter-sound recognition, build vocabulary, teach meaning, etc. Since these are the students' own words, they will enjoy learning more about them. Flashcards can be made with the word on one side of the card and the definition on the other. For visual learners, the definition can be a picture they have drawn.

    Variation: Have students underline each word they read correctly when the story is intact. When a word has three lines drawn under it, the student makes a flash card for that word and adds it to his growing recipe box collection.

7. When students become proficient with the Language Experience method, find real stories for them to learn to read. Choose stories that contain many of their word file words.

Using the Language Experience Method with a Group

If a significant number of your students are reading below grade level, you can adapt the Language Experience method for group work.

1. Provide an in-school experience for the entire class. *Examples:* taking a walk around the school grounds; viewing a film; selecting books at the library; hearing a guest speaker. This is the essential first step, since we can never assume that all children share similar experiences outside of school.

2. While the rest of the class is writing and drawing about the experience, call your students with reading problems together to create a group story about it. Have each student dictate at least one sentence for the story. Print the sentences *exactly as they are dictated.* Print each student's name at the end of his or her sentence.

3. Continue by following steps 3–7 of "Using the Language Experience Method with One or Two Students"

on page 87, adapting the steps as necessary for group work. Your goal is to have *all* of the students in the group learn to read *all* of the sentences in the story.

Variation: Start with Art

Try this version of the Language Experience method with students who have trouble coming up with ideas for stories, and those who have had limited learning experiences outside of school. It's also a brain-compatible way for visual-global learners to create interesting stories.

1. Provide the class with a common experience.

2. Afterward, have students create drawings about the experience and arrange them in the proper sequence to make individual or group stories. All students will enjoy this experience, so you may wish to include everyone.

3. Once students have completed their drawing stories, have them dictate one or two sentences for each drawing. To include more details in the writing, suggest that students first add more details to their drawings. Better sentences come more easily from this process. Print the sentences *exactly as they are dictated.*

4. Continue by following steps 3–7 of "Using the Language Experience Method with One or Two Students" on page 87, adapting the steps as necessary.

Improving Fluency

Fluency is a goal for all readers. Fluent readers apply decoding skills automatically so they can concentrate on getting the meaning of what they are reading. They recognize many words by sight. They constantly make predictions about what's coming up, and they correct themselves if what they are reading is not making sense. They understand how to adjust their reading pace and strategies for different types of reading material.

Without fluency, comprehension is impaired. It is nearly impossible for non-fluent readers to remember the words and ideas they try to read. They are so concerned with pronouncing the words correctly that they have little time to think about comprehension. Furthermore, they are interrupted too often by teachers and peers who help them. Never help struggling readers unless they ask for it. Encourage them to use a trick most fluent adult readers apply automatically: They guess or skip unfamiliar words, coming back to them later when the meaning of the entire sentence becomes more clear.

Silent fluency is much more important than oral fluency. If kids understand the meaning of what they read, but their reading aloud is flawed, do not remediate! The only valid test of reading ability is comprehension.

Believe it or not, some kids can read with increased fluency if they move one arm around in a big circle, ride a stationary bike, or pace while reading! Even more fascinating, students can often read words if they visualize them in color, see them on colored paper, or read with the aid of a colored transparency sheet laid right over the words on the page. This might be related to scotopic sensitivity. See page 34.

The Carbo Recorded Book Method*

Dr. Marie Carbo has adapted the learning styles model created by Drs. Rita Dunn and Kenneth Dunn and applied it to reading. Her recorded book method, described in *Teaching Students to Read Through Their Individual Learning Styles,* combines teacher-made recordings of reading selections with a tactile-kinesthetic approach to learning skills and vocabulary. It works with any reading material, from basal readers to literature to subject matter text, and it can put your insecure readers on the path to improved fluency and comprehension in a matter of days.

Check with the publishers first to get permission to make the recordings. Explain that you will use them to support the printed materials only.

You will need to purchase a large quantity of blank audiocassettes, since you will record only three to four minutes per side.** Students will rewind the tapes several times to listen to a designated segment. If you put more than one segment on a side, kids will waste a lot of time trying to find the right segment. The cassettes should be white so you can write the story name and page numbers directly on the shells without needing labels. Simply type the words *white shell blank audio tape* (or *audio cassette*) into an Internet search engine to get a list of suppliers.

You will also need several audio cassette players, or a listening station with four to six headsets attached.

If you don't have time to record all of the cassettes you need, get help. There are probably some parents who would like to volunteer at school but find it difficult to come in during the school days. Taping stories is a task they can do at home after appropriate instruction. Teach them the three-step method described in "How to Record the Stories" on pages 89–90. Or see if other teachers at your grade level are willing to work as a team. Each of you can record several stories and share. Student teachers and paraprofessionals—or even retired teachers, actors, or librarians—can also make the recordings.

All cassettes should become part of a story library available to all teachers, so never record over existing stories

---

* Adapted with permission from *Teaching Students to Read Through Their Individual Learning Styles* by Marie Carbo, Rita Dunn, and Kenneth Dunn. Englewood Cliffs, NJ: Allyn & Bacon, 1986.

** When technology makes cassette tapes and players obsolete (which will happen eventually), use the available technology to make the recordings.

once you are finished with them. You may want to see if your school is willing to purchase an inexpensive cassette duplicating machine (available at some of the discount merchandise stores). The cost is minimal compared to other intervention methods.

Tip: If you want to group kids for reading, try grouping them by learning style (auditory, visual, tactile-kinesthetic) instead of reading ability. This allows you to teach the text to the whole class while conducting learning-style compatible activities for vocabulary and reading skills with smaller groups.

The Carbo Method Step-by-Step

1. Choose a few high-interest stories to teach to the whole class. (Struggling students' self-esteem improves when they are able to use the same reading material as their peers.) Record them following the method described below in "How to Record the Stories."

2. Choose several students you think might respond to this method. Take them aside, introduce a story you have recorded, and read the entire story aloud to them.

    Read the entire story aloud to your struggling readers only. Successful readers will not want to hear it. Because they enjoy predicting story outcomes while they are reading, they won't want to know in advance how it ends. Be sure to tell the kids who hear the whole story not to share the content with other readers—that would spoil it for them. You could also record the story and have struggling readers listen to the recording.

    Tips: If the story is too long to read aloud or record, read the first five or six pages and describe the rest of the story. If you're doing a novel, read the first one or two chapters aloud, summarize the rest, and use a story map (see pages 97–100) to give students an idea of what to expect.

3. Direct students' attention to the first paragraph of the selected story. Give them a few moments to browse through the rest of the story and make some predictions about what will happen based on pictures, chapter titles, etc.

4. Have the students listen to side one of the first cassette—the first two to three minutes of the story. While they listen, they should read along with the text, either silently or in a soft voice. They should also physically track the printed page by scooping each phrase—moving the index and middle fingers of their dominant hand under the phrase. This tactile-kinesthetic scooping motion helps to create fluency.

    Tip: For students with visual perception problems who have trouble keeping their place, provide a bookmark or other tracking guide.

5. After students have successfully learned to read the first part of the story, teach reading skills and vocabulary

in the context of that section. Use any of the methods described in this chapter or create your own. Hands-on activities will help struggling readers learn more easily. Dr. Carbo's book, *Teaching Students to Read Through Their Individual Learning Styles,* is full of such strategies. See "References and Resources" at the end of this chapter.

6. Continue in the same manner with the rest of the tapes until the story is done. Teach skills and vocabulary after each segment by using visual and tactile-kinesthetic methods described in this chapter and in Chapter 4.

    Tip: If making and/or using the tapes seems overwhelming, try this method with some students: Read the story as if you were recording it. As explained in "How to Record the Stories" below, read the page number aloud each time you start a new page, pause for a few seconds, read in phrases, and so on.

How to Record the Stories

1. Select a high-interest story slightly above the students' instructional reading level. Set aside a block of quiet time for recording.

2. Record three to four minutes of the story on each side of the cassette. According to Dr. Carbo, this is the maximum length you should always use, even with older readers. Students will constantly be rewinding the cassette to listen to each segment multiple times. They will get confused if there is more than one segment to a side, and they will get impatient if a segment is too long.

    - Speak clearly into the microphone from a distance of about eight inches; any closer may result in strange noises on the recording. Be as expressive and enthusiastic as if you were reading aloud to the class.

    - Each time you start a page, read the page number aloud in a soft voice. Then say, "Now look over the text and pictures on this page." Pause for a few seconds.

    - Read in phrases, pausing briefly between phrases. This helps students to group words and ideas together more naturally. It is especially beneficial for those who can read isolated words but have poor comprehension. If you think a word will be unfamiliar to the students, pause briefly before and after saying it.

3. End each tape by saying, "This is the end of this recording. Please rewind it for the next listener."

Record a few practice cassettes and try them out with your students. If students are not making noticeable progress with a recorded segment after listening to it properly two or three times, either the material is too challenging, the recorded segment is too long, or the reading pace is too fast. Adjust and try again. Keep multiple cassettes for the same story in zip-lock plastic bags.

Convincing Reluctant Readers to Use the Carbo Method

Some students may resist listening to each segment two or three times. Others may be unable to hear their own progress after using this method. Try this strategy with those students so they can hear for themselves how they sound after they listen to the taped segment one, two, and three times. Some readers may not need all three repetitions; this strategy will help you make that call as well.

1. Before they have seen or heard the story, give them a blank cassette and have them record themselves reading the first segment of the story cold, with no preparation. They should mark the end of their reading by putting a small piece of masking tape on the cassette window.

2. Have them listen to your recording of the first story segment.

3. Have them record themselves reading the first story segment again, after they have heard your recording once. They should also mark that reading with masking tape.

4. Repeat steps 2 and 3 twice more.

5. Listen together as each student plays his or her recording. You should both be able to hear how well the student reads after no preparation and then after one, two, and three times of listening to your recording. The student's progress should be obvious.

6. Based on what you hear, decide with the student how many repeat listenings are best for him or her.

It isn't necessary to repeat this process with every student or every story. Once should be enough to motivate students to use the recorded book method—including the repeated listenings—without much further prodding on your part.

Scenario: Jim

Jim was a fifth grader with a negative attitude about reading—understandably, because his reading skills were very poor. It was painful to listen to him try to read aloud. He often hesitated, confused words, and started phrases and sentences over. His heavily furrowed brow indicated how hard he was working and how frustrated he felt.

Jim was going to a special reading teacher every day. His teacher, Ms. Abbrogado, had learned about the Carbo Recorded Book method and was using it with kids like Jim to improve their fluency and comprehension. She had

provided all the students with a blank tape of their own on which they could record how they sounded before and after they listened to the reading tapes she had prepared.

Shortly after Thanksgiving, Jim started nagging Mrs. Abbrogado about wanting to take his tape home and leave it there. Each time he asked, she refused, carefully explaining how she needed to keep the tape at school so Jim could re-use it for each story. By his fifth request, her patience had run out, and she finally asked the question she should have asked at first.

"Why do you need this tape at home?"

"Because," Jim replied with a little grin on his face, "I want to give it to my grandma for Christmas!"

"Oh!" the teacher replied sheepishly. "Why didn't you say so?"

Jim had finally developed some self-respect regarding his reading ability. He was even ready to share his reading with his beloved grandma.

Whisper Reading*

This highly effective one-on-one method for improving fluency makes an impression on several senses simultaneously. It can be used instead of recorded books if cassettes are not available. Whisper Reading is also an excellent coaching strategy for parents to use with their children at home, so be sure to offer to teach it to interested parents.

1. Choose a story the student is already somewhat familiar with, either one you have already read to the class or one the student has read on her own.

2. Sit slightly behind the student to the right, close enough so you can point to the material being read.

3. Have the student read the story (or part of the story) aloud. Meanwhile, read along with the student.

   - *Read directly into the student's right ear.* Lower your voice when the student is reading confidently. Raise it slightly when assistance is needed.

   - Read with fluency at a rate slightly slower than you would use if reading independently, but not as slow as the student would normally use. Tell the student not to worry about keeping up with you. Explain that she will read faster as time progresses. As the student's fluency improves, pick up your pace so you are always reading just a little faster than she is.

   - Don't worry if the student reads some of the words incorrectly. If she substitutes a word which could fit in a particular sentence because it has a meaning

* Adapted from a method used by Theresa Catalina, reading specialist, Port Huron, Michigan, from R.G. Heckelman, "Using the Neurological-Impress Remedial Reading Technique." *Academic Therapy Quarterly,* Summer 1966, pp. 235–239.

similar to the actual word, take this as a sign that she is successfully trying to make meaning happen. If she asks you for help with a word, simply say the word instead of asking her to sound it out.

- As you and the student read the material, point to the phrases being read. **Tip:** Make a scooping motion with your finger from the beginning to the end of each phrase. This emphasizes the importance of reading in phrases rather than calling out individual words.

4. Afterward, ask the student to tell you one thing she remembers from the story. Then page together through the remaining pages, predicting what might happen the next time you read together. Do not ask specific questions about the story.

Follow these steps for 10–15 minutes, 3–5 times a week, and you and the student should notice improved fluency and comprehension within one month.

Teaching Oral Reading

For some reason, we have always assigned a lot of importance to children's ability to read aloud fluently without benefit of practice beforehand. This strikes me as strange, considering that adults rarely put themselves in this uncomfortable position. Think of the last time you were asked to read a passage in your place of worship or at a meeting of an organization you belong to. You probably insisted on having the chance to rehearse several times before the actual reading. Many adults get flustered when reading aloud to a group, and we certainly appreciate an opportunity to prepare ahead.

Kids are no different. It's grossly unfair for us to evaluate their reading fluency or comprehension on the basis of something they read aloud at a moment's notice. Even gifted students are sometimes terrible oral readers, since their minds race so far ahead of the words they are trying to read. There is nothing worse than struggling readers listening to other struggling readers read poorly! For kids to become better oral readers, they need to hear good models.

Teachers play a major role in creating a learning environment that nurtures reading development. We model our love of reading by reading aloud to students of all ages daily—including adolescents. When your students hear you model all the elements of good reading, they realize that reading is more than word-calling and are likely to become more willing to learn the skills necessary to read independently with expression. Reading aloud an entire novel a little bit at a time provides numerous opportunities to link the story's content to the rest of the curriculum. The positive effect of reading aloud is reflected in the excited way students anticipate the next section and ask

you to squeeze your read-aloud into the schedule whenever possible.

In schools where students move between classes, reading aloud to them daily is still possible, but it requires purposeful planning. Read aloud your favorite passages of a story or play, newspaper articles that connect to something kids are studying, or reports about what is happening in science.

This section describes several highly effective techniques for teaching oral reading. Try any and all; invent more of your own. Do whatever you can to communicate that reading is one of life's great pleasures—and that reading aloud can be enjoyable for both the reader and the listener.

Buddy Reading

1. Give students an overview of the story or book they will be reading.

2. Read the entire story (or first chapter) aloud to the kids who need to hear it before reading it.

3. Before any discussion, questions, or vocabulary, pair struggling readers with more competent readers, but *never with the very best readers.* That type of pairing is not effective for either partner.

4. Assign each pair a small portion of the text to read aloud with their buddies. Guide them to divide the section fairly so each reads about an equal amount. Explain that when they are finished reading, they should talk to each other about what they think the main character's problem is. Or assign one or more of the other Essential Questions (see page 100).

5. Be sure to provide group discussion time frequently. If the whole class is reading the same story or novel, use the Name Card method (pages 14–17) to ensure that all students are fully involved in the discussion.

6. Repeat steps 4 and 5 until the selection is completed. *Do not* ask struggling readers to read aloud to the entire class. This round-robin method is rarely effective and is often painful for both the exceptionally capable readers and those who find reading extremely difficult.

Buddy reading is also a helpful strategy for parents to use when reading aloud with their kids at home, so be sure to offer to teach it to interested parents.

Rehearsed Reading*

You can use this method to replace ineffective round-robin reading in both the literature and content areas.

* Vacca, Richard, and JoAnne Vacca. *Content Area Reading.* 4th edition. Glenview, IL: HarperCollins College Publishers, 1993. Used with permission of HarperCollins College Publishers.

1. Instead of calling on students at random to read aloud, assign each student a specific passage a day in advance.

2. Give students time to rehearse their passages, either alone or with a reading buddy. Be available to coach students in how to read with good volume and expression. Assign the practice experience as homework if there is someone at home to help.

3. When readers are ready, move students into higher thinking levels. Tell students they should also prepare *one* question to ask the class about their assigned section. Give each student a copy of the "Question Starters" handout (page 93), circling or underlining ahead of time the prompts you want them to use for a particular story.

    Tip: For added interest, have students ask their questions *before* beginning their oral readings as well as at the end. Knowing what question they will eventually have to answer boosts the audience's interest and attention levels. A more alert audience makes the reader feel more valued and intelligent.

4. On the following day, have students read their rehearsed passages aloud to the group, one at a time. While each student is reading, the others should have their books *closed,* using a finger or bookmark to hold their place. This allows the reader to make minor substitutions or changes without the whole group pouncing on him to point out errors.

    Tip: Some highly visual learners won't be able to listen effectively without looking at the text. Allow those kids to keep their books open, but make them promise not to help the person who is doing the reading.

5. Allow time at the end of each reading for questions and responses.

Choral Reading

Choral reading is an enjoyable way for students to improve fluency and learn to add expression to their oral reading. Certain texts include selections designed for choral reading; many readings in your regular curriculum may be adapted for this purpose. Type *choral reading* into an Internet search engine to find numerous selections.

1. Model reading aloud with expression an appropriate selection. Demonstrate proper phrasing, tempo, enunciation, rhythm, and volume.

2. Have students follow your model as you direct them. Point out any visual cues to how particular lines and words should be read. *Examples:* Sections written in capital letters are usually read in unison, although the entire piece may be chanted that way. Larger or bold print means louder voices.

3. As students become more capable choral readers, assign small parts to individual students, rows, boys, girls, etc. It's also fun to add more voices with each line.

4. Add hand and body movements after the text is perfected.

5. Have students practice and polish a collection of readings and perform them for other classes or at times when parents are visiting the class.

After kids have had some experience reading fun pieces, have them use choral reading for oral reading times. Teams can choral read dialogue or take turns with paragraphs. Use your imagination—and use choral reading often.

Poetry lends itself well to choral reading. Try the following selection with your students and see how they like it.

The Kids at Our School*

We're the kids at *[insert school name]* School
We think we're great
We think we're cool.
Our teacher's number one BIG RULE is:
"TRY AS HARD AS YOU CAN!"

We learn to follow our own school rules,
We read and write and calculate, too.
Our parents ask us each day, "Will you
TRY AS HARD AS YOU CAN?"

We try to please in every way,
To be real good at work and play!
'Cuz we love to hear *[insert teacher's name]* say,
"THEY TRY AS HARD AS THEY CAN!"

Improving Comprehension

Comprehension is the ability to understand what one reads. It can be aided by many techniques, some of which are described in this section.

Comprehension depends on the reader being able to *connect* what is being read to prior knowledge and *predict* upcoming events. Prediction creates a purpose for reading, and students enjoy seeing how accurately they can foresee what will happen next in a story. Use story maps (see pages 97–100) to help visual and tactile-kinesthetic learners see the big picture.

Story Detectives

1. Make a copy of the "Predictions" handout (page 94) and use it to prepare a list of predictions for the story.

---

* Adapted from the work of Sue Rebholz, Shorewood, Wisconsin. Used with permission.

Question Starters

LITERAL THINKING

"Summarize . . ."

"See . . ."

"Find . . ."

"Give an example of . . ."

"List . . ."

"Explain in your own words . . ."

"Demonstrate . . ."

"Give a definition of . . ."

INTERPRETIVE / CREATIVE THINKING

"Compare . . ."

"State and defend your opinion of . . ."

"Create . . ."

"Design . . ."

"Analyze . . ."

"Give the pros and cons of . . ."

"Judge . . ."

"Classify . . ."

"Imagine . . ."

"Find similarities and differences . . ."

"Categorize . . ."

"Predict . . ."

"Contrast . . ."

Predictions

NAME: _____

FOR: _____
(story title)

Prediction	Yes	No	Maybe
_____	☐	☐	☐
_____	☐	☐	☐
_____	☐	☐	☐
_____	☐	☐	☐
_____	☐	☐	☐
_____	☐	☐	☐
_____	☐	☐	☐
_____	☐	☐	☐
_____	☐	☐	☐
_____	☐	☐	☐
_____	☐	☐	☐
_____	☐	☐	☐
_____	☐	☐	☐
_____	☐	☐	☐
_____	☐	☐	☐
_____	☐	☐	☐
_____	☐	☐	☐
_____	☐	☐	☐

You will be asking students to respond to your predictions based on what they learn from the title, chapter titles, and/or pictures. Some of your predictions should be accurate, others highly improbable, and others somewhere in between.

2. Divide the class into small groups.

3. Have students read the title of the story and, based on the title, predict what events might occur. Or have them browse through the story and make predictions based on the chapter titles or pictures.

4. Give each student or group a copy of the predictions you completed in step 1. Have them respond to each prediction by checking YES (they think the event will happen), NO (they don't think it will happen), or MAYBE (they think it may possibly happen). Tell the students to be prepared to give reasons for their choices.

5. Get feedback from all groups and collate responses using an overhead transparency or wall chart.

6. Keep the predictions on display as the story is read. Check regularly to see how accurate the predictions were.

KWPL*

This easy-to-use method motivates students to really want to read. It can be used for a reading selection—and also for any social studies, science, or thematic unit introduction—with a high degree of success. The Name Card method (pages 14–17) is very effective when used with KWPL.

1. Draw four columns on the chalkboard or on a large piece of chart paper to use as the group chart. Give each column a heading, as shown below.

---

* Adapted from Donna S. Ogle, "KWL: A Teaching Method That Develops Active Reading of Expository Text." *The Reading Teacher* 39 (October 1986), pp. 564–570. Used with permission.

Leave plenty of room for writing beneath each heading. Be sure to emphasize the K in Know, the W in Want, the P in Predict, and the L in Learned, as shown.

Important: Complete steps 2–4 *before* having students read the selection.

2. Give students their own desk copies of the KWPL chart (page 96). Have them work with partners to brainstorm all they KNOW about the designated topic. Use the Name Card method to get responses to write in the "What We Already Know" column on the group chart.

3. Have students work with partners to decide what they WANT to know about the topic. Use the Name Card method to list their questions in the "What We Want to Know" column on the group chart.

Include questions that may arise from disagreements about "What We Already Know." *Example:* If the topic is alligators, one student might say, "An alligator has a very long snout," and another student might protest, "No, that's not an alligator, that's a crocodile." At this point, that topic becomes a question and moves into the "What We Want to Know" column, rewritten as a question: "Do alligators have long snouts?"

4. Have students use their own charts to PREDICT the answers to their "What We Want to Know" questions. It's okay if partners have different predictions. Use the Name Card method to include their predictions in the "What We Predict We Will Learn" column on the group chart.

5. Have the students read the selection. During the reading, students check out the accuracy of their individual predictions. They can use a plus sign (+) to indicate an accurate prediction and a minus sign (–) to indicate an incorrect prediction. In this way, students become emotionally involved in what happens in the selection.

6. Discuss the reading. Then ask the student partners to write what they have LEARNED in the "What We Have

What We Already **K**now	What We **W**ant to Know	What We **P**redict We Will Learn	What We Have **L**earned

KWPL

NAME: _____

FOR: _____
(story title)

What We Already **K**now	What We **W**ant to Know	What We **P**redict We Will Learn	What We Have **L**earned

Learned" column on their charts. Use the Name Card method to complete that column on the group chart.

7. Discuss all four columns of the chart.

After students have experienced this process several times under your direction, they might enjoy working with partners on the same activity with a different selection, without using the group chart. Have more copies of the KWPL chart available.

More Prediction Ideas to Try

■ If a story has pictures, have students page all the way through it, making predictions about the events, the main problem, the crisis, and the resolution. Several times during your reading of the story, stop, have the students close their books, and ask them to make predictions about what's going to happen next.

■ After students read a story (or you read it to them), have them close their books. Read the story again, leaving out words here and there. Have students predict and say the missing words. To turn this into a written exercise, copy a selection from the story, covering certain words. Write a list of possible word choices at the bottom of the page and have students "fill in the blanks" from the list of choices.

■ Some students enjoy writing their predictions and checking their accuracy as a story progresses. After students start reading a story, have them stop from time to time to predict the following:

– upcoming events

– the next word in a sentence

– a repeatable refrain (see "Predictable Books," page 85)

– how the story will end

– what might happen if a character chooses a different course of action.

■ After completing a story, invite students to imagine:

– what happens after the story ends

– what would have happened if a character had chosen a different course of action

– how a character from this story might behave in a different story.

■ Discuss how clues in a story lead to solutions and sometimes surprise endings. Have students reread a story a second time and locate those foreshadowing clues.

Visual Organizers

For global thinkers, visual organizers are a brain-compatible way of improving reading comprehension. Story maps and character maps help them to get the big picture of the selection. Compare-and-contrast circles clarify similarities and differences within categories of information.

Story Maps and Character Maps

The more closely a story fits an expected, familiar structure, the easier it is for readers to grasp and remember the most important ideas. Before discussing the elements of a story, chart them on a story map; see page 98 for an example. Add spokes to the various shapes and use the Name Card method (pages 14–17) to invite students to contribute details about each element.

Character maps are another way to visually organize important information about a story. Use a separate character map for each major character; see page 99 for an example. Add spokes and have students contribute the details during a class discussion, again using the Name Card method.

Once you have modeled the use of both charts, students might enjoy working with partners to complete charts for stories they read. Copy the examples and use them as handouts.

The "Handy" Story Map*

This variation on the story map is perfect for younger kids. Give them blank sheets of paper and have them trace around one of their hands (fingers spread, palm down). Then have them fill in their "handy" maps with the following information about a story you have just read:

■ Thumb: Story title

■ Index finger: Setting

■ Middle finger: Main character

■ Ring finger: Main character's major problem

■ Pinkie: Main character's major action to resolve the problem.

* Brenda Goffen, consultant in special education, Highland Park, Illinois.

Story Map

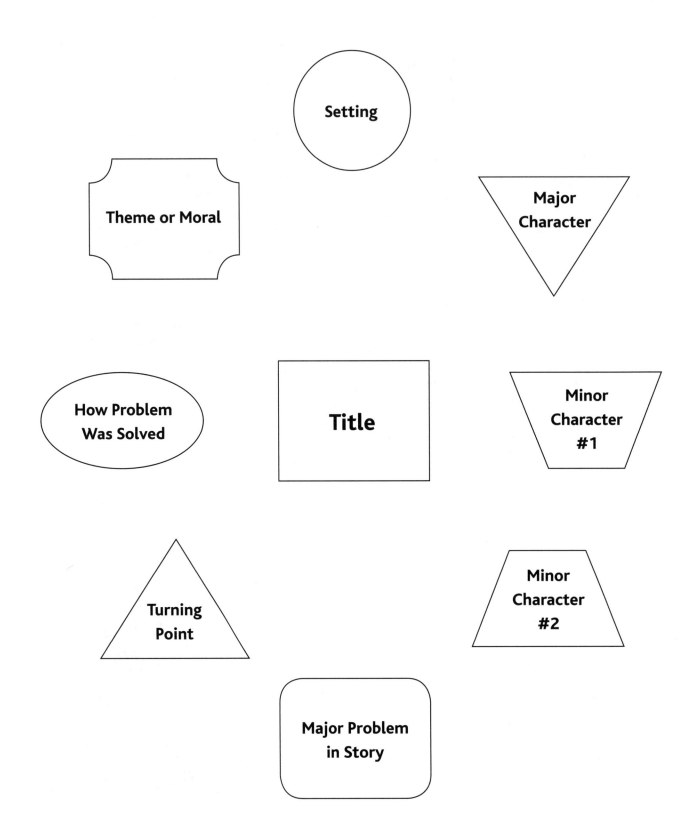

Setting

Theme or Moral

Major Character

How Problem Was Solved

Title

Minor Character #1

Turning Point

Minor Character #2

Major Problem in Story

Character Map

Physical Appearance

How Character Changed by the End of Story

Positive Qualities

What Character *Should* Have Done

Name

Negative Qualities

Effect on Other Characters

First Major Action

Second Major Action

Or they might use their maps to fill in the following information as you read a story aloud:

- Thumb: Major problem
- Index finger: First important event
- Middle finger: Second important event
- Ring finger: How the problem was solved
- Pinkie: What happened after the problem was solved
- Wrist: How the story ended.

Students might eventually use their maps to make sure stories they write contain all the essential elements.

Compare-and-Contrast Circles

Two simple circles can be used to illustrate similarities and differences within categories of information.

1. Draw two large intersecting circles on the chalkboard and begin a class discussion, or have students draw their own circles and work independently.

2. List attributes of one element in the left section, attributes of another element in the right section, and attributes both elements share in the overlapping section. *Examples:* characters in a story; characters' behaviors; events or experiences; the author's style; the use of personification, simile, etc.

3. To identify similarities, refer to the information in the overlapping section. To identify differences, refer to the information in the right and left sections.

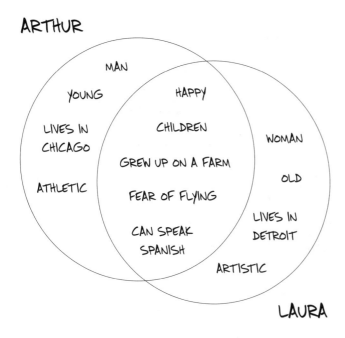

ARTHUR

MAN
YOUNG
LIVES IN CHICAGO
ATHLETIC

HAPPY
CHILDREN
GREW UP ON A FARM
FEAR OF FLYING
CAN SPEAK SPANISH

WOMAN
OLD
LIVES IN DETROIT
ARTISTIC

LAURA

Using a Story's Illustrations

Visual learners enjoy approaching a story's content by way of its illustrations. Try this strategy with your global thinkers and those who are artistically inclined. Have students:

1. Describe what they actually see in an illustration.

2. Predict what might happen next in the section, based on the illustration.

3. Compare illustrations about the same topic from different sources. (This requires some research.)

4. Find the similarities and differences among illustrations.

5. Study illustrations of the same story by different artists. Compare and contrast.

6. Decide which illustration best captures the essential meaning of the selection.

7. Identify any illustration that seems out of place or irrelevant. Give reasons for their opinion.

8. Find other events that should have been illustrated, and create the illustrations.

Essential Questions

Asking consistent and predictable questions about a story can strengthen the comprehension skills of your emerging readers. When you limit the number of questions you ask to those that are essential for understanding the material, students learn to prompt themselves with each new selection. These are the questions I use:

- "What was the basic problem that the character(s) had to solve?"
- "How did they solve that problem?"
- "How might you have solved the problem, if you had been in the character's situation? Give details."

You may use your own questions, but keep them brief and consistent. To make the information more accessible to visual learners, create a simplified version (with fewer shapes) of the story map on page 98.

1. For the first several stories, ask only the first question ("What was the basic problem?"). Have reading buddies talk about the story until they can identify the basic problem. Call the class back together to discuss the problem. Use the Name Card method (pages 14–17) to call on students for the discussion.

2. After students have mastered the identification and description of the basic problem, add the second question for subsequent stories. Have reading buddies address both questions ("What was the problem?" "What was the solution?"). When the large group convenes, expect all students to have answers to both questions.

3. Once students are comfortable with the first two questions, add the third question ("What would you have done to solve the problem?").

In this way, students learn to approach each new story with the same questions. They automatically engage in comprehension activities while they are reading. Once students are adept at using the three essential questions, you can add other questions about the basic elements of fiction, such as setting, characters, plot, and action. Add them slowly, one at a time.

Try these essential questions for nonfiction:

- "What is the main topic of the selection?"
- "What major problem is being experienced by those involved?"
- "What causes of the problem are explained?"
- "What has been done already to solve the problem?"
- "What have been the effects of any action taken so far?"
- "What might you suggest as a more effective solution to the problem?"
- "What might be the author's purpose in writing the selection?"

Creative Dramatics

An ideal comprehension tool for tactile-kinesthetic learners, creative dramatics is often overlooked because some teachers feel funny about using this technique. I encourage you to try a few of the following suggestions, just to see how they work with your students. You will probably find that the benefits outweigh your doubts or discomfort.

- Some kids have problems articulating their thoughts. An invitation to "show us what you are trying to say" may lead to a better description. Have students act out scenes from their lives that are related to what the characters in a story are going through. (*Example:* If the characters are dealing with an aging grandparent, students can act out short skits about their own problems with older relatives.) When students connect their reading with personal experiences, their reading becomes more meaningful and memorable.

- Have them dramatize story events; predict and act out upcoming events; act out vocabulary words; and/or portray specific characters. Older students can work in groups to demonstrate ways in which a character changes during a story.

- Have one student play the role of a major character in the story. The other students ask questions and the character answers in the first person. It's easy to move students into interpretive levels of thinking when they

start asking questions about how a character feels, or those that demand that judgments be made.

Kids who become adept at dramatization can actually create plays from story material. They often enjoy videotaping the results to show the folks at home or students in other classes.

Variation: Readers' Theater

Some teachers find the Readers' Theater method more comfortable than creative dramatics. It's also very easy to implement.

Students read a story aloud as if it were a play. Each student takes a part (one part is always the narrator). All of the "he said," "she said" are eliminated. Students can use the Rehearsed Reading technique (page 91) to prepare their part before reading it to an audience. For more information about Readers' Theater, see "References and Resources."

Summarizing

Use a fishbone graphic to teach summarizing skills. Write it on the chalkboard or create a simple handout. Students complete the fishbone by finding and filling in answers to the categories—Who, What, When, Where, Why, and How—and by identifying the main topic of the selection. Afterward, they use that information to write a summary statement.

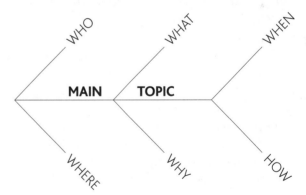

Sequencing

Arranging story events in their proper order requires logical, analytical, and sequential thinking, which makes it a frustrating task for global thinkers. Begin teaching sequencing by having kids relate a series of action steps for some activity they know well (*examples:* getting dressed for school, tying their shoes, making a peanut butter and jelly sandwich). They can draw the events themselves or describe them as someone else writes them down, taking care to deliver them in the correct order or sequence. If they turn out not to be in the correct order or sequence, have the students who drew or spoke them cut apart their pictures or sentences and rearrange them so they are. Once students have learned the concept of sequencing from this activity, you can apply it to a story.

Following is a proven way to teach global thinkers how to sequence events in a story or those related to a historical era.

1. Have reading buddies list the events of a story on writing paper in no particular order. They should begin each event on a new line and leave spaces between. Model how to tell when a new event is being described by thinking out loud.

2. Have the students cut apart the event statements, then arrange them in their proper sequence by moving them around.

3. When the events are in their proper sequence, have the students number them and tape them to a larger sheet of paper, in order.

4. The students can now write the story or read it aloud in its proper sequence.

Variation: Comic Strips

1. Find a fairly long comic strip the student understands and enjoys. (*Examples:* a brief story from a comic book; a strip from the Sunday comics.) Read it with the student.

2. Number each segment, then cut the segments apart and mix them together.

3. Have the student arrange the segments in the proper sequence by following the numbers. Mix and repeat several times.

4. When the student is capable of sequencing the segments independently, find a new strip, read it together, and cut it apart *without* first numbering the segments. Help the student reassemble the segments, then mix them together and have the student reassemble them without help. Repeat several times.

5. Practice with several more strips over time until the student understands this process and can complete it independently.

6. Demonstrate how students can do this with stories they read by drawing their own pictures and arranging them in their proper sequence.

Variation: Storyboards

Divide a large sheet of paper into several sections. Show students how to draw or write story events in each section in sequence. Let tactile-kinesthetic learners draw pictures on separate sheets of paper and physically rearrange them in the proper sequence.

Reciprocal Teaching*

Reciprocal Teaching is an instructional procedure designed to enhance students' comprehension of text. The procedure is best characterized as a dialogue between teacher and students. The term "reciprocal" describes the nature of the interactions, since one person acts in response to the other. This dialogue is structured by the use of four strategies: *questioning, summarizing, clarifying,* and *predicting.* The teacher and students take turns assuming the role of dialogue leader.

Reciprocal Teaching Purpose and Components

The purpose of Reciprocal Teaching is to facilitate a group effort between teacher and students, as well as among students, in the activity of bringing meaning to the text. These strategies were selected because they not only promote comprehension, but also provide opportunities for the students to monitor their own comprehension. Instruction that is conducted for the purpose of increasing students' awareness and regulation of their own activity is referred to as metacognitive instruction.

■ **Summarizing** provides the opportunity to identify, paraphrase, and integrate important information in the text. Text can be summarized across sentences, across paragraphs, and across the passage as a whole. When the students first begin the Reciprocal Teaching procedure, their efforts are generally focused at the paragraph level. As they become more proficient, they are able to integrate larger portions of text. (*Note:* The fishbone graphic on page 101 can help with this component.)

■ **Questioning** reinforces the summarizing strategy and carries the learner one more step along the comprehension activity. When students generate questions, they first identify the kind of information that is significant enough that it could provide the substance for a question. Then they pose this information in a question form and self-test to ascertain that they can indeed answer their own question. Question-generating is a flexible strategy to the extent that students can be taught and encouraged to generate questions at many levels. For example, some school situations require students to master supporting detail information; others require students to infer from text or apply information from text to new problems or situations. (*Note:* The "Question Starters" handout on page 92 and the Thinktrix critical thinking model on pages 70–71 can help with this component.)

---

* This section and the one that follows are adapted from a manual regarding Reciprocal Teaching prepared by A.S. Palincsar, Y. David, and A.L. Brown. Used with permission of Annemarie Sullivan Palincsar.

■ **Clarifying** is an activity that is particularly important when working with students who may believe that the purpose of reading is saying the words correctly, and who may not be particularly uncomfortable that the words and, in fact, the passage are not making sense. When teaching students to clarify, their attention is called to the many reasons why text is difficult to understand; for example, new vocabulary, unclear referent words, and unfamiliar or difficult concepts. They are taught to be alert to the effects of such impediments to understanding and to take the necessary steps to restore meaning: reread, read ahead, and ask for help. (*Note:* The graphic organizers in this chapter can help with this component.)

■ **Predicting** requires students to hypothesize about what the author might discuss next in the text. In order to do this successfully, students must activate the relevant background knowledge that they already possess regarding the topic. The students then have a purpose for reading; to confirm or disprove their hypotheses. Furthermore, the opportunity has been created for the students to link the new knowledge they will encounter in the text with the knowledge they already possess. The predicting strategy also facilitates use of text structure as students learn that headings, subheadings, and questions imbedded in the text are useful means of anticipating what might occur next. (*Note:* The "Predictions" handout on page 94 can help with this component.)

In summary: Each of these strategies was selected as a means of aiding students to construct meaning from text and monitor their reading to ensure that they are, in fact, understanding what they read.

While the eventual goal is flexible use of the strategies, they are typically used as follows: The discussion leader generates questions to which the group responds. Additional questions are raised by other members of the group. The leader then summarizes the text and asks other members if they would like to elaborate upon or revise the summary. Any clarifications are discussed. Finally, in preparation for moving on to the next portion of text, the group generates predictions.

Literature-Based Reading

All of the strategies described in this chapter work with real literature as well as with basal reading materials. Some teachers use real literature for their entire reading program. Of course, if you do this, you will need to make absolutely certain that the assigned reading, phonics, and writing standards for your grade are all included in your program.

■ Whatever model or method you use, set aside at least 30 minutes per day for reading real literature. Don't call it "free reading" or "recreational reading." What does that say about the rest of the reading that goes on in your classroom? Always remember that the purpose of *all* reading instruction is to empower students to one day read anything they choose. In some classrooms, kids spend less than seven minutes during a typical reading period actually reading. How would you like it if someone nabbed your book, magazine, or newspaper after seven minutes and made you do skill work?

■ Help your students choose slightly challenging books by applying the Three-Finger Rule. After they select a book they think they would like to read, they open it to a page somewhere in the middle—preferably one with few or no pictures. Then they read the page, holding up one finger each time they come to a word they can't read or understand. If by the end of the page they are holding up three (or more) fingers, the book is probably too difficult for independent reading and they should make another selection. However, they may look at the book for other reasons.

■ Do away with any rule that forbids students to select a book they have already read or one that is too easy for them. Adults frequently do both.

■ Before giving reluctant readers a story to read, tell them the story. This gives them a big picture to keep in mind as they read. Or read the story aloud until students know enough about it to pique their interest. Let them read independently from that point on.

■ Consider showing a film version (video or DVD) of a story before and after your students read it. Later, have students compare the book and film in terms of their similarities and differences. (Remember to allow analytic readers to choose not to see the film before they read the story themselves.)

■ Avoid written book reports! Nothing is more likely to extinguish a growing flame of positive attitudes toward reading than a required written book report. All of the language arts and writing objectives you believe are practiced in book reports can easily be experienced in other types of lessons.

■ One teacher begins each class session with an activity called "Let's Talk About Books." Students pair up to talk about the books they are reading or to read aloud a favorite passage. The teacher also works with a student partner, giving them some uninterrupted time together. All of her students are more motivated to read.

■ Set aside a regular time for students to informally share books they are reading, even books they haven't finished. Don't adults do that all the time? Have you ever had a friend refuse to hear you talk about a book because you hadn't finished reading it yet?

■ Give each student a copy of the "Books I Want to Read" chart (page 105). Explain that they should take it out whenever their peers share information about books they are reading. If they hear about a book they might want to read, they list it on their chart. When they visit the library, they carry their chart with them. Then they can select books independently without asking the question many librarians dread: "Do you have any good books?"

How to Lead Group Discussions of Novels

Do whatever it takes to make class discussions about books challenging, engaging, intelligent, and meaningful. Those teachers who have been trained in Socratic questioning, seminar leadership, or the Great Books programs know how to pose challenging questions, probe for students' reasoning, direct students to find evidence for their opinions and conclusions, and keep discussions open by continuously asking questions rather than judging the rightness or wrongness of student responses. For another helpful model of higher-level thinking, see Frank Lyman's Thinktrix (pages 70–71).

1. Start each discussion by having students summarize the novel so far and describe the part they have just finished reading.

2. Have them analyze and critique the characters' actions and decisions up to this point.

3. Have them predict events and actions that may happen in upcoming chapters. They should give reasons for their predictions.

4. Whenever possible, facilitate students' personal involvement in the novel. Structure debates where they take sides and argue a particular character's point of view. Then have them switch roles and take the opposite viewpoint. Or invite students to discuss the similarities and differences between their lives and the characters' lives. Call only on volunteers for this activity. Students should not have to share information about their private lives unless they choose to share it.

How to Use the Reading Response Journal

Students who have a positive attitude about writing might enjoy keeping an ongoing journal about a book they are reading. The Reading Response Journal is an excellent way to help students apply critical thinking to what they are reading. Students might write in their journals at the end of each reading session, or during the reading process when their ideas are still fresh.

Tips: Don't require a written response every day. Even for students who like to write, this can quickly become an unpleasant chore. Remember that spelling accuracy and writing mechanics are not important in journal writing. Keep the focus on thoughtful reflection.

1. Give each student several copies of the "Reading Response Journal: A Record of My Thoughts" handout (page 106). Explain that they may use several lines to respond to a particular event.

2. Some students appreciate topic suggestions, preferring those to the open-ended "write about whatever you want." You might design visual cues for specific types of responses.* Create handouts featuring each visual cue. *Examples:*

■ Write about what you see happening in the selection you will be reading today. When you finish reading, comment on the accuracy of your predictions.

■ Write what you are thinking about the characters and events.

■ Write about how what you are reading reminds you of your own experiences.

■ Tell about something from a character's point of view.

■ Write a letter to one of the characters. Tell what you like about him, respond to something he has done, and offer a suggestion about something he might do differently.

■ Write down your questions about things in the story you don't understand. Be prepared to ask them in class or discuss them with your teacher during conference.

■ Make predictions about what you think will happen next in the story.

---

* Adapted from a method used by Linda Holt, teacher, Maui, Hawaii.

Books I Want to Read

This List Belongs To: _____

Author or Call Number	Title	Short Description

 # Reading Response Journal

A Record of My Thoughts

My name: _____

Title of the book I'm reading: _____

Author's name: _____

Date I finished
reading the book: _____

Date I finished
reading the book: _____

Event	My Reaction

Teaching the Skills of Reading

Even when we teach the skills of reading in the context of the literature rather than as isolated skills, direct instruction is necessary to ensure comprehension and transfer. The following five steps will help you to teach any new reading skill effectively. **Tip:** Model any strategy by thinking out loud while using a transparency on an overhead projector. Then your students can see that even the teacher uses strategies to be a good reader.

1. **Get ready to teach the skill.** Activate students' background knowledge about the skill. Have them discuss where they have seen it or used it, and what they think it means.

2. **Describe the skill.** Give the name of the skill, tell how it is useful in this particular reading selection, and explain how it might be used in other learning situations such as newspapers or magazines. Have students repeat the information to a partner and be able to put it in their own words.

3. **Apply the skill.** Demonstrate when and how to use the skill in the context of the current selection, thinking out loud the whole time. Accompany your demonstration with visual organizers.

4. **Have students practice the skill.** Practice, practice, and more practice is the key to mastering any new skill. Allow students to work individually, in pairs, or in small groups to apply the skill in practice exercises, keeping in mind that the number of practice examples should not exceed 12 during any one practice session. Have students practice only one skill at a time until they can demonstrate competency.

5. **Transfer the skill.** The transfer of a skill learned in reading to other subject areas or learning contexts does not happen automatically. You must purposefully demonstrate the use of the skill in the new context.

Using Practice or Workbook Pages More Effectively

Group your visual-tactile-kinesthetic learners in pairs for practice exercises. Assign tasks that easily convert to hands-on activities.

Example: When a practice page calls for matching words and their meanings, give each pair of students a copy of the page and a sheet of colored paper. Student A cuts the practice page in half vertically. Then Student A cuts apart the words and Student B cuts apart the meanings. Both students place their pieces on the colored paper and rearrange the pairs until they are satisfied that each word is matched to its proper meaning. (Experiment with different colors of paper; allow individual students to continue to use any color they feel enhances their ability to stay on task.) Next, Student B writes the answers on an uncut practice page. Both students sign off on the page to indicate that they have done the work together.

Periodically, you can present an exercise in paper-and-pencil format to see if the students are ready to make the transition to accomplishing the task without actually cutting apart the pieces.

The following strategies can also increase students' interest in doing practice or workbook pages:

■ Any practice pages you use with your students should teach or reinforce skills that make sense within the context of what they are reading. Skip those pages for which you can't find a contextual connection, or rearrange the skills to teach them in meaningful contexts.

■ All practice pages must be accompanied by clear directions. Read and discuss them with the students. Provide concrete visual examples of what the finished work should look like.

■ If some kids have difficulty understanding the directions for a practice page, offer them one at a time. Have students demonstrate their understanding of each direction before you add others.

■ Get students excited about practice pages by offering the Five-in-a-Row opportunity: Anyone who completes five consecutive questions or examples neatly, legibly, and correctly may stop practicing! This works best when students work independently rather than with partners.

Questions and Answers

"When can I start using these strategies, and how long should I use them?"

All of the strategies presented in this chapter are intended to be used in conjunction with any reading or writing program you are currently using. In other words, you don't have to wait until they are approved or adopted by your school or district. You can start implementing them today with students who are not experiencing success with present methods. If other students also want to try these strategies on occasion, you can allow this, but your target students should use them consistently until they are ready to make a full-time transition to the adopted program. If they never become ready for that transition, remember that they were not doing well with the adopted program in the first place, and they are probably farther ahead because of your modifications than they would have been without them.

"How can I find time for all of these activities when I barely have enough time to teach my regular reading program?"

Contact the publisher's representative for your reading program. (A representative has been designated by the publisher as a resource person for your school district.) Ask if you're expected to include in your teaching all of the activities and elements suggested in the teacher's manual. If you are told that yes, you must include everything, ask for a free demonstration in your school with kids at all grade levels. In my experience, this often leads publishers to acknowledge that there is room for some flexibility. Also, keep in mind that students shouldn't spend their precious learning time on tasks they can't do successfully. Substitute some of the activities and strategies described here for those that are frustrating your students.

"Won't some of these active learning strategies make my hyperactive students more uncontrollable?"

Plan for students to work in 10–15 minute segments with time off in between. If students need to calm down, have them listen to soothing music for a few minutes before returning to the task at hand. Keep classroom lights low as well. Make perks available for students who maintain on-task behavior. Finally, be aware that kids who are experiencing success at tasks are generally less hyperactive than kids who are not.

"How can I use real literature with students who read far below grade level?"

All kids enjoy good stories. Since all the strategies used with basal reader stories can be used with real literature, reluctant readers may be even more positively motivated through the literature. Try using colored overlays from the Irlen Institute to see if the overlays help make the words stand still. See "References and Resources."

REFERENCES AND RESOURCES

See also the "References and Resources" for chapters 7 and 8.

Brain and Reading video series (www.ascd.org). Three videos and a Facilitator's Guide introduce educators and parents to the principles of brain-compatible learning and how they apply to reading. The Facilitator's Guide includes handouts, overheads, and background readings to expand on the ideas in the videos. 1-800-933-ASCD (1-800-933-2723).

Brown, Hazel, and Brian Cambourne. *Read and Retell: A Strategy for the Whole Language/Natural Learning Classroom.* Portsmouth, NH: Heinemann, 1990. Describes a strategy for improving reading comprehension.

Carbo, Marie. *What Every Principal Should Know About Teaching Reading: How to Raise Test Scores and Nurture a Love of Reading.* Syosset, NY: National Reading Styles Institute, 1997. Classroom-based, research-proven examples of how to strengthen reading programs using students' reading styles, how to achieve high reading gains, how to evaluate reading programs, and how to start an exemplary reading program.

Carbo, Marie, Rita Dunn, and Kenneth Dunn. *Teaching Students to Read Through Their Individual Learning Styles.* Englewood Cliffs, NJ: Allyn & Bacon, 1986. Helps teachers assess and accommodate students' reading styles and teach reading skills in ways that are friendly to tactile-kinesthetic learners.

Clay, Marie M. *Reading Recovery: A Guidebook for Teachers in Training.* Portsmouth, NH: Heinemann, 1993. Describes the Reading Recovery program, which has been dramatically successful in helping struggling readers become more capable readers.

Cunningham, Patricia, and Richard Allington. *Classrooms That Work: They Can All Read and Write.* 3rd edition. Boston, MA: Allyn & Bacon, 2003. Integrates phonics and literature-based process writing and reading instruction for a balanced approach to literacy.

Davis, Sandra. "Teaching the Reading of a Novel to Secondary Students with Learning Disabilities." *Illinois Reading Council Journal* 17:2 (1989), pp. 11–15.

Fountas, Irene C., and Gay Su Pinnell. *Guided Reading: Good First Teaching for All Children.* Portsmouth, NH: Heinemann, 1996. The leading book in the field of guided reading, which helps teachers diagnose and remediate reading problems.

Great Books Foundation (www.greatbooks.org). Great Books Workshops for adults teach *shared inquiry,* a collaborative, question-driven method of discussion. 1-800-222-5870.

Harvey, Stephanie, and Anne Goudvis. *Strategies That Work: Teaching Comprehension to Enhance Understanding.* Portland, ME: Stenhouse Publishers, 2000. Excellent presentation of specific strategies classroom teachers can use to improve comprehension.

Heckelman, R.G. "Using the Neurological-Impress Remedial Reading Technique." *Academic Therapy Quarterly* (Summer 1966), pp. 235–239.

HOTS: Higher Order Thinking Skills (www.hots.org). A general thinking skills program for Title I and LD students in grades 4–8 that accelerates learning, test scores, and social confidence. Demo unit available to download. 1-800-999-0153.

International Reading Association (IRA) (www.reading.org). Books, brochures, videos, and journals to support the teaching of reading and writing. 1-800-336-READ (1-800-336-7323).

Irlen, Helen. *Reading by the Colors: Overcoming Dyslexia and Other Reading Disabilities Through the Irlen Method.* New York: Perigee, 1991. Describes the Irlen Method for improving reading skills and explains what it can and can't do.

Irlen Institute (www.irlen.com). Diagnostic testing and help for children and adults with perceptual reading and learning problems, available in certified testing centers nationwide. For some children, the use of colored overlays or lenses for their glasses (the Irlen method) dramatically improves their learning success. 1-800-55-IRLEN (1-800-554-7536).

Learning Ally (www.learningally.org). This organization makes available taped recordings of most textbooks and some literature used in schools throughout the United States. Their fees are nominal. 1-800-221-4792.

Lyman, Donald E. *Making the Words Stand Still.* Boston: Houghton Mifflin, 1986. Writing from his own experience, Lyman describes the anguish that kids with LD feel as they try to learn, then describes his own unique teaching methods.

National Reading Styles Institute (NRSI) (www.nrsi.com). Home to Marie Carbo's books (see above) and other reading support materials. 1-800-331-3117.

Ogle, Donna S. "KWL: A Teaching Model that Develops Active Reading of Expository Text." *The Reading Teacher* 39 (October 1986), pp. 564–570.

Palincsar, A.S. "Reciprocal Teaching." In *Teaching Reading As Thinking* by A.S. Palincsar, D.S. Ogle, et al. Alexandria, VA: Association for Supervision and Curriculum Development, 1986.

Palincsar, A.S., and A.L. Brown. "Reciprocal Teaching: Activities to Promote Reading with Your Mind." In *Reading, Thinking, and Concept Development: Strategies for the Classroom.* T.L. Harris and E.J. Cooper, eds. New York: The College Board, 1985.

Parents Active for Vision Education (P.A.V.E.) (www.pavevision.org). Helps parents and educators locate services to diagnose reading problems that stem from vision problems.1-800-PAVE-988 (1-800-728-3988).

Read • Write • Think (www.readwritethink.org). A partnership between the International Reading Association (IRA), the National Council of Teachers of English (NCTE), and the MarcoPolo Education Foundation. Go online for lesson plans, standards, student materials, a calendar of classroom activities and online resources associated with events and literacy and literature, and more.

Readers' Theater (www.evan-moor.com). Scripts and plays to help students practice reading aloud with fluency and expression. 1-800-777-4362.

Reading Recovery (www.readingrecovery.org). Designed by Marie M. Clay, this program has been highly effective with first-grade students whose reading skills are grossly inadequate. When the program is carried out as it was designed, the long-term reading gains enable most students to read at or near grade level for their remaining years in elementary school. Reading Recovery is most effective when it is available to all students who need it and is used as a supplement to good classroom teaching. Consult Marie Clay's book, *Reading Recovery: A Guidebook for Teachers in Training* (see page 108).

Simmons, Deborah C., and Edward J. Kameenui, eds. *What Reading Research Tells Us About Children with Diverse Learning Needs: Bases and Basics.* Mahwah, NJ: Lawrence Elbaum Associates, 1998. A comprehensive text on how to teach reading to struggling readers.

Stauffer, Russell G. *The Language Experience Approach to the Teaching of Reading.* New York: HarperCollins, 1980.

SuccessMaker (www.pearsonschool.com). Scalable digital courseware for grades K–8. Individualizes instruction to the specific needs of each student by automatically presenting instruction at the level at which a student is ready to learn, creating a successful learning experience. Aligns with district, local, and national standards, and is supported by a comprehensive management system. Used in more than 16,000 schools in the United States and 1,500 abroad. Courseware is available in customizable bundles. Program costs vary, depending on the software purchased, the range of grade levels to be covered, and the amount of professional development services requested.

Tibbett, Teri. *Listen to Learn: Using American Music to Teach Language Arts and Social Studies (Grades 5–8).* San Francisco, CA: Jossey-Bass, 2004. Offers teachers a dynamic way to use the history of American music to engage their students. Features a variety of activities that encourage students to write about their favorite music, investigate songs as poetry, research the lives of famous musicians, and more. Includes a music CD.

Vacca, Richard T., and JoAnne L. Vacca. *Content Area Reading: Literacy and Learning Across the Curriculum.* 8th edition. Boston, MA: Allyn & Bacon, 2004. Reading, writing, speaking, and listening processes to help students learn subject matter across the curriculum. This respected text is designed to be an active learning tool, complete with real-world examples and research-based practices, and has been updated to incorporate topics related to contemporary issues such as content standards, assessments, No Child Left Behind, and Reading First.

Winebrenner, Susan with Dina Brulles. *Teaching Gifted Kids in Today's Classroom: Strategies and Techniques Every Teacher Can Use.* Minneapolis: Free Spirit Publishing, 2012. Chapter 4, "Extending Reading and Writing Instruction," gives several suggestions for implementing and managing a flexible and responsive reading program.

CHAPTER

7

Teaching Reading: Sounds, Vocabulary, and Spelling

Most students can benefit from learning about letter-sound associations. Students with learning problems may have a great deal of trouble learning phonemic awareness and phonics because the sounds are often taught in isolation, and meaningful context is absent. Sometimes, these global learners are better off learning about phonics after they have learned to read by some other method, such as those described in Chapter 6. The thing to avoid is early failure in phonics, which leads to students concluding that they are not smart enough to learn to read.

Phonemic Awareness

Phonemic awareness is the ability to recognize that spoken words are made up of a sequence of individual sounds. The focus is on the structure of the words and the understanding of the relationship between the sounds that letters make, without any attention to meaning. Phonemic awareness abilities include the understanding and application of these concepts:

- Words are made up of individual sounds or blends.
- Words can begin or end with the same sound.
- Words can have the same sounds within them.
- Words can rhyme.
- Words have syllables.
- Removing or substituting letters or sounds can create other words.

- Some sounds are pronounced as blends.
- Sentences are comprised of groups of words.

Whatever work with sounds students could do with their eyes closed falls into the category of phonemic awareness.

Phonics Instruction

Phonics is a system in which readers learn the relationships between letters and their sounds in order to recognize and pronounce words, as well as being able to read and spell in isolation, in the context of words, and in sentences. Because poor word identification skills inhibit readers' ability to obtain meaning from text, the knowledge of phonics affects many areas of learning. For struggling learners, the essential issue is not *whether* they need phonics, but *when and how* phonics should be included in their reading program.

Students who appear totally confused and unable to learn sound/letter relationships in kindergarten through second grade should be taught to read by a more holistic method that will lead to successful outcomes. For these students, formal instruction in the rules of phonics should be postponed until they perceive themselves as successful readers. Somewhere during the second or third grade, you might offer to teach them some magic tricks that will enable them to pronounce unfamiliar words and improve their spelling ability. (Most seven- and eight-year-olds love tricks.) Students of all ages learn phonics much more easily when they are developmentally ready.

Global learners cannot learn sounds in isolation. It makes no sense to deprive them of meaningful reading experiences until they master the phonics component. Instead, we must teach all phonics-related skills in the context of meaningful words, phrases, and sentences. Whenever possible, use tactile-kinesthetic learning tasks that include a healthy dose of musical-rhythmic activities. And always remember how illogical and unreliable our phonics system is. *Example:* Why spell fish "f-i-s-h"? Why not spell it "g-h-o-t-i"? "Gh" as in lau<u>gh</u>, "o" as in w<u>o</u>men, and "ti" as in na<u>ti</u>on = fish!

Techniques for Teaching Letter-Sound Recognition

Letters

- Teach consonants before vowels because they usually say their own name. Teach consonant sounds as they are usually heard rather than the exceptions.

- Teach each consonant sound in the context of a specific picture and corresponding cue word. Students can visualize the picture to remember the sound. **Tips:** Tactile-kinesthetic learners prefer action words as their cue words ("s" as in "ski," "r" as in "run," "p" as in "play"). Auditory and visual learners prefer nouns.

- Teach each vowel in the same way as consonants, focusing on its sound in the context of a picture and cue word.

- For vowel sounds that say their own name, have students act out each cue word as it is said. The cue words, with pictures, might be:

  "a" as in "race"   "o" as in "blow"

  "e" as in "lean"   "u" as in "music"

  "i" as in "ride"

I have selected these as cue words because they are action words, they are easy to act out, and the target letter appears only once. You can also use cue words where the target letter appears more than once, as long as it has the same sound. Feel free to choose different cue words, but follow the same criteria. Once you select a cue word for a particular vowel sound, don't change it. Don't teach vowel sounds using the confusing terms "long" and "short."

- For other vowel sounds, the cue words, with pictures, might be:

  "a" as in "pat"   "o" as in "knock"

  "e" as in "jet"   "u" as in "tug"

  "i" as in "pitch"

- Make up a little story for each cue word to enhance the mental picture. For example, in teaching "tug," you might tell a story about a boat that has to pull a big ship with (name a currently popular hero, heroine, or action figure) aboard. He or she is tugging the ship away from the tug at the same time the tug is tugging it forward. (The sillier the story, the better.)

- After teaching sounds in the context of words, work on letter recognition. Show students a letter while saying its sound. Immerse students in one sound at a time, perhaps spending as long as three days on a single sound. Have students notice the letter when they see it in words. Serve snacks that start with the letter; play games in the classroom and at recess that start with the letter; and so on. Consistently connect the letter to its cue word. Never demonstrate a letter in isolation ("puh-puh-puh"). Always refer to its cue word ("puh as in play" or "puh–puh-lay").

- Make flashcards for the letters. Use cards of one color for consonants, cards of another color for vowels that say their own name, and cards of a third color for vowels that have a different sound than their name.

- Have students trace over the letters with the second and third fingers of their writing hand while saying the sounds aloud. This works best if they can feel the letters. Use letters made with sandpaper or soft wax crayons, or have students trace the letters in shoeboxes of sand or salt. Have students use large motions to write the letters in the air; have them write the letters on each other's backs or on their own arms.

- Include all of the senses in learning the sounds. *Examples:* Have kids punch out sounds and words in the air, sing a song with the target words, or dance or act out sounds as they say the words.

Word Families*

- When students can say some letter sounds, move on to word families. *Example:* If they can almost always recognize the short "a" in pat, say, "If you know 'pat,' you know 'hat' and 'fat' and 'rat' and 'sat.'"

- Teach families of words with similar sounds together. Print the target sounds in colored chalk, markers, or ink. Use one color for each family.

- Collect word families on notecards in a word box. Highlight the target sound with a particular color to reinforce the visual image of the family pattern.

- Make learning about word families a tactile-kinesthetic experience: Use plastic letters on a magnetic board

---

* Some ideas in this section are from Linda Holt, teacher, Maui, Hawaii. Used with permission.

and change the initial consonants. Have students keep written lists of the word families, perhaps using different colors for each family.

- Create a silly story filled with family words. *Example:* "The purple turtle went to see the nurse because he got hurt going around the curve." Have students add more words; invite them to help you make up similar stories for other word families.

- Have students write stories using as many family words as possible. They can use highlighter pens to illustrate the repetitive pattern. Collect their stories in a book, make copies, and send them home for kids to read aloud.

- Once students understand simple word families ("cat," "hat," "sat"), change the short vowel but keep the consonants the same. *Example:* "If you know 'cat,' you know 'cot' and 'cut.'" Next, work with blending sounds. *Examples:* "flat," "clap," "trap."

- Reinforce the family words until students recognize the sounds and can speak them automatically.

- Design games and other enjoyable ways for students to practice their sound-letter skills. Most kids learn skills through games in an amazingly short period of time.

Working with Words*

Give students a group of letters that make up a word they will learn in today's lesson. Have students arrange the letters to make several shorter words. Dictate the words you want them to make, or provide a written list of the words.

Example: If the target word for the day is "weather," give all students all seven letters. Don't tell them what the target word is. Say that they are "word detectives" and their job is solving the mystery of how all of these letters will fit together to make one word. Direct them to use the letters to make "the," "wet," "hat," "her," "wreath," "where," and so on until someone figures out that all of the letters together make "weather."

Variation: Have students work in small groups to create as many words as possible from the letters in a five-minute period. One student acts as group recorder and writes down all of the words. The team with the most words wins. Award bonus points for using all of the letters in one word.

The Word Wall*

The Word Wall is a large bulletin board or a designated spot on the white or black board that is never erased. Each

week, you add five new words to the wall that students need for that week's reading and writing activities. Write the words on pieces of colored paper (or in colored markers or chalk) and arrange them alphabetically by the first letter only. Each day, select five words from the Word Wall for students to practice. Have them rhythmically chant and clap the letters in each word three times, then write the word and chant and clap again what they have written. For variety, use Arm Tap spelling (see page 119). Include any words from the "Working with Words" activity above. Students might also practice words from the Word Wall using vocabulary flashcards (see page 113).

Using Music, Rhythm, and Movement

- Raps and rhymes help kinesthetic students learn letter sounds more easily. Look for products that teach kids chants for phonics rules.

- Use rhythm cues to teach sounds and syllables. You might have students punch the air with their fists or clap each time they hear a syllable in a word. *Example:* As you and the students say "pizza" together, fists go up on "piz" and "za."

- Have kids write words in the air using large hand/arm movements, or in different media such as shaving cream, finger paints, or salt, or in different colors, or on each other's backs.

- Clapping the letters also helps kids remember correct spellings, as does hitting their arm for each syllable. Especially for global learners, rhythm clues are far more effective than the traditional syllable rules.

- It helps some students to act out a word while saying it repeatedly.

Using Typewriters and Computers

Allow students with phonics and spelling problems to type out the words they are trying to learn. They should type each word three times, checking for accuracy each time. For tactile-kinesthetic learners, touching the letters on the keyboard reinforces the sounds of the letters. Ask parents or friends to donate their typewriters to your classroom instead of throwing them away!

Building Reading Vocabulary

If you went into your class tomorrow and gave a pop quiz on all of the vocabulary words you have taught since the beginning of the year, what do you think the results would

---

* "Working With Words" and "The Word Wall" are adapted from Patricia Cunningham and Richard Allington, *Classrooms That Work: They Can All Read and Write.* New York: HarperCollins, 1994. Used with permission.

be? Liberal estimates run as high as 50 percent, but most teachers predict somewhere between 20–35 percent. Since it's highly unlikely that our students will remember *all* of the vocabulary words we teach them, and since they won't all remember the *same* 20–35 percent, it makes more sense to teach a smaller number of words so well that 100 percent of the students remember 100 percent of the same words!

Traditional methods of studying vocabulary have been largely ineffective for struggling students. As the mother of one second grader watched her daughter copy vocabulary words and their definitions from the glossary of a book, she asked, "What does that word mean? The one you just finished writing?" The child responded, "I don't know, Mommy. I don't have time to learn the words. I'm just supposed to copy them."

Contrary to popular practices, global learners should *not* be taught the vocabulary from an upcoming reading selection *before* they read the text, since they find it very difficult to learn anything outside its meaningful context. Help students pronounce unusual names before reading, but don't teach vocabulary words until they appear in the context of a chapter. Above all, remember that global learners benefit most from visual teaching methods. Adding tactile-kinesthetic activities enhances the learning process even more.

Finally, please remember what we adults do when we come to an unfamiliar word in something we're reading: We spend a brief moment trying to infer the meaning from that context, and if that doesn't work, we skip it! I've always wondered why we keep this secret from kids for so long. If we really want kids to be good readers, we have to give them lots of experience making educated guesses.

Vocabulary Flashcards

Make sure that students have seen and heard the vocabulary words in context *before* you have them work with flashcards.

- To create basic flashcards, have students write the vocabulary word on one side of the card and the meaning on the other. Some students might prefer to draw a picture of the meaning instead of writing it.

- To create more effective flashcards, have students write the word on the left side of the card and the meaning on the right, then cut the cards apart in jigsaw puzzle patterns. The mental image of the word will be reinforced by the jigsaw pattern. Matching words and meanings adds a tactile-kinesthetic component.*

- Have students group their vocabulary flashcards by categories or word families.

- Turn vocabulary mastery into a game. Students will need their own sets of basic flashcards (with their initials on each card). Group kids with similar words into pairs and give each pair a game board, dice (or spinner), and playing pieces. To take a turn, a student reads a vocabulary word and tries to give the meaning. If the meaning is correct, the student receives the card. (Or have them play the other way: read the meaning, give the word.) The person with the most cards at the end of the game wins. The initials make it easy to return the cards to the original owners when the game is over.

The Vocabulary Attributes Chart**

Vocabulary attributes charts can help students visualize and understand words and their meanings. Rather than teaching words as they arbitrarily appear in selections, you group words that share common attributes and teach them together. This method is equally effective with any subject area.

1. Make several copies of the Vocabulary Attributes Chart on page 114.

2. Decide on a category of words that share common attributes. *Example:* "Nouns that describe things." Print a noun in the center box of each chart, using red ink.

3. Create four subcategories of information that could describe attributes of words in that category. *Examples:* For nouns that describe things, subcategories might be "looks like," "usual uses," "unusual uses," and "synonyms." Print these in the boxes at the top and bottom of the chart, using red ink. These attribute boxes will stay the same for every word in the category.

4. Have students brainstorm attributes for each category. Record them in blue ink.

5. When each chart is complete, hang it up where kids can see it. All of the charts for a specific category should be displayed together.

See page 115 for four examples of how this chart might look when completed. The Wagon and Rose examples show nouns and their attributes. The Mission San Diego example shows how this chart might be used for history. The Tyrannosaurus Rex example shows how it might be used for elementary science.

After students have experienced this process several times under your direction, they might enjoy working with partners on this activity.

---

* Marie Carbo, Rita Dunn, and Kenneth Dunn. *Teaching Students to Read Through Their Individual Learning Styles.* Englewood Cliffs, NJ: Allyn & Bacon, 1986.

** The charts in this section are adapted from *New Directions in Vocabulary* by Barbara Abromitis. Carbondale, IL: Blue Ribbon Press, 1992. Used with permission.

Vocabulary Attributes Chart

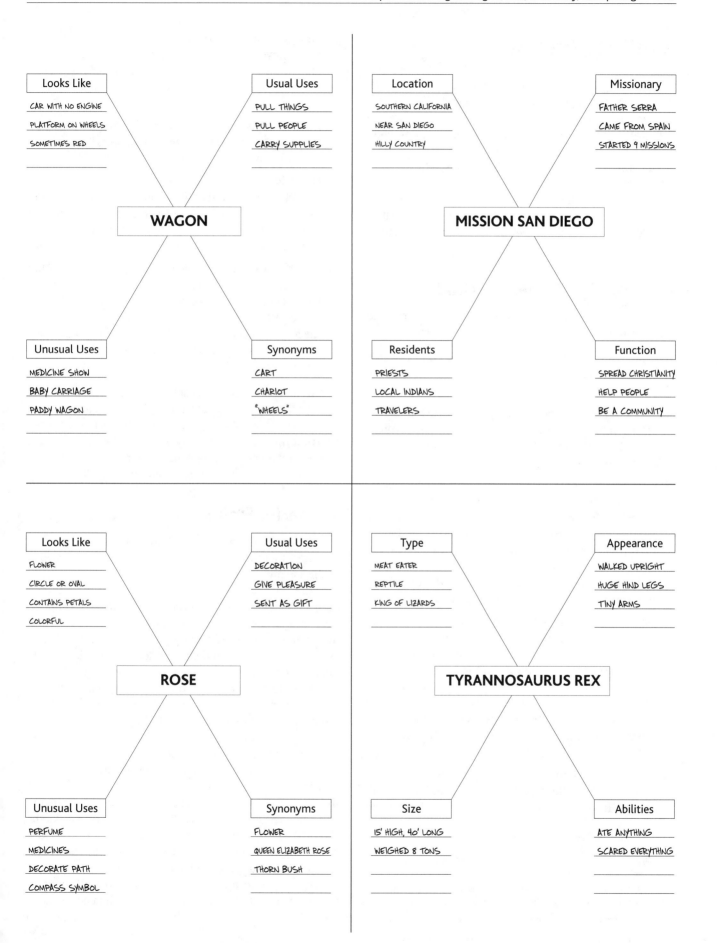

WAGON

Looks Like
- CAR WITH NO ENGINE
- PLATFORM ON WHEELS
- SOMETIMES RED

Usual Uses
- PULL THINGS
- PULL PEOPLE
- CARRY SUPPLIES

Unusual Uses
- MEDICINE SHOW
- BABY CARRIAGE
- PADDY WAGON

Synonyms
- CART
- CHARIOT
- "WHEELS"

MISSION SAN DIEGO

Location
- SOUTHERN CALIFORNIA
- NEAR SAN DIEGO
- HILLY COUNTRY

Missionary
- FATHER SERRA
- CAME FROM SPAIN
- STARTED 9 MISSIONS

Residents
- PRIESTS
- LOCAL INDIANS
- TRAVELERS

Function
- SPREAD CHRISTIANITY
- HELP PEOPLE
- BE A COMMUNITY

ROSE

Looks Like
- FLOWER
- CIRCLE OR OVAL
- CONTAINS PETALS
- COLORFUL

Usual Uses
- DECORATION
- GIVE PLEASURE
- SENT AS GIFT

Unusual Uses
- PERFUME
- MEDICINES
- DECORATE PATH
- COMPASS SYMBOL

Synonyms
- FLOWER
- QUEEN ELIZABETH ROSE
- THORN BUSH

TYRANNOSAURUS REX

Type
- MEAT EATER
- REPTILE
- KING OF LIZARDS

Appearance
- WALKED UPRIGHT
- HUGE HIND LEGS
- TINY ARMS

Size
- 15' HIGH, 40' LONG
- WEIGHED 8 TONS

Abilities
- ATE ANYTHING
- SCARED EVERYTHING

Spelling Instruction*

Students might ask: "Why do we have to learn to spell? We can use a computer with a spellchecker!" The obvious answer is that knowing how to spell allows us to read and write with greater ease. Also, there are many times when people have to complete an application or write a paragraph without the aid of technology. Poor spelling creates a poor first impression.

Learning to spell involves much more than memorization alone. Most students can become competent spellers if we teach them in ways that are compatible with their learning styles.

The Spelling Styles Method**

If you don't teach spelling, you may use this method to teach vocabulary words.

1. Choose four 10- to 15-word spelling lists that are reasonably similar in difficulty. Don't announce ahead of time which lists will be used.

2. Tell your students that you're going to take four weeks off from formal spelling. During that time, you're going to teach them how to use their learning styles to become better spellers.

3. Give each student copies of the "Spelling Styles Chart" handout (page 118) and the "Spelling Styles Record Sheet" handout*** (page 117). Explain that for the next four weeks, they will use these charts to identify their preferred learning styles in order to achieve the best possible spelling results. Reassure them that they will record their own scores privately and that none of the scores will count toward their spelling grade.

4. Give the entire class a pretest of week one's spelling words. Insist that everyone take the test and do the best they can, even though they haven't had a chance to study the words in advance. Again, reassure them that their scores will be private. Even you won't see them. Tell students that if they get just one wrong, they can pair up with another student with a similar score, select a list of challenging words to study, and learn the visual style along with the rest of the class.

5. Have students correct their own tests and record their scores in *blue* in the "V-Pre" (Visual Style, Pretest) column of the record sheet by coloring in the column up to

and including the number they spelled correctly. Afterward, have them look at their Spelling Styles Chart. Model the steps listed in the "Visual Style" box as you teach them. Explain that this is how visual learners study spelling.

6. Have students work in pairs to study the week one spelling words the visual way. Monitor all pairs to make sure they are using the style correctly.

7. On Friday, give the week-one test again. Have students correct their own tests and record their scores in *red* in the "V-Post" (Visual Style, Post-Test) column, as in step 5. This will show how well they can spell as a visual learner would.

8. Over the next three weeks, repeat steps 4–7 for the other three quadrants of the styles chart, using the remaining spelling lists. Have students record their pretest and post-test scores on the record sheet. By the end of the fourth week, the colorful bar graph will show each student the studying style that gives him or her the best results.

Challenge students to practice their preferred learning style method in other areas (*examples:* learning state and world capitals, vocabulary words, number facts, etc.). Keep referring them back to the styles chart. When you return to the regular spelling program, encourage students to set and record their own goals for each week's spelling list.

Scenario: Elaine

It took me years to realize that I had never actually *taught* spelling; I merely *tested* it! One November, I finally decided to change my approach.

Eight-year-old Elaine had never gotten a score higher than 35 percent on any spelling test. Since most of her peers were already well set in their spelling patterns, and since their grades weren't changing much from week to week, I announced that I would use the next four weeks of spelling time to teach the whole class about spelling styles.

I knew that Elaine studied her spelling words at home (her mother had confirmed that fact for me), but the results were invariably disappointing. During our four-week experiment, Elaine discovered that she was a visual-tactile-kinesthetic (multisensory) learner.

When the learning style discovery activity ended, I asked Elaine to set a goal each week for how many words she would learn to spell with 80 percent accuracy or higher by using her strongest modality. For the first week, she chose 10 words. I choked back what I wanted to say—"Oh, no, that goal is too high! You would have to spell eight words correctly to get 80 percent, and the most you've ever gotten right on a formal spelling test is three!" Instead, I helped her to chart her goal. Then I coached her in using the multisensory style to study the 10 words she selected

---

* Spelling is discussed in this chapter because it requires working with sounds. However, it is perfectly appropriate for you to teach spelling in the context of reading or writing, because spelling is an integral part of achieving literacy.

** The Spelling Styles method and the "Spelling Styles Chart" handout on page 118 are used with permission of Anita DeBoer, consultant in education.

*** Adapted from the work of Doris Brown, special education teacher, retired. Used with permission.

Spelling Styles Chart

Visual Style

★ Look at the word; say it aloud, pronouncing all the sounds

★ Close your eyes and see it

★ Open your eyes and write the word

★ Check for accuracy; write again

★ Look up to the left and see the word in a bright color

★ Hide your written sample; write again; check for accuracy

★ Hide sample; write again using a different bright color pen or pencil; check

★ Repeat these steps with all other words

★ Write each word several times; check each time

Tactile-Kinesthetic Style

★ Look at the word; trace it with your index finger; say the letters

★ Draw a box around the word that follows the letter shapes; notice what the drawing reminds you of

★ Write the word in shaving cream, salt in a box, finger paint, pudding, etc.

★ Punch out the letters in the air; say each letter with each punch

★ Use Arm Tap spelling

★ Sing, act, or dance the word (in your mind is OK)

★ Use sandpaper letters; trace words with your index finger while saying the letters aloud

★ Write the word in the air; write it on paper and check accuracy

★ Hide your written sample; write again; check for accuracy

★ Repeat these steps with all other words

★ Write each word several times; check each time

Auditory Style

★ Say the word

★ Sound it out, saying each letter or blend

★ Spell it aloud; write it as you spell it aloud

★ Check for accuracy; write again; check

★ Sing the letters to the tune of a song or jingle you know

★ Enunciate each letter clearly or blend slowly

★ Repeat these steps with all other words

★ Write each word several times; check each time

Multisensory Style

(Visual/Tactile-Kinesthetic/Auditory)

Use strategies from the other three boxes. Suggested combinations:

★ Look at the word; pronounce all sounds

★ Visualize it with your eyes closed

★ Trace the letters with your finger; make sandpaper words if needed

★ Draw a box around the word

★ Sing, act, or dance the word

★ Write the word with your fingers on a partner's back

★ Write in colored chalk or markers; use other media

★ Repeat these steps with all other words

★ Write it after you study it each way; check for accuracy each time

Spelling Styles Record Sheet

NAME: _____

Number of words	V-Pre	V-Post	T-K Pre	T-K Post	A-Pre	A-Post	Multi-Pre	Multi-Post
15								
14								
13								
12								
11								
10								
9								
8								
7								
6								
5								
4								
3								
2								
1								

My strongest learning style is (check one):

☐ Visual ☐ Tactile-Kinesthetic ☐ Auditory ☐ Multisensory

from the spelling list. I affirmed her "Yes I Can" attitude—and watched in amazement as she got all 10 words correct on the test. She happily recorded her results, and I sent a note home to announce her victory.

Elaine gradually increased her goal until she was studying 15 words each week. She maintained good grades in spelling for the rest of the year.

Caution: The goal increase must be the student's idea, *not* the teacher's!

More Techniques for Teaching Spelling and Learning Sounds

Arm Tap Spelling

Have students spell words on their arm. They should extend the arm they don't write with and use the index and middle fingers of their writing hand to tap out each clustered sound, then slide out the whole word at the end.

Example: Model "arm spelling" the word "arithmetic." Tap "A" (pause) "R-I-T-H" (pause) "M-E" (pause) "T-I-C" (pause), then say the whole word as you slide your two fingers down your arm from shoulder to wrist.

After much guided practice, students should be able to use this technique silently to figure out how many syllables are in a word and how it is spelled.

The Fernauld Word-Tracing Method*

1. Ask students to identify a word they would like to spell accurately in their writing. (It's best to do this at a moment when a student needs a particular word—as in "Teacher, how do you spell _____?")

2. Using a soft, waxy instrument (like a thick crayon), print or write the word on a 4" x 6" card. The letters should be raised off the surface of the card.

3. Have students trace over the word with the index finger of their writing hand, saying the word aloud as they trace it. Multisyllabic words should be pronounced in syllables. After several practices, students should be able to turn the card over and write the word from memory.

Functional Spelling

Struggling students are more motivated to learn something they consider meaningful and important. It makes sense to concentrate their spelling efforts on the words they need to function in their own writing.

1. Have students keep lists of their frequently misspelled words.

2. When they have collected five words, have them use the Spelling Styles method (page 116) to study the words.

3. Have partners test each other. Words that are mastered are dropped from the list; new words are added until the list is five words long again.

If students keep their word lists in a small spiral notebook, they will have a cumulative record of the words they learn. If they staple a progress chart to the back cover, they can record the number of words they spell correctly on each test. Use a bar graph or line graph for their records.

Spelling Baseball

Spelling baseball is a particular favorite of learners who need to move around. Students get to run the bases as they progress through the game.

1. Create two teams of students, with a range of spelling abilities on each team.

2. Draw a large baseball diamond on the board at the front of the room.

3. Have students go to bat and choose the level of difficulty of the word they will try to spell. A simple word is a single; a challenging word is a home run.

4. Each correct spelling is a base hit or home run. Each incorrect spelling is an out. Teams score a point each time one of their players comes home; after three outs, the other team is up to bat.

Of course, you can use this format to review any content, not just spelling.

Spelling Bees and Other Contests

It is imperative that students be allowed to use their preferred learning style in spelling bees and other contests.

- If they are visual, allow them to write out the word rather than spell it aloud.

- If they are tactile-kinesthetic, let them write the word in sand or salt.

The only fair requirement is that *all* students be given the same amount of time to come up with the correct spelling. If these special allowances make your students ineligible for regional or national competitions, either conduct your own local spelling bee or have a separate competition for volunteers to qualify for those competitions.

Studying Misspelled Words

Avoid circling spelling errors for visual learners, since that calls more attention to errors than to words spelled correctly. Instead, fold a piece of writing paper into three columns. Have students write their spelling words in the left column.

---

* Fernauld, Grace. *Remedial Techniques in Basic School Subjects: Methods for Teaching Dyslexics and Other Learning Disabled.* Austin, TX: PRO-ED, 1988. Used with permission.

On test day, have them fold that column over to the back and take the test in the middle column. Afterward, have them write the correct spellings of any words they got wrong in the right column (on the same line as in the test column).

Giving Partial Credit*

Some of your students will continue to struggle with spelling, despite your best efforts to the contrary. Instead of marking a misspelled word entirely wrong, give partial credit for each correct letter written in the right space.

Questions and Answers

"Shouldn't all students learn phonics in the primary grades?"

Many adults (including me and perhaps including you) learned to read by methods other than phonics, and we read well. We should teach phonics when students are ready to learn them—usually when they are capable of discriminating between sounds. If a student's auditory memory function is impaired, or if some other form of LD makes it difficult or impossible for a student to understand and use phonics, use other methods described in this book to teach the skills needed for reading. Postpone teaching phonics until students perceive themselves as capable readers.

"What if some kids miss out on important vocabulary or skills because they aren't doing the same tasks as the other students?"

Teach them the grade-level vocabulary in another format. *Examples:* Incorporate the words into crossword puzzles or checkerboards (students can't move their checker until they say the meaning of the word on a particular square). Structure their skill work to give them practice in the skills that all the other students are working on, but in a more hands-on manner.

"What grade should students like Elaine get when their goal is very low?"

Students who accomplish the goal they set should get a C until their goal gets into the regular range for a B or an A. When we gift students with an A for results that are far below grade-level expectations, we communicate that we never expect them to be able to do grade-level work. A grade of C for reaching one's self-set goal is much better than a low or failing grade received for a low percentage score. As students like Elaine move their goals up into levels more commensurate with grade-level standards, higher grades may be earned.

"Isn't there a time when students should just have to memorize things, like spelling words, simply because they need to know them?"

If students have the ability to memorize, the answer is yes. If they have a form of LD which adversely affects their ability to memorize, the answer is no. For those kids, the only way they can learn to spell correctly is with learning aids—much as we would use a language translator in a foreign country for words and phrases we were unable to remember automatically.

REFERENCES AND RESOURCES

See also the "References and Resources" for chapters 6 and 8.

Abromitis, Barbara. *New Directions in Vocabulary.* Carbondale, IL: Blue Ribbon Press, 1992.

Accelerated Vocabulary (www.renlearn.com). Students learn new words in context through reading, then use this computer program that offers quizzes on books from many popular series to help stimulate vocabulary acquisition. Also allows teachers to provide each student with an individualized list of learned vocabulary words. 1-800-338-4204.

Carbo, Marie, Rita Dunn, and Kenneth Dunn. *Teaching Students to Read Through Their Individual Learning Styles.* Englewood Cliffs, NJ: Allyn & Bacon, 1986. Helps teachers assess and accommodate students' reading styles and teach reading skills in ways that are friendly to tactile-kinesthetic learners.

Clicker (www.cricksoft.com/us). A talking word processor that allows students to start writing with a picture, then helps them turn it into text. 1-866-33-CRICK (1-866-332-7425).

Cunningham, Patricia, and Richard Allington. *Classrooms That Work: They Can All Read and Write.* 3rd edition. Boston, MA: Allyn & Bacon, 2003. Integrates phonics and literature-based process writing and reading instruction for a balanced approach to literacy.

Fernauld, Grace. *Remedial Techniques in Basic School Subjects: Methods for Teaching Dyslexics and Other Learning Disabled.* Austin, TX: PRO-ED, 1988.

Gentry, J. Richard, and Jean Wallace Gillet. *Teaching Kids to Spell.* Portsmouth, NH: Heinemann, 1993. Describes many strategies for teaching spelling. Includes useful lists of Latin and Greek stems, 500 words students commonly need in their writing, extensive sections on invented spelling, and strategies for teaching phonics.

International Dyslexia Association (www.interdys.org). An international organization dedicated to the study and treatment of dyslexia. Many of their methods are successful for kids with reading problems, whether or not they

---

* Brenda Goffen, consultant in special education, Highland Park, Illinois.

have been diagnosed as dyslexic. Formerly the Orton Dyslexia Society. (410) 296-0232.

Promoting Vocabulary Development: Components of Effective Vocabulary Instruction. Austin, TX: Texas Education Agency, 2002. One of five downloadable PDFs available in the Red Book Series of the Texas Education Agency's Reading Initiative program (www.tea.state.tx.us). The series provides information and resources on reading topics (including vocabulary development, comprehension, and content-area reading) to assist parents, educators, school board members, and others with an interest in education and children's reading development.

Simon S.I.O. (Sounds It Out) (www.donjohnston.com). Very helpful in teaching phonemic awareness and phonics. The program engages students with an animated personal tutor. 1-800-999-4660.

Stevenson Learning Skills (www.stevensonlearning.com). Materials that take a multisensory approach to teaching reading and related skills, as well as math facts and concepts. 1-800-343-1211.

Winsor Learning (www.winsorlearning.com). A source for multisensory phonics instruction based on the Orton-Gillingham approach, which has been an integral part of special education instruction for decades. 1-800-321-7585.

Word Quests for Word Seekers (www.wordquests.info). An online resource providing etymologies for English words derived from Latin and Greek.

The Word Within the Word (www.rfwp.com). Michael Clay Thompson's vocabulary building curriculum that uses etymology, not memorization, in a systematic approach to the study of vocabulary. Student and teacher volumes are available, each containing 30 lessons, as well as class sets and alternative test books (to reduce the possibility of cheating). Published by Royal Fireworks Press. (845) 726-4444.

WordMaker (www.donjohnston.com). This phonics, phonemic awareness, and spelling program based on the work of Dr. Patricia Cunningham helps kids remember words they have learned and use them in their writing. 1-800-999-4660.

Write:OutLoud (www.donjohnston.com). Helps younger and older students by saying words as they are being typed, so students can both read and hear what they have written. 1-800-999-4660.

Teaching Writing

Just as children learn to read by reading, they learn to write by writing. Almost all students can learn to write if we are flexible about the methods and the technology they can use. Remediation of handwriting or other writing skills beyond third grade without technology assistance is often a waste of the learner's time. There are many software programs available that can speak words as students write them, or prompt students to recognize a word for which they are searching. See "Assistive Technology" on pages 79–80.

Our goal should be to enable students to communicate in ways that are fluent and meaningful for them. When students perceive that writing lets them share exciting and important ideas, they may be more willing to do whatever it takes to learn how to write. This chapter describes many strategies and techniques that can turn your reluctant writers into willing and even eager writers.

What to Do When Students Hate to Write

Frustrated students think they hate to write, but what they really hate is revising. When we give them more painless ways to complete their writing assignments, they develop more positive attitudes about writing.

From the first day children enter school, language experiences shape the way they perceive all communication skills. You might start by simply asking your students to write down a few ideas about something they did, saw, or heard. Obviously, students who aren't yet literate can't write real sentences. However, it's important for them to *think* they can so they begin to develop the critical understanding of the relationships between thinking, speaking, writing, and reading. As teachers, we must encourage them to write in any way they can. Some will just scribble; others will draw pictures; still others will write symbols that are incomprehensible to anyone but them. At this very early stage, the only criterion for acceptability should be whether they can read what they have written.

I once worked with a group of three-year-olds who had just returned to preschool after a flood that had put most of their homes underwater. I asked them to write about two things that had happened to them in the flood and to draw a picture about it. As they came up to read their stories, I modeled for them how a reader glances down at the text and looks up at the audience. By the time the third child came up, everyone was reading in this manner, even though most of their writing was illegible.

Scenario: Walter

Walter was in a preschool class for four-year-olds who had been labeled "at risk." Each day, his teacher asked the class to write in their journals; at the end of the day, she translated their writing into acceptable English. When I suggested that she stop translating, she expressed concern that her students wouldn't see good models of writing without her help. I explained that good models wouldn't be meaningful to the children until they themselves understood the thinking-speaking-writing-reading connection.

The teacher agreed to give it a try. The next day, she observed that Walter was spending an inordinate amount of time hunched over his journal. Curious about his entry, the teacher asked Walter to share what he had written with the class. Walter came up to stand beside the teacher. She looked over his shoulder and saw a series of chicken scratches that made absolutely no sense to her.

Then Walter started to read: "Last night before I went to bed . . . ." He suddenly stopped reading, giggled self-consciously, put his hand over his mouth, and said, "Oops,

I made a mistake!" He then turned his paper upside-down (which for him was right-side-up) and continued reading his journal!

Emerging writers have a code that they understand perfectly well. When we interrupt their coding to show them the correct way to write, we may compromise their ability to achieve correctness at a developmentally appropriate time.

Journal Writing

Journal writing is an important part of literacy development at any age. Most teachers allow students' journals to illustrate their writing progress over time. Although it's valuable to teach students the importance of keeping written records of their thoughts and experiences, the idea of having to write something every day can become very stressful for kids who find writing difficult in the first place.

- Tell students to write a journal entry at least twice a week on whatever days they choose. This allows reluctant writers to skip some days when they just don't feel like writing.

- Many kids appreciate a suggestion from you about possible writing topics, but always allow students to choose their own topic if that is what they prefer.

- As you review student journals, respond in writing from time to time. This emphasizes the use of the written word as a communication device.

- If you want students to be candid in their journal entries, suggest a signal or symbol they can use to indicate when they don't want you to read a certain entry.

- Above all, avoid correcting what students write in their journals.

What to Do When Students Don't Know What to Write About

How often have you heard someone say, "The really good writers always write from personal experience"? Yet we teachers continue to compile lavish collections of story starters to aid creativity. This type of assignment is purely inauthentic to struggling writers, who have yet to learn that writing is only part of the thinking-speaking-writing-reading connection.

In one class I worked with, we spent two days compiling a list of possible writing topics. On the first day, we filled the entire chalkboard with ideas students brainstormed during a 20-minute period in response to the question, "What can I write about?" On the second day, we took a six-foot piece of butcher paper and divided it into four sections: "About Me," "About People I Know," "About People I Don't Know," and "Made-Up Stuff." Next, we put every item on the brainstormed list into one or more of these sections. Then we titled the chart "What I Can Write About" and taped it to a wall.

Students were encouraged to write their first story about a topic from the "About Me" category; subsequent stories could come from any other category. The chart stayed up all year. Whenever anyone said "But I don't know what to write about!" we would simply point to the chart and say, "Check out our chart!" The claims of not knowing what to write about ceased almost immediately.

WHAT I CAN WRITE ABOUT

About Me	About People I Know	About People I Don't Know	Made-Up Stuff

Improving Fluency by Just Writing

When students complain that they can't get started writing about a topic, suggest that they try the following:

1. Write your topic at the top of a sheet of paper.

2. Now just write for three to five minutes *without lifting your pencil from the paper.* You can write anything that comes to mind, even if it doesn't relate to your topic. If you really can't think of a single thing, write, "I can't think of anything to write." Keep looking back at your topic. Let your pencil do the work for you.

3. When the time is up, go over everything you have written. Underline any ideas that might be related to your topic.

4. Write the ideas you underlined on a clean sheet of paper. Skip several lines between each written idea. Work with a partner to brainstorm and list supporting ideas and details.

5. Use your ideas, supporting ideas, and details to write several sentences. Reorganize as needed into one or more paragraphs.

See "Making Writing Visual and Global" (pages 126–129) for ways to help students organize sentences into paragraphs.

Writing Programs

Which writing program should you use? If your district has adopted a program, you may not have a choice. If your district has not adopted a program, take a look at what is available from various publishers and other sources.

At the time of this writing, the 6+1 Trait Writing Model is the program of choice in many schools across the country. The current evolution of the six-trait rubric developed by the Northwest Regional Educational Laboratory in Portland, Oregon, the 6+1 Trait Writing Model teaches what are now considered to be the seven most important traits of writing. They are:*

- **Ideas and content.** This trait includes the main idea or theme, supporting details, clear purpose, and compelling information. Ideas must be of high quality.

- **Organization.** This trait includes an engaging lead-in, logical order of ideas, smooth transitions, and a satisfying conclusion.

- **Voice.** This trait includes the writer's personality, feelings, honesty, and sincerity. The reader/listener should believe what the writer is saying.

- **Word choice.** This trait includes using memorable phrases, words that are appropriate for the intended audience, and specific parts of speech. Writing succinctly is the desired goal.

- **Sentence fluency.** This trait includes rhythm and meter, variety in sentence length, rhyme, alliteration, and an easy flow of ideas through the entire piece.

- **Conventions.** This trait includes appropriate grammar, correct spelling, meaningful punctuation, and effective paragraphs.

- **Presentation.** This trait includes the form and layout of the text, and the ease of its readability.

For more information about the 6+1 Trait Writing Model, see "References and Resources" at the end of this chapter.

The Writing Process**

The Writing Process helps students learn to write by emulating the methods used by professional writers. Just as in real-life writing, students are allowed to create many drafts without having to polish each one to the publication stage. Ultimately, they select a few to finalize for other eyes to be able to read and understand.

Give each student a copy of the "Steps to Good Writing" handout (page 125). Teach each step explicitly. Model any steps for which students need clarification. Be available to answer questions, teach skills, and provide encouragement.

Caution: It is imperative that students regularly select a piece of their writing to take all the way through the editing and publishing stages. When elementary students are rarely expected to correct mechanics and spelling in their writing, teachers in the upper grades may conclude that some students exhibit significant lapses in their skills and may blame the Writing Process for those inadequacies. Some states have abandoned the Writing Process as a result. Whatever program, model, or method you use to teach writing, make certain that your students will be able to demonstrate solid skills to their future teachers.

Scenario: Damien

Damien was a fourth grader who had been diagnosed as having LD. When I met him, he was very fluent in expressing his ideas verbally, but when it came to writing he dug in his heels and insisted, "I can't write! I hate writing!"

This situation with certain students—fluency in thinking and speaking combined with dramatic weakness in their ability to write down their thoughts—can often indicate

---

* 6+1 Trait Writing Model is a registered trademark of Northwest Regional Educational Laboratory (NWREL). Used with permission from Northwest Regional Educational Laboratory, Portland, Oregon.

** Originated more than 30 years ago in San Francisco as the Bay Area Writing Project, the Writing Process has since been refined by many authors and teachers including Nancy Atwell, Lucy McCormick Calkins, Donald H. Graves, and Donald M. Murray. See "References and Resources" at the end of this chapter.

Steps to Good Writing

1. Getting Ready: Pre-Writing

- Listen to soothing instrumental music in a slightly darkened room as your ideas flow.

- Brainstorm your ideas about the suggested topic into a visual picture on paper.
  Do this in any way that feels comfortable. You might use a web or a mind map.

2. Writing

- Choose a subtopic from your picture, web, or mind map.

- Write your ideas in sentences as you think of them.

- At this stage, don't worry about putting your ideas in the correct order, using the correct spelling, or using the right punctuation, capitalization, or grammar. Just write!

- Continue this process until you are out of ideas.

3. Revising

- Read aloud to another student what you have written.

- Ask your listener to comment on **one** idea in your writing. Invite your listener to ask **one** question about something that is unclear.

- Have your listener make one suggestion about how to make your written piece better. You may accept or reject the suggestion.

- To make changes, cut-and-paste your piece, trying out different arrangements of the sentences and ideas. If you are working on paper, you can literally cut the sentences apart and tape them together in different orders. (Use removable tape). If you are working on a computer, use the word processing program to make your changes. You might save different versions of your piece and compare them.

4. Editing

- Work with a partner or the teacher to correct spelling, mechanics, and so on.

- If you feel that your writing needs a lot of help, focus on one skill at a time until you master it. Add other skills one at a time, knowing that all previously mastered skills should also be evident in your work.

5. Publishing

- For every 3–4 pieces you write, you must choose **one** to publish.

- Polish your chosen piece so it can be understood by other eyes.

- Write your final copy in pen (on a clean sheet of paper) or on a computer.
  If you use a computer, be sure to use any available programs to check your spelling and grammar.

- Arrange with the teacher to sit in the author's chair and share your work with the class.

Repeat the writing and revising steps until YOU are satisfied with your writing.

that the students are twice exceptional: gifted in some areas of learning while experiencing learning difficulties in other areas. For more on this topic, see "Being Gifted and Having Learning Challenges at the Same Time" on page 28.

Like many kids with LD, Damien was a terrible speller, and his mental fluency was severely compromised by the halting manner in which he wrote. He would carefully consider each word, trying to determine whether he could come even remotely close to the correct spelling. He would lose track of his ideas in the middle of his sentences. He felt hopeless about his weaknesses and dreaded any writing assignment.

His teacher and I had decided to use the Writing Process with his class. We were curious about how that method would affect Damien.

First, I had to convince Damien that during the initial stages of the process, fluency was the only goal. Although he was skeptical, he soon figured out that I meant what I said, and he opened up on paper with such fervor that I faced a new challenge: how to stop him! He chose to write about his favorite activity—his family's annual summer camping trip to a remote site with lots of fishing. During their typical two-week outing, their routine was relatively constant from day to day. Damien wrote a bed-to-bed story for each day of their most recent vacation. He wrote furiously for the entire writing period every day for two weeks.

Finally, he agreed to choose one of his days to work through the other steps of the Writing Process. I assured him that he could finish the rest of the story some other time. Obviously, Damien was no longer resistant to writing. Like many other struggling writers, he had found success with the Writing Process.

Ways to Support the Writing Process

Encourage Inventive Spelling in First Drafts

Learning how to be an accurate speller is a developmental process. We have all noticed that the English language appears to contain more spelling exceptions than rules. Imagine how frustrating it must be for a child with learning difficulties to try to remember arbitrary rules that make no logical sense!

All spellers go through several stages, from having no awareness of sound-letter relationships to being able to spell correctly most of the time. As kids learn the importance of finding the right letter to represent a certain sound, they are actually engaged in phonics learning of the highest degree. Just watch a young writer struggle to sound out words in the first stages of the writing process, and you can actually see the sound-spelling connection happen.

If students are allowed to use guesstimates during the draft phases, this will definitely help them to become more fluent writers. Of course, they should be expected to demonstrate accurate spelling in the finished product.

Really weak spellers should be allowed to use spellchecker programs for part of the product. Alternatively, you might have them use dictionaries and other print sources to correct their spelling in the first paragraph of a piece. When some degree of spelling fluency is reached, increase your expectations for spelling accuracy one paragraph at a time. Remember that many adults use spellchecker programs routinely. There is no reason why we can't train weak spellers to use a combination of software and print sources to increase their spelling accuracy.

Use Writing Software

Computer programs for writing help struggling writers develop and organize their ideas so their writing flows more fluently. There are several kinds of programs available. Some type the words as students speak them into a microphone. Some allow students to hear what they have typed. Spellchecker, word-prediction, and thesaurus programs also improve writing fluency. The more easily frustrated writers achieve fluency, the more quickly their resistance to writing fades.

Two popular writing programs are Inspiration and Kidspiration. Both use graphic organizers to build and strengthen writing skills. See "References and Resources." See also the writing, reading, and spelling programs described in the "Assistive Technology" section in Chapter 5 (pages 79–80).

Use the Sentence Construction Chart

If students get stuck trying to write complete sentences, show them how to use the chart at the top of page 127. It's especially effective with visual learners. Of course, not every sentence will have all of the elements on the chart. But all sentences should have at least a subject ("Who or What") and a verb ("Does or Did").

Making Writing Visual and Global

The Paragraph Centipede

Primary students enjoy this graphic approach to writing a cohesive paragraph—and, with practice, their writing shows dramatic improvement. Have them work in groups.

1. On a large sheet of blank paper, draw the body of a centipede. It should be large enough to allow for writing, and also for several legs to be attached. On another

---

* Morsink, Catherine Voelker. *Teaching Special Needs Students in Regular Classrooms.* Boston: Little, Brown and Co., 1984.

Which	Who or What	Does or Did	What or Whom	Where
MY	DOG	LICKED	THE MAIL CARRIER	ON THE ARM

sheet of paper, draw legs that are long enough and wide enough to fit a printed sentence. Make copies for each group of one body and several legs. **Tip:** Laminate the pictures so they can be reused.

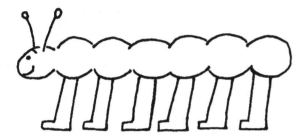

Adapted from James F. Baumann and Maribeth C. Schmitt, "Main idea-pede," in *The Reading Teacher,* March 1986, p. 64. Copyright by the International Reading Association. Used with permission.

2. Tell the students the main idea of the paragraph they are about to write. Have them write the idea on the centipede's body.

3. Have each group brainstorm as many details as they can to describe the main idea of the paragraph. Each student might suggest a detail and write it on a leg. If some students can't write, designate one student in each group to act as a recorder, putting each new detail on a separate leg. Explain that for now, fluency is the *only* goal. They shouldn't worry about correctness, spelling, mechanics, or the relevance or order of ideas.

4. After the groups have brainstormed several details, the selection process begins. Have students take turns reading the main idea (body) followed by their detail (leg). Students hold the leg up to the body while reading, and the group decides together whether a student's detail supports the main idea. Details that are meaningfully connected are put in one pile; details that aren't are discarded.

5. When the groups have identified several details that fit, they decide on the sequence by ordering the legs from left to right. They keep rearranging the legs until everyone agrees on the sequence. At that point, they number the legs in order. Students take back their own legs and correct spelling, grammar, and punctuation,

perhaps with the help of others in the group. (Have extra legs available for students who need them.)

6. The corrected legs are attached to the body in sequence, and everyone writes a complete paragraph and reads it aloud.

Variation: The Paragraph Organizer

Try this approach with students in grades 4–12. It's the same basic concept as the Paragraph Centipede but less babyish in appearance. Have the students work in pairs or small groups.

1. Give each pair or group a copy of the "Paragraph Organizer" handout (page 128). Tell them to write the main idea in the space indicated. (Or you can write it in before you make the copies.)

2. Have students brainstorm supporting details, writing each detail on a new line in the "Ideas for Sentences" column of the chart. Make sure they understand that they are to put each idea on a new line (so the ideas can be cut apart easily in step 3). Explain that at this stage, fluency is the *only* goal. Tell them not to write anything yet in the "Sequence" column.

3. Tell students to cut the sentences apart, hold each sentence up to the main idea, and discard any that don't fit.

4. Have them sequence the remaining details and number each one (using the box under the "Sequence" heading). Have them edit their sentences.

5. The final sentences are taped together in the correct sequence, and students write their paragraphs by copying the sequence on a clean sheet of paper.

Story Maps

The story and character maps on pages 98 and 99 may also be used to plan written descriptions of stories and characters. Students simply create sentences from each of the details charted on the map.

Paragraph Organizer

The main idea: _____

_____

Sequence	Ideas for Sentences

"Hand In" a Perfect Sentence*

Students can do their own proofreading with this simple tool. Have them trace around one of their hands (fingers spread, palm down). Then have them write the following on the digits:

- Thumb: *Capitals*

- Index finger: *Punctuation*

- Middle finger: *Spelling*

- Ring finger: *Neatness*

- Pinkie: *Subject* (for staying on the subject)

As students proofread a piece of their writing, they can use the hand prompts by touching each finger in turn and asking the following questions, one for each finger:

- "Does the sentence begin with a *capital* letter?"

- "Does it end with a *punctuation* mark—a period, question mark, or exclamation point?"

- "Is the *spelling* correct?"

- "Is the writing *neat* and readable?"

- "Does it have something to do with the *subject* I am writing about?"

Variations: You can use the hand visual in countless ways in many different subject areas. Two variations for writing are:

- Each finger represents the components of a good narrative—"Who?" "What?" "When?" "Where?" "Why?"—and the palm says "How?"

- To help students elaborate on character and scene descriptions, each digit is labeled with one of the senses—"What do we *see*?" "What do we *hear*?" "What do we *touch*?" "What do we *smell*?" "What do we *taste*?"—and the palm says "What do we *feel* (what emotion)?"

---

* Brenda Goffen, consultant in special education, Highland Park, Illinois.

Evaluating the Writing of Students with Learning Difficulties

Give each student a folder to be used exclusively for writing. Attach a "Writing Portfolio Record Sheet" (page 130) to the inside flap of the folder. Help each student select one writing skill in need of significant improvement. Explain that except for the target skill and previously mastered skills, you will not notice other types of errors.

As the student shows significant improvement in the target skill, have a conference to decide what skill to focus on next. Tell students that they are expected to maintain competence in all of the skills they have previously mastered as they add new skills one by one.

Teaching struggling writers to use writing rubrics can be very effective in helping them internalize guidelines for good writing. Check to see what the publisher of your language arts or writing program offers. Find and use rubrics sanctioned by your district; go online to find free rubrics (see "References and Resources"). Be aware that complex rubrics can overwhelm emerging writers. The best approach is to use just one category at a time until some fluency is achieved. As other categories are added, students are expected to maintain the progress they have made in previous categories. For more information on assessment, see Chapter 12.

How to Handle Penmanship and Handwriting

All kids who can write should be taught printing and cursive writing when they are developmentally ready, not at any specific arbitrary age. They should then be allowed to develop and use the writing style that is easiest and most legible for them—even if it is a combination style.

What can we do about the horrible handwriting of some of our struggling students? We can celebrate the fact that technologies are available to help them become legible writers! For kids whose LD makes writing nearly impossible, consult your district's technology expert to discover how to make the appropriate technology available. Sometimes, if technology assistance is written into a student's Individual Education Plan (IEP), special education funding will pay for it.

As in grammar, spelling, or mathematics, it is never okay to postpone children's interaction with meaningful writing while we wait for them to develop better handwriting skills.

Writing Portfolio Record Sheet

FOR: _____
(student's name)

Target Skill	Date Begun	Date Mastered	Comments

How to Teach Letter Formation

You can use this procedure to teach both manuscript and cursive writing.

1. Model writing the letter as you think out loud the sequence of the strokes. *Example:* "To form the small letter 'a,' I put my pencil where the 1:00 would be, draw a circle moving counterclockwise toward 12:00 and all around the clock, and come back to 1:00. Without lifting my pencil, I draw back down the right side of the circle until I get to 5:00 and then make a little tail off to the right."

2. Have the student put his hand over yours as you write the letter several times and think aloud the strokes.

3. Have the student trace over the letter you make, thinking aloud the strokes. (Some students find sandpaper letters or other types of raised letters especially helpful for this step. Some kids love to have letters and words written on their backs with other kids' fingers, toothbrushes, etc.) For variety, have the student form the letter in the air, using large, exaggerated motions. If you have a pointer that shows a beam of light, let students use that as well.

4. Have the student copy the letter several times, thinking aloud the strokes.

5. Have the student close his eyes and visualize the letter in colored lights, looking up and to the left.

6. Have the student write the letter without copying it, thinking aloud the strokes and checking for accuracy.

7. Have the student practice writing the letter several times, whispering the sequence of the strokes. By now, the student should be able to write from memory.

When teaching blended letters, have the student practice writing them in real words.

Finally: Please remember that there is no life situation at which one can fail if one can't read or write cursive! All important forms ask for printing. So legibility and fluency should be the goal, but the style belongs to the student.

More Tips for Teaching Handwriting

Handwriting is more likely to improve with practice in actual writing than with exercises. However, if you are expected to teach handwriting as a separate subject, you should find the following tips helpful.

- Make sure that students' papers are properly positioned. Left-handed students should tilt their paper almost 15 degrees to the right so they can hold their pencils without hooking their hand to write straight.

- Teach all written symbols (letters, numbers) using the same sequence of strokes each time. Model the correct method often—on the board, an overhead, with large movements in the air.

- The Italic Handwriting Series has been successful for some students with handwriting difficulties. The letters have no loops and fewer flourishes, so the transition from manuscript to cursive is greatly simplified. Legibility and writing fluency are greatly improved. See "References and Resources."

- In *Making the Words Stand Still,* Donald Lyman includes a precise written alphabet. He suggests having students practice letters in the following families together: straight-line letters; straight and slanted letters; circle letters; circle-and-straight-line combinations; circle-and-curve combinations. See "References and Resources."

- Teach and use cursive writing as early as your students can handle it, since cursive writing improves the flow of learning. Some students with learning difficulties can actually be *more* fluent with cursive writing because its connectedness increases the fluency of thought.

- Have kids practice their handwriting by tracing raised letters, then filling in dotted-line versions. If students have trouble feeling the way letters are formed, have them work in various media: salt, sand, shaving cream, finger paint. They can also practice writing letters on each other's backs or in the air with large arm movements, using the arm of their writing hand.

- If spacing between words is a problem, have students place dice, other small objects, or one or two fingers between words to get an idea of the right amount of space to leave.

Questions and Answers

"Won't kids be unable to write in real-world situations if they always use the crutches described in this chapter?"

Students who develop a positive attitude about their writing ability may eventually learn to write in more traditional ways. Those who never develop this attitude will always have problems with writing. Your goal should be to help your students perceive themselves as capable writers, using whatever methods are available to you.

I am aware of no standardized test on which students are not allowed to draw some type of graphic before they start writing. If visual learners need graphic assistance for their entire life, it's better for them to learn such crutches than to grow up believing there is only one correct way to write—a way they can't master.

There are numerous colleges and universities that provide assistance to students with learning difficulties. Our job is getting our students to want to continue their education. We should use any tool within our reach to make that happen.

"My students with LD resist journal writing. What can I do to help them?"

Try using the Goal Setting strategy described on pages 65–68. This will give your students a sense of control over how much and what they write.

In my opinion, teachers often overdo journal writing. Some students are asked to journal for most or all of their subjects on a given day. I wonder how adults would feel if someone asked us to reflect in writing about every aspect of our daily lives! Give your students with learning difficulties choices about how often they will have to write in journals.

REFERENCES AND RESOURCES

See also the "References and Resources" for chapters 6 and 7.

Atwell, Nancie. *In the Middle: Writing, Reading, and Learning with Adolescents.* Portsmouth, NH: Heinemann, 1987.

—*In the Middle: New Understanding About Writing, Reading, and Learning.* 2nd Edition. Portsmouth, NH: Boynton/Cook, 1998. Atwell reflects on her ten years' of teaching experience since writing the first edition of *In the Middle.*

Bellamy, Peter C., ed. *Seeing with New Eyes: Using the 6+1 Trait Writing Model.* 6th Edition. Portland, OR: Northwest Regional Educational Laboratory, 2005. Based on NWREL's 6+1 Trait Writing Model, this guidebook helps teachers use the traits of good writing as a framework for instruction and scoring of prewriters as well as competent ones. While the main audience is teachers of grades K–2, the model can also be used effectively with older students in special education and limited English language proficiency classes. Available from www.nwrel.org. 1-800-547-6339.

Calkins, Lucy McCormick. *The Art of Teaching Writing.* New Edition. Portsmouth, NH: Heinemann, 1994. The latest edition of Calkin's celebrated book on teaching writing to elementary students.

Cunningham, Patricia, and Richard Allington. *Classrooms That Work: They Can All Read and Write.* 3rd edition. Boston, MA: Allyn & Bacon, 2003. Integrates phonics and literature-based process writing and reading instruction for a balanced approach to literacy.

Dahlstrom, Lorraine M., M.A. *Doing the Days: A Year's Worth of Creative Journaling, Drawing, Listening, Reading, Thinking, Arts & Crafts Activities for Children Ages 8–12.* Minneapolis: Free Spirit Publishing, 1994. Includes 366 journaling activities for beginning writers, plus 1,000 more related activities, many hands-on.

—*Writing Down the Days: 365 Creative Journaling Ideas for Young People.* Revised and updated edition. Minneapolis: Free Spirit Publishing, 2000. A year's worth of writing topics linked to the calendar year.

Daily Oral Language (DOL) (www.greatsource.com). The teacher's manual for this program contains a year's worth of sentences (two per day) with errors in them. When using DOL, I write each day's sentences on the board, and students confer with their buddies to decide where the errors are. I use the Name Card method (pages 14–17) to call on students to come to the board to fix one error. The group responds "thumbs up" or "thumbs down" to indicate their agreement or disagreement with the solution. If most disagree, I ask someone else to suggest a change. The class then votes on the changed version. Some teachers use anonymous sentences from student writing as the samples. Please remember that this is called Daily *Oral* Language. Many teachers have turned this into a writing assignment, which I believe defeats its potential for appealing to global learners. 1-800-289-4490.

Graves, Donald H. *Writing: Teachers & Children at Work.* 20th Anniversary Edition. Portsmouth, NH: Heinemann, 2003. Many people feel that this book revolutionized writing instruction.

Heiden, Corlene. *Writing Right.* Carbondale, IL: Blue Ribbon Press, 1993.

Inspiration Software (www.inspiration.com). Inspiration (for older students) and Kidspiration (for younger kids) create graphic organizers from text students enter so they can see what they are thinking. The programs then help students transfer information from the graphic organizers to written documents. 1-800-877-4292.

Italic Handwriting Series by Barbara Getty and Inga Dubay. Portland, OR: Portland State University Continuing Education Press. A comprehensive handwriting program for grades K–6. Available from Allport Editions (allport.com).

Keyboarding programs for writers with learning difficulties:

- SpongeBob SquarePants Typing (www.Broderbund. com). Ages 7 and up. A wet and wacky romp through the world of keyboarding that both kids and adults will enjoy. Features multiple levels of challenges and two modes of play. 1-800-395-0277.

- Type It (www.epsbooks.com). Grades K–12. Linguistically oriented touch-typing system for beginners. 1-800-225-5750.

- Type to Learn and Type to Learn Jr. (www.smart kidssoftware.com). Grades 1–6. Comprehensive keyboarding course. 1-888-881-6001.

- UltraKey 5.0 (www.bytesoflearning.com). All ages. Teaches touch-typing and safe keyboarding using voice, animation, video, and virtual reality. Provides options that adapt to a broad range of age groups and special needs. 1-800-465-6428.

Lyman, Donald E. *Making the Words Stand Still.* Boston: Houghton Mifflin, 1986. Writing from his own experience, Lyman describes the anguish that kids with LD feel as they try to learn, then describes his own unique teaching methods.

Merit Software (www.meritsoftware.com). This educational software company sells products for home and school use including Grammar Fitness, Write It Right, ESL Fitness, and Vocabulary Fitness. 1-800-753-6488. Merit also maintains several interactive Web sites where students can learn basic writing skills for free. They are:

- www.englishgrammarconnection.com. Online lessons help improve students' English grammar skills.

- www.essaypunch.com. Takes users through the actual steps of writing a basic essay.

- www.paragraphpunch.com. Takes users through the actual steps of writing a basic paragraph.

Morsink, Catherine Voelker. *Teaching Special Needs Students in Regular Classrooms.* Boston: Little, Brown and Co., 1984.

Murray, Donald M. *Learning by Teaching: Selected Articles on Writing and Teaching.* Montclair, NJ: Boynton/Cook, 1982. Writing and teaching from the perspective of a working writer and teacher who is one of the pioneers of a process approach to teaching writing.

Rico, Gabrielle Lusser. Writing the *Natural Way: Using Right-Brain Techniques to Release Your Expressive Powers.* Revised edition. New York: Tarcher/Putnam, 2000. Demonstrates a visual technique to increase fluency for writers and turn the task of writing into the joy of writing. Revised edition is newly illustrated and includes updated, field-tested exercises.

Rubistar (rubistar.4teachers.org). A terrific free tool for teachers who want to use rubrics but don't have the time to develop them from scratch. The site is also available in Spanish; click the Rubistar en Español window. A project of the High Plains Regional Technology in Educational Consortium (HPR*TEC), one of ten RTECS funded by the Department of Education.

6+1 Trait Writing (educationnorthwest.org/traits). The Northwest Regional Educational Laboratory's (NWREL's) unique approach to presenting the Six-Trait Writing model and training teachers in its use. Teachers and students can use this framework to pinpoint areas of strength and weakness as they continue to focus on improved writing. (503) 275-9572.

Reading and Learning in the Content Areas

The content areas that extend the curriculum beyond reading, writing, and math present special problems to struggling learners, who usually have a negative attitude about the difficult reading they encounter in literature, science, health, social studies, and other curricular areas. Some students actually have a physiological response to any phrase that includes the word *read:* Their stress level rises, and their defense mechanisms are activated. I try to substitute synonyms whenever possible, such as skim, scan, find, locate, etc.

If you think you're not a reading teacher, think again! When a student has trouble with a particular subject, part of the problem is related to poor reading skills. So we are *all* reading teachers, since we *all* need to know how to help kids read and understand specific content. Although it is almost certain that rapid advances in technology will one day allow people to receive information from a variety of sources that don't require reading, today's students must be able to use textbooks and lectures effectively, and that is what we must teach them.

To help students with learning difficulties become more successful in the content areas, we can get them hooked by allowing them to choose a topic that already interests them or seems likely to interest them. We can teach them to approach all content-area reading with the question, "How can I transform these words into pictures so I can remember the information visually?" We can enable them to use their learning style strengths as they obtain and share information. We can give them ways to gather, identify, and organize the *maximum* amount of information with the *minimum* amount of reading. (Remember,

if they're not learning the way we teach them, let's teach them the way they learn!)

This chapter focuses on the explicit teaching of strategies for reading and studying in the content areas. As you try them with your students, keep in mind the acronym WHOLISTIC (see page 57) to be sure you are incorporating as many strategies as possible that are user-friendly to global learners. If these strategies seem like a lot of work that would take up too much time, please don't be discouraged. Once your students know how to learn, you'll save time later on. Use as much time as necessary to help students learn these strategies so they can use them independently. Since you will be teaching the strategies in the context of the required standards, no learning time will actually be lost.

Scenario: Elizabeth

By the time she reached the tenth grade, Elizabeth had lost faith that she would ever be successful in school, and she was seriously considering dropping out. Her failure was not from lack of trying. She went to school nearly every day, carried an assignment notebook which she dutifully filled out before leaving each class, brought home books from every subject every night, and spent 30 minutes per class per night on homework. Neither she nor her frustrated parents could understand why she kept getting low grades.

Elizabeth usually spent most of her homework time taking copious notes from her state-owned textbooks, which she was not allowed to write in. She filled several spiral notebooks, copying her textbooks almost word-for-word.

To prepare for a test, she copied the notebook for that subject. Because she was unable to distinguish between important and unimportant information, she just wrote everything down, copied it over, and hoped for the best.

During the second semester, Elizabeth's physical science teacher demonstrated some visually oriented ways to take notes and showed the class how to create and use graphic organizers. One day Elizabeth came home excited after an unusually successful experience in school. The class had watched a film, and everyone had been encouraged to take notes in a learning-style compatible manner. Elizabeth had chosen a simple mapping technique, and she was going to use her notes to study for the next day's quiz. As she told her parents, "I now realize I'm a visual learner. When I take notes and study in the way that matches my learning style, I can actually understand the material! For the first time in my life, I feel really prepared for a test." Then she added, "Maybe these methods will make me smarter in my other classes, too."

Getting Ready to Learn

How many learning-how-to-learn strategies do your students know? On page 136, you'll find a chart you can copy and use to track their progress. Use the "Not Yet" column to identify strategies they need to learn, "Learning Now" to indicate strategies you're currently teaching, and "Knows How" for strategies they have mastered. Enter dates to mark their progress over time; update the charts as students acquire new strategies. Older students can keep their own records.

This form can be adapted to keep track of the study and organizational skills described in Chapter 11.

Simple Mapping

Scenario: Simple Mapping in Action

On a day when I was demonstrating model lessons in a middle school, I visited a class of 12 students whose learning disabilities were significant enough to warrant their placement in a self-contained special education class. Their frustrated teacher greeted me by saying, "I sure am glad to see you! We've been working on outlining for our last six meetings and the kids still don't get it! How can you help?"

I had two immediate but unspoken reactions to her question. First, I knew that most of her students were probably global learners. Outlining is something only analytical thinkers are comfortable with. Second, I wondered why she was wasting so much valuable teaching time on an obsolete skill. Outlining is not something most of us need to do in our everyday lives; organizing information is.

It took only 15 minutes for those kids to learn how to organize information in a brain-compatible way.

The students were using a duplicated exercise: three paragraphs describing three types of bats (the mammal kind). Their job was to identify each type with a Roman numeral, find three details about each type, and list the details as A, B, and C under each numeral.

I placed each student with a partner and asked them to quickly skim (not read) the paragraphs to identify one type of bat. Calling on one student at random, I asked him to respond. Predictably, he identified the vampire bat.

The teacher signaled me from her desk. "The vampire bat is the one described in the *second* paragraph," she whispered, "and I expect students to identify them in their proper order."

"Don't worry," I whispered back. "It will all work out in the end."

Using colored markers, I drew a red circle and wrote "Vampire Bat" in the center. Next, I asked the partners to *skim* the appropriate paragraph to find two to three details about vampire bats. I cautioned them to find at least that many, because I would call on them at random until several details were mentioned. I told them they would have 60 seconds, and that gave their sharing a sense of urgency which kept them nicely on task the entire time. When the time was up, I called on several students at random and charted their responses as spokes on the red circle.

We repeated this process for the next two bats, using a blue triangle for the fruit bat and a green square for the flying fox. (You've probably guessed that the reason for using different colors and shapes is so the information will make a lasting impression on the kids' brains.)

Next, I said, "Now, what your teacher wants you to do is organize this information the way the ancient Romans did! So look at the first paragraph and identify the bat. Since it's the fruit bat, we'll print a Roman numeral I in the blue triangle for the fruit bat. Next, let's identify the first fact and label it with a capital A. The second fact is B, and so on."

We repeated the same steps until we had a picture of the details for all three bats. (See page 137 for how it looked.) Finally, we transferred the information to the correct blank spaces in the outline form at the bottom of the exercise page, and our global learners were on their way to learning how to outline in a learning-style compatible manner—backwards from the whole to the parts!

By now, the kids had caught on that outlining was easy if they were allowed to do it in a way that was comfortable for them—visually and holistically. Next, someone asked a shocking question: "Could we please do another one?" Their teacher, shaking her head in disbelief, quickly passed out another example. Working on their own, it took most pairs only 12 minutes to complete the second outline in the same manner as the first.

LEARNING HOW TO LEARN

STUDENT'S NAME: _____

Strategy	Not Yet	Learning Now	Knows How
Previewing content before reading or studying			
Using survey techniques such as noticing pictures, graphs, italics, etc.			
Reading chapter questions before reading the text			
Predicting important information			
Taking notes in learning-style compatible manner			
Summarizing what was learned			
Understanding and remembering vocabulary			
Remembering what was learned			
Using various forms of reference materials			
Transferring learning to other situations			
Working and learning independently			
Asking for help when needed			

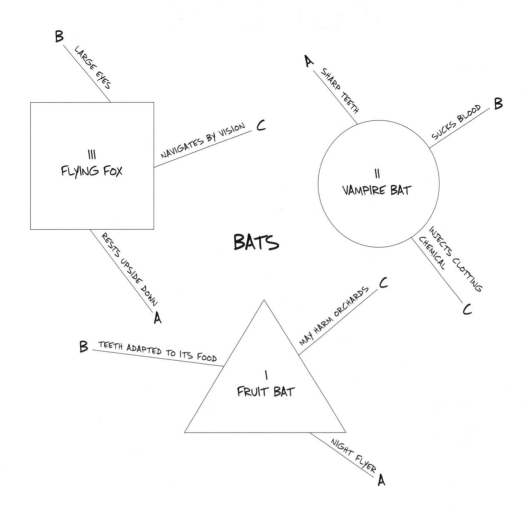

Using Simple Mapping

Mapping is the use of visual aids to facilitate learning. A simple map is a visual organizer. A visual organizer is any learning tool that allows students to visualize information. Graphic organizers, mind maps, flowcharts, timelines, diagrams, cartoons, pictures, Venn diagrams—all are visual organizers. They enable global learners to *skim* written text for indicators that important information is present, *skim* a particular section for the necessary information, and record that information in a visual way, creating a mental picture of what they need to learn. They can glean a lot of information with a minimal amount of actual reading, which they greatly appreciate. Recall that global learners must see the big picture before focusing on any of the parts.

1. As you lecture or talk, draw what you are saying onto a simple picture format. Use as many shapes and colors as you can, and think out loud (see "Metacognition," page 68) as you draw. In this way, students will be able to repeat the process you are modeling.

2. Demonstrate how to summarize information into short phrases as spokes attached to a shape. Never write complete sentences, as that will encourage students to copy word-for-word what they read.

3. Show students how to use these maps not only to illustrate important information, but also as study guides to help them remember what they have learned.

4. Give students experience in using simple mapping with many types of information sources—books, videos, DVDs, etc. Once global learners develop their own personalized version, they will become more confident about taking notes from a wide variety of sources.

Even if some students are already using other note-taking methods successfully, encourage them to try this method once or twice. Give them the "Simple Mapping" handout on page 138. Explain that once they know how to do simple mapping, they will have it in their toolbox if they ever need another way to learn especially difficult information. All students should be allowed to use whatever methods lead to the best possible learning outcomes.

Vocabulary Mapping

The Vocabulary Attributes Chart is a visual organizer for vocabulary. Described in detail on pages 113–115 in the context of building reading vocabulary, it's equally effective for teaching vocabulary in any of the content areas.

Simple Mapping

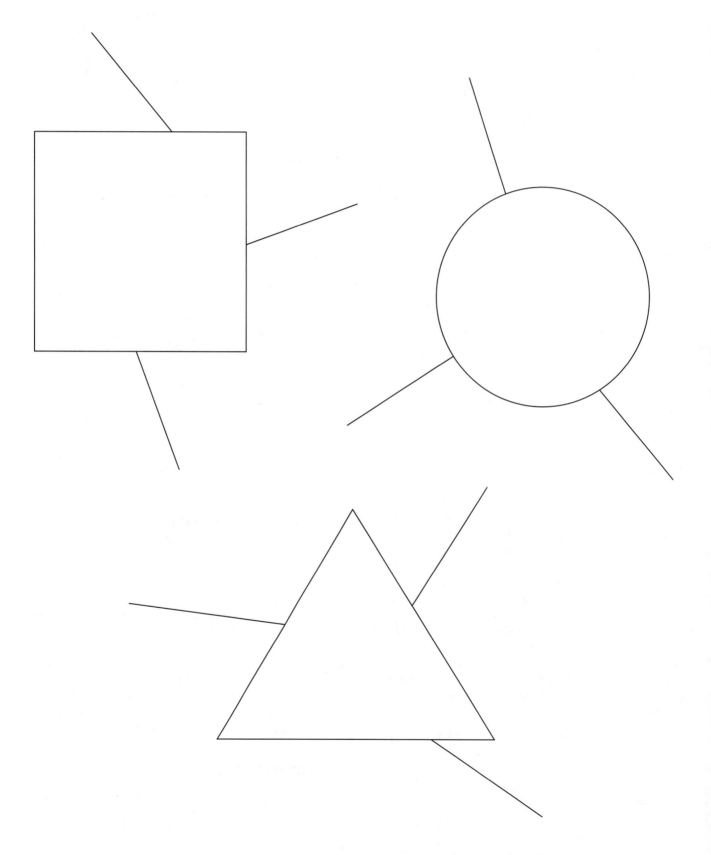

In one sixth-grade class, the teacher was trying to teach the vocabulary of ancient Rome. He was very frustrated because the kids could *write* the definitions but couldn't *remember* what the words meant. We categorized the words into several groups (*example:* "words describing jobs in the Roman culture"). Then we created a Vocabulary Attributes Chart for each group. The chart for the job of senator looked like this:*

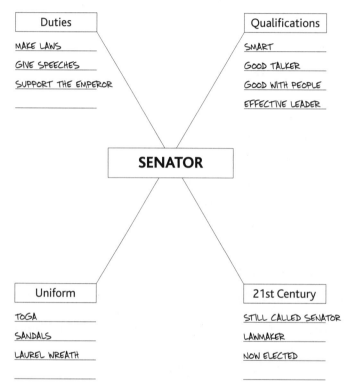

Duties
MAKE LAWS
GIVE SPEECHES
SUPPORT THE EMPEROR

Qualifications
SMART
GOOD TALKER
GOOD WITH PEOPLE
EFFECTIVE LEADER

SENATOR

Uniform
TOGA
SANDALS
LAUREL WREATH

21st Century
STILL CALLED SENATOR
LAWMAKER
NOW ELECTED

Understanding Material from Texts and Lectures

Many teachers don't realize that students need successful reading strategies in order to get meaning from text, lecture, or discussion material in the content areas of social studies, science, nonfiction material, and/or thematic units. The strategies that work best are somewhat similar to and somewhat different from the strategies used to get meaning from literature. Teach students to use these strategies metacognitively. See pages 68–69. It's very helpful when they think out loud the process they are using to understand what they need to learn.

1. **Before reading:** Students must activate prior knowledge so they can make connections between what they already know and the new material about to be learned. Have students:

- Brainstorm what they already know about the topic. (See "KWPL" on pages 95–97.)

- Describe and discuss the purpose for learning the material.

- Survey the entire chapter, noticing important features such as pictures, maps, charts, diagrams, italics, and bold print. Make predictions along the way. (Use the "Predictions" handout on page 94.)

- Read the questions at the end of each section before reading the section. This alerts the brain to what's important to notice while reading.

- Read and pronounce the vocabulary words. Students should wait to learn or study words they don't know until they have read or heard the content. *Caution:* Writing dictionary definitions has been found to be completely ineffective in helping kids remember vocabulary words. It's much more effective to discuss the words in the context of the text and have kids write about the vocabulary in their own words. Graphic organizers such as the Vocabulary Attributes Chart on page 114 are a big help to visual learners.

- Locate places and events on a map.

- Watch a DVD, video, or other visual representation of the material about to be learned. This helps visual learners connect new information to the pictures now stored in their memory.

2. **During reading:** Students must make sure they understand what they are reading or hearing. Anything they don't understand must be clarified. Have students:

- Notice headings and other features (pictures, maps, charts, diagrams, italics, bold print) that identify important information.

- Get as much information as they can by skimming. (See "Skimming and Summarizing Written Material" on page 140.)

- Look away after a section is finished and say out loud, or write a summary of, what has been read or heard. (This may be done with a learning partner.)

- Use graphic organizers such as the Content Organization Chart (page 141) or the "3S TN (Qs)" handout (page 144).

- Learn to ask questions about the text. (See "Reciprocal Teaching" on pages 102–103 and the "Question Starters" handout on page 92.)

- Check out earlier predictions. (Use the "Predictions" handout on page 94 or the P column in KWPL; see pages 95–97.)

- Summarize often what they are learning. (Use graphic organizers for this, such as the fishbone on page 101.)

* Adapted from *New Directions in Vocabulary* by Barbara Abromitis. Carbondale, IL: Blue Ribbon Press, 1992. Used with permission.

3. **After reading:** Students must be able to demonstrate their understanding of the text by answering the questions they surveyed in the before reading step. They should also be able to connect information from several sections of text throughout the section or chapter. Have students:

- Confirm or refute original predictions.

- Summarize the major ideas in the whole piece by outlining, using a graphic organizer, or simply drawing what they want to remember.

- Think about how this section is connected to what they have learned before.

- Go back to their notes and combine the information there to describe five big ideas to remember from the entire section.

Skimming and Summarizing Written Material

Have students:

- Notice and read the heading for any new section.

- Locate and read all questions that will have to be answered for that section.

- Skim the first and last paragraphs of a section.

- For other paragraphs in the section, read the first and last sentences and any key words that are italicized or highlighted in some way. Locate the information for the italicized terms. Illustrate one or two key points using a graphic organizer.

- Write down the answer to a required question as soon as they recognize it.

- To summarize a section, combine the key points from all paragraphs into one or two statements.

- Write an introduction and conclusion for the summary.

Reciprocal Teaching (see pages 102–103) is another strategy that can strengthen students' reading comprehension in the content areas. Try it as a way to improve understanding of material from texts and lectures.

The Content Organization Chart

Global students need a way to organize their thinking as they are taught new content. For the brain to learn new information, it must first be able to connect it to what it already knows. Because the brain is a pattern-seeking device, we need to teach in patterns.

The Content Organization Chart (page 141) is slightly different from simple graphic organizers because once the categories are in the visual forms, they remain the same for all other examples within that subject area. The chart lends itself to any subject area at any grade level. *Examples:*

- the seasons

- the systems of the human body

- plants of a certain category

- the elements in a story or novel

- processes in mathematical equations

- the steps in a scientific experiment

- communities

- types of energy

- regions of the world

- types of government systems

- famous people from any category

- animals of a certain category

- artists of a certain style

- composers of a certain type of music

- the planets of the solar system

- the people of any country

- the states or provinces of any country.

P.S. You're right—the Content Organization Chart looks exactly like the story map and character map in Chapter 6! This basic format can be used for many different purposes.

Using the Content Organization Chart

The step-by-step description that follows illustrates how you might use the chart to teach a unit on regions of the world for which a single textbook serves as a primary information source. Once you have walked your students through this process, you can easily adapt it for use with many texts at a time and also with lectures, CD-ROMs, videos, or any other information sources.

1. Prepare a large wall chart version of the Content Organization Chart on page 141, drawing each geometric shape in a different color.

2. Group students in discussion buddy pairs. Give each student a personal copy of the Content Organization Chart. Explain that you will be using the wall chart to model what they should write on their handouts.

3. Tell students that they will be learning about their own world region. (*Example:* If your school is in Wyoming, they will learn about the Great Plains.) Print the name in the center square of the wall chart. Students should write it on their charts, too.

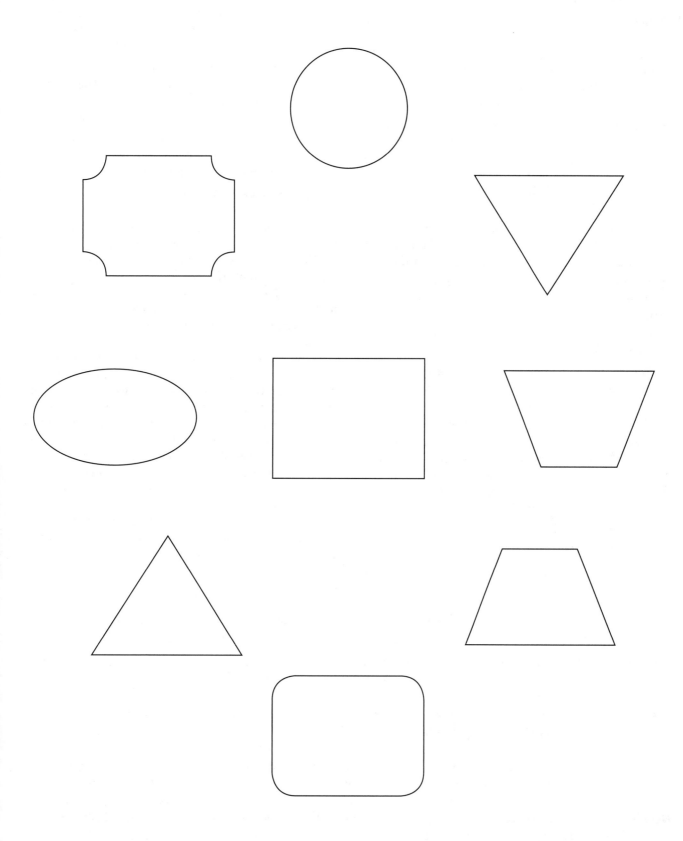

4. Instruct students to open their textbooks to the Table of Contents and locate the chapter on the selected region.

5. Have the students survey the chapter by browsing through it, noticing how the text is organized and asking each other questions about the pictures, charts, and other features. They don't have to answer the questions they ask. They should also read any questions that are listed in the chapter.

6. Tell them to turn back to the chapter beginning. Ask them to study the first page and notice the way(s) the text signals the presence of important categories of information. Print the name of the first category (*example:* "Location") in the circle at the top of the wall chart.

7. Direct students to skim the "Location" section in the text, and to print or write three facts about that category on their charts. They should record the facts on spokes they draw attached to each figure on the chart.

8. Use the Name Card method (pages 114–117) to call on students until you have four to six details about "Location." Write them on the wall chart. Direct the students to add any details to their own charts that they don't already have written there.

9. Call students' attention to the way the text signals the next category of information. Print the name of the category in the next shape on the wall chart, working clockwise; students also add it to their charts.

10. Repeat steps 7 and 8 for the new category. Proceed in the same way until all of the categories have been charted. Call students' attention to the fact that they now have a completed Content Organization Chart they can use to prepare for any discussion or test on that particular world region.

11. For the next region, hand out new copies of the Content Organization Chart. You'll also need a fresh wall chart. Now choose a world region *as different as possible* from the area where the students live. Print the name in the center square of the chart. Tell the students that textbooks present information in very similar ways—from chapter to chapter, and from subject to subject.

12. Using the Name Card method, call on one student to *predict* a category of information that will be described for the new region. Write it on the wall chart—*in the same shape you used for that category on the first chart.*

13. Direct students to turn to the index in their textbooks, find the page that describes the predicted category, and chart the details for that category.

14. Repeat steps 8–10 for the new region.

By the third region, many of the discussion buddies will be ready to complete their own charts by using the textbook and/or other sources independently. Continue working with pairs that still need your assistance. Consistently point out that the same categories should always appear in the same places on the chart. *Example:* If "Location" was the top circle in the first chart, it should be the top circle in all charts.

Tips: Always have plenty of copies of the Content Organization Chart on hand. Once students realize the many benefits of this process, they will want to use it often. When you give a test, hand out blank copies of the chart and tell students to fill them in with as many details as they can remember before starting the test. Since they will already have a visual image in their brain of a completed chart, they should be able to recall much more information about the topic than if they had used traditional note-taking methods.

Variation: Older students might prefer using a chart without geometric shapes. Below is an example of a chart for studying the systems of the human body.

Body System	Organs	Functions	Diseases	Caring For
Circulatory	Heart, arteries, veins	Pump blood to and from the heart	High blood pressure; blockages	Weight control; exercise; no smoking
Respiratory	Nose, lungs, bronchia, diaphragm	Deliver oxygen to blood; breathing	Cancer; emphysema	Same as above
Digestive	Stomach, liver, gall bladder, intestines	Intake food; deliver nutrients to cells; eliminate waste	Ulcer; bile disease; cancer	Low-fat foods; low dairy; lots of water
Nervous	Brain, spinal column, nerves	Intellectual; controls other organs	Cancer; stroke	Avoid falls; lifelong learning

3S TN (Qs): Note-Taking for Global Learners

Older students who need a visual way to take notes from books, videos, and lectures will benefit from this technique, which combines elements from several other strategies you may recognize. The beauty of 3S TN (Qs) is that the note-taking method *becomes* the study guide at the same time it is being used to prepare for a test or discussion. Any discussion can benefit from students taking notes ahead of time.

In the acronym 3S TN (Qs), S stands for Survey, Skim, and Study; TN stands for Take Notes; and (Qs) stands for Questions.

1. Group students in discussion buddy pairs. Give each student a "3S TN (Qs)" handout (page 144).

2. Help students learn to **S**urvey the chapter or unit (in textbooks, on CD-ROM, on videos or DVDs, etc.; the format of the material doesn't matter). For every feature they notice, they should ask themselves a **Q**uestion. They don't have to answer the questions. Eventually, student pairs should be able to do this step independently, and should be allowed to add or change the information on their charts to match the information on the chart you are creating from students' responses. You chart can be an overhead transparency or a wall chart that will remain visible to students during the entire unit.

3. Have students work with their discussion buddies to **S**kim a section and answer this **Q**uestion: "What's the *most* important idea the section describes?" They should write their answer in the left-hand column of the chart, under "Topic." If students need help finding the main idea, have them use the fishbone graphic on page 101.

4. Instruct students to write several details about the topic in the right-hand column of the chart, using brief phrases (not complete sentences).

5. Use the Name Card method (pages 14–17) to call on kids for their topics and explanations. Invite several pairs to share. Assure the students that as long as they have the general gist of the idea, they don't need to use the exact words anyone else uses.

6. Continue in the same manner until students have taken a full page of notes.

The Two-Column Strategy for Studying

To use the "3S TN (Qs)" chart as a study guide, students should follow this procedure:

1. Cover each column with a sheet of paper.

2. Partner A uncovers the first topic and predicts the details that have been recorded about it.

3. Both partners check to see if the prediction is correct. If it is, they switch roles, and Partner B uncovers the second topic and predicts its details. If the prediction is incorrect, Partner A tries again.

4. When all of the topics have been discussed, the partners repeat the process, this time uncovering the details first and predicting the topic.

In this way, students learn the information from both perspectives: topic and details.

Be prepared to model "3S TN (Qs)" several times with students who have difficulty choosing the right topics and coming up with descriptions.

Variation: Create a new handout, labeling the left-hand column "Question" and the right-hand column "Explanation." Students take notes in the "Explanation" column for one segment of information at a time, then look back over their notes and create a question for each major point. They study those notes in the same way as described in steps 1–4 above.

Questions and Answers

"Won't all of this drawing and mapping slow students down so much that they won't be able to complete their assignments?"

Think of all the time kids waste when they don't know how to learn. It takes forever for them to find their books, paper, and pencils. Then they have to locate the right place to begin, after which they usually ask numerous questions of you and their classmates. As the use of graphic organizers becomes more automatic, your students may need less time to complete their learning tasks.

"How is the Content Organization Chart different from plain mapping or other graphic organizers?"

Many graphic organizers or maps simply create a visual representation of printed text. The Content Organization Chart (pages 140–142) is designed to illustrate the similarities between various chapters or units. When students see and understand those similarities, they begin to anticipate them for upcoming content. Over time, they understand the importance of connecting new knowledge to what has been learned in the past.

"Shouldn't I teach vocabulary words in the same order as they appear in the written material?"

You may teach them as they are introduced and used in the text, but keep in mind that students with learning difficulties cannot learn more than a few words at a time. That

3S TN (Qs)

You can use this form to help you take notes and study the information for discussions and assessments.

- **S**urvey an entire selection to get the big picture. Ask **Q**uestions as you survey. You don't have to write the answers. Just think about them and tell them to your partner.

- **S**kim a small section of text at a time. Ask **Q**uestions as you skim to be sure you are noticing the most important information.

- When you find something you want to remember, **T**ake **N**otes in phrases. Constantly ask yourself **Q**uestions to make sure the information is important.

- **S**tudy your notes using the two-column strategy. Ask **Q**uestions and answer them verbally.

TOPIC	DETAILS

means you'll have to wait until later to teach some of the words. If you teach words by categories using the Vocabulary Attributes Chart (pages 113–115), you'll be able to teach some words from the present context as well as other words with similar attributes from other contexts.

"Won't there be some occasions when students will have to read an entire text rather than selectively skimming and mapping or charting?"

If and when that time comes, students can still use visual organizers to make the text material easier to learn and understand. It's likely that students will eventually have many study methods at their disposal besides traditional reading and note-taking. Always remember that students will succeed at real world tasks only if they perceive themselves as capable learners. Use whatever means you can to actualize their positive perceptions. The more successful students are with skimming methods, the more likely it is that they will develop and maintain more positive attitudes about reading in general.

A high school English teacher in Midlothian, Illinois, devoted much time and effort during the school year teaching her students how to create visual mind maps of what they wanted to write before they actually started writing. She demonstrated how this strategy would enable them to be fluent in the idea-generation stage and more focused when they actually began to write. While supervising a written college entrance exam for some of her students, she was gratified to see that several of the kids were using the mapping strategy to plan the paragraph they had to write. The teacher knew then that she had taught them a skill they could use to survive in writing tasks even when she would not be there to coach them.

Any support techniques that your students with learning difficulties can learn from you will make them more confident adults and more capable students in post-high school learning situations.

REFERENCES AND RESOURCES

Abromitis, Barbara. *New Directions in Vocabulary.* Carbondale, IL: Blue Ribbon Press, 1992.

Parks, Sandra, and Howard Black. *Organizing Thinking: Book 1.* Grades 2–4. Pacific Grove, CA: Critical Thinking Press and Software, 1992. Students learn how to analyze and use information more effectively and create their own organizers to improve comprehension and retention in any subject. —*Organizing Thinking: Book 2.* Grades 5–8. Pacific Grove, CA: Critical Thinking Press and Software, 1990.

Thinking Maps (www.thinkingmaps.com). Visual teaching tools that foster and encourage lifelong learning. The maps provide a common visual language for learning within and across disciplines. 1-800-243-9169.

Vacca, Richard T., and JoAnne L. Vacca. *Content Area Reading: Literacy and Learning Across the Curriculum.* 8th edition. Boston, MA: Allyn & Bacon, 2004. Reading, writing, speaking, and listening processes to help students learn subject matter across the curriculum. This respected text is designed to be an active learning tool, complete with real-world examples and research-based practices, and has been updated to incorporate topics related to contemporary issues such as content standards, assessments, No Child Left Behind, and Reading First.

Improving Students' Success in Math

For all the years I've been in education, the math pendulum has swung back and forth between emphasis on computation and emphasis on problem-solving. Of course, the most effective programs have a healthy combination of both. With struggling learners, we must make sure they can keep up with grade-level standards even while they are still learning the basics at an automatic recall level. Otherwise, they will find themselves so far behind expected standards that they may never catch up. Most 21st-century jobs require excellent mathematical skills, which makes math literacy as essential as any other literacy requirement.

The language of mathematics is just as symbolic as the language of reading, and we know that students with learning difficulties have a hard time with symbolic language. In general, struggling students exhibit some, many, or all of the following characteristics when it comes to math:

- They have difficulty seeing and hearing numbers correctly. Reversals and substitutions are common. For some kids, the numbers seem to move on the page.

- They may be able to recite numbers fairly well, but they lack intuitive understanding about numbers and what they represent. They have very little number sense.

- They fail to perceive patterns and relationships (*examples*: quantities represented by numerals; coin sizes and values; which signs represent which operations).

- Forming the numerals takes so much energy that there is none left for figuring out solutions. They misread and miswrite, have trouble counting, and

can't stay within the lines. Motor problems make their papers sloppy and inaccurate. They mix up columns and digits. It's hard for them to keep their place on a page; this is made worse if work must be copied from the board. They lose manipulatives.

- They have difficulty remembering number facts or vocabulary, problem-solving procedures, or previously learned material. Rapid-fire mental math is painful or impossible for them.

- Word problems are particularly daunting since they include *three* layers of symbols: numbers, words, and operations. Students lose their train of thought in the problem-solving process.

- They are confused by new math problems that include multiple concepts on each page of the textbook.

- They do the same problem over and over or use only one problem-solving method repeatedly (this is called *perseveration*).

- They can't ignore distractions like the sound coming from a group of students working with the teacher.

Many children develop an intuitive understanding of mathematical concepts during their preschool years. As they observe their world, they learn to understand numerals and the quantities they represent, how to divide things up fairly, and the appropriate clock times for going to bed, getting up, and eating meals. Since the brain seeks patterns, effective teaching in math focuses on demonstrating the presence of patterns and helping children connect new ideas to those they already understand. Since global learners must see the whole picture before understanding the parts, teaching them effectively requires moving from concrete, hands-on learning to the abstract applications of computation and other step-by-step procedures.

Students should not be required to learn the basics before engaging in problem-solving. Just as kids learn to read by reading and to write by writing, they learn math by "mathing"—using mathematical concepts in scenarios based on real-life events. When teaching math to global learners, always begin with a concrete situation (*example:* "How many crackers should we take out of the box so all students can have one cracker?"). When it is not possible to create an actual situation, use manipulatives to represent the problem. Ideally, you should move students with learning difficulties to the computation phase only after they understand the concepts involved. Some students respond well to memory tricks like "Does McDonald's Sell Cheeseburgers" on page 154, because these tricks make abstract instructions more concrete.

When the National Council of Teachers of Mathematics (NCTM) revised its standards in 2000, it gave equal importance to computation and problem-solving. The introduction to *Principles & Standards for School Mathematics* says, "Students need to learn a new set of mathematics basics that enable them to compute fluently and to solve problems creatively and resourcefully."

The NCTM standards are extensive, and they will probably change again in the future. (To access the current standards, see "References and Resources" at the end of this chapter.) When you add in your own state's standards, the process of bringing all students to proficiency levels may seem overwhelming. While successful students learn math concepts relatively quickly, and they easily see the connections between them, students with learning difficulties take a long time to learn math, and they often fail to understand the connections between concepts, which makes retention elusive. Many math series complicate math instruction for struggling learners even further because too many math concepts are presented in one lesson or on one practice page. Very little time and only a page or two are devoted to explaining and developing new concepts. As a result, some students are more confused than ever.

It's essential to give students who are emerging into an understanding of mathematical concepts as much time as they need to learn how to manipulate objects so they can solve problems that have meaning in their daily lives. (*Examples:* dividing up treats for a birthday party; using money to buy real objects in a classroom store; physically manipulating shapes to see their relationships—these real-life scenarios must precede the shift to the use of abstract numerals.) We must also remember to focus on what kids are doing well, not on their frustrations. Be patient! All good things take time, and for struggling students, a little more time may be just what they need.

This chapter presents strategies and techniques that facilitate math learning for students who find math difficult. Try several with your students until you find one or two that make a noticeable difference in their success with math. Again, the phrase to remember is Dr. Kenneth Dunn's: "If students cannot learn the way we teach them, then we must teach them the way they learn." The self-talk that should be ever-present in students' minds is, "If this method is not making sense to me, I'll ask the teacher to help me try other methods until we find the one that works for me!" Look back at the acronym WHOLISTIC (see page 57) as a reminder of how to promote learning success for struggling students in any subject area.

Ways to Get Struggling Students Hooked on Math

- Stay with hands-on learning until understanding is achieved, then help kids discover the skills they need to solve the same problem. In other words, they should see and manipulate the problem first with concrete objects, then translate the information into the symbolic language of numbers. Whenever possible, allow students to work together as they learn.

- Remember that math happens all day long, not just during math period. Take every opportunity to show how math is present in *all* subjects. (*Examples:* the cost of fighting a battle; the number of calories people consume in a given day; how sound is measured in music.) Connect math at school to students' lives at home. (*Examples:* Have students observe and graph the TV-watching habits of family members; have them draw their bedroom or living room on graph paper, make furniture cut-outs, and rearrange them to learn about scale.)

- Call attention to how math is used in literature. Use math scenarios from stories you read aloud; fairy tales, folk tales, and children's books abound with potential scenarios. Ask a librarian for suggestions. (How about the math in *Alice's Adventures in Wonderland*?) Have students create word problems from the books they are reading or from classical favorites. Find songs, poems, and jingles that incorporate repetitious math patterns; use novels and stories as math-related discussion-starters. *Example:* A story about a runaway teenager can lead to an authentic exploration of how much it costs to live on one's own.

- Use the students' own names and actual events in their lives in math problems.

- Since global learners need to see the big picture before learning the parts, always show them how a completed problem or task will look. *Example:* When you want students to fill in a grid of number facts, show global kids the completed grid and have them work backwards to understand the relationships and patterns.

- Use music, rhymes, raps, and/or jingles to help kids learn number facts in a way that is both fun and effective.

- Have students set their own goals for what part of a math task they will attempt or how many problems they will solve within a given time period. (See "Goal Setting" on pages 65–68.) If this doesn't motivate them to work on math, you might try allowing them to accumulate points they can trade in for incentives. If they meet their goal, they get all of the possible points. If they achieve 70 percent or higher of their goal, they get 70 percent of the possible points. If they beat their own goal, they get bonus points.

- Consistently emphasize that asking questions and making mistakes is the only way to learn.

- Teach estimation and expect students to use it in as one consistent step in all the math they do.

- Have students solve several problems using one strategy, and one problem using several strategies. When they see that there are many ways to solve the same problem, they no longer fear messing up on the one right way.

- Revisit ideas often after they have been learned. Each math period should include a review of something kids already know.

- Find and use whatever technology is available and approved by your technology support people and your administrators. This includes software, calculators, and other support systems. *Example:* A program called Fastt Math (see "References and Resources") is said to significantly increase fluency with all math facts. Research has shown these effects to be long-lasting. There are (or will be) other programs that can make a positive difference in your students' attitudes and aptitudes. Ask your technology support person for assistance.

Teaching Techniques to Try

- Always take the time to show students how the skills they are learning are used in real life, both on and off the job.

- Show an example of the problem as it would look when it was completed. Often, global learners can understand better when they can see the end first.

- Choose and use consistent color cues for algorithms. *Example:* In fractions, if the numerator is always green and the denominator is always red, the colors can help students remember and use the language of mathematics, which can be very confusing.

- One teaching method that is often successful with struggling students is the Concrete to Representational to Symbolic to Abstract sequence of instruction. The concrete stage uses manipulatives. The representational stage uses pictures and other visual aids which relate directly to what was done with the manipulatives. The symbolic stage demonstrates how the concrete and representational stages appear numerically. The abstract stage follows naturally as the students first engage in guided practice and eventually should be better able to practice independently what they have learned. All stages should include thinking out loud so students are metacognitively aware of what they are learning. See pages 68–69.

- Another teaching method that has found favor among teachers and students is Cognitively Guided Instruction (CGI). Teachers use Socratic questioning to lead students to describe their thinking about how they solved a problem. Students learn that there are many ways to solve problems, to value risk-taking in their thinking, and to honor the thinking of their classmates. CGI is based on the belief that children's knowledge is central to instructional decision-making. The teacher is the guide on the side rather than the sage on the stage. Students who are taught using CGI appear to have a deeper understanding of the way math works than do kids who spend most of their time with computation. Training in how to use CGI is available from the National Center for Improving Student Learning and Achievement in Mathematics and Science (NCISLA). See "References and Resources."

- Model how to do a problem as you metacognitively think out loud the steps you are going through. (See pages 68–69.) Repeat this process several times and always follow the same steps in the same order.

- Use the Name Card method (pages 14–17) to check homework and to check for understanding as you teach. Use the cards to send kids to the board to demonstrate math examples. Now and then, allow students to go to the board with their math discussion buddy. After writing the problem on the board, the students explain how they got their answer. Then the whole class votes to show if they disagree with that particular answer. One secondary geometry teacher told his students that when they put work on the board, they could choose do it correctly or incorrectly. That way, if the class disagreed with an answer, the students could explain that they knew it was wrong but were just trying to fool their classmates. This gave kids a way to save face if they put the wrong answer on the board.

- As often as you possibly can, have students describe in writing what they are thinking as they solve their problems. This practice is extremely useful in demonstrating that there are many ways to solve a given problem, and that every child's thinking deserves to be heard and processed. Take class time to discuss these descriptions and have kids appreciate and enjoy each other's mathematical thinking.

- Teach in small chunks so kids get lots of practice with only one step at a time. Don't expect struggling students to do concept development and computation simultaneously. Supply a learning aid, such as a number facts grid, until kids have grasped the meaning of a new concept. Make they sure they understand the words you are using to describe the concepts. *Example:* When teaching *perimeter,* make sure students understand what *perimeter* means before asking them to compute actual perimeters.

- Be sure to teach and assess often in the same format that will be used on any high-stakes tests students will have to take. They must be familiar with the format so they are not distracted by it. *Example:* If students will have to fill in bubbles on answer sheets, use that format during your own assessments.

- Assign number values to letters of the alphabet. Have students compute the cost of different words and sentences.

- Bring mail-order catalogs to class. Give each student a mystery amount of money to spend on purchases from a catalog. Instruct them to include tax and shipping when deciding what to buy.

- Bring restaurant menus to class. Have students practice ordering, computing the bill (including tax and tip), and averaging the cost of each person's meal.

- Dissect a daily newspaper for math applications. One day's paper could keep your class busy for a week. If you don't know how to create lessons from the newspaper, contact the editors of the Education section and ask for lesson plans.

- Have students figure out time changes throughout the world, including the loss or gain of an entire day when one crosses the International Date Line.

- Involve students in the study of economics. The National Council on Economics Education is eager to share free materials for use with students in primary grades through high school (see "References and Resources"). You might even go into business. Math comes alive when the entire class gets involved in manufacturing, selling, and earning a profit.

- Whenever feasible, let students choose a smaller number of problems to do within an assigned time period. It's better to assign problems by the available time than to assign the same number of problems to all students. Encourage students to use the Goal Planning Chart (page 66) to set and reach goals.

- Use math games whenever possible to bring some excitement to math. In deference to your kinesthetic learners, choose games where kids move around. Too many paper-and-pencil activities are frustrating for struggling students.

- Use whatever tricks are available to you. See "Finger Multiplication" (page 153) and "Fingermath" (page 151). Both are fabulous aids that students can take into any testing situation with them, since the only tools they need are their own fingers!

- Find and consistently use any available technology and software to help kids learn math. Programs like SuccessMaker bring fun and a little mystery into the math period. See "References and Resources" for this and other suggestions.

For more ideas, check your teacher's manual. If there is someone in your school or district with "math" in his or her title, call and ask for assistance. Invite colleagues to eat their lunch in your room; bring chocolate; brainstorm ideas.

Teaching the Basics

Computation

- Always show the solution first so students can see the whole pattern at once. After the pattern has been shown several times, begin asking students to compute the solution independently.

- Never ask struggling students to copy work from the board or textbook. Math is about number relationships, not about accurate copying.

- Use number lines when kids begin to work with numbers, as well as when introducing new concepts. Commercially produced number lines are available in almost every educational catalog of teaching tools. Or use a large clock face with hour and minute markings as a number line; some kids find it easier to count back-and-forth on a clock face. Use colored markers for the 5-minute chunks and different-colored markers for the 15-minute chunks.

- Give kids lots of practice in writing the numbers correctly. The "How to Teach Letter Formation" strategy and "More Tips for Teaching Handwriting" on page 131 can easily be adapted for this purpose.

■ Always expect kids to estimate a reasonable solution before they do any computation.

■ For practice problems, less is more. Never assign more than seven to ten practice problems. Motivate students by offering this option: They may stop practicing as soon as they complete five consecutive problems correctly.

■ Allow students to use graph paper for computation problems to keep columns straight. Prepare sturdy templates for students to use while working problems. Templates can expose one problem at a time or one column in computation. Draw circles in colored ink around the problems' numbers so kids don't think those digits are part of the problem.

■ Find and use software that makes number facts mastery happen faster for some students.

Teaching the Facts

Follow this sequence to teach addition and subtraction facts. **Tip:** Always start with concrete objects before moving to numerals.

1. Teach the doubles.

■ Have students make equations for the doubles' facts.

■ Have students make word problems using everyday situations.

■ Have students share their word problems. Encourage them to explain their thinking processes out loud. Try having them act out the problems to enhance their understanding.

■ Have students journal about the process and then discuss their thinking about it.

■ Send home some work that repeats the same process, with a letter to parents explaining it. Invite feedback from parents.

2. Repeat this process for the doubles plus 1. *Example:* "If 5 + 5 = 10, then 5 + 6 = one more than 10, or 11. Likewise, if 5 – 5 = 0, then 6 – 5 = one more than 0, or 1."

3. Repeat this process for the doubles plus 2, the doubles plus 3, and so on.

4. Repeat this process for the doubles minus 1, the doubles minus 2, the doubles minus 3, and so on.

Expanded Notation

Use expanded notation to make sure kids understand the numbers they are using in their math problems. *Example:* "36 + 42" would be rewritten as "30 + 6 and 40 + 2." Add either the 1's or the 10's first: 30 + 40 = 70; 6 + 2 = 8. The answer is 78.

If regrouping is necessary, as in 39 + 25, follow the same process: 30 + 9 and 20 + 5. 9 + 5 = 14; 30 + 20 = 50; 50 + 14 = 54.

Once kids understand the expanded notation method, it is much easier for them to grasp the related algorithm.

Partial Sums

Another quick way to solve an addition problem is by doing partial sums. *Example:* For 49 + 57: Add the 1's first: 9 + 7 = 16. Add the 10's next: 40 + 50 = 90. Add both sums: 16 + 90 = 106.

Number Facts

■ Teach the facts in families. *Examples:* all of the combinations that add up to 10 (2 + 8, 8 + 2, 3 + 7, 7 + 3 . . .); all of the facts that are associated with each other (6 – 4 = 10, 10 – 6 = 4, 10 – 4 = 6 . . .).

■ Teach addition and multiplication together, since they are two sides of the same concept. Teach subtraction and division together for the same reason.

■ Demonstrate everything with manipulatives. Think out loud and have students do the same.

■ Call students' attention to the ways in which number facts are used in their real lives.

■ Make number facts a game during every math period. Fold pieces of paper into a certain number of sections, then challenge students to write one complete math fact family in each section. Have kids set their own goals for how many sections of paper they can complete.*

■ Enlist parent helpers to prepare number facts flashcards. An entire fact is written on the front of a 5" x 7" card and cut in two in a unique jigsaw pattern, with the problem on one part and the solution on the other. This is especially helpful for visual learners, who can link the facts to the patterns.

■ When learning the multiplication facts from 1 to 10, most students already know (or easily grasp) the 0's, 1's, 2's, 5's, and 10's. Next, add the twins: 3 x 3, 4 x 4, 6 x 6, 7 x 7, 8 x 8, and 9 x 9. Now they know 56 of the 100 multiplication facts, and learning the rest is relatively easy. *Example:* To find 8 groups of 7, think "7 groups of 7 = 49; one more group of 7 is the same as 49 + 7, or 56."

■ Give each student personal laminated copies of number facts grids. Indicate notable patterns (odd numbers,

---

* Susan Flynn, teacher, Christianburg, Virginia.

even numbers) with different colors. Have students use the grids to estimate the reciprocal processes (subtraction for addition, division for multiplication). *Example:* "Divide 14 by 3. Is 14 a number in the 3 line? No? Then what is the closest number?"

Recording the Number Facts

Many commercial products are available to teach kids the number facts, but I have found a simple homemade method that works just as well for students who reach the upper grades without knowing their number facts. It is easily adaptable for teaching other types of facts.

1. Make a cassette or digital recording of the number facts, one series at a time. Say the facts in order, pausing briefly after each one. Example: "6 . . . 12 . . . 18 . . . 24 . . . 30 . . . 36 . . . 42 . . . 48 . . . 54 . . . 60."

2. Students listen to the recording and turn it off after the first three facts ("6 . . . 12 . . . 18").

3. Students chant the first three facts several times, holding up one finger for the first fact ("6"), two for the second ("12"), three for the third ("18"), and so on. In this way, they can see that 2 x 6 = 12, 3 x 6 = 18, and so on.

4. When students master the first three facts, they add the next one, listening to the recording only as far as "24." They chant "6," "12," "18," "24," holding up one, two, three, and four fingers in order.

5. Students continue to repeat this sequence, adding one more fact each time until they can chant the 6's through 60 (10 x 6). When they are successful at this, they try starting at 6 x 5 = 30, holding up all fingers of one hand simultaneously. Counting then to 36 and beyond, they can shortcut the process for facts above 5 times the number.

6. Repeat the same process for the other tables through 9. Later, show kids how to start with the twins to work forward or backward so they don't have to start from the beginning of the sequence each time.

7. Prepare another recording that contains the fact families. *Example:* "6 x 3 = 18, so 3 x 6 = 18, and 18 ÷ 3 = 6, so 18 ÷ 6 = 3."

Fingermath

In my workshops about teaching kids with learning difficulties, participants are always amazed by the Finger Multiplication strategy (see page 153). Many have asked for similar strategies for other math operations. I recommend a technique called Fingermath.

Fingermath is related to the workings of an abacus, which in turn are related to the workings of the fingers of both hands. I would use it with students who are not able to become fluent with memorized number facts despite months of practice. Fingermath allows students to use all ten fingers to add, subtract, multiply, and divide numerals up to at least 100. Once fluency is reached (after lots of practice), students have a method they can use in both testing and real-life situations to perform basic number operations quickly and accurately. (One fan calls it "a calculator you can sneak into the SAT.")

The Complete Book of Fingermath by Edwin M. Lieberthal was published in 1979 and (at the time this book went to press) is still available through online resources and in some libraries. It contains many examples of how to use this method, with illustrations. I recommend that you consult the book, then teach this wonderful method to your own students.

19 Is as High as I Go*

With this method, students never have to add higher than 19.

Write out a problem of two-digit numbers to add. Whenever you get to 10, strike a slash through the number and write the leftover as a small digit. *Example:*

1. Add the 1's column.

$$
\begin{array}{r}
78 \\
55^{3} \\
69^{2} \\
+ 47 \\
\hline
9
\end{array}
$$

8 + 5 = 13; slash the 5 and write a tiny 3 beside it

3 + 9 = 12; slash the 9 and write a tiny 2 beside it

2 + 7 = 9; write the 9 in the 1's place of the sum

2. Add the 10's column.

$$
\begin{array}{r}
^{2}78 \\
^{4}55 \\
^{0}69 \\
+ 47 \\
\hline
49
\end{array}
$$

Count the slashes in the 1's column: 2
Write 2 above the 7 in the 10's column: 2 + 7 = 9

9 + 5 = 14; slash the 5 and write a tiny 4 beside it

4 + 6 = 10; slash the 6 and write a tiny 0 beside it

0 + 4 = 4; write the 4 in the 10's place of the sum

---

* Rita McNeeley, teacher, Port Huron, Michigan.

3. Add the 100's column.

Count the slashes in the 10's column: 2

$^2 78$

55

69

+ 47

249

Write 2 in the 100's place of the sum

TouchMath*

TouchMath is a program that has helped many tactile-kinesthetic learners understand basic math operations. It provides hands-on learning without actual manipulatives.

Each digit from 1–9 is drawn with the same number of dots (touchpoints) as the number it represents. The numbers 6–9 are drawn with circled dots, each representing two dots.

1. The 1 is touched at the top while counting "One."

2. The 2 is touched at the beginning and end while counting "One, Two."

3. The 3 is touched at the beginning, middle, and end while counting "One, Two, Three."

4. The 4 is touched and counted from top to bottom on the down strokes while counting "One, Two, Three, Four."

5. The 5 is touched and counted in the order shown: "One, Two, Three, Four, Five." You might call "Four" the "belly-button" to help students remember it.

6. The 6 begins the use of dots with circles. The encircled dots are touched and counted twice. So the 6 is touched and counted from top to bottom: "One-Two, Three-Four, Five-Six."

7. The 7 is touched and counted from top to bottom: "One-Two, Three-Four, "Five-Six," followed by the single dot at the top left, "Seven." You might call "Seven" the "nose" to help students remember it.

8. The 8 is touched and counted from left to right, counting the "head" first and the "body" second: "One-Two, Three-Four, Five-Six, Seven-Eight."

9. The 9 is touched and counted from top to bottom: "One-Two, Three-Four, Five-Six, Seven-Eight," followed by the single dot at the left (the "nose"), "Nine."

Students learn addition and subtraction by touching the numbers to reinforce the concept of how many. To add numbers, count all of the dots and circled dots.

Addition example: To add 3 + 6: 3 dots + 6 dots (each circled dot on the 6 counts as 2 dots) = 9. Students count "1, 2, 3, 4–5, 6–7, 8–9."

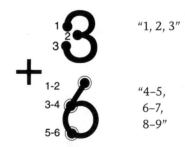

---

* *TouchMath.* 4th edition. Innovative Learning Concepts, Inc. Used with permission.

Subtraction example: To subtract 3 from 8, touch the top number (8), then count backwards from there by touching the dots on the 3 ("7, 6, 5"). The answer is the same as the last dot touched. (There are no touchpoints on the top number in TouchMath subtraction.)

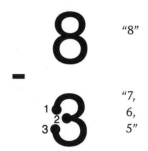

The complete TouchMath program also includes work with multiplication and division as well as time, place value, and other concepts. Teachers are reminded to always have students repeat the problems and answers aloud to help them memorize the number facts and enhance their ability to transfer what they have learned to more conventional ways of doing arithmetic. For more about TouchMath, see "References and Resources."

Multiplication and Division

Number Arrays

The following array represents 3 groups of 4, or 3 times one group of 4, or 3 x 4. Once kids understand this, they learn the reciprocals: 4 x 3 = 12; 12 ÷ 3 = 4; 12 ÷ 4 = 3.

Nines on My Fingers*

Write the numbers from 1–10 on sticky colored circles. Have students stick the circles to the backs of their fingers in order from left to right. The left pinkie is 1, the left ring finger is 2, etc., all the way to the right pinkie, which is 10.

To compute 9 x 4, the student holds up both hands, palms facing out.

1. Bend the left index finger (4). The fingers to the left of the bent finger represent the 10's. Three 10's = 30.

2. The six fingers to the right of the bent finger (including thumbs) represent the 1's. Six 1's = 6.

3. Add the 10's and 1's together. 30 + 6 = 36, so 9 x 4 = 36.

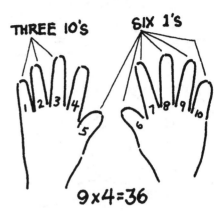

Try 9 x 7. Bend the right index finger (7). There are six 10's to the left of the bent finger and three 1's to the right of the bent finger, so 9 x 7 = 63.

Finger Multiplication**

To use this method, students must know the multiplication tables from 0–5. There are two combinations in this method that are exceptions (6 x 6 and 6 x 7), and they should be left until last to demonstrate.

Write the numbers from 6–10 on two sets of sticky colored circles (two 6's, two 7's, etc.). Have students stick the circles to their fingertips. The pinkies are 6's and should be the same color; the ring fingers are 7's and should be another color; the middle fingers are 8's (another color); the index fingers are 9's (another color); the thumbs are 10's (another color). **Tip:** Instead of sticky circles, you can also use watercolor markers to write the numbers on the students' fingers.

To compute 7 x 8, the student holds up both hands, palms sideways, facing in, pinkies between the hand and the floor.

1. Place the 7 finger of either hand against the 8 finger on the other hand. The touching fingers, together with all of the fingers below them on both hands, represent the 10's. Five 10's = 50.

2. Multiply the number of remaining fingers on one hand by the number of remaining fingers on the other hand to find the 1's. 3 x 2 = 6.

3. Add the 10's and 1's together. 50 + 6 = 56, so 7 x 8 = 56.

---

* Adapted from Nancy S. Bley and Carol A. Thornton, *Teaching Mathematics to Students with Learning Disabilities.* 3rd edition. Austin, TX: PRO-ED, 1995. Used with permission.

** Adapted from Martin Gardner, *Entertaining Science Experiments with Everyday Objects.* New York: Dover Publications, 1981. Used with permission of the author.

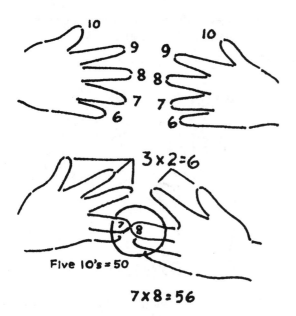

7 X 8 = 56

Try 9 x 7. Touch a 7 finger against a 9 finger. All touching fingers and those below them = six 10's = 60. Multiply the remaining fingers; 3 x 1 = 3. Add the 10's and 1's: 60 + 3 = 63, so 9 x 7 = 63.

Exceptions:

- 6 x 6: Touching pinkies: Two 10's = 20. Multiplying free fingers: 4 x 4 = 16. 20 + 16 = 36, so 6 x 6 = 36.

- 6 x 7: Touching pinkie and ringer finger: Three 10's = 30. Multiplying free fingers: 4 x 3 = 12. 30 + 12 = 42, so 6 x 7 = 42.

Teach these two last, since they have an addition step at the end.

Partial Products

Partial Products in multiplication is related to Expanded Notation in addition and subtraction (see page 150). *Example:* 46 (40 + 6) x 23 (20 + 3).

1. Multiply the 1's: 3 x 6 = 18.

2. Multiply the lower 1's x the upper 10's: 3 x 40 = 120.

3. Multiply the lower 10's x the upper 1's: 20 x 6 = 120.

4. Multiply the 10's: 20 x 40 = 800.

5. Add 18 + 120 + 120 + 800 to get the answer: 1,058.

Division Made Easy

With this method, students learn that division is progressive subtraction. They remember the steps by chanting a mnemonic, "**D**oes **M**cDonald's **S**ell **C**heeseburgers,"* while

adding tactile-kinesthetic support. Methods like these can make abstract algorithms easier to remember and use.

1. Students write the division problem, extending the division box by adding a vertical line at the right down the page.

$$25 \overline{)\,2991}$$

2. Students chant "**D**oes" to remind themselves that the first step in the process is to **D**ivide. Simultaneously, they draw the division sign (÷) in the air. They estimate how many groups of 25 cheeseburgers can be made from a batch of 2991 cheeseburgers. Any estimate will do, as long as the total used does not exceed the available supply. *Example:* "I can divide 2991 into groups of 25 at least 100 times."

3. Students chant "**M**cDonald's" to remind themselves that the next step in the process is to **M**ultiply. Simultaneously, they draw the multiplication sign (x) in the air. They multiply the estimate (100) by the number of cheeseburgers in each group (25), using up 2500 cheeseburgers.

$$25 \overline{)\,2991} \quad 100$$
$$\phantom{25 \overline{)}\,}2500$$

4. Students chant "**S**ell" to remind themselves that the next step in the process is to **S**ubtract. Simultaneously, they draw the subtraction sign (–) in the air. They subtract the number of cheeseburgers they have grouped (2500) from the original available number of cheeseburgers (2991) to see how many cheeseburgers are left to be grouped. They discover that 491 are left.

$$25 \overline{)\,2991} \quad 100$$
$$\phantom{25 \overline{)}\,}2500$$
$$\phantom{25 \overline{)}\,}\underline{491}$$

5. Students chant "**C**heeseburgers" to remind themselves to **C**heck the remainder of cheeseburgers to be sure there are enough left to make more groups of 25. Simultaneously, they clap once loudly, signaling that the entire process is about to begin again.

---

* Dave Wurst, teacher, Indian Prairie District, Illinois.

6. Students repeat steps 2–5 until the remainder is so small that there are not enough cheeseburgers left to make any more groups of 25. Whatever is left is the remainder. The total number of groups is determined by the sum of all of the groups that have been made. Answer: 119 R 16.

```
        25 ) 2991
             2500    100
             ----
              491
              250     10
             ----
              241
              225      9
             ----    ----
               16    119
```

7. Use the same steps to illustrate that any number may be used to estimate, as long as there are enough items to form the required groupings.

```
        25 ) 2991
              250     10
             ----
             2741
              250     10
             ----
             2491
             1250     50
             ----
             1241
              250     10
             ----
              991
              250     10
             ----
              741
              500     20
             ----
              241
              225      9
             ----    ----
               16    119
```

When kids are ready for the shorter regular method for long division, they can use the same prompts, with a slight variation (treat "cheeseburgers" as two words):

Does = **D**ivide
Ask: "How many 25's in 2? 0. So how many 25's in 29? 1."

```
              01
        25 ) 2991
```

McDonald's = **M**ultiply
1 x 25 = 25

```
              01
        25 ) 2991
              25
```

Sell = **S**ubtract
29 – 25 = 4

```
              01
        25 ) 2991
              25
             ----
               4
```

Cheese = **C**heck to see that the remainder (4) is not larger than the divisor (25).

Burgers = **B**ring down next digit and **B**egin again.

Continue until the final remainder is smaller than the divisor and there are no digits left to bring down.

```
              01
        25 ) 2991
              25
             ----
               49
```

Fractions

For some students, the study of fractions is extremely confusing, since the 1-to-1 correspondence they have come to depend on in whole-number computation is no longer present. The acronym WHOLISTIC (see page 57) can help you to remember how to teach global learners virtually any content, including fractions.

- Have students find examples of fractions used in real life. Organize by categories on a chart.

- Create classroom situations in which kids need to use fractions. *Example:* Dividing treats for a class party; dividing art materials for a project.

- Teach fractions first with concrete examples, such as filling a marked measuring cup with water, before moving on to visual aids that show equivalencies.

- Remember that hands-on activities and manipulatives always work best for struggling students.

Decimals

For many students with learning difficulties, decimals may be more confusing than fractions.

- Have students find examples of decimals used in real life. **Tip:** Have them look through the newspaper. Organize by categories on a chart.

- Use different-colored blocks to show the equivalents.

- Give students practice using money—counting, buying things, making change, etc. Use play money including coins.

Liquid Measures*

Draw a large circle that looks like a capital G. Inside the G, draw four circles that look like capital Q's. Inside each Q, write two capital P's. Inside the circle of each P, write two C's. Draw the outline of a milk gallon around the entire figure. Now students have a way to quickly understand

---

* Adapted from a strategy used by Melissa Matusevich, teacher, Montgomery County, Virginia.

liquid measures: 2 cups = 1 pint; 2 pints = 1 quart; 4 quarts = 1 gallon; and so on.

Linear Measures

Draw a long rectangle and divide it into three parts. Label it "The Yard," as in schoolyard. Draw a large foot in each section to show that 3 feet = 1 yard. Draw 12 "1's" in each foot to show that 12 inches = 1 foot.

Word Problems

Create and display a permanent Problem-Solving Strategies Chart that describes the following:

- Make a model, diagram, drawing, table, or graph.
- Guess what the answer might be; compare your answer to your guess.
- Look for a pattern and use it.
- Work backwards from the solution to the beginning of the problem.
- Make an organized list.
- Use simpler numbers.
- Write an equation.
- Act it out.
- Use a combination of strategies.
- Create your own strategy.

When teaching a word problem, start with a hook that ties the concepts in the problem to the students' personal lives. Use their real names in problem scenarios. Walk them through the following steps:

1. Read the problem aloud. Restate it in your own words.

2. Think about the problem. What do you know about it? What information does it give you? Take notes, draw pictures or diagrams, or use a graphic organizer to record your thoughts.

3. Think about what the problem is asking you for. What do you need to find out?

4. Look at all of the available information. Be sure that you understand all the words or symbols.

5. Discard any unnecessary information.

6. Estimate the answer.

7. Choose a problem-solving strategy from the Problem-Solving Strategies Chart. Notice that the list says you can also create your own strategy.

8. Solve the problem using the appropriate operation or operations—addition, subtraction, multiplication, and/or division.

9. Compare your solution to your estimate. Does the solution make sense? Is your computation accurate?

10. Try to get the same solution using another method.

Using the Problem-Solving Box

Once students have chosen a problem-solving strategy, they may use the Problem-Solving Box on page 157.

Describe and demonstrate how this handout should be used: Students should write each step in the left-hand column of the chart, then write a reason for that step in the right-hand column.

Have students work in pairs to solve a problem and complete the handout, saying the steps and reasons out loud as they write them. Have them begin with simple problems they already know how to solve. Later, they can move on to more challenging problems.

As always, pair struggling math students with helpful average students, not with the top math students. Ask the pairs to report to the class about the problem-solving methods they used.

You might find or create step-by-step processes for some or all of the problem-solving strategies listed above under "Word Problems" (and on your classroom Problem-Solving Strategies Chart). Student pairs using the Problem-Solving Box could follow these processes or consult them when devising their own problem-solving strategies and steps.

Problem-Solving Box

Steps to solve the problem	Reasons for each step

Questions and Answers

"Math has never been my strongest teaching area. What can I do to strengthen my math teaching skills?"

While researching the revised and updated edition of this book, I was amazed at how much help is available from software and over the Internet for teaches who want to do a great job of teaching math. Check the "References and Resources" and spend some time exploring the Web sites. Take a class from someone like Marilyn Burns, or study some videos or DVDs from the library of Ms. Math, Rachel McAnallen. Study your teacher's guide for tips. Call the publisher directly when you need assistance.

"There is so much pressure to get through all of the assigned math standards that I can't find time to help the kids who fall behind catch up. What can I do to make sure they don't get lost forever?"

Remember the old Chinese proverb: "I hear and I forget, I see and I remember, I do and I understand!" I think the best thing to do is to teach today's new concept(s) to the entire class as a direct instruction lesson. Then, as stronger math students take the time to practice what has been taught today, take a group of struggling math students aside and teach them, visually and kinesthetically, their number facts, all the basic operations, basic geometric shapes, and other essential concepts—and make it fun! My belief is that kids who have had a positive experience in math this year are going to be more successful on the math portions of any test than students whose daily failures have convinced them that they can't ever understand math.

"How will it look if these students have to use their fingers to help them compute when they are adults?"

About as acceptable as it is for you to use the spell-check feature on your computer! Besides, solar-powered calculators that fit into a pocket, purse, or backpack are available for less than $10—very reasonable for most students. Don't worry about the future. Let's focus on teaching our students to love math!

"Don't all students eventually have to commit the number facts to memory?"

If there is no impairment of a student's memory processing, it's reasonable to expect the student to memorize the number facts. If a student's memory is impaired, this expectation may not be reasonable. In either case, developing a genuine affection for math as a holistic learning experience is far more important than learning number facts.

"Some of my students always perform terribly on timed tests. What can I do so their test scores come closer to reflecting what they really know?"

Instead of having all students try to complete an arbitrary number of problems in a certain amount of time, give your struggling students control over their own progress. (See the Spelling Styles method on pages 116–119 for an example of how you can give students control.) The first time they take a test, they chart their own outcomes on a bar graph. Each subsequent time, they predict how many more right answers they can add to their own record, then place a small dot on the graph to represent their new goal. (Emphasize the importance of setting realistic goals.) After each test, they chart their outcomes in permanent color, perhaps drawing a dotted line between the goal and the outcome. Give incentives for making steady progress and beating their own records.

REFERENCES AND RESOURCES

Algeblocks (www.etacuisenaire.com). Grades 6–12. Hands-on algebra with manipulatives. Classroom kits and training videos are available. 1-800-445-5985.

A+ Math (www.aplusmath.com). Helps students improve their math skills interactively. Offers online interactive worksheets, flashcards, and games covering a variety of topics. The site also has custom flashcards and worksheets that can be printed.

Bley, Nancy S., and Carol A. Thornton. *Teaching Mathematics to Students with Learning Disabilities.* 4th edition. Austin, TX: PRO-ED, 2001. A gold mine of information about and strategies for helping students with learning disabilities learn math.

Buchholz, Lisa. "Learning Strategies for Addition and Subtraction Facts: The Road to Fluency and the License to Think." *Teaching Children Mathematics* (March 2004), pp. 362–367.

Burns, Marilyn. *About Teaching Mathematics: A K–8 Resource.* 2nd edition. Sausalito, CA: Math Solutions Publications, 2000. Creative ways to teach math to reluctant learners.

Carpenter, Thomas P., and Elizabeth Fennema. *Children's Mathematics: Cognitively Guided Instruction.* Book and CD. Teach math metacognitively to very young students by linking new knowledge to what they already know. Portsmouth, NH: Heinemann; Reston, VA: NCTM, 1999.

Cawley, J.F., et al. "Arithmetic Computation Abilities of Students with Learning Disabilities: Implications for Instruction." *Learning Disabilities Research and Practice* 11:4 (1996), pp. 230-237.

Council for Economic Education (www.councilforeconed .org). Nationwide network promoting economic literacy with students and their teachers. Request free materials to teach economics to students of all ages. (212) 730-7007.

Daily Mathematics (www.greatsource.com). Grades 1–8. Students develop vital skills in just five to ten minutes a day. 1-800-289-4490.

Dix, Tonya. "Doing Business with Math." *Teaching PreK–8* (January 1992), pp. 56–57.

Educational Songs That Teach (www.twinsisters.com). Ages 6–12. Kids learn addition, subtraction, multiplication, and division with musical/rhythmic assistance. (Additional school subject areas are available; all products are on CD.) 1-800-248-8946.

ERIC Education Resources Information Center (www.eric. ed.gov). This online information center offers many articles on teaching students with a wide variety of learning disabilities. Look for ERIC digests on math-related issues.

FASTT Math (www.tomsnyder.com). Grades 2 and up. Research-validated methods help struggling students develop fluency with basic math facts in addition, subtraction, multiplication, and division. The software provides an adaptive program that increases fact fluency in customized, ten-minute daily sessions. Examination packets, including a disk that shows how the lessons work, are available for the asking. District site licenses are available. 1-800-342-0236. (Tom Snyder Productions is a Scholastic company.)

Gardner, Martin. *Entertaining Science Experiments with Everyday Objects.* New York: Dover Publications, 1981.

Georgia Standards (www.georgiastandards.org). Managed by the Georgia Department of Education, this site offers a year's worth of lesson plans for a variety of grades and subjects. Its Teacher Resource Center provides links to dozens of math-related sites and products.

Hands-On Equations: Making Algebra Child's Play (www. borenson.com). Grades 3–8. A visual and kinesthetic teaching system for introducing algebraic concepts. Students balance both parts of equations to understand the concept of "equal." In addition to its products, the company offers instructional workshops throughout the United States. 1-800-993-6284.

Hart, Leslie A. *Anchor Math: The Brain-Compatible Approach to Learning.* Village of Oak Cree, AZ: Books for Educators, 1992. This book will help you teach your students about numbers and math in a way that will turn them on to learning math.

Higher Order Thinking Skills (HOTS) (www.hots.org). Program designed to build the thinking skills of educationally disadvantaged students in grades 4–7. Combines the use of computers, drama, Socratic dialogue, and a detailed curriculum to stimulate thinking processes. Computers are used to intrigue students and get them involved, not to present content. 1-800-999-0153.

Kamii, Constance. *Implications of Piaget's Theory* and *Using Piaget's Theory* (store.tcpress.com). Books and videotapes of educational strategies for early elementary–aged students based on Jean Piaget's scientific ideas of how children develop logico-mathematical thinking. 1-800-575-6566.

Lieberthal, Edwin M. *The Complete Book of Fingermath.* New York: McGraw-Hill, 1979. This book is out of print but worth tracking down on the Internet and in libraries. Search for ISBN 0070376808.

The Math Forum (www.mathforum.org). Affiliated with Drexel University, this site features dozens of math lessons on fractions and other concepts. Click on "Ask Dr. Math" to ask your own questions and search through questions that have already been posted on the site.

Math Notes (www.mathsongs.com). This series of audio CDs uses a sing-along format to teach math concepts to kinesthetic learners. Each CD comes with a book of math objectives and directions for using the material in the classroom, as well as a copy of the song for use as an overhead master. No previous math skills are required to use the songs. (979) 849-4413.

Math Solutions Professional Development (www.math solutions.com). Founded by educator Marilyn Burns, Math Solutions offers resources that provide the help you need to improve math instruction. 1-800-868-9092.

MathLine Concept-Building System (www.howbrite.com). A manipulative that combines the number line with the abacus; a mechanical calculator that shows how math operations actually work. 1-800-505-MATH (1-800-505-6284).

Meagher, Michael. *Teaching Fractions: New Methods, New Resources.* Columbus, OH: ERIC Clearinghouse for Science, Mathematics, and Environmental Education (ERIC/CSMEE), 2002. ERIC # ED478711. Available at www.eric.ed.gov.

National Center for Improving Student Learning and Achievement in Mathematics and Science (NCISLA) (www.wcer.wisc.edu/ncisla). Home of Cognitively Guided Instruction (CGI) and source of teacher training in the method.

National Council of Teachers of Mathematics (NCTM) (www.nctm.org). Books, journals, materials, videos, and collections of math lessons for many topics and grade levels. NCTM Standards *(Principles & Standards for School Mathematics)* are available in print, on CD, and online (standards.nctm.org). 1-800-235-7566.

Pallotta, Jerry, and Rob Bolster. *The Hershey's Milk Chocolate Bar Fractions Book.* New York: Scholastic, 1999. Using Hershey Chocolate bars to teach basic fractions makes a yummy lesson!

Problem Solver workbooks (www.mheonline.com). Grades 1–8. Teaches all ten generic problem-solving strategies. Teachers photocopy notebook problems for students. 1-800-334-7344

Rowan, Thomas, and Barbara Bourne. *Thinking Like Mathematicians: Putting the NCTM Standards into Practice: Updated for Standards 2000.* Portsmouth, NH: Heinemann, 2001.

Shake and Learn (www.shakeandlearn.com). Products that use music and movement to teach academic standards. *Shake and Learn: Mathematics* includes a music CD with kinesthetic cues, lesson plans, reproducibles, and extension activities. Also available: *Shake and Learn Mathematics* DVD. From SALT Productions, Inc. 1-800-884-3764.

SuccessMaker (www.pearsonschool.com). Scalable digital courseware for grades K–8. Individualizes instruction to the specific needs of each student by automatically presenting instruction at the level at which a student is ready to learn, creating a successful learning experience. Aligns with district, local, and national standards, and is supported by a comprehensive management system. Used in more than 16,000 schools in the United States and 1,500 abroad. Courseware is available in customizable bundles. Program costs vary, depending on the software purchased, the range of grade levels to be covered, and the amount of professional development services requested.

Teacher to Teacher (www.mathforum.org/t2t). A question-and-answer service for teachers and parents who have questions about teaching math.

TouchMath (www.touchmath.com). Multisensory teaching approach that bridges manipulation and memorization. 1-800-888-9191.

TouchMath. 4th edition. Colorado Springs, CO: Innovative Learning Concepts, Inc.

Trade-Offs (www.ait.net/catalog). Grades 5–8. Fifteen 20-minute video programs and a teacher's guide to explain basic economics to middle school students. From the Agency for Instructional Technology. 1-800-457-4509.

The 24 Game (www.24game.com). This mathematics-teaching tool demonstrates that math can be powerful, engaging, and most of all, fun. The answer is always 24, which alleviates students' anxiety about finding the right answer and puts the emphasis on the process—the method behind the math. 1-800-242-4542.

The University of Chicago School Mathematics Project (UCSMP) (ucsmp.uchicago.edu). Offers information, training, and teaching assistance. Materials are available for all grade levels. (773) 702-1130.

Helping Students Get Organized and Learn Study Skills

As if students with learning difficulties don't face enough challenges, they are often profoundly disorganized and don't know how to study. Good organization and study skills are essential to success in school and in life. Following are tips and strategies you can demonstrate and coach—concrete skills you can teach your struggling students and all others who could use some extra help in these areas.

Bringing Order into the Disorganized Lives of Students with Learning Difficulties

Teacher: "Manuel, please number your paper from one to ten."

Manuel: "Do they have to be in order?"

That really happened . . . don't you love it? Comments like this one illustrate what a big job it is to help struggling students get their learning act together. We ask them, "Did you do your homework?" "Did you remember to take home what you were supposed to study last night?" "Did

you study for the test?" "Did you bring the materials you need today from home?" Predictably, the answer is "No," "I forgot," "What test?" or "What materials?" This causes no end of frustration for everyone involved.

We could all benefit from methods that make our lives more efficient and rewarding. Many students with learning difficulties are terribly disorganized. When we realize that students' organizational styles reflect their learning styles, we can appreciate the different ways in which they perceive and deal with organization issues. Organizational skills must be taught in the same explicit manner as any other skill. Start small and build slowly on one success at a time.

Above all, assume nothing. Never assume that these kids have study and organizational skills but choose not to use them. Never assume they were ever actually taught how to be organized and efficient. And even if they were taught these things, never assume they remember! Choose simple procedures, use them consistently, never give more than one or two directions at a time, offer sincere, specific praise when it is earned, and *make sure there is a written version* so visual learners can refer to a handout that contains all the important information you want them to remember. *Examples:* directions for specific tasks, things to remember to take home or bring back to school, party or field trip information, etc.

Teach Students to Think SMART

Teach your students an acronym they can use throughout the day to prepare for successful learning. Write the following on the board or create a handout:

Smart students use learning strategies.

Materials are ready (books, paper, folders, pencils, etc.).

Assignment notebook is available.

Remember to ask questions when you don't understand.

Think positively ("I can do it!").

Before beginning an activity, students say to themselves, "I can learn if I think SMART." Then they review what the acronym means. Reinforce the acronym daily.

Use Routines

Create and follow routines for everything. Spend lots of time during the first two weeks of the school year reinforcing these routines so students follow them automatically without reminders from you. Using key words ("line up") or signals (hand cupped behind your ear for "listen to me") should lead instantly to the expected routine. For students who don't respond well to verbal directions, provide visual checklists or picture directions for them to follow.

The more predictable and consistent your daily procedures are, the better struggling students will be able to cope with them. Start with simple routines that span a short period of time so students get frequent positive feedback. Begin with a one- or two-item routine; have students check off each item as it is completed. Add more items one at a time as students are ready for them.

Example: One of your students has great difficulty making transitions between tasks. Instead of keeping the entire class waiting, give that student a prearranged signal three to five minutes before the transition will take place. At your signal, she stops what she is doing and consults a checklist that the two of you prepared together. She goes through the procedures one-by-one:

1. Finish the word or exercise you are working on, but don't start any new part of your work.

2. Check to make sure that your name is in the upper right-hand corner of your paper.

3. Put your paper in the color-coded folder for that subject. Put it in the left pocket if the work is done, the right pocket if it isn't.

4. Put your pencil in the pencil slot at the top of your desk.

5. Put your books in your desk or dishpan container.

6. Watch and listen to the teacher for the signal on what to do next.

At this point, the student should be ready to move on to the next activity with the rest of the class.

Tip: If your students use color-coded pocket folders for each subject, have them write "Completed Work" on the left pocket and "Work Being Done" on the right pocket.

Promote the Checklist Habit

The simple act of creating and using checklists can bring order into many students' lives. See page 163 for examples. If kids need to bring certain things from home to school each day, a checklist attached to the door they use when leaving home can serve as a reminder. If a pencil hangs by a string nearby or is attached with Velcro, they don't have to waste time searching for a writing instrument. They can look quickly through their backpacks and check off each item as they notice it.

Checklists may be kept in a designated folder or taped to students' desks. If kids have lockers, prepare checklists to hang inside that remind them of what they need to bring to each class. Students with learning difficulties should be allowed to visit their lockers before each class.

Give students Daily Task checklists to use at their desks. (See page 26.) Checking off tasks as they're completed can be very satisfying. Award partial credit for partial success.

More Ways to Get and Keep Students Organized

- Use color everywhere you can to help kids with their organization. There can be different-colored folders for each subject area, different-colored writing tools to indicate the type of correction that is needed, color categories on the Content Organization Chart (page 141), etc.

- If students in your school change classrooms for different subjects, give each student a dishpan or other plastic container. Students leave everything they need for other subjects in their homeroom but carry with them what they need for the subject they are going to (paper, writing tools, water bottles, text and workbook, etc.). When they arrive at the math room, for example, they simply slide this container into the desk they are using. Since the student who just vacated the desk has taken his or her container, there is room for them to do this.

- Help students prioritize tasks by listing them in order of importance and working their way down the list. They can feel good about accomplishing the most important tasks, even if they can't finish them all.

THINGS TO BRING TO SCHOOL EACH DAY

Item	Monday	Tuesday	Wednesday	Thursday	Friday
Books I brought home					
Pencils, pens, paper					
Homework					
Lunch or lunch money					
Permission slip					
Other_____					

THINGS TO BRING TO CLASS EACH PERIOD

Item	1st	2nd	3rd	4th	5th	6th	7th	8th
Book								
Homework								
Pencils, pens, paper								
Other_____								

- Working at a desk may be overwhelming for kids with attention problems. Set them up at a table with a study carrel. They can work independently there and rejoin the class for discussions and group activities.

- Rather than expecting students to organize all of their things at their desk, provide another place in the classroom where their books and corresponding work folders can be color-coded, organized, and stored. (*Examples:* A magazine file box can hold everything the student needs for one subject—math book, papers, folder.) Ask parents to help supply aids that may be purchased commercially (pencil cups, zippered pockets for folders, plastic boxes with lids, etc.).

- If at all possible, give students with LD a duplicate set of textbooks to keep at home, reducing the chances that they will lose their textbooks between home and school. Some teachers even provide their most hyperactive students with a second desk in the classroom, giving those kids another acceptable reason to move their bodies.

- Attach things that often get misplaced to students' desks with pieces of Velcro. *Examples:* books, pencils, pens, erasers . . . anything that can be dropped.

- Create a backwards timeline for longer-term assignments. Coach parents to use this method at home as well. *Examples:* If a story is due on Friday, show students how to plan the number of sentences they need to write on Thursday, Wednesday, Tuesday, and Monday, in that order. If a mobile display of the characters in a book is due in two weeks, work with the student to plan each day's activities, starting on the morning of the due date. Be sure to include those tasks on the student's daily checklist (see page 26).

■ Use assignment notebooks that are consistent from class to class. Parents and other caregivers should be told to expect that the notebook will come home every day, whether or not the student has homework. So part of the home routine should be to check the notebook with the student for homework assignments. If a backwards timeline is in progress, that should go home, too, perhaps stapled to the assignment notebook so it returns to school the next day.

Teaching Students How to Study

Look back at "Getting Ready to Learn" on page 135. Do your students know these learning-how-to-learn strategies? Use the chart on page 136 to track their progress and determine which strategies you need to teach directly—or teach again.

Material from Texts and Lectures

Teach students how to use these strategies and techniques metacognitively. (See pages 68–69.) It's very helpful when they think out loud the process they are using to learn.

Skimming and Summarizing Written Material

1. Notice and read the heading for any new section.

2. Locate and read all questions that will have to be answered for that section.

3. Skim the first and last paragraphs of a section.

4. For other paragraphs in the section, read the first and last sentences and any key words that are italicized or highlighted in some way. Locate the information for the italicized terms. Illustrate one or two key points using a graphic organizer.

5. As soon as you recognize the answer to a required question, write it down.

6. To summarize a section, combine the key points from all paragraphs into one or two statements.

7. Write an introduction and conclusion for the summary.

Use Graphic Organizers

Use any graphic organizers with which your students are comfortable. Demonstrate how notes can be taken in short phrases and drawn rather than written out. Students who learn this method can often visualize the graphic organizer as they are taking a test, which helps them to remember lots of information.

You may use the Content Organization Chart on page 141 as a graphic organizer for taking general notes on any topic. Simply retitle it the Note-Taking Chart.*

Use Notecards

Teach students how to use notecards to take notes and organize information.

1. Give each student four to six notecards. Have them write a heading on each card. *Example:* If students are studying the Spanish missions of California, they might choose four—perhaps San Luis Obispo, Santa Barbara, Santa Cruz, and San Juan Capistrano. Each location becomes a heading on a notecard.

2. Show students how to take notes in phrases or by paraphrasing what they read, hear, or observe. Insist that they not write complete sentences.

3. Have students take notes on the appropriate cards. *Example:* As they learn information about San Luis Obispo, they locate the notecard with that heading and record the information there. As they learn information about Santa Cruz, they record it on the notecard with that heading.

In this way, note-taking becomes a kinesthetic experience. Kids with learning difficulties find this much easier than writing everything on a piece of paper and reorganizing it later.

Students can also use notecards to prepare and study for tests. On one side, they write a question about a word or idea they need to know, using blue or black ink. On the other side, they write or draw the answer, using red ink. They can use the cards to review material on their own or with a partner. If they answer a question correctly, that card goes into a discard pile. If they answer incorrectly, it goes back into the main deck so it will come up again soon. The notecards should be shuffled each time they are used.

For middle school and high school students, please see "3S TN (Qs): Note-Taking for Global Learners" on page 143.

---

* All of the reproducible handouts in this book, including the Content Organization Chart, are included as digital content. All may be customized to meet your needs and printed out for use in your classroom or group.

Five Quick Memory Tricks

Mnemonics

There are times when students need to simply memorize something. Information is more easily retrieved from memory when the learner uses a mnemonic (memory device) to store it in the brain. Teach any mnemonic meta-cognitively by thinking out loud and expecting students to do the same.

Example: "I need a mnemonic for remembering the planets in the order of their distance from the sun. I'll start by making a vertical list of all the planets. Then I'll think of a word or phrase for each planet that starts with the same letter as the planet. My goal is to link the words into a sentence I can remember."

Mercury	**M**ary's
Venus	**V**ery
Earth	**E**nergetic
Mars	**M**usic teacher
Jupiter	**J**oyfully
Saturn	**S**old
Uranus	**U**s
Neptune	**N**ew
Pluto	**P**ianos

"Now, every time I want to remember the names of the planets in the correct order, I'll recall the sentence and remember that the first letter of every word or phrase is the same as the first letter of the planet's name."

Challenge students to create their own memory sentences.

Verbal Repetition

Just as in the old blab schools of colonial days, students' memories are enhanced when the entire group chants together what they are trying to learn. Add rhymes or rhythms (beats) and the chances of remembering get better.

Acronyms

An acronym is a word or phrase made from the first letters of the words or phrases that students are trying to remember. One of the most famous classroom acronyms, HOMES, stands for the names of the Great Lakes: Huron, Ontario, Michigan, Erie, Superior. Another, NEWS, helps students remember the four directions: North, East, West, South.

Chunking

Chunking reduces the strain on short-term memory. Instead of trying to learn and remember many individual things,

one learns them in sets or groups. Example: Have students learn the number facts in sets of three. To learn the 3's, students chant "3, 6, 9; 3, 6, 9; 3, 6, 9," then "12, 15, 18; 12, 15, 18; 12, 15, 18," then "3, 6, 9, 12, 15, 18; 3, 6, 9, 12, 15, 18; 3, 6, 9, 12, 15, 18," and so on.

The Location Method

In this rather silly but effective method, students remember items on a list by imagining that each is located at a different place in a familiar room. Example: To remember the names of three types of plant-eating dinosaurs, a student might visualize herself placing a brontosaurus on the sofa, a stegosaurus on the piano, and a sauropod on top of the TV. She would then visualize herself retrieving the items in the same order.

Homework

Homework is one of the biggest stressors for students with learning difficulties. Often, they don't complete their homework, or they forget to bring it back to school. There are several reasons why homework is such a problem for them. Sometimes they don't remember the lesson long enough to do the related homework. Sometimes they simply don't know what to do. Sometimes their home situation is chaotic, without adult supervision, and they have no place to do their homework and no one to turn to when they need help.

Ways to Improve the Homework Situation for Struggling Students

- If you know that any of the conditions described above are present—the inability to remember lessons, lack of support at home—never punish a student for not finishing homework.

- Talk to parents and caregivers to reassure them that it's not their job to be the teacher, and they should guard against overhelping their kids. Let them know how you want them to communicate with you if their child is having trouble understanding and doing the homework. (For more on this topic, see Chapter 14.)

- Assign homework by elapsed time rather than as quantities of work to be done. Instead of assigning numbers of pages to be read or problems to be solved or activities to be completed, tell students to spend 15 minutes reviewing math concepts or 20 minutes writing a story. Give them permission to stop working when that time has passed. You might send home a note explaining the elapsed time homework and asking a parent or caregiver to initial the homework as proof that the time was spent.

- Give students credit for any homework they bring back to school. If you assign homework by elapsed time, you might give full credit for working for the assigned amount of time, and partial credit for working for less time. I don't recommend awarding extra credit for working extra time. Some parents end up expecting their kids to work longer to please the teacher, which leads to a power struggle at home.

- Try not to take credit away from students whose homework is not done. When partial credit is given for partial homework, students are more likely to complete at least some of their homework. To make the point that homework helps learning outcomes, some teachers give bonus points or extra credit for completed and returned homework, but never take away already-earned credit from students who do not return their homework.

- The credit students earn in any particular subject should reflect their progress at school from one marking period to another. This is preferable to averaging grades over the span of a marking period. If you were being evaluated, you would want full credit for any improvement you have made from one observation to the next. You would not want the person evaluating you to average his or her observations over time.

- For longer-term assignments and projects, help students create and use a backwards timeline. Have them record their timeline on the "Monthly Homework and Project Calendar" (page 169).

Use Assignment Notebooks

Provide and use assignment notebooks that are consistent from class to class. *All teachers should use identical assignment notebooks with their struggling students.* Pages 167–168 include a two-page "Homework Assignments" form you may copy and use if you and your colleagues agree that it works for your philosophy and school. (Make two-sided copies to save paper; add any special instructions to the second side.) If this isn't the right form for your school, design or find one that everyone can accept.

Show students how to cross off completed assignments and star those that still need their attention. Or they could use a color-coded system—blue or black for completed, red for still not done. Teach parents or caregivers what their responsibilities are vis-à-vis the notebook:

- Parents/caregivers should expect the assignment notebook to come home every night, regardless of whether the student has homework.

- They should ask to see the notebook and have the student explain the assignments for that day.

- They should consult the backwards timeline to check the progress of any long-term assignments.

Use a Calendar

Some kids prefer a calendar to an assignment notebook. It helps them to see the big picture of a longer-term assignment from start to finish (due date)—or, working backwards, from finish to start. It also helps them to see at a glance what steps toward completing an assignment are coming up in the next week or few weeks.

For students who want to work with calendars (or those you think would benefit from trying this strategy), make copies of the "Monthly Homework and Project Calendar" on page 169. Make ten copies for each student if this is the start of the new school year, fewer if you're further into the year. Point out that these pages don't have any months or dates on them, then show students how to add this information (the month at the top, the dates in the upper right-hand corners of each box). Next, model how to write homework assignments beside the "H." Then show how to write the name of a project beside the "D" on its due date—and, working backwards, how to record the homework assignments related to that project.

Tests

Most students with learning difficulties do not do well on tests of any kind. Either they are very anxious and perform poorly, or they have given up hope and perform poorly. It's easy to have a defeatist attitude when one has seldom or never enjoyed success. You can help your struggling students change their attitude, their approach, and their experience.

Start by giving each student a copy of the "How to Prepare for a Test" handout (page 170). Teach this content as you would a lesson in any subject area. The information is certainly just as important. Take time to discuss and explain each step. You may want to add, delete, or change steps to meet the needs of your students.

Ways to Improve Testing Outcomes for Struggling Students

Use Goal Setting

Just as students can use goal setting (see pages 65–68) to predict how much work they will do, they can use it to predict their performance on tests.

Have students set a personal goal for each test: How many items do they think they can complete within the designated time? Have students write their goal as a ratio at the top of their test paper: predicted number of items to amount of time. *Example:* 10 questions in 30 minutes = 10/30.

Homework Assignments

NAME: _____ **TODAY'S DATE:** _____

Subject	Assignment	Check if completed or explain why incomplete
Reading		
English		
Writing		
Math		
Social Studies		
Science		
Health		
Foreign Language		
Applied Arts		

continued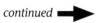

Homework Assignments
(continued)

Circle what to take home	Circle what to bring back tomorrow
Books:	**Books:**
Math	Math
Reading	Reading
Social Studies	Social Studies
Science	Science
English	English
Foreign Language	Foreign Language
Other: _____	Other: _____
Supplies:	**Supplies:**
Pencils	Pencils
Colored Pencils	Colored Pencils
Markers	Markers
Pens	Pens
Paper	Paper
Ruler	Ruler
Assignment Notebook	Assignment Notebook
Other: _____	Other: _____

Parent's/Caregiver's signature shows I spent _____ working on all homework.
                                                        time

Parent's/Caregiver's Signature: _____

Comments from parent/caregiver: _____

_____

Monthly Homework and Project Calendar

DIRECTIONS: Write in the month and dates. Write homework assignments next to the **H** using black or blue pencil or pen. Write project names next to the **D** (for Due Date) using red pencil or pen. Then work backwards from the due date and write in the homework you need to do to finish your project on time.

MONTH: _____

Sunday	Monday	Tuesday	Wednesday	Thursday	Friday	Saturday
H D	H D	H D	H D	H D	H D	H D
H D	H D	H D	H D	H D	H D	H D
H D	H D	H D	H D	H D	H D	H D
H D	H D	H D	H D	H D	H D	H D
H D	H D	H D	H D	H D	H D	H D

How to Prepare for a Test
Ten Tried-and-True Tips

Hardly anyone likes tests, but everyone has to take them!
Here's how to make sure you're ready to do your best at test-taking time.

1. Before you leave the classroom, be sure you have asked questions about any words or ideas you don't completely understand.

2. Before you leave school, be sure you have all the materials you need to study for the test: your book, your notes, any extra material the teacher has given you, the homework hotline number or Web site address, and so on. (What else do you need?)

3. At home, find a quiet spot to do your studying. If it helps you to concentrate, play soothing music at a very low volume while you study. Don't take phone calls, answer email, watch TV, play computer games, or instant message (IM) anyone. Just study.

4. In your book, review chapter and section headings, words in italics or bold print, pictures, charts, graphs, etc. If you took notes, review those, too.

5. Take notes while you study. Use graphic organizers, different colors, acronyms, mnemonics, or anything else that will help you remember the material.

6. Practice sample problems or exercises.

7. If you study with someone else, make sure to leave some time to review the material again by yourself.

8. Before you go to bed, put all the things you need to bring to school tomorrow in one place. (In your backpack? On the kitchen table? Next to the door?) Be sure that you have pencils or pens for the test. Is there anything else you will need? What about books? A calculator? What else? Have everything ready.

9. Go to sleep at a reasonable time.

10. Set your alarm so you wake up early enough to eat breakfast before you leave.

BONUS: QUICK TIPS FOR TEST TIME

- When you get the test, take three deep breaths. Each time you exhale, think to yourself, "I'm ready for this test. I prepared for it, and I will do well!"

- On the back of your paper (or on a piece of scratch paper), quickly write down anything you think you'll need for the test. Jot down key ideas, dates, vocabulary words, and names. Sketch simple maps and vocabulary maps.

- Skim the whole test. Then go back and complete the easier items first.

- As you work through the rest of the test, never spend more than two minutes on one item if it doesn't make sense to you or if it seems very hard. Make a mark in the margin so you can come back to that item if you have enough time.

For a while, correct the items the students tried to do without scoring them down for any missed items. As several weeks of success go by, gently encourage kids to raise their goals slightly. The lowest grade students should get on tests structured this way is a C, because they are learning to set and accomplish real goals.

Address Test Anxiety

- Talk about test anxiety with students who experience it. What is it? Where does it come from? What does it feel like? What are the symptoms?

- Talk about the importance of getting enough sleep the night before a test, and eating a healthful breakfast on the morning of a test.

- Demonstrate deep breathing techniques.

- Demonstrate progressive relaxation—visualizing different parts of the body releasing stress.

- Allow students to listen to soothing music through headphones during tests.

- Teach positive affirmations students can repeat to themselves before and during tests.

- Make sure that every student has a copy of the "How to Prepare for a Test" handout (page 170).

Teach Test-Taking Strategies and Tips

Teach and model the following test-taking strategies. They will help to relieve test anxiety and provide the comfort of having a plan.

For any test:

- Take some time when you first get the test to look over all the items. Begin with sections that you think you will do well on, then go on to other sections as time permits.

- Read the directions carefully. If you don't understand the directions, ask the teacher

- Ask the teacher if it's safe to guess on the type of test you are taking. (Sometimes it is, and sometimes it isn't.) If it is, then guess when you don't know the answer.

- Once you answer a question, don't change your answer later unless you are positive that your first answer is wrong.

- Never spend too much time on a problem. If you don't have a plan for solving the problem in mind within two minutes, move on to the next problem. Make a little mark by the number of any questions you skip so you can find them easily later.

For true/false tests:

- Statements with words like "always," "never," "completely," "only," and so on are almost always false.

- If any statement in a series of statements is false, the whole series is false.

- Guessing "true" is usually safer than guessing "false."

For multiple choice tests:

- Answer the easiest questions first.

- Don't spend too much time on any one item.

- Cover the answers, read the question again, and come up with your own answer, then compare it to the ones that are available.

- Read the beginning of the question separately with each of the choices, and think of them as true/false choices.

- Eliminate any choice you know to be incorrect.

- If two or more options seem true, and another option is "all of the above," choose "all of the above" as your answer.

- If any two options are the opposite of each other, choose one of them.

For short answer tests:

- Look over all the questions first and jot down key words for everything you know.

- Come back and write sentences or complete phrases about the key words you wrote.

For essay questions:

- Take a few minutes to draw a graphic organizer and jot down your thoughts.

- Write a few sentences about each topic. Keep re-reading the topic sentence to make sure the details you write are related to just that topic.

- It's better to have a few sentences for each of the required paragraphs than to spend all your time on just one paragraph. Leave open spaces between each paragraph as you are writing so you can fill in the space later with other sentences that fit.

Questions and Answers

"Where am I supposed to find time to help these kids with organizational tasks?"

A good time to do this is when the other students are working in cooperative groups. (Those students shouldn't need your constant help then because they are supposed to be helping each other. Therefore, to take ten minutes to help students with learning difficulties should not create a hardship for the rest of the class, since you will return to them shortly.) If you remember that kids' ability to learn content will improve when their study and organizational skills are in place, you can give yourself permission to use regular teaching time for this purpose.

"What can I do when kids lose their forms and checklists?"

Make duplicates to send home; keep one copy at school. Students should always keep their organizational tools for school at school.

"Isn't it possible that some kids are just lazy and could do much better if they only applied themselves to the learning jobs they have to do?"

Think of something you tried to learn to do over time with little or no success. No matter how hard you tried, the task never seemed to get any easier. What happened over time to your motivation? Much of what looks like laziness is really hopelessness and frustration. When we keep sending the message to our students that we are confident they can learn certain strategies that will make their learning come more easily, they may find the courage to try again. As soon as one strategy brings promising results, be sure to respond with specific and sincere praise. Use that success to encourage students to try a few more strategies. When we don't focus on matching the students to the most helpful strategies, the students have no alternative but to conclude they are simply not able to learn. We must prove that is not the case.

"Many of my students get little or no help from parents. How can my students learn all they need to know without parental support?"

The older I get, the more I understand how to differentiate between expending energy on things I can and cannot change. The only way you *might* be able to change parents' behavior is to send home positive messages about their children. And even if you are never successful in improving your students' situation at home, you can keep demonstrating your firm belief that with the right match of strategies to their learning styles, amazing progress can be made, with or without parental assistance.

REFERENCES AND RESOURCES

Heacox, Diane. *Up from Underachievement: How Teachers, Students, and Parents Can Work Together to Promote Student Success.* Minneapolis: Free Spirit Publishing, 1991. Describes a step-by-step program that helps students in all grades break the failure chain.

Learning to Learn (www.learningtolearn.com). A research-based learning and thinking skills system, recommended for national use by the U.S. Department of Education. Students move away from rote learning towards inquiry-based learning and acquire skills that help them use their natural visual learning abilities. Delivered in schools through teacher training. 1-800-288-4465.

Levine, Mel. *Keeping a Head in School: A Student's Book About Learning Abilities and Learning Disorders.* Cambridge, MA: Educators Publishing Service, 1991. Helps students develop and use effective strategies for getting better results with schoolwork.

Parks, Sandra, and Howard Black. *Organizing Thinking: Book 1.* Grades 2–4. Pacific Grove, CA: Critical Thinking Press and Software, 1992. Students learn how to analyze and use information more effectively and create their own organizers to improve comprehension and retention in any subject. —*Organizing Thinking: Book 2.* Grades 5–8. Pacific Grove, CA: Critical Thinking Press and Software, 1990.

Pieces of Learning (www.piecesoflearning.com). Publisher of books on differentiation, standards-based teaching, assessment, and raising student achievement including Carolyn Coil's *Becoming an Achiever: A Student Guide* and *Motivating Underachievers: 220 Strategies for Success.* 1-800-729-5137.

Study Guides and Strategies (www.studygs.net). Information on improving study habits. The site also contains dozens of how-to pages that demonstrate guidelines for test taking, paper writing, organization, using the Internet, etc. All the information is in the public domain.

Success by Design (www.successbydesign.com). A good source of assignment notebooks and student planners for grades K–12. 1-800-327-0057.

RECOMMENDED READINGS FOR STUDENTS

Carlson, Richard. *Don't Sweat the Small Stuff for Teens: Simple Ways to Keep Your Cool in Stressful Times.* New York: Hyperion, 2000.

Covey, Sean. *The Seven Habits of Highly Effective Teens: The Ultimate Teenage Success Guide.* New York: Simon and Schuster, 1998. Ages 13 and up. For teens, parents, grandparents, and any adult who influences young people.

Fox, Annie, and Ruth Kirschner. *Too Stressed to Think? A Teen Guide to Staying Sane When Life Makes You Crazy.* Minneapolis: Free Spirit Publishing, 2005.

Johnson, Spencer. *Who Moved My Cheese? for Teens: An A-Mazing Way to Change and Win!* New York: Putnam Publishing Group, 2002. Presents the author's parable about change framed in a story about a group of high school friends trying to handle change in their lives.

Moser, Adolph J., illustrated by Dav Pilkey. *Don't Pop Your Cork on Mondays: The Children's Anti-Stress Book.* Kansas City, MO: Landmark Editions, 1998. Ages 9–12. Explores the causes and effects of stress and offers practical approaches and techniques for dealing with stress in daily life. Recommended for kids, parents, teachers, and clinicians.

Romain, Trevor. *How to Do Homework Without Throwing Up.* Minneapolis: Free Spirit Publishing, 1997. Ages 8–13. Kids learn a variety of simple techniques for getting homework done. Serious suggestions delivered with wit and humor.

Schneider, Meg. *Help! My Teacher Hates Me: A School Survival Guide for Kids 10 to 14 Years Old.* New York: Workman Publishing, 1994.

Whitney, Brooks. *School Smarts: All the Right Answers to Homework, Teachers, Popularity, and More!* Middleton, WI: Pleasant Co. Publications, 2000. Ages 9–12. Part of the American Girl Library.

Williams, Julie, illustrated by Angela Martini-Wonde. *A Smart Girl's Guide to Starting Middle School: Everything You Need to Know About Juggling More Homework, More Teachers, and More Friends.* Middleton, WI: Pleasant Co. Publications, 2004. Grades 5–8.

Assessing What Students Have Learned

CHAPTER 12

One of the greatest challenges today's educators face is how to assess the learning of students who begin a school year at an achievement level substantially below grade-level expectations. In the past, schools created and used assessment systems for students with special needs that were significantly different from those applied to most other students. Grading for special education students was often adjusted, with their effort taken into consideration as a way to give them higher grades for their work. The goal was to keep their self-esteem high in the hope that eventually that might lead to actual improvement.

Sometimes, students at the bottom of the academic barrel were allowed to fail when interventions were not successful. Some teachers rationalized that those students were choosing to fail by not responding to all the help that was offered, and that it was reasonable to allow students to experience the consequence of their choices. When parents of these kids were not responsive to the school's efforts to improve their children's achievement, some educators concluded that the blame lay with the family, and not the school.

With the No Child Left Behind legislation and increasingly rigorous state standards, the expectation now is that every student will attain achievement levels mandated by your state, while the school as a whole will achieve Adequate Yearly Progress (AYP). Schools that fail to meet these standards may experience serious sanctions from the state and federal government.

Teachers, students, and parents have all been profoundly affected by the way assessment is done in our schools. All instruction is now driven by the data that describes what students are learning. Educators at all levels have worked hard to align what is taught with the expected standards, assess students often, and find ways to intervene as soon as achievement slips. Interventions are offered in several layers. Tutoring for struggling students happens before and after school, during school breaks, and over summer vacation. Coaching is available for teachers in strategies to help needy kids reach grade-level standards. Teach, assess, use the data to decide how to intervene . . . teach, assess, use the data to impact instruction . . . The cycle seems endless.

Results have been impressive in some schools. The Center for Performance Assessment provides leadership and assistance to schools in their efforts to reach the expected goals. Director Douglas Reeves describes the Center's goal as "90/90/90": If there are schools with 90 percent minority populations and 90 percent of students receiving free or reduced lunch, yet 90 percent of students are meeting or exceeding standards, than those same results should be within reach for any school. The center's Web site offers fascinating testimonials from 90/90/90 schools that have learned to meet AYP goals, along with the names and email addresses of contact people in those schools. (See "References and Resources" at the end of this chapter.) The attitude of these schools toward their students is clear: "You can, you will, and we will help you."

In his work with administrators, Reeves describes conditions that have a positive impact on student achievement:

■ a curriculum focused on standards, with at least half the instructional time spent on developing literacy

174

- frequent, structured meetings that focus on student achievement; attention to achievement data; willingness to change direction when strategies are not working

- involvement of the entire building staff on improving achievement

- teacher assignment based solely on what works best for the students

- writing across the curriculum.

This chapter describes ways in which teachers and students can work together to bring all students up to assessment levels considered acceptable by your state. These high expectations require all educators to examine, and perhaps change, their grading and assessment practices.

Ways to Improve Student Achievement

Assessment is much easier when students are successful learners. The following tips and guidelines can help you help your students to get satisfactory results on assessments.

- Continuously communicate high expectations for all students in your school.

- Activate prior knowledge so students can see how what they are about to learn is connected to what they already know and understand. For suggestions, see "Understanding Material from Text and Lectures" on page 139.

- Before teaching the content, always share with your students the exact standards to be learned. At the end of the lesson, come back to those standards to reinforce how the lesson related to them.

- Show struggling students how to use goal setting so they can feel more in control of their learning and assessment outcomes. (See pages 65–68.) You might try what one school did: Start a "Yes I Can" campaign. Have students make buttons to wear that describe their specific goal(s) for the upcoming grading period. Display charts in the room that list students' goals, but not their progress. This allows students to recognize and reinforce each other's goal-related behaviors. When students work toward a goal, they declare, "Yes I Can!" When students notice a classmate working toward a goal, they declare, "Yes You Can!" Students keep their own private records of actual progress toward their goals. If your school has a button-making machine, you can also make "Yes I Can" buttons for your students to wear.

- Whenever possible, assess in the same format used on your state assessments. *Example:* If the state tests require students to fill in bubbles on answer sheets, use bubble answer sheets for your classroom assessments.

- Assess often and adjust your instruction accordingly. Be sure your assessment procedures accurately demonstrate progress over time.

- Use assessments that are more descriptive than judgmental or punitive. *Example:* Rather than just writing a grade as the number of examples or problems that were incorrect, indicate the number that were correct, and include comments that help the student understand what she can do to improve her results next time on a similar task.

- When using rubrics, be sure your students understand the language level. Offer rubrics in stages instead of all at once. *Example:* If a writing rubric includes four categories—clarity, accuracy, idea development, meaningful sequence—concentrate on clarity until students are scoring at average or higher numbers. Then slowly add the other categories one at a time. As students become more comfortable with using rubrics independently, their assessment outcomes will improve.

- Continuously adjust instruction based on feedback from your observations and assessments.

- Find and use (or create and use) student self-assessment tools that show progress over time. See the Report Card Chart on page 185.

- Actively involve students in communicating with their other teachers and their families about their achievement, focusing on improvements over time.

- If you're faced with a choice between computer-assisted learning and no learning, use the technology. Keep working with students to help them learn independently, but don't hesitate to use whatever works. Students who have enjoyed some success in school will do better on assessments of all kinds than those who have only experienced failure.

Scenario: Noah

Noah was a seventh grader who had become increasingly negative about school in recent years. His mom sadly remembered how eager he had been to go to kindergarten. She also recalled how dismayed she had been to learn that his progress in school was seriously hampered by his inability to do simple things, such as understand letter-sound relationships or write his letters and numbers neatly.

Noah had always learned by listening to the conversations of older kids and/or adults, and he had been an avid fan of educational television. He loved surprising people with the information he knew just from watching those shows. Although he could tell great stories that demonstrated his creative imagination, he became sullen when he was expected to write down his thoughts neatly, legibly, and accurately.

His teachers in elementary school had offered him opportunities to work on shorter assignments or choose fewer spelling words. Although their gestures were sincere, Noah always rejected them because he worried that the other kids would find out about the special arrangements and tease him. His grades were never good, although his fourth-grade teacher gave him all A's because he tried so hard. Since he knew his A's meant something different for him than for most other kids his age, he didn't take much pride in them.

When Noah reached middle school, he became a troublemaker. Perhaps the recognition he received for that role from his teachers and peers was safer than being recognized for his inadequacies with the regular seventh-grade work. He still watched shows on educational television, but he didn't talk about them anymore.

The Grading Dilemma

"I *hate* report cards!" is a claim often made by frustrated teachers, who have long known that traditional methods of grading leave much to be desired. Regardless of how well we keep records of student progress, the act of giving grades causes a lot of anxiety and worry. We wonder how adequate (and accurate) grades are and how effectively they communicate the actual progress our students are making. We realize that no matter how hard we try to be totally objective, we are often influenced by students' behaviors and attitudes.

Many parents also hate report cards. Few understand the often confusing and inconsistent information report cards bring. They know that some teachers give higher grades to kids who work really hard, while others conform consistently to the grading scale the school has adopted. Teachers' comments are often cryptic and full of jargon incomprehensible to parents. Remarks like "Your son is not working up to potential," "Your daughter needs to use her time more wisely," and "Your child could do much better if she only applied herself" are so trite that their meaning has been lost. For grades to have true significance for parents (and students), they must be interpreted the same way by all people who see them.

Most kids have no idea what grades actually mean and are clueless about the number of hours their teachers spend trying to assign grades that are accurate and fair. Whenever I saw my students counting the total number of letter grades, check marks, or plusses and minuses,

I wanted to scream, "No, that's not the way you're supposed to receive those grades!"

Struggling students hate report cards even more than teachers and parents. Once they realize that there won't be much good news for them to carry home at report-card time, they develop a negative attitude about grades in general. Low grades don't usually motivate students to work harder and do better in the future.

Glossary of Terms

Assessment: Determining a student's competency and progress.

Authentic assessment: Evaluating students' learning with meaningful tasks that are directly connected to what they have been taught.

Averaging: Evaluating students' learning based on the average of all the work they have done over a particular time period.

Curve: Arranging grades so students' work represents a range from excellence to failure.

Evaluation: Making a judgment about the degree to which students have met criteria.

Grading: Assigning a quantitative value to students' work.

Performances, exhibitions, and/or demonstrations: Active illustrations by students that demonstrate what they have learned beyond paper-and-pencil activities.

Portfolio: A collection of a student's work in several formats over time to evaluate progress made since a starting point.

Reporting: Communicating information about students' progress to parents and to the students themselves.

Rubric: Description of standards against which students' work will be judged.

Traditional assessment: Paper-and-pencil tasks that require students to write their responses to test questions in traditional formats, such as true/false, multiple choice, and essay.

Traditional vs. Authentic Assessment

In the 1990s, authentic assessment was the goal in many schools. Teachers were expected to design real-world-type tasks that would allow students to demonstrate their acquisition of knowledge and skills. The No Child Left Behind legislation and state standards have brought about a return to more traditional assessment methods. In some cases, a student's performance on just one high-stakes test can determine his or her success or failure for an entire school year. Authentic and traditional assessment methods can be used together by teachers who are comfortable with both.

For many years, teaching to the test was considered unethical. Now we know that it is only ethical to test what has been taught! Such authentic assessments should enable us to diagnose students' strengths and weaknesses effectively and provide specific learning experiences, which will lead to improved achievement.

Effective assessment practices include attention to these beliefs:

- All students can be successful learners when their learning style strengths are respected.

- Stimulating, meaningful curriculum motivates students to work hard; grading alone may not.

- Students should not be graded during the learning process. (Would you want to be evaluated while you were learning to use a new teaching strategy?)

- Grades are somewhat effective as incentives but are almost never effective as punishment. *Example:* A zero for late or incomplete work does not motivate students to work harder.

- Low grades cause most students to withdraw from learning. Zeroes entered in grade books should be changed to higher grades when students are able to show growth. Partial credit should be available whenever possible. (Even Olympic judges in some events throw out the lowest score!)

- Reporting grades as averages is unfair. Reporting should always focus on a student's current levels of achievement at the time the report is made!

- Methods that compare students to each other are not helpful for struggling students. Methods that compare students' performance to specific criteria are more fair and effective.

- When students perceive that only a few can get the highest grades, there is no incentive for students to help each other improve their learning. Avoid grading curves. All students should be able to earn high grades; all students should get the grades they have earned.

- A separate grade for effort should never be given.* Only the student knows how much effort he has expended on an activity.

- Opportunities to earn credit for improvement, rather than achieving finite criteria, provide higher incentives for learning.

- Grading and assessment methods should enable students, parents, and teachers to plan for improved outcomes on the next attempt.

- Teachers should coach students on how to explain their grade reports to their parents. In this way, parents—and students themselves—have a much better understanding of what the reports really mean.

- Students should be expected to continue working on a task until high-quality work is achieved. It's *much* more effective for students to work on fewer tasks to higher quality levels than to work on many tasks to unacceptable quality levels.

- Honors credit should be available to any student at any level who completes the type of product worthy of honors' level expectations.

More Ways to Improve Student Achievement

Watching Students Learn

Systematically observing students in the school environment is a highly effective way to assess performance. At first, you may have to force yourself to record your observations as you watch the kids at work and play; after a while, this will become so automatic that you won't be able to see something without wanting to record it.

It's perfectly all right if your students know that you're watching them, as long as you explain your purpose and how you intend to use your notes. Following an initial adjustment period, they will become oblivious to your recording methods. Be sure to use audio and videotapes whenever they might enhance your observations or be useful for sharing your data with parents and teaching specialists.

On page 178, you'll find a Daily Observations Record Sheet you can copy and use to keep track of your students' performance. Create a master copy with the names of all of your students and make multiple copies to have on hand. Data from these observations is useful in parent-teacher conferences as well as for staff meetings regarding program adjustments for particular students. An example of how you might use the record sheet is shown on page 179.

---

* Kohn, Alfie. *Punished by Rewards.* New York: Houghton Mifflin, 1993, p. 208.

DATE: _____

Student's Name	Observed Behavior	+ = Improving − = Losing Ground Ø = Staying the Same	Comments

DAILY OBSERVATIONS RECORD SHEET

DATE: MONDAY, NOVEMBER 15

Student's Name	Observed Behavior	+ = Improving − = Losing Ground ∅ = Staying the Same	Comments
CHARLOTTE	SPELLING	+	CHOSE 10 INSTEAD OF 4 WORDS TO STUDY; 80% CORRECT
BRIAN	SOCIAL SKILLS	−	PHYSICALLY ATTACKED SARAH ON PLAYGROUND
MARIA	MATH	+	REALLY GOT INTO MEASURING ACTIVITY
RUDY	MATH	∅	EARLIER PROGRESS IN KNOWING MATH FACTS CONTINUES
ALONZO	READING	+	COMPLETED 2ND BOOK THIS MONTH
KRISTIN	SPELLING	−	CAN'T SEEM TO TRANSFER WORDS SPELLED CORRECTLY ON TEST TO OTHER WRITTEN WORK

Portfolios

Creating a portfolio is a systematic procedure that allows students to collect and display their work in a given subject area over time, much as an artist might. Portfolios emphasize students' strengths and illustrate how they learn rather than what they know. They allow attention to be paid to effort and progress, providing much more information about what students have achieved than grades and test scores alone. Students (and their parents) can more easily see how much progress they have made.

A portfolio might include a combination of regular work and work that represents any or all of the following:

■ the same type of activity done at various intervals over time

■ an unusual idea

■ an in-depth understanding of a problem or idea

■ a resourceful or clever use of materials

■ evidence that a student has stayed with a topic for a long time and learned a lot about it

■ products beyond paper-and-pencil tasks.

Portfolio products can take virtually any form, from written papers and tests to drawings, photographs, audios, videos or DVDs, certificates, reviews, CD-ROMs, and even three-dimensional objects. (*Example:* A math portfolio might include data about surveys students have conducted, observations about where and how math is used in everyday life, visual representations—even 3-D—of something kids have designed that applies math functions, and descriptions of experiences with enrichment activities.) Each product should meet the following basic criteria:

■ It should be selected by the student as an example of work the student is proud of or otherwise believes represents high-quality work.

■ It should be edited and polished to pre-established levels of mastery, as described by rubrics that students refer to continuously as they work to achieve higher levels of performance. Unedited work can be sent home, but it should be stamped "Not Edited."

Once you have started using portfolios, set aside class time weekly for students to work on them. They should use that time to review the work they have done since the last selection time, choose something new that they feel should be included in their portfolio, and make any necessary changes or modifications which would enable that piece to stand as a representation of their best effort.

To keep parents up-to-date on how their children are doing in school, send them regular portfolio reports more often than report cards. Have children bring home their latest portfolio product to show their parents; be sure to coach students on how to describe their work to their parents. Include a "Portfolio Product Report"* (page 181) for parents to complete and return. Students fill out the first

---

* Adapted from the "Texas Portfolio Record Sheet" with permission of the Texas Education Agency.

part of the form, and parents fill out the rest. **Tips:** Introduce this form during a parent-teacher conference. Tell parents that giving sincere verbal encouragement and celebrating small successes will motivate their children more than monetary or other tangible rewards. Discourage parents from chastising their children or removing home privileges for unacceptable schoolwork.

Performances, Exhibitions, and/or Demonstrations

In some schools, students are asked to perform what they have learned in real-life settings. Educators in favor of using performance assessments argue that they are a more reliable indicator of student growth in learning than objective tests. The problem is that performances are more difficult to create and evaluate than traditional assessments. The chart below illustrates some differences between traditional testing and performance assessments.

TRADITIONAL TESTING COMPARED TO PERFORMANCE ASSESSMENT

Skill to be mastered	Traditional testing	Performance assessment
Math computation	Tests with paper & pencil Word problem solution	Using a catalog of merchandise, make a written plan to spend $1,200. Be sure to include tax and shipping costs. Do not exceed $1,200 and do not spend less than $1,175 total.
Biography	Read a biography of a famous person Write answers on Biography Report Sheet	With a partner, choose two biographies of people who lived during the same time period. Use an interview process to present what you learn. You play the role of one of the people, your partner plays the other, and you interview each other about events in your life. For added interest, dress up as the people you are portraying.
Government	Complete a flow chart that shows how the balance of power works in U.S. government to prevent misuse/abuse of power	Select a historic event in which persons in the U.S. tried to take more power than they were entitled to under the Constitution. Prepare a series of newspaper articles to illustrate how checks and balances stopped the potential abuse of power.

Portfolio Product Report

To be filled out by the student:

Name: _____ Date: _____

Name/title of product: _____

Description of product: _____

_____

Why did you choose to include this product in your portfolio?

_____

_____

_____

How does this product demonstrate that your schoolwork is improving?

_____

_____

_____

To be filled out by the parent/caregiver:

How did your child share information about this product with you?

_____

_____

_____

How did you acknowledge/celebrate your child's progress?

_____

_____

_____

Student's Signature: _____

Parent's/Caregiver's Signature: _____

Please give this form to your child to return to school. Thank you!

Rubrics

Rubrics are guides for assigning quantitative values to various levels of student performance in a particular area of work. They allow students to clearly understand exactly what is required of them. Peer partners may work together to help each other assess which level of performance has been attained and determine what is needed to move to a higher level. Scores are earned in each category, and total scores may translate into letter grades or point totals. Three examples of how rubrics might look are shown below.

Thousands of free rubrics are available on the Internet if you prefer not to create your own or don't have the time. Type "free rubrics" into a search engine and explore the various Web sites listed. See "References and Resources."

SAMPLE RUBRICS

COUNTING RUBRIC (KINDERGARTEN)

Counting	4 Points	3 Points	2 Points	1 Point
Counts from memory up to ___ (number).	Counts easily to and beyond the target number.	Counts to target number without any errors.	Counts to target number with 2 or fewer errors.	Unable to count to target number.
Points Earned				

READING COMPREHENSION (ELEMENTARY SCHOOL)

Reading	4 Points	3 Points	2 Points	1 Point
Main idea	Completely understands main idea; can describe it in own words; is able to use inferential material to draw conclusions.	Can describe main idea in own words, mostly using material directly found in story to do so.	Appears to understand the gist of the story but is unable to prove assertions using material in the story.	Totally missed the main idea of the story; has an incorrect notion of what the main idea is.
Points Earned				

WRITING (GRADES 5 AND UP)

Writing	4 Points	3 Points	2 Points	1 Point
Paragraph about favorite place	Easy to understand; uses detail and description; flows logically; uses correct grammar, mechanics, and spelling.	Clear message, good flow with some detail and description; flows fairly logically; usually uses correct grammar, mechanics, and spelling.	Organization not totally clear; few details or description; logic difficult to follow; makes many errors in grammar, mechanics, and spelling.	Lacks ability to communicate thoughts in writing.
Points Earned				

Student-Designed Rubrics

Students can be taught how to create their own rubrics before they actually begin a project or activity. One teacher offered her sixth-grade students an opportunity to choose a project about ancient civilization from eight alternatives. Groups were formed of students who had chosen the same type of project. One group decided to create dioramas to illustrate the agora, the open marketplace of ancient Greece. The students looked at some dioramas that another class had done, found some information in a book on art projects about making dioramas, and created the following rubric to use to evaluate each person's diorama.

1. Container is large enough for all objects to be in clear view.	YES	ALMOST	NO
2. Finished display is three-dimensional.	YES	ALMOST	NO
3. Figures stand in a sturdy fashion.	YES	ALMOST	NO
4. Main display has detail and is interesting to view.	YES	ALMOST	NO
5. Background is detailed and flows into display.	YES	ALMOST	NO

The students referred to their rubric often during the construction of their dioramas. They were encouraged to continue filling out rubric ratings until all of their elements could lead to a "yes" response. In some cases, the final grade was tied to how many "yes" and "almost" responses were circled for the final product. Best of all, the teacher's job was much easier, since most of the adjustments to the products were completed before she received the finished products.

Struggling Students and Standardized Tests

Standardized tests are especially challenging for students with learning difficulties, who are suddenly expected to do many things that are difficult for them under the best of circumstances. They must read quickly, come up with answers, write, and solve several problems, all within a limited amount of time. Obviously these students need all the help we can offer.

- Give every student a copy of "How to Prepare for a Test: Ten Tried-and-True Tips" on page 170. (These tips can benefit all of your students, not just struggling students.) Review and discuss each tip with the class. Explain that these strategies have worked for other students.

- Teach your students the STAR strategy for test success:*

    Survey the test to get an idea of how much time you can spend on each question. Mark any questions you think you can answer quickly.

    Take time to read the directions CAREFULLY.

    Answer the questions. Start with an easy one to boost your confidence. Skip the ones you can't answer.

    Reread the questions and your answers. Make any needed changes. Return to any questions you've skipped and try again.

- Many students with learning difficulties do much better on standardized tests when they are allowed to take the tests in the same environment in which they have been learning. If they usually work seated on the floor or while listening to music, they should be allowed to take tests under those conditions.

- Struggling students may also achieve better test results if they are permitted to read test questions aloud or have the questions read to them. You might arrange for those who want these considerations to take the test in another room, with an adult monitor present.

- Students with learning difficulties should not take tests with finite time limits. If you need to hold them to time limits to include their tests in those of the rest of the class, of course you must do so. However, at a later date you may want to give the kids the same test again without imposing a time limit. These results would count only for your information and would not, of course, be reported to the testing company. For many struggling students, taking untimed tests they are permitted to read aloud (or have read aloud to them) while seated comfortably in an environment with soft music and low lights leads to much more accurate profiles of what they have learned.

Scenario: Seth

Seth, a second grader, always took a long time to work through any kind of test. He was so poky that he rarely completed even half of a timed test. Not surprisingly, the profile his teachers and parents got from his standardized test results was woefully inadequate and didn't come close to reflecting Seth's real abilities.

---

* Adapted from *School Power: Study Skill Strategies for Succeeding in School*, Revised and Updated Edition, by Jeanne Shay Schumm, Ph.D. Minneapolis: Free Spirit Publishing, 2001. Used with permission of the publisher.

For example, on one standardized test, Seth considered the following question:

Which is harder?
a) a feather
b) a sidewalk
c) a headboard
d) all of them.

Seth reasoned that a feather is hard to throw, a sidewalk is hard to walk on, and his headboard is hard when he hits his head on it, so he chose "d) all of them" as his answer. Naturally, he didn't get any credit for it.

When global thinkers take multiple-choice tests, they can invariably find reasons why *all* choices are correct. The following suggestions will allow you to learn much more about what your students know than standardized measures can tell you.

Ways to Make Assessment More Meaningful for All Students

- Allow and encourage struggling students to use their strongest learning style to demonstrate what they have learned.

- Have an open invitation for students to be able to earn credit for their work if they can show their thinking, even when their response is not what you expected.

- When grading papers, mark correct responses instead of wrong responses. Write the score as a fraction, with the number correct over the total number of problems. *Example:* A score of 6 correct out of 10 would be written as 6/10.

- When giving letter grades that relate to percentages, calculate the percent correct of the number of items completed rather than of the entire assignment.

- Provide open-ended opportunities for kids to retake tests or redo assessments until they have achieved acceptable levels of performance. *Caution:* Be sure that this doesn't create lazy study habits in more capable students. Make attractive alternate activities available for those who reach acceptable levels of performance promptly.

- Provide school-wide incentives for kids to bring up their grades. See "Use the BUG Roll" below.

Use the Report Card Chart

The Report Card Chart on page 185 encourages students to take more control over their own assessment goals. It's best to begin using this chart at the start of the new school year, but you can also start using it at the end of the first or second report card periods.

Make a copy of the chart for each student. Fill in the student's scores (stanines or percentile ratings) from the end of last year. Explain and demonstrate how much progress is expected during a typical school year. *Example:* If students scored in the 25th percentile in math computation at the end of last year, encourage them to set a goal of 50 percent or higher for this year to bring them into the proficiency range. The goal for the first report card might be 35 percent, the second 40 percent, and the third 50 percent or higher.

Explain how students can set goals for their own achievement in each subject for your class. Then help students set specific goals for each report card. When the report card is issued, show students how to write their actual progress in a different color on their chart so they can see whether they reached their goals. Repeat this process between report cards until the end of the school year.

The Report Card Chart helps students understand how one gets from one goal to another. Because the goals they set are their own, students are more motivated to move ahead than if they wait to see what the teacher gives them in each grading period. Of course, you can help your students with the process, but this method works best if the goals belong to them.

You might use the Report Card Chart in conjunction with the Goal Planning Chart (page 66) and the "Yes I Can" strategy described on page 119.

Use the BUG Roll*

Traditional grading systems are unfair in many ways. One of their most glaring weaknesses is that they do not always reward significant progress. Consider the typical classroom situation in which Student A moves from an average of 92 to 93 and gets recognized on the high honor roll for a net improvement of 1 percent. Meanwhile, Student B moves from an average of 42 to 68—a growth of 24 percentage points—and gets no recognition whatsoever.

The "BUG Roll"—the "BUG" stands for "Bringing Up Grades"—has motivated many struggling students to improve their grades. Although schools keep their top honor roll intact, a BUG Roll is added. To get on the BUG Roll, students must improve one letter grade in any subject area without going down to a lower grade than the one they

---

* Felice Kaufmann. Talk given at the Illinois Gifted Education Conference, December 1987. Used with permission.

Report Card Chart

STUDENT'S NAME: _____   **CURRENT GRADE IN SCHOOL:** _____

	Reading Skills	Reading Comprehension	Math Skills	Math Computation	Problem-Solving	Writing	Other
End of Last Year							
Start of School to First Report Card							
First to Second Report Card							
Second Report Report Cards							
Second to Final Report Cards							

BUG Roll Certificate

Be it known that

_____

has earned the right to join the group of students

who have been able to *Bring Up Grades*

in the manner prescribed by our school.

Congratulations!

earned in the previous marking period for any other subject. In an extreme scenario, a student who failed every subject in the first grading period would earn a position on the BUG Roll if she moved from an F to a D in science while still getting F's in every other subject! Struggling students perceive that they have a good chance for positive recognition, while they would have no chance if they had to move from F's to much higher grades to get on the regular honor roll.

Students who make the BUG Roll realize some of the same perks that are given to regular honor roll students. Both groups enjoy seeing their names listed on an honor scroll that is placed where visitors can easily notice it. (The regular honor roll students are listed on one scroll, the BUG Roll students on another, but they are displayed side by side.) Both groups get tokens that entitle them to special privileges, such as days off from homework, purchases from the school store, or admission to special school functions. In some schools, special buttons are made and presented to kids as they become eligible for the BUG Roll. In one middle school, I heard students asking each other what subjects they were going to get bugged in!

If you would like to implement the BUG Roll in your classroom or school, you'll find a certificate you can use to honor your students on page 186. Be sure that regular honor roll students continue to be honored in special ways for their achievements as well.

Questions and Answers

"When should I give my struggling students A's?"

It is my feeling that struggling students should get C's or B's for accomplishing goals that are realistic for them. They should not get A's until their goals (and achievements) move into the same range other students must reach before they can earn A's. When kids realize that we're giving A's to them for work that is significantly below grade-level expectations, they may conclude that we believe they aren't capable of earning higher grades on their own. A well-earned C—which in the past might have been a D or an F—is much more likely to build self-esteem than a higher grade that is not earned.

"In college and the workplace, people are compared to each other constantly. When are these kids going to get practice experiencing comparisons if we personalize all of the assessment techniques we use in the classroom?"

Before students are ready to have their learning and productivity compared to anyone else's, they must have confidence in their ability to succeed. We are not abandoning standards when we personalize assessment procedures. Rather, we're empowering more students to be successful because they know what we expect before they start

their work, and certainly before they hand it in. Today's workplaces combine collaboration and competition, and students should experience both. Balance is the key.

"How can we expect parents to respond to assessment practices that bear little or no resemblance to what they are used to?"

Parent re-education is an important component of any educational change. Parents shouldn't have to interpret new assessment practices on their own. When we introduced cooperative learning and whole language, we probably shared our rationale and practices with parents. Coach students in how to explain the new practices to their parents, emphasizing what they most enjoy about them. Send home bulletins and newsletters. Be proactive; keep parents informed.

REFERENCES AND RESOURCES

bertiekingore.com (www.bertiekingore.com). The Web site of Bertie Kingore, Ph.D., a national consultant who has worked with students, their teachers, and their parents for over 30 years. She continues to work in classrooms to model the differentiation of instruction for all learners. Her site is dedicated to providing educational materials that enrich learning experiences for all students.

Kaufmann, Felice. Talk given at the Illinois Gifted Education Conference, December 1987.

Kimeldorf, Martin. *Creating Portfolios for Success in School, Work, and Life.* Minneapolis: Free Spirit Publishing, 1994. Exercises lead students in grades seven and up through the process of preparing four different types of portfolios: personal, student, project, and professional. The companion Teacher's Guide suggests ways to implement and evaluate portfolios at various grade levels and adapt them for students with special needs.

Kohn, Alfie. *Punished by Rewards.* New York: Houghton Mifflin, 1993.

Leadership and Learning Center (www.leadandlearn.com). Chairman and founder Dr. Douglas Reeves identifies five factors present in schools with performance at or above the 90th percentile in which 90+ percent of the students come from combined minorities and 90+ percent of the students are on free and reduced lunch. They are: strong emphasis on achievement, focus on essential curricular areas, frequent assessments with multiple chances for students to show improvement, writing across the curriculum, and use of consistent rubrics across all classes for assessment. Call for more information and a list of schools that qualify. 1-866-399-6019.

Learner Profile (www.learnerprofile.com). This computerized assessment management tool allows you to track your students' grades and assignments, organize student information, and develop reports on your computer or on a handheld PDA. 1-800-733-2828.

Product Guide Kits (www.curriculumproject.com). A unique collection of assessment rubrics that help students plan how to earn high grades for their projects and products. 1-800-867-9067.

Rubistar (rubistar.4teachers.org). A terrific free tool for teachers who want to use rubrics but don't have the time to develop them from scratch. The site is also available in Spanish; click the Rubistar en Español window. A project of the High Plains Regional Technology in Educational Consortium (RTEC), one of ten RTECs funded by the Department of Education.

Schumm, Jeanne Shay, Ph.D. *School Power: Study Skill Strategies for Succeeding in School,* Revised and Updated Edition. Minneapolis: Ph.D. Minneapolis: Free Spirit Publishing, 2001.

CHAPTER

13

Teaching Students How to Behave Appropriately

Scenario: Armen

Armen had been in the gifted program all through elementary school. His frustrated teachers recognized his exceptional intelligence despite his dismal record of class work completion, and most were happy to have him leave their rooms for the half-day each week of "Challenge Class." They understood that one reason Armen resisted the work was because it wasn't *his* work, it was *their* work. Like other gifted kids, Armen would have been thrilled to do work that represented new learning for him. As his teachers moved him from the regular curriculum into projects connected to his passionate interests, he became more productive.

When Armen entered junior high school, the teachers there tended to perceive him as "lazy, stubborn, and someone who needs to be taught the lesson that in the real world, we don't always get to work on what we like!" Therefore, Armen spent most of his school time in an isolated cubby adjacent to the office, where he enjoyed entertaining teachers and other visitors. His teachers would not let him back into their classes until he promised to do his work. Some even asked him to write "I will not waste my time in school" hundreds of times—a significant waste of his time in school. The futility of their methods became apparent when, on March 30th, Armen lost the privilege of attending the school picnic on May 31st! Two months before school ended, the system had run out of ways to punish Armen. What would they do with him for the next two months?

Looking Dumb vs. Being Bad

High on the list of things we are all concerned about is classroom discipline. When we are pushed to define the word "discipline," it appears that what we worry about most is maintaining control! Discipline is not supposed to ensure mindless obedience. Rather, effective discipline should make good habits routine so students can maintain proper behavior independently.

All students are behaving at every moment of the day. When we say that someone is "misbehaving," we really mean that they are not behaving the way we want and we would like their behavior to change.

Why do some kids behave badly in school? One powerful reason is to avoid the embarrassment of being seen as dumb, stupid, or incapable of learning. Every time we put kids in the position of fearing exposure for their learning inadequacies, we make them choose between looking dumb and being bad. The choice is obvious. Therefore, the simplest way to solve behavior problems is to help students become capable and successful learners.

When students perceive that they are unable to learn, their reactions may progress through three stages:*

- In stage one, students are confused about their struggle and either withdraw into a quiet shell or begin to act out through excessive movement or behavior

---

* From "Child and Context: Reactive Adaptations of Learning Disabled Children" by R.G. Ziegler, *Journal of Learning Disabilities* 14:7 (August–September 1981), pp. 391–393, 430. Used with permission.

they know will lead to punishment. As frustrations continue, they may fear any new work task. They also may generalize that they are incapable in areas where they were formerly strong.

- In stage two, disengagement occurs and the students' goal is simply to avoid the pain of seemingly impossible tasks. Procrastination is noticeable and kids may complain about activities, calling them "dumb" or "stupid." In an attempt at self-preservation, students often exhibit an "I don't care" attitude, which probably means "I don't care to expose myself to the possibility of feeling inadequate again."

- In stage three, denial and negativism are prevalent. Since it is no longer acceptable for the students to perceive that they are just dumb, it is safer to exhibit an attitude that students who cooperate with the school game are the ones who are really dumb.

You probably know from personal experience how hard it is to make a change of any kind. Many adults remain in unhappy situations because they fear that a change will be even more miserable. If change is hard for us, imagine how tough it must for kids. Once students are labeled "difficult," it may actually be more comfortable for them to stay that way than to change their behavior from bad to good. No wonder it sometimes appears that students are trying to sabotage their own lives and our sincere efforts to help them. Anything you suggest to them must be perceived as safe enough to try. They must believe that they are in control and you are acting as a guide, not as an authority figure.

Sometimes students' misbehavior seems rooted in difficult home situations that we as teachers feel powerless to change. It's tempting to give up on kids when we don't get the cooperation or support from home that we know would make a big difference. Here's the bottom line: You have little or no control over what happens at home. What you *can* control is what happens to your students at school. I suspect that many parents who have never come to a parent-teacher conference have negative memories of their own school years. I believe that if we call those parents on a regular basis with good news about their children's achievement and behavior, school will seem like a friendlier place and those parents might become more willing to get involved in their children's education. It's certainly worth a try.

When we attempt to coerce children by scolding, threatening, revoking privileges, lowering grades, giving detentions, or calling their parents, we begin a vicious cycle, and the only predictable outcome is revenge. Students may appear to comply for a short time, but the loss of their dignity usually leads them to plan and carry out some way to get back at us. Often their retaliation is passive—forgetting things, appearing helpless, blaming others. Eventually their behavior forces you into another act of coercion, and the cycle continues. Educational psychologist Raymond Wlodkowski has summarized this cycle in the chart shown below.

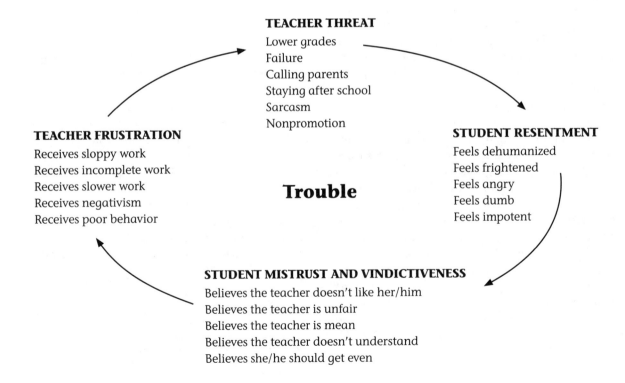

TEACHER THREAT
Lower grades
Failure
Calling parents
Staying after school
Sarcasm
Nonpromotion

TEACHER FRUSTRATION
Receives sloppy work
Receives incomplete work
Receives slower work
Receives negativism
Receives poor behavior

Trouble

STUDENT RESENTMENT
Feels dehumanized
Feels frightened
Feels angry
Feels dumb
Feels impotent

STUDENT MISTRUST AND VINDICTIVENESS
Believes the teacher doesn't like her/him
Believes the teacher is unfair
Believes the teacher is mean
Believes the teacher doesn't understand
Believes she/he should get even

From Wlodkowski, Raymond J. *Motivation and Teaching: A Practical Guide*. Washington, D.C.: National Education Association, 1986. Used with permission.

There are teachers at all levels of experience who believe that student behavior is an issue separate from curriculum or teaching methods. In fact, we are not supposed to control our students. We are supposed to guarantee their learning. To do this, we must understand that behavior management, teaching methods, and curriculum are intertwined.

If I were your principal, I would not let you send kids to my office until you had filled out a form that looked something like this:

STUDENT'S NAME: _____

GRADE: _____

TEACHER'S NAME: _____

Describe what you as the teacher have done to match your lessons to this student's most successful learning style:

_____

_____

_____

_____

_____

Give evidence that the work you are expecting this student to do is neither too difficult nor too easy for the student:

_____

_____

_____

_____

_____

Describe the incident that prompted you to send this student to my office:

_____

_____

_____

_____

_____

_____

By the time they completed this form, most teachers would realize there is more they could try in the classroom before sending the student to a higher authority.

This chapter describes several effective alternatives to coercion. If these strategies seem overwhelming to you—if you feel that you lack the time or resources to implement them with your students—then ask yourself what kind of results you're achieving with what you're doing now. If you keep doing what you're doing, you'll keep getting what you're getting! Now is a good time to replace any methods that are not working well with those that will allow you to work smarter, not harder.

Remember that it took your students a long time to develop and practice their inappropriate behaviors. Progress toward change may be slow, with frequent setbacks. Real classroom behavior management is about changing the behavior of the adults! Changes in students come *after* changes in teachers and parents.

Intervening with Inappropriate Behavior

If I were part of an accreditation team assessing a school's discipline program, I would evaluate it inversely to the size of the discipline manual. I believe that the thicker such a manual is, the less effective a discipline program will be. There are many discipline programs in use today by individual teachers and by entire schools and school systems. And yet the offices of those in charge of school discipline are always full of repeat offenders and other kids who seem unaware that rules even exist, let alone that they are expected to follow them. We can change this. Read on to learn how.

Help All Students Feel That They Belong

Plan several activities for the beginning of a year or semester that are specifically designed to help all students feel like they belong to the group. See Chapter 1 for suggestions.

Teach to Students' Learning Style Strengths

If your students can't learn the way you are teaching them, you can either wait until they come around to your way of teaching, or you can teach them the way they learn. Have you ever been thrust into a learning situation where the activities didn't make sense and you felt less than capable? See chapters 4 and 5 for strategies you can use to empower *all* of your students to learn more effectively. Remind your students often that it's safe to make mistakes as long as they learn from them.

Establish and Use Predictable Routines

Effective classroom teachers know from experience that the time they take at the start of every school year to make classroom routines automatic for their students is time well spent. I know one high school math teacher whose students were extremely well trained in how to hand in their papers—first by rows, and then across all rows. He felt confident that he could record their grades without even looking at their names because every paper was where it was supposed to be! I'm not advocating this level of routine for all teachers, but it certainly is helpful to the teacher and comfortable for the students when everyone knows what to do with just a word or signal from the teacher.

Students with learning or social difficulties often create havoc for substitutes. Understanding that part of the problem is their uneasiness with the interrupted routine should help you to come up with creative solutions.

Example: Leave detailed information on the established routines, including schedule, procedures, a request to maintain the established routine and schedule as much as possible, and the name of a person to contact in an emergency. Perhaps you could send a particularly disruptive student to work in a time-out area, another teacher's classroom, or the office of a person responsible for discipline—not as a punishment but as a preventive measure.

Establish and Reinforce Simple Classroom Rules

In my experience, the longer the list of classroom rules, the more likely that kids will choose a misbehavior that is not specifically listed. (*Example:* If a rule states "No running in the halls," a student might skip down the hall, then argue that the rules don't forbid skipping.) The solution is to keep the rules simple and highly visible. Post them on a chart prominently displayed in your room, and give your students frequent verbal reminders.

I have four favorite rules that get the job done:

1. Treat others in the same way you want to be treated.

2. Don't bother anyone. (Chart examples.)

3. Don't call attention to yourself. (Chart examples.)

4. Do your work.

If students break a rule, ask them privately to identify which rule their behavior violates. If they can't identify that their behavior is against the rules, ask them to sit alone until they can either stop the undesirable behavior or talk with you about the needed change. Explain the effect the misbehavior has on others, including you, and outline the consequence that will be applied if they fail to choose more appropriate behavior. Tell them they can rejoin the class after they complete a "Behavior Change Plan" (page 192).

Be Consistent and Fair

- Avoid overusing negative or hostile eye contact. Make sure that every student also receives positive facial expressions from you on regular occasions.

- Anticipate situations that are likely to cause problems, and brainstorm possible solutions with the student before the next similar event. *Example:* "Eric, we have to go into the auditorium for a program in an hour. Let's think of a plan so when you feel unable to sit and listen, you can leave before you call attention to yourself."

- Set up conditions that allow students to save face. *Example:* If you know that a student will resist a request to clean up the floor around her desk, work up to it gradually by preceding it with other requests the student is less likely to object to. "Josie, please pass out these pencils for me . . . . Thanks. Now would you please take the lunch count to the office for me . . . . Thanks. Now please pick up all the papers on the floor around your desk and put them in this box . . . . Thanks."

- Help complainers by acknowledging that you hear their complaints and challenging them to come up with workable solutions. Either they will think of good solutions or they will stop complaining! **Tip:** Ask them to write down all of the details they can think of so you can understand the complexity of their problem. Chances are the complaints will end soon.

Make Sure that the Curriculum Is Stimulating and Worth Learning

We can't really make kids do anything; we can only make opportunities available to help motivate them to engage in the learning tasks we are offering. See pages 70–72 for specific strategies that will help you provide a meaningful and challenging curriculum.

Keep Talk to a Minimum

For some kids with behavior disorders and/or language processing problems, too much teacher talk is frustrating and even annoying. Create several nonverbal cues that indicate what you want kids to do or stop doing, and use them instead of words whenever possible. Be sure to fully explain and model the meaning of each signal. *Examples:*

- To indicate that a student should stop a particular behavior: Raise your hand above your head, count

Behavior Change Plan

MY NAME: _____

DATE: _____ **TIME:** _____

What I did that was wrong:	**What I wanted to happen:**	**What really happened:**
To get what I want, I must stop:	**What I can do to behave more appropriately:**	**What I need from my teacher to help my plan:**

"One," and hold up one finger for ten seconds. Add two more fingers at ten-second intervals (counting "Two" and "Three") if the behavior doesn't change.

■ To indicate that a student should move to the time-out place: Use a referee's time-out hand signal.

■ To indicate that someone has made an appropriate behavior choice: Give a thumbs-up or high-five.

You might also teach your students how to signal when they want you to change your behavior. One teacher tells her class, "If you are feeling like you need to move, please stand beside your desk. If you need a break, pantomime the time-out sign, and if you think we're too serious and need to lighten things up a little, wink at me." Students are more likely to honor your requests when the process works both ways.

Help Students to Stay Calm

■ Be aware of situations that are likely to overstimulate students. Strive for a good balance between stimulating and calming activities.

■ At the beginning of each work period, have students move through a controlled exercise or rhythmic activity to release pent-up energy. There are many commercial products (audios, videos, DVDs) available for this purpose.

■ Talk the class through an exercise where they alternately clench and relax many parts of their body, from their head to their toes.

Teach Students How to Handle Anger

Kids who fly off the handle without apparent provocation may not know how to express their anger in more acceptable ways. Hand out copies of "Things You Can Do Instead of Staying Angry" (page 195) for students to keep at their desks. Tell them they might initial the tips that work best for them, or circle the ones they would like to try the next time they get angry. Give positive reinforcement each time you notice students who have handled their anger appropriately.

If we want our students to handle their anger in healthy ways, we need to set a good example. Kids need to understand that their behavior leads to certain positive and negative consequences. One of those negative consequences should not be a teacher who gets upset. Keep in mind that many struggling students, especially those with severe emotional problems, really can't choose more appropriate behaviors without direct instruction, proactive counseling,

and support from qualified professionals. Deal with misbehavior quickly and fairly; apply logical consequences rather than threats and punishments.

Teach Students How to Monitor Their Self-Talk

When kids engage in negative self-talk, it adversely affects their behavior and productivity. You can help your students to develop a short script they can keep at their desks. Anytime they catch themselves using negative self-talk, they should take several deep breaths and read the script to themselves. After reading, they should close their eyes and visualize themselves in the more positive situation. *Example:*

■ Negative self-talk: "What if the teacher calls on me and I don't know the answer? What if the kids think I'm dumb? I'd better make them notice me first for something else."

■ Positive self-talk: "Stop! I'm going to take three deep breaths and remember that the teacher doesn't call on anyone until we've had a chance to talk to our partner. I have a nice partner who always helps me think of what to say. I'll rehearse my answer so when I get called on, I'll be able to have a good answer!"

Coach students to notice times when their behavior is correct and helpful and silently congratulate themselves for their success. Their self-talk might sound something like this: "I'm proud of myself for not touching anyone on my trip to and from the board." Arrange a non-verbal signal to use with students when you notice praiseworthy behavior so you can let them know it's time for some silent self-praise.

Use the WDEP Model

Based on William Glasser's work in reality therapy, the WDEP model (**W**ant, **D**oing, **E**valuate, **P**lan) is a helpful guide to dialoguing with students who are engaging in inappropriate behavior. It can lead to a "Behavior Change Plan" (page 193).

The setting should be a private conference between you and the student. Sit beside the student rather than across from him. Suggest that you and he can become partners in finding a solution to his problem. Visualize the problem in the empty space across from you both. Make sure the student understands that the purpose of your meeting is not to punish, but to make a plan for appropriate behavior that is more likely to get the student what he wants or needs.

Things You Can Do
Instead of Staying Angry

____ Close your eyes and count to 10 forwards and/or backwards. Or try counting backwards from 100 by 3's. You can't stay angry when you're concentrating on a learning task.

____ Think positive words: "calm," "open-minded," "ready to learn," "peaceful," "happy."

____ Put your opinion in an I-statement. Tell the other person how what they have said or done makes you feel. Like this: "I feel ____ when you _____."

____ Try to see the problem from the other person's point of view. How would you feel if you were that person?

____ Ask the teacher or another student for help in getting over your anger.

____ Calm down with a relaxation technique. Take a deep breath, hold it as you count to six, and let it out slowly as you count to six. Repeat several times.

____ Go to the listening center and listen to soothing music for a while.

____ Get the time-out pass. Take a voluntary time-out in the classroom or another time-out place.

____ Close your eyes and picture yourself in a place where you feel calm. Notice the details of this calming place and think of how you love to be there.

____ With the teacher's permission, run up and down a flight of stairs several times.

____ Think of how you would feel if the other person expressed anger at you the way you want to express it.

____ Remember that no one can *make* you feel angry. *You* are in control of how you choose to respond to a certain situation.

____ Think of a joke. Say some silly tongue-twisters. SMILE! It's hard to stay angry when you're smiling!

Other ideas that work for me:

____ _____

____ _____

____ _____

____ _____

____ _____

____ _____

Tell the student that you are going to check in with Radio Station WDEP. Ask the following questions and listen respectfully to any and all responses:

- "What do you **W**ant to have happen?"
- "What are you **D**oing to get what you want?"
- "**E**valuate how well your behavior is helping you reach your goal. Is what you are doing against the class rules? If so, which rule or rules?"
- "Think of a **P**lan to change what you're doing so your new behavior has a better chance of helping you get what you want or need."

Try hard to avoid jumping in with a solution unless the student asks for your input. Then make just *one* suggestion at a time that specifically addresses *only* the behavior that is the focus of this conference. Arrange to meet again in a day or two to see how well the plan is working and, if necessary, to guide the student to create a different plan.

Scenario: Charlie

Charlie was a seventh grader with a behavior disorder. He simply could not keep his hands to himself. Not only did he touch other kids at every opportunity; he sometimes hurt them. He was contrite immediately after each incident, but he seemed unable to translate being sorry into more appropriate behavior. It occurred to me that "keep your hands to yourself" was too vague an expectation for Charlie to understand.

Charlie and I met and agreed that he would carry a Kush ball whenever he left his desk to remind him not to touch other kids. In between trips, he could use the ball to help get rid of his omnipresent excess energy.

I showed Charlie how to keep track of his own progress on a chart he would keep at his desk. He would earn and record a plus (+) each time he left his desk and returned without touching anyone, and a minus (–) each time he touched someone. As soon as he accumulated three plusses and no more than two consecutive minuses, he would earn ten minutes of free drawing time, since Charlie loved to draw.

I attached a small chart to his desk and demonstrated how to enter a plus when he met his no touching goal and a minus when he didn't. I explained that for the first few days, I would reinforce his behavior with a thumbs-up or thumbs-down signal.

The first time he left his desk and returned, I gave him a thumbs-up. He entered a plus on his chart.

The second time—thumbs-down. He had "accidentally" touched Brian at the pencil sharpener. I walked over to Charlie's desk and we had a brief conversation:

Me: "I noticed you touched Brian, so what mark will you record this time?"

Charlie: "It wasn't my fault. He touched me first!"

Me: "You're not recording whose fault it was; you're recording whether or not you touched someone."

Charlie: "That's not fair."

Me (without emotion): "Please record the minus you earned, and then we'll make a plan so the same thing doesn't happen again."

Charlie: "Okay—but it's still not fair."

After Charlie grudgingly recorded a tiny minus, I asked him to suggest a plan that would lead to more success the next time he left his seat. He decided that he would wait until no one else was at the pencil sharpener.

Charlie went on to record another plus, then two minuses in a row. After he had recorded the second minus, I prompted him:

Me: "You know, if you have to record a minus the next time you leave your desk, the first two plusses won't count. Remember, our agreement requires you to have three plusses with no more than two minuses in a row. So tell me your plan to be sure not to touch anyone the next time you leave your desk."

Charlie: "I guess I should carry that ball you gave me with both hands."

Me: "Sounds like a good plan. Hope it works."

Charlie held on tightly to his ball during each subsequent time he left his desk, and he was soon able to record the next plus. I bestowed his reward immediately, and Charlie looked proud as he took his ten minutes to draw a picture of a kid desperately hanging on to a Kush ball as he walked around the room.

In subsequent days, Charlie learned to record his tallies without my direct assistance, and he earned far more plusses than minuses. After several successes, we upped the ante to four, then five plusses in a row. It's not essential that kids record their marks totally honestly. The very act of being responsible for recording one's behavior ultimately leads to behavior change.

+	–	–	+	+	+	+	–	+	+	–	+
				Reward				**Reward**			

Helping Students Learn to Choose Appropriate Behavior

Catch Them Being Good and Doing Well

- Regularly scan the class to notice and reinforce students' appropriate behaviors. If students perceive that the only time they get your attention is when they are doing something wrong, the problem is obvious. Simply calling everyone's attention to what's being done right can motivate students to borrow teacher-pleasing behaviors from other kids. Purposefully notice kids when they are behaving appropriately, and support that behavior in encouraging terms. *Example:* "I notice that half the class is ready for directions. I'd love to see the rest of the class be ready, too." It's probably better not to use specific students' names in your praise. Such kids may become targets for the hostility of others.

- When you have coached a student to change a particular behavior, notice the preferred behavior privately as soon as it happens, even if at first it means leaving something else you are doing. Increase the duration of time between praising statements until eventually the student chooses the appropriate behaviors automatically.

- Praise is much more effective when it is focused on students' actions rather than on their personalities. *Examples:* Instead of "You're such a good boy, Joseph," say "Joseph, your improved behavior this week must be the result of all of your hard efforts." Instead of "This is the best class I've ever had," say "Class, we are getting so much more work done when you follow the class rules and are considerate to each other."

Notice What Events Usually Precede Inappropriate Behavior

Keep an anecdotal record of misbehaviors for at least a week. Notice what happens immediately before the inappropriate behavior, and look for patterns. Use the behavior charts on pages 201–204 to diagnose the student's unmet needs and intervene accordingly.

Use Awareness Tallies

If students appear unaware that their behavior needs to change, use this strategy for a short time.

1. Identify and describe a behavior you would like a student to change.

2. Gather baseline data about the student's behavior. If the child's parent or caregiver approves, one way to do this is by making a video. Simply set up a camera on a tripod and aim it at the target student; turn it on after the student stops noticing it. You can count the number of infractions at a later time, when you don't have to monitor the rest of the class.

3. Remember that a picture equals a thousand words. Don't show the video to anyone but the student (except, perhaps, the parents or guardians at a conference). When you show it to the student, use only a short segment and make sure that the student can view it in privacy. Have the student tally how many times she sees herself engaging in the inappropriate behavior within a 10–15 minute time period.

   Variation without video: Have the student tally how many times she engages in the inappropriate behavior during a given time period. Afterward, discuss the frequency of the behavior with the student. Ask her to set a goal for the next tally period of fewer times than she recorded during the first period.

4. Repeat this process until the number of times the behavior is observed declines to a manageable amount.

ANECDOTAL RECORD

Type of misbehavior	What came just before it	How I dealt with it
BLURTING OUT INSULTS TO ANOTHER STUDENT	CURRENT EVENTS DISCUSSION WITHOUT USING NAME CARD METHOD	REALIZED STUDENT FEARED EMBARRASSMENT, PICKED UP AND USED NAME CARDS

AWARENESS TALLY

Date/Time	Inappropriate behavior	During what class activity	Tally # of times
4/6 9:45–10:15	TALKING OUT OF TURN	CLASS DISCUSSION ABOUT NOVEL	ЖЖ

Use I-Messages

Rather than blaming students for their behavior, tell them how you feel about it. *Example:* Instead of "If you don't stop calling Jason a 'retard,' you're going to have to work in the office!" say "I worry that Jason will be embarrassed when you call him unpleasant names."

Follow this with a statement of exactly what you expect this student to do. *Example:* "I need you to tell me a plan before recess of how you will solve this problem. If you can't come up with a plan, I'll make one for you."

Model the Behavior You Want Students to Emulate

1. Decide which positive behavior you would like the student to learn. *Important:* Introduce requests for behavior change one at a time. Do not add other requests until each new behavior has been learned.

2. Model exactly what you want the student to do as you softly talk out loud the steps you are taking. *Example:* "I'm walking down the aisle on my way to the rug for a meeting with the teacher. I'm keeping my arms at my sides so I won't touch anyone. When I get all the way to the rug without touching anyone, I will say to myself, 'Congratulations to me for getting from my seat to the rug without touching anyone! I'm terrific!'"

3. Ask the student to perform the same task while you softly talk him through it.

4. Have the student perform the same task as he verbally coaches himself through it.

5. Have the student perform the same task as he thinks or whispers the self-talk.

The student should keep a tally chart at his desk so he can mark each time he completes the task correctly. If it seems necessary, you may have him choose a mutually acceptable reward he can earn after a certain number of tallies.

Use Recorded Sound Cues

Special education teachers have long used a method of cueing students with sounds at random intervals. At the moment the students hear the sound, they monitor and record their behavior. The method works best when students are able to do a certain task but appear unable to stay on task. After a 15–20 minute training session, students seem able to stay on task longer; after extensive practice, some students are able to monitor their behavior at the sound without having to formally record it. What's fascinating is that good results can be achieved even if students are inaccurate in the way they record their behavior! Although this method rarely distracts other students, headphones may be used if you or the student wants the cueing to be private. Most students can be weaned from the procedure after they have used it for several weeks or months.

STUDENT BEHAVIOR TALLY

Date/Time	Appropriate behavior	Tally # of times	Self-compliment
2/11 12:15–2:00	WALKED TO RUG WITHOUT TOUCHING ANYONE ELSE	ЖЖ	"I DID IT! HURRAY FOR ME!"

SOUND CLUES CHART

Tone #	What I am doing when I hear the tone	Yes (Correct behavior)	No (Incorrect behavior)	New Plan
1	WRITING A SENTENCE	+		
2	LOOKING OUT THE WINDOW		−	START WRITING AGAIN

1. Make a cassette or CD recording of a pleasant-sounding beep, heard intermittently every five to six minutes.

2. Train students to stop what they are doing at the sound of the beep and ask themselves:

   ■ "What am I doing?"

   ■ "Is this what I am supposed to be doing at this time?"

   If the answer to the second question is "yes," students tally a response in the YES column of a tally chart and silently congratulate themselves. If the answer is "no," students tally that response and plan how to get back on the right path.

3. Monitor the responses at regular intervals. You may want to let kids earn incentives for a certain number of YES tallies. There should be no punishment for NO tallies.

Directly Teach Social Skills

1. Identify a skill the student lacks. Discuss with the student how having the skill will make interaction with others more positive.

2. Model how the skill should be used or have other kids model it.

3. Ask the student to describe the components of the skill as modeled correctly.

4. Have the student role-play the skill with you or another student as you coach her through it.

5. Have the student role-play the skill as she verbally coaches herself through it.

6. Have the student role-play the skill as she whispers the self-talk.

7. Provide numerous opportunities for the student to continue practicing the skill.

8. Each time you notice the student using the skill correctly, go to her and say, "I noticed that you were [describe the skill] correctly. Good work!" Consistent,

immediate positive feedback is essential to having the student form the habit of using the skill.

9. Whenever the student lapses into inappropriate behavior, ask her to think out loud all the ways in which she could have behaved appropriately. Then, to add a little humor, have her wonder aloud why, in this situation, she was so silly as to not have chosen the correct way to behave. Have the student end this little exercise with a plan for how to make a better choice the next time.

Set Up an Opportunity Cost Procedure

Although I prefer to focus on positive reinforcement and overlook negative consequences, sometimes consequences are powerful deterrents to behavior. As a last resort, set up an opportunity cost procedure. The concept is simple: When students fail to take the opportunity to follow their behavior management program, it costs them something.

Example: A third grader named Miguel was extremely aggressive at recess. We created a behavior management program in which Miguel could earn points for not being physically or verbally abusive to anyone during recess. He started each 15-minute recess with a credit of 15 tally marks, one for each minute. Each time I had to call him over to note an infraction, he watched me cross out some of the points: three for not following recess rules, five for being aggressive toward anyone. For every recess where he lost no points, Miguel's entire class got a bonus of five minutes at the end of the day to just talk to each other. In this way, his peers helped him ignore opportunities for negative behavior. Every time Miguel preserved his original 15 points, he chose the perk of carrying a ball outside for recess.

Use Behavior Charts

All human behavior is driven by our attempts to have our needs met. People who behave in positive ways most of the time are those who perceive that their important needs are being met. Inappropriate behavior signals that people perceive that their important needs are not being met. See Chapter 4 for information on how to meet your students' basic learning needs—and improve their behavior.

Several behavioral psychologists including William Glasser, Rudolf Dreikurs, and Donald Dinkmeyer have theorized that adults can help shape young people's behavior in positive ways by:

1. observing the inappropriate behavior,

2. diagnosing what unmet need it reflects,

3. intervening to meet the need, and

4. avoiding situations that reinforce inappropriate behaviors.

The four charts on pages 201–204 will help you to do this in your classroom and provide students with what they truly need:

- to *belong*

- to feel *worthy and important*

- to be able to have the *freedom to make choices*

- to experience *fun and enjoyment.*

Before consulting the charts, before activating your school's discipline plan, and before focusing on inappropriate behaviors, ask yourself these three questions:

1. Am I providing opportunities for students to learn in brain-compatible ways by attending to their learning style needs?

2. Is the curriculum appropriately challenging for the student—not too easy and not too difficult?

3. Does the student understand the relevance and importance of what I am expecting him or her to learn?

If you answer "no" to one or more of these questions, follow the suggestions found throughout this book to create more appropriate learning experiences. If you can answer "yes" to all three questions and a student continues to exhibit negative behaviors, move on to the charts and the intervention suggestions. Be sure to notice that certain information appears on several charts because the student may have more than one unmet need.

1. When you have identified a student whose inappropriate behavior is causing problems, keep an anecdotal record for five school days. Record exactly what you observe the student doing, as well as what event immediately preceded the behavior.

2. Look over the first column of each behavior chart until you find one that describes many of the inappropriate behaviors the student is exhibiting. Look next at the title of the chart. This tells you which basic need the student perceives is not being met.

3. Look in the second column for suggested ways to solve the behavior problem. Try one or two solutions at a time. If possible, keep a simple record of what you try and how the student reacts. Check the third column to learn what not to do.

4. Meanwhile, try to change the event that appears to instigate the inappropriate behavior.

5. Work with the information on one chart for two weeks. By then, you should know if you chose the correct chart. If you didn't choose the correct chart, repeat steps 1–4 using a different chart.

Use Behavior Contracts

When my granddaughter Brooke was five years old, she and her parents came to visit us. They stayed for three days, and on the morning they were supposed to return home, Brooke indicated rather emotionally that she wanted to stay longer with her grandma and grandpa. It was a very busy time for me, and on several previous visits Brooke had desperately needed her mommy and daddy almost as soon as they walked out the door. She promised not to repeat that behavior this time.

"Well, if you want to stay, you have to sign a contract," I said.

Her eyes widened and she asked, "What does that mean?"

"I write out the expectations I have for your behavior," I explained. "If you agree to do what I ask, you have to sign the contract. When you sign the contract, it means that you promise to do exactly what it says."

"Okay."

I took out a piece of paper and wrote down three expectations. I added a line to the left of each one so Brooke could initial it.

_____ 1. I promise not to cry for my mommy at night. If I want to talk to my mommy, I'll tell Grandma during the day.

_____ 2. I promise not to cry when I have to go to bed.

_____ 3. I won't ask how many days are left until I go home. Instead, Grandma and I will mark off every day on the calendar so I can count the days myself.

We read through the contract together and she very seriously printed her initials next to each item. Then we put the contract on the refrigerator with a magnet, Brooke kissed her parents good-bye, and we started a highly satisfying five-day stay together. During that whole time, she never engaged in the inappropriate behaviors I had feared. Whenever I took her someplace with me and someone asked her, "Are you being a good girl while you are staying with Grandma?" she would reply seriously, "Yes, I am, because we have a contract!"

The need to be accepted as you are; to be a sought-after member of a desired group or class.

Inappropriate Behaviors (indications that the need is not being met)	Interventions (ways to meet the need)	Actions/Responses to Avoid
■ Demands much teacher attention and time; always needs help.	■ Recognize him for his strengths and chat with him about his outside-of-school interests to demonstrate that you care about him as a person even though he sometimes misbehaves.	■ Choosing teams or cooperative groups publicly.
■ May be shy, fearful, tentative OR		■ Threats and punishments.
■ May be bossy, a show-off, or class clown.		■ Anything that looks like rejection.
■ Nosy; wants to know everyone's business.	■ Immediately recognize positive behaviors.	■ Ignoring the student.
■ May express anger; bullies.	■ Have her tutor younger kids.	■ Giving in to power struggles.
■ May destroy things that belong to others.	■ Use the Name Card method; occasionally paraphrase his responses.	■ Giving too much help; this may enable the student into helplessness.
■ Complains that "no one likes me."	■ Showcase her strengths in group learning situations.	
	■ Give him important jobs.	

BEHAVIOR CHART 2: THE NEED FOR SELF-WORTH

The need to feel worthy, important, and competent; to feel that your abilities are appreciated and that success is attainable.

Inappropriate Behaviors (indications that the need is not being met)	Interventions (ways to meet the need)	Actions/Responses to Avoid
■ Expects and gets failure; gives up when frustrated.	■ Create a learning environment in which mistakes are invited.	■ Helping too much; students can learn helplessness.
■ Speaks negatively about himself.	■ Teach the link between effort and outcomes.	■ Doing for the student what she can do for herself.
■ Makes excuses—whines, cries, complains, worries.	■ Model positive thinking and attribution statements.	■ Repetition; drill; sameness.
■ Procrastinates; exhibits an "I don't care" attitude.	■ Match learning tasks with the student's learning style strengths.	■ Threats; punishment; sarcasm; public teasing.
■ Puts down other students who are successful.	■ Present tasks that are slightly challenging and worth doing.	■ Assigning extra work when regular work has not been completed.
■ Rarely produces work; is disorganized; copies from others.	■ Connect new learning to previously mastered concepts.	■ Rejection.
■ Directs attention away from herself; blames others; tattles.	■ Focus on only one deficit area at a time.	
■ Withdraws; may not speak if spoken to.	■ Teach him how to set short-term daily goals.	
■ Is frequently absent or tardy.	■ Use the Name Card method; occasionally paraphrase her responses.	
	■ Incorporate his interests into his schoolwork.	

BEHAVIOR CHART 3: THE NEED FOR FREEDOM, AUTONOMY, AND CHOICES

The need to feel in control of what happens to you; the freedom to make choices and decisions about what affects you.

Inappropriate Behaviors (indications that the need is not being met)	Interventions (ways to meet the need)	Actions/Responses to Avoid
■ Constantly seeks attention.	■ Offer meaningful choices whenever possible.	■ Expecting all students to do the same work in the same way.
■ Blurts or calls out; makes strange noises.	■ Learn about her personal interests and chat daily for one or two minutes about them.	■ Power struggles; authoritarian statements like "Because I say so."
■ Interrupts or talks loudly.	■ Incorporate his interests into his schoolwork.	■ Threats, punishments, and extra work.
■ Tattles; teases.	■ Demonstrate how knowledge increases personal power.	■ Ignoring students when they are behaving appropriately.
■ Tells tall tales and other untruths.	■ Use the Name Card method; occasionally paraphrase her responses.	■ Totally negative parent conferences.
■ May bully or fight.	■ Assign him important jobs in the classroom and school.	■ Allowing students to set teachers and parents against each other by reporting information third-hand. Parents and teachers should communicate directly about sensitive issues.
■ Sounds angry and argumentative much of the time; challenges authority.	■ Harness her leadership ability.	
■ Pushes the rules to the outer limits; seeks exceptions.	■ Model, teach, and reinforce desirable behaviors including anger control strategies.	
■ Complains "I don't want to do this. Why do we have to do this?"	■ Help him set his own short-term goals for improvement.	
■ Procrastinates; is forgetful.	■ Ask her to describe the consequences of inappropriate behaviors to make sure she understands them.	
■ Accuses the teacher and the system of unfairness.	■ Use nonverbal cues to signal recognition of negative behaviors and reinforcement of positive behaviors. *Examples:* "When I tug my ear, that means you need to choose a more appropriate behavior. When I nod at you, I am noticing that you made a good choice."	
	■ Apply consequences without anger.	
	■ Let bullies know that the school's authority extends beyond the school and grounds.	

BEHAVIOR CHART 4: THE NEED FOR FUN AND ENJOYMENT

The need to have fun; time and opportunities for laughter, play, and entertainment.

Inappropriate Behaviors (indications that the need is not being met)	**Interventions** (ways to meet the need)	**Actions/Responses to Avoid**
■ Silliness; giggling. ■ Class clown; makes others laugh. ■ Plays with toys and other objects. ■ Tells lots of personal stories.	■ Understand that giggling is one way to release excess energy and anxiety. ■ Incorporate fun into regular school tasks, as well as at recess and play time. ■ Add variety to schoolwork. ■ Use game formats to teach needed information.	■ Being serious all of the time. ■ Predictable activities that rarely allow for variety. ■ Sending messages that there is only one correct way to do things.

You might want to move beyond the other tally formats suggested in this chapter to a formal behavior contract. The power of a behavior contract is amazingly strong. There's something about signing their name to a piece of paper that makes students take promises seriously. Even very young students can learn to use behavior contracts.

1. Identify the inappropriate behavior that you want the student to stop doing.

2. Collect baseline data for several days to establish how often the behavior occurs.

3. Meet with the student to share the data you've collected. Describe the behavior you have observed and ask the student to explain why the behavior is inappropriate. If he can't provide an explanation, do it for him. Suggest a behavior you would like him to exhibit instead of the inappropriate behavior. *Be very specific in describing the behavior you want;* model it if necessary.

4. Give the student a copy of the "Behavior Contract" (page 206). Include a description of the desired behavior and the number of times the student should exhibit the behavior. (**Tip:** Have the student choose this number goal, and start small!) Explain that he should make a tally mark on the contract each time he is able to exhibit the behavior. Agree on an incentive the student will earn when his behavior matches or exceeds the contract.

   Notice that this contract asks the student to tally how many times he succeeds, not how many times he fails. Working to *increase* the frequency of what we *do* want is more effective than working to *decrease* the frequency of what we *don't* want.

5. Be prepared to deliver the incentive as soon as possible after the student satisfies the terms of the contract.

Tips:

- Keep the behavior contract between you and the student only. Don't involve parents, since you'll lose control over the contract terms.

- Make the initial contract short-term. On later contracts, you can gradually extend the time and increase the number of tallies needed to earn the incentive.

- Don't worry if kids don't record their behavior accurately. The act of recording in itself can lead to improved behavior.

- If the inappropriate behavior is causing harm to other kids or seriously interfering with the progress of the class, you may also need to identify a consequence to be imposed at the time the harm is done. Keep the consequence separate from the contract; it should not interfere with the contract's continuation.

Improving Behavior for the Whole Class

Although ideally we want to move away from external motivation for doing well in school, whole-class programs can be remarkably effective in persuading kids who misbehave to conform to reasonable expectations.

Some teachers give points to the whole class when all students have met certain clearly defined and explained behavior expectations, usually for a given class or subject rather than for an entire school day. Points may also be given to rows or small groups of kids seated together.

You might award points for categories including attendance, bringing in homework, following class rules, completing expected tasks, etc. Only *give* points—never take them away. Your students will soon begin putting pressure on their peers who are keeping them from getting the points. (It's fun to watch them take over some of the things you used to do to get positive results from everyone in the class.) Tally points regularly and let kids cash them in for treats, coupons, and/or privileges ranging from extra recess time to class parties.

With very young students, you might want to hand out colored cards or other tokens each time you recognize their good behavior. Just before class ends, have them turn in their cards or tokens for an incentive of their choice.

With older students, try the "Positive Points" system.* Each student gets a "Positive Points" card he or she uses to tally points earned by achieving personal behavioral goals. Whenever you notice a student engaging in a goal-related behavior, you acknowledge it verbally. (*Examples:* "Tracy, I noticed that you kept all of your materials together in your folder today. Give yourself five positive points." "Jeffrey, I noticed that you followed directions. Give yourself three positive points.") You and the class decide in advance how many points a behavior is worth and work together to create a list of incentives (menu items) with specific point values. Vary the menu often to keep interest high. A card that is lost or destroyed is not replaced that day; points are not carried over from week to week; once points have been earned, they cannot be taken away later for inappropriate behavior. At the end of the week, students exchange their points for incentives of their choosing. Or they might pool their points toward a treat or activity for the whole class.

---

* Leslie Bersman and Michelle Westley. "Reinforce First: An Effective Approach to Promote 'Positive' Behavior in Behavior Disorder Classrooms." Paper presented at the Council for Exceptional Children (CEC) Conference, Denver, CO, April 1994. Used with permission.

Behavior Contract

Made between _____ **and** _____
student's name   teacher's name

for the period _____ **through** _____
starting date   ending date

The behavior I am agreeing to demonstrate:

_____

_____

_____

_____

_____

The incentive I am trying to earn:

_____

_____

The price of the incentive (number of tallies I need): _____

TALLY BOX

Student's signature: _____

Teacher's signature: _____

Scenario: Mrs. Swanson's Smiley Face Program*

When teacher Charlotte Swanson was faced with an unusually difficult kindergarten class, she initiated a Smiley Face program. Kids won smiley tokens when they followed class rules and lost them if they broke a rule.

Mrs. Swanson was always careful to be calm and matter-of-fact when she had to take back a token. "Look, you just lost a smiley," she would say. "Can you tell me why? Can you make a plan so you don't lose another one for the same reason?" Occasionally kids could earn back lost tokens by doing something nice for someone else, or by showing lots of effort on a particular piece of work.

Students could exchange their tokens for prizes at scheduled times, and they had to count their own smileys when choosing what they wanted at the Smiley Store. Later in the year, Mrs. Swanson made smileys in different denominations and used them to teach kids how to make change. Students even had some say about what should be available for purchase at the Smiley Store.

Mrs. Swanson was delighted with the results of her program. She was especially pleased to see her students helping each other avoid inappropriate behavior.

Class Meetings

William Glasser's philosophy includes a belief that students can usually solve their own problems. Class meetings provide a way for students to discuss their problems in the classroom and work together to identify solutions. One type of class meeting can be used to deal with behavior problems. The emphasis is on finding a group solution to the group problem; care is taken not to identify anyone as guilty, find fault, or mete out punishment. Regular meetings help the class monitor the effectiveness of the solution.

1. Students sit in a circle or other arrangement so they can all see one another.

2. A student or the teacher states a problem, taking care to simply describe it without naming names or assigning blame for the problem.

3. The teacher assures all students who want to contribute information or thoughts about the problem that they will have a chance.

4. Students speak directly to each other rather than to the teacher. *Example:* Instead of saying, "Rosemary said that no one was trying," a student would look at Rosemary and say, "You said that you thought no one was trying."

5. Each new speaker paraphrases what the previous speaker said before making his own contribution.

6. Students and the teacher suggest several solutions. The teacher keeps the discussion going by asking students to give reasons for their suggestions and by soliciting other ideas. The teacher tries to be just one of the group instead of its focal point. The teacher (or a designated student) records all ideas on chart paper.

7. Anyone is allowed to object to any suggestion they find unacceptable, including the teacher. Unacceptable suggestions are deleted from the list.

8. The class votes on the remaining suggestions and agrees to try the one that gets the highest rating. **Tip:** Don't discard the other suggestions, as they may be considered in subsequent meetings.

9. Students make a verbal commitment to abide by the agreed-upon solution.

10. The class meets again in three to five days to assess how well the solution is working. If it is doing the job, the group congratulates itself in some way and continues to use the solution. If it is not doing the job, the group consults the list of suggestions remaining from the first meeting and chooses another to try.

Variation: Small Group Meetings

Each student has the chance to state her perception of the problem without interruption. Each new speaker paraphrases what the previous speaker said. Suggestions are generated only after all kids have stated the problem from their point of view.

With one particularly difficult class, I asked the students to write out their versions of the problem, urging them to include all the details so I would be sure to have the correct information. A funny thing happened a few days later: I noticed a dramatic decrease in the number of students who were complaining about other students. I specifically heard a student named David say, "No, no—don't tell her! She'll make us write about it. Let's just forget it!"

Conflict Resolution and Peer Mediation

Many schools are using programs that are designed to reduce conflict before it escalates into violence. Some programs train teachers to mediate conflicts, but the most exciting programs, such as the one described in Fred Schrumpf's book *Peer Mediation*, train students in these skills. (See "References and Resources" at the end of this chapter). When such programs are used successfully, the number of incidents involving inappropriate behavior drops dramatically, as does the number of "discipline referrals."

Help your students learn to deal directly with each other when arguments or disagreements arise. Coach

---

* Charlotte Swanson, teacher, Elgin, Illinois. Used with permission.

them through the process of thinking through the problem, explaining it clearly and simply, trying to imagine how the other person feels, and coming up with possible solutions in preparation for meeting face-to-face. "Getting Ready to Talk: For People in Conflict" (page 209) invites students to put their thoughts on paper. Completing the handout, bringing it into a conflict resolution meeting, and consulting it during the meeting are excellent ways to keep things on track.

Using the Time-Out

Time-outs are often used when students are unable to choose appropriate behaviors. The purpose of the time-out is to convince disruptive students that they only have two choices: to be in their regular class and follow the behavior expectations, or to be away from the regular class to sit and wait. In most cases, a time-out is preferable to sending kids out into the hall or to the office of the person who enforces discipline in the school. Try these procedures if your school does not have a staffed time-out room.

1. Set up an area in your classroom where kids can't see what is going on in the regular learning area. This is the time-out place. Students can either send themselves there when they feel they are about to erupt, or you can send them there when their behavior warrants their physical removal from the group. The time-out place should contain only a chair and a desk or table—nothing rewarding or very interesting.

   Students should stay in the time-out place for a reasonable minimum number of minutes (5–15) or until they feel they have enough self-control to rejoin the class. When a student returns from the time-out place, don't call attention to him, even in congratulations, since that attention may lead the student to create similar situations for similar attention.

2. If serious inappropriate behavior continues, consider an out-of-class time-out. Have the student go to another classroom or to the office of an administrator or counselor for at least one class period.

   A student who is sent to an out-of-class time-out carries a note from herself and the teacher describing the reason she was asked to leave class. She may use this time to cool down, work on regular schoolwork (not punishment-type assignments), or complete a plan for changing her behavior, which gives her the opportunity to get along better in class.

3. For emergencies, allow students to choose a voluntary time-out when they feel their emotions rising to a danger point. Tell them that when they have such feelings they should take the Time-Out Pass (an actual object available for kids to use) and go to a time-out place,

either in your room, another teacher's room, or a designated area in the school.

One teacher set aside an area in the classroom for students who felt the need to work alone when they perceived they would be too overstimulated if they worked with the group. This became a reasonable alternative environment for kids who were distracted by cooperative learning, as well as a haven for kids who simply preferred more solitary working conditions.

4. If misbehavior persists beyond the time-out arrangements, the principal or a designee enters the picture and arranges a one-day suspension. When the student returns to school, he goes to the time-out location and completes a "Behavior Change Plan" (page 193) that is mutually acceptable to the student and the teacher.

Used this way, the time-out is not a punishment. Rather, it's a chance for students to learn how to develop more appropriate behaviors. What a nice alternative to having the teacher throw the kid out! Think about it: Even in our homes, we look for a place to go so we can calm down before we reenter a tense or stressful situation.

The Responsible Thinking Process: A School-Wide Behavior Management Model*

Based on the work of Edward E. Ford, the Responsible Thinking Process teaches students how to take responsibility for their own behavior choices. An individual is trained to serve as the teacher in the Responsible Thinking Classroom (RTC). (Many schools have found that non-certified people, such as parent volunteers, can do an excellent job in this role.) Classroom teachers, the principal, the school counselor, and the RTC teacher work together. When any adult observes a student breaking a rule, the adult asks the student a series of questions:

1. "What are you doing?"

2. "What are the rules? Are you following or breaking the rules?"

3. "What happens when you break the rules?" (In schools that use the Responsible Thinking Process, all students know the answer to this question: "I go to the RTC.")

---

* Adapted from *Discipline for Home and School, Book One: Teaching Disruptive Children How to Look Within Themselves, Decide the Way They Want to Be, and Then Think of Ways to Achieve Their Goals Without Violating the Rights of Others* by Edward E. Ford. Revised Third Edition. Scottsdale, AZ: Brandt Publishing, 2003. Used with permission of Edward E. Ford.

Getting Ready to Talk
For People in Conflict

My name: _____

Name of person I argued or disagreed with: _____

My explanation of the problem:

_____
_____
_____
_____

How the other person probably feels about the situation:

_____
_____
_____
_____

To solve this problem, I am willing to:

_____
_____
_____
_____

4. "Is that what you want to have happen?"

5. "What do you want to do now?"

6. "What will happen if you disrupt again?" (There is just one possible answer: "I will go to the RTC.")

In most cases, after a few weeks of using the Responsible Thinking Process, only the first and sixth questions are necessary.

If the student refuses to engage in this dialogue, the adult asks, "Do you want to work at this or not?" If she still refuses to engage, the adult says, "You need to go to the RTC."

If the student engages in the dialogue, settles down temporarily, but disrupts again later, the adult asks, "What are you doing?" (question #1), then "What did you say would happen if you disrupted again?" (referring to question #6), followed by "Where do you need to go now?" (to the RTC).

The student is sent to the RTC, along with a referral form describing the disruption. She is not allowed to return to the class she disrupted until she has written a plan to deal with her problem behavior. She can go to other classes or other school events but must spend all of the disrupted class time in the RTC until she completes her written plan. In other words, if the student disrupts math class, she cannot return to math class until she completes her plan.

When the student arrives in the RTC, she may take whatever time she needs to calm down and prepare to write her plan. For highly volatile kids, this cooling-down time is very welcome.* When the student is ready to write her plan, the RTC teacher gives her a form to use. (Forms for primary students and those in grades 3–12 are found on pages 211 and 212.) The teacher may read and explain the questions on the form, but the student must write her own plan, which must clearly and specifically describe how she will deal with this problem in the future. Younger students and those unable to write may draw pictures reflecting on what they did and what they will do next time. In some cases, the RTC teacher may write the plan as the student dictates.

Once the student has completed her plan, she returns to the class she originally disrupted. She sits quietly in a designated place until the teacher can find a few moments to sit down with her and review her plan. The student explains the plan to the teacher, who may offer suggestions and alternatives. When the plan is accepted, the student is officially back in the class.

Schools in which the Responsible Thinking Process is working well have seen a 60 to 70 percent drop in referrals to the RTC, which means that more students who used to get into trouble frequently have learned how to avoid repeat incidents in their classrooms.

You may be wondering if some kids act out just to go to the RTC. Edward Ford says that in his experience this rarely happens, because most kids would rather be where the action is instead of sitting quietly by themselves in a time-out room. Some middle school and high school teachers worry that students will miss too much class time if they go to the RTC. We might instead consider how much instructional time the other students are missing because of the disruptive students' behaviors.

If you decide to try the Responsible Thinking Process with your students, be sure to use the forms exactly as they appear here. For more information, see "References and Resources."

Dealing with Bullying in Your Class and School

When we read the appalling stories of students who attack, injure, and even kill their schoolmates, we invariably learn that they have something in common: At some point, they were bullied. We all probably have our own memories of similar situations, so we can empathize with the pain these kids must feel.

Any plan to prevent school violence must teach all students to respect individual differences. In fact, that's what most of this book is about. One of the interesting things I've discovered during my years of giving workshops for teachers is that the very act of differentiating the curriculum—providing learning activities for students based on their individual learning needs—communicates that it's okay to be different. It teaches students to respect themselves just as they are, which in turn makes them more open to respecting others.

Bullying comes in many forms, from teasing to taunting, mocking, name-calling, insults, nasty emails and IMs (instant messages), threats, and physical violence. Kids bully for many reasons—to feel powerful and in control, to be the center of attention, because they have been bullied themselves, because they get pleasure from other people's pain, because they feel little or no empathy for others. It's a myth that kids bully because they have low self-esteem.

If bullying is a problem at your school, it's almost impossible to stop it without a dedicated school-wide program that is accepted and supported by everyone in your school community, from the administration to the students and their parents. A program I especially recommend is the Olweus Bullying Prevention Program. Dan Olweus is

---

* Another option in the Responsible Thinking Process is the "chill-out pass," which is given to students who are easily upset. Students can show their pass to the adult in charge, then go to the RTC to chill out. Students learn to monitor their own feelings in the classroom and leave before it's too late. Wouldn't we all prefer this to in-class explosions?

Responsible Thinking Process
Student Plan (Primary Grades)

NAME: _____ **DATE:** _____

CLASSROOM TEACHER: _____ **GRADE:** _____

What did I do that was against the rules? (Write or draw your answer in the space below.)

What is the rule?

What happens when I break the rules?

What am I going to do the next time the same problem occurs? (Write or draw your answer.)

Responsible Thinking Process
Student Plan (Grades 3–12)

NAME: _____ **DATE:** _____

CLASSROOM TEACHER: _____ **GRADE:** _____

Describe exactly what happened.

_____

_____

Does your description match that of the person in charge? *(Circle one)*	YES	NO

What was the first question the person in charge asked you?

_____

What was the rule you broke or the procedure you didn't follow?

_____

_____

Did your action keep other students from doing what they were supposed to do? *(Circle one)*	YES	NO
Did your action keep the person in charge from doing something he or she needed to do?	YES	NO
Have you ever written a plan before to deal with this same problem?	YES	NO

If you have written a plan about this problem before:

Would you like to see a copy of that plan to help you write a new plan?	YES	NO

What changes will you make now so your plan can be successful?

_____

_____

---

continued ➡

The next time you have the same problem, how will you deal with it? Write a plan below:

_____

_____

_____

_____

What might make it difficult for you to follow your plan?

_____

_____

_____

If you are really serious about following this plan, what changes should the person in charge see?

_____

_____

_____

What support do you need to help you with this plan?

_____

_____

_____

In detail, describe how you will make up the work you missed while you were in the RTC.

_____

_____

_____

STUDENT'S SIGNATURE: _____

RTC TEACHER'S SIGNATURE: _____

CLASSROOM TEACHER'S SIGNATURE: _____
(indicates acceptance of the plan)

a professor of psychology at the University of Oslo. When a series of bullying-related suicides shocked Norway into awareness of the problem, Olweus responded by creating a comprehensive program that is now widely used and respected. For more information about this and other anti-bullying programs, see "References and Resources."

Questions and Answers

"Shouldn't kids just know how to behave more appropriately in school?"

Never assume that students know how to substitute good behavior for bad. Students need to work with an adult to learn such basic skills as taking turns, sharing, asking for help, accepting suggestions, apologizing when necessary, and accepting praise or compliments. Several excellent books, including Arnold Goldstein's Skillstreaming series and Dorothy Rich's *MegaSkills,* can help you teach social skills directly. See "References and Resources."

"How can I find time to try these interventions? When am I supposed to do all of the record-keeping involved?"

Try keeping a log for several days of the amount of time you spend disciplining students with significant behavior problems. Then ask yourself if that time wouldn't be better spent teaching kids how to more successfully manage their own behavior. If students need to come to class early or stay beyond regular dismissal time, it's appropriate to use those times to teach the elements of the management systems. You'll probably observe that the amount of time needed per student actually decreases when the time is spent on management rather than punishment.

"We have some parents who object to using behavior contracts or time-outs with their children. What can we do?"

A conference between parents, teachers, the principal, and appropriate support staff may help all parties reach agreement on the need for certain interventions. Students themselves might be asked to describe for their parents the positive effects they think such interventions have upon their behavior and productivity. Perhaps parents could benefit from reading articles or books that justify the use of certain interventions. When parents understand that the goal of these techniques is not to punish but rather to teach students how to assume more responsibility for themselves, negative attitudes may change.

"My students' parents want to be involved in their behavior contracts. Why do you recommend that parents not be involved?"

A behavior contract should only relate to a child's behavior at school, and any incentives or consequences specified in the contract should only be given at school. When parents are expected to apply consequences at home for a child's inappropriate behavior at school, the teacher loses control of the situation. Parents can help by spending one-on-one time with their child—reading aloud, playing a game the child enjoys, or just talking about each other's experiences during the day. Parents can also make sure that the child spends time at home on daily work related to learning. In addition, parents can be invited to use any of the forms in this chapter for home-related behavior change needs.

REFERENCES AND RESOURCES

Bersman, Leslie, and Michelle Westley. "Reinforce First: An Effective Approach to Promote 'Positive' Behavior in Behavior Disorder Classrooms." Paper presented at the Council for Exceptional Children (CEC) Conference, Denver, CO, April 1994.

Boodman, Sandra G. "Teaching Bullies a Lesson." *The Washington Post.* June 5, 2001.

DeBruyn, Robert L., and Jack L. Larson. *You Can Handle Them All: A Discipline Model for Handling over 100 Different Misbehaviors at School and at Home.* Manhattan, KS: Master Teacher Inc., 1984. Available from www.masterteacher. com; 1-800-669-9633.

Discipline with Dignity (www.disciplineassociates.com). The skills and strategies you need to deal with disruptions while teaching kids responsibility for their own actions. 1-800-772-5227.

Dreikurs, Rudolf, and Vicki Soltz. *Children: The Challenge.* New York: Plume, 1990.

Faber, Adele, and Elaine Mazlish. *How To Talk So Kids Will Listen & Listen So Kids Will Talk.* New York: Avon Books, 1999. 20th anniversary edition. Strategies to enhance communication between adults and youngsters.

Ford, Edward E. *Discipline for Home and School, Fundamentals.* Scottsdale, AZ: Brandt Publishing, 2004.
—Discipline for Home and School, Book One: Teaching Disruptive Children How to Look Within Themselves, Decide the Way They Want to Be, and Then Think of Ways to Achieve Their Goals Without Violating the Rights of Others. Third Edition. Scottsdale, AZ: Brandt Publishing, 2003.

Froschl, Merle, et al. *Quit It! A Teacher's Guide on Teasing and Bullying for Use with Students in Grades K–3.* New York:

Educational Equity Center; Wellesley, MA: Wellesley College Center for Research on Women; Washington, DC: NEW Professional Library, 1998. Available from Educational Equity Center, www.edequity.org; (212) 243-1110. Also available from the Wellesley Centers for Women, www.wcwonline.org; (781) 283-2500.

Glasser, William. *The Quality School: Managing Students Without Coercion.* Revised edition. New York: HarperPerennial, 1998.

Goldstein, Arnold P., et al. The Skillstreaming Series (www.researchpress.com). Books, skill cards, CD-ROMs, and videos help kids learn appropriate social/interactive skills and make good behavior choices. The series includes *Skillstreaming in Early Childhood, Skillstreaming the Elementary School Child,* and *Skillstreaming the Adolescent.* 1-800-519-2707.

Gootman, Marilyn E. *The Caring Teacher's Guide to Discipline: Helping Young Students Learn Self-Control, Responsibility, and Respect.* 2nd edition. Thousand Oaks, CA: Corwin Press, 2000.

Hall, R. Vance, and Marilyn L. Hall. *How to Negotiate a Behavioral Contract.* 2nd edition. Austin, TX: PRO-ED, 1998.

The Honor Level System (www.honorlevel.com). A school discipline system that stresses positive reinforcement for appropriate behavior and academic achievement. Created to meet the needs of one middle school in Washington more than 20 years ago, the program is now used with more than 90,000 high school, junior high, middle school, and elementary students in the United States. Free trials are available. 1-800-441-4199.

How Difficult Can This Be? The F.A.T. City Workshop: Understanding Learning Disabilities (www.shoppbs.org). Hosted by Dr. Richard LaVoie, seen on PBS, this documentary program looks at the world through the eyes of a learning-disabled child. A must-see for all teachers—great for staff meetings. Also available: *Last One Picked . . . First One Picked On,* hosted by Dr. LaVoie, addresses the social problems kids with LD often face. 1-800-531-4727.

Kreidler, William J. *Creative Conflict Resolution: More than 200 Activities for Keeping the Peace in the Classroom.* Glenview, IL: Good Year Books, 1984.

Lane, Pamela S. *Conflict Resolution for Kids: A Group Facilitator's Guide.* Washington, DC: Accelerated Development, 1995.

Managing the Disruptive Classroom (www.ait.net). A program for teachers based on reality therapy, produced by the Agency for Instructional Technology (AIT) and Phi Delta Kappa. Includes a 60-minute video program and a 32-page facilitator's guide. 1-800-457-4509.

Migliore, Eleanor T. "Eliminate Bullying in Your Classroom." *Intervention in School and Clinic* 38:3 (2003), pp 172–176.

Moorman, Chick, and Nancy Weber. *Teacher Talk: What It Really Means.* Saginaw, MI: Personal Power Press, 1989. A guide to using "teacher talk" to manage students and their problems in the classroom.

Olweus Bullying Prevention Program (www.clemson.edu/olweus). A comprehensive, school-wide program designed for use in elementary, middle, or junior high schools.

Powers, William T. *Behavior: The Control of Perception.* 2nd edition, revised and expanded. New Canaan, CT: Benchmark Publications, 2005.

Responsible Thinking Process (www.responsiblethinking.com). A behavior management and classroom discipline process that teaches respect for others by fostering responsible thinking; (480) 991-4860.

Rich, Dorothy. *MegaSkills: How Families Can Help Children to Succeed in School and Beyond.* New and expanded edition. Boston: Houghton Mifflin, 1998. Teaches the basic skills needed to be competent in life.

ricklavoie.com (www.ricklavoie.com). The Web site of Dr. Richard Lavoie, a nationally recognized expert on learning disabilities and host of the *How Difficult Can This Be?* and *Last One Picked . . . First One Picked On* videos (see above). His books, videos, articles, and workshops are fabulous resources for anyone who lives and works with students with learning difficulties. He really understands these kids, and he helps parents and teachers do the same.

"Schoolwide Prevention of Bullying" booklet. Portland, OR: Northwest Regional Educational Laboratory, 2001. Available to download at educationnorthwest.org/resource/798. To order additional copies, call 1-800-547-6339.

Schrumpf, Fred, Donna K. Crawford, and Richard J. Bodine. *Peer Mediation: Conflict Resolution in Schools.* Revised edition. Champaign, IL: Research Press, 1997.

Sjostrom, Lisa, and Nan D. Stein. *Bullyproof: A Teacher's Guide on Teasing and Bullying for Use with Fourth and Fifth Grade Students.* Wellesley, MA: Center for Research on Women; Washington, DC: NEA Professional Library, 1996. Available from the Wellesley Centers for Women, www.wcwonline.org; (781) 283-2500.

Ziegler, Robert G. "Child and Context: Reactive Adaptations of Learning Disabled Children." *Journal of Learning Disabilities* 14:7 (August–September 1981), pp. 391–393, 430. Explains the condition of "learned helplessness."

14

Working with Parents as Partners in Their Child's Learning

When parents* are supportive of the school's goals and communicate this support to their children, those kids have a much better chance of succeeding in school than kids whose parents are unsupportive and uninvolved. As teachers, we need to help parents understand that being a team member in the goal of educating their children can have positive results for everyone.

Having a child with severe learning difficulties can be challenging and stressful. Parents typically move through a series of emotions and attitudes, ranging from "Won't someone please help my daughter learn?" to "Why aren't the teachers doing their job?" to "What's wrong with this lazy kid?" On first finding out about their child's learning problems, some parents react with denial. Others, recognizing the similarities between their child's situation and their own history of struggling to learn, may think, "Look at me! I made it and I'm doing fine. Why can't my child do the same?" Still others may decide, "The schools I attended never helped me with my problem. If my child has the same thing, the school won't help him either." They may either become extremely demanding and hostile, or they may withdraw entirely to save themselves from more pain.

Other problems arise when teachers assume that parents from disadvantaged socioeconomic groups don't care about their children's education. In fact, many of these families are vitally interested in having the educational system help their children find the pathway out of poverty. At the same time, they may fear losing control of their children's values and destiny if they let the school take over too much.

Some parents are reluctant to expose what they perceive to be their own language and learning inadequacies. For others, their children's school experience is so different from what they remember or think it should be that they feel increasingly isolated and uninformed. Some parents have experienced nightmarish school meetings at which no one on staff had anything kind to say about their child. Parents who feel that the system isn't being fair may come to view the school as an enemy.

In other words, there are many reasons why some parents resist getting involved with their children's school or meeting with school personnel. Nevertheless, it is totally unproductive for teachers and administrators to conclude, "Well, I've done everything I could, and Albert's mom never comes to a single conference. If she doesn't care about his success in school, why should we?" Even if we are dealing with a situation where the adults really don't want to get involved, we can't assume that the child doesn't want to learn! There are many schools where formerly unsuccessful students are experiencing school success despite bleak conditions at home.

---

* Parents, caregivers, other relatives, foster parents—any adult a child lives with can be a partner in his or her learning.

It's not enough to say that your school *wants* parent involvement. Your school must *work* proactively and assertively to extend invitations to parents for specific kinds of participation and provide the required training. Virtually any kind of parent involvement boosts student achievement, from helping to create learning materials for the classroom to joining a committee, from going on a field trip to volunteering in the child's classroom. When parents are present in school activities, they send a clear message to their children that school is worthwhile and valuable. This chapter describes several ways to reach out to parents and make them welcome at school.

Ways to Promote Parent Involvement at School

- All communication with parents, whether verbal or written, should be available in the language spoken in the home. Efforts by your school to provide this service will go a long way toward making parents feel that the school is truly interested in communicating with them.

- Regularly send home notes to parents in which you recognize something positive their child has done at school. When families have a history of hearing only bad or gloomy news about their children, the arrival of good news about any behavior, event, or work product can begin to reverse the fearful or negative impressions some parents have about school in general.

- Frequently send home classroom or school newsletters. When written in a folksy manner without educational jargon, newsletters are an effective communication tool. If students themselves write some of the articles, you can be sure that the parents will at least read those! As a regular feature, you might describe activities that are designed for parents and students to do together. *Examples:* Go through the house to find items that begin with certain letters or rhyme with certain words. Use family experiences as the impetus for Language Experience stories dictated by the child (see pages 86–88). Poll family members on their food preferences, TV-watching habits, job-related issues, etc.

- Make your school family-friendly by raising awareness about the positive aspects of diversity. Diversity provides opportunities to learn about and appreciate our similarities and differences. Invite all families, including those from majority groups, to share information about their cultures, traditions, and observances with the students and each other.

- Invite people from all cultures represented in your school to screen school communications, spot potentially insensitive content, and suggest improvements.

- Arrange for translators to be present at school meetings so parents for whom English is a second language can easily follow the agenda and receive the necessary information. If possible, have your school purchase or borrow a system that allows translators to speak through microphones to listeners wearing headsets. (You've seen this sort of thing in use during televised United Nations meetings.) All meeting documents should be available in the language spoken in the home.

- Fewer than half of America's households today fit the traditional family model. Therefore, it's important for us to accept many different kinds of family arrangements as normal, simply because those are the environments from which our students come. Avoid addressing verbal and written communications to "Mom and Dad."

- Be sensitive to the emotional trauma certain well-meaning assignments might cause. *Examples:* Asking students to discover their family's roots can be upsetting for adopted children or those whose families escaped from or disappeared in some holocaust in another land. Having students write their autobiographies can be disturbing to someone whose earlier life was something he or she would rather forget. Don't assume that all kids celebrate Christmas and Easter or take family vacations. When you ask kids to report on personal or family data, make several choices available.

- Avoid attributing a child's inappropriate behavior to his family situation. Since we can do very little to change what's going on in the family, the least we can do is reduce the stress that the child experiences at school. When children become more positive about going to school and participating in school activities, this diminishes one source of aggravation and frustration for the family in trouble.

- Consider making home visits to families who don't come to school when they are invited.

- Offer conferences at nontraditional times so people who work different shifts also have opportunities to attend.

- Help parents connect to parent support groups in your community. If possible, attend a few meetings yourself to get an insider's perspective. Call ahead for permission to sit in on the group.

- Find out about literacy programs in your community. Some parents resist school involvement out of fear that their illiteracy might be revealed. Learning to read along with their children can be a mutually satisfying experience.

- Offer classes in effective parenting, even if only a few people show up. Advertise the fact that there will be translation services, and list the languages that will be available. Be sure to present the classes in a positive light. Explain that they're being offered as opportunities to learn something new and connect with other parents, not because the adults don't know how to parent. Emphasize that everyone benefits from new learning. (You might mention the teacher-training seminar you attended recently.)

- Offer information nights on learning styles, cooperative learning, or other educational topics, slipping in a little advice on creating and maintaining positive parent-child relationships.

Homework Issues

Students who regularly do homework have a better chance for school success than those who don't. However, we can't assume that all kids have equal access to conditions in the home that help to make homework a positive experience.

Parents play a critical role in determining whether and how effectively children do their homework. Damaging cycles develop when parents nag kids to do their homework or take on a teaching role. Often, when parents who really are classroom teachers try to teach their own children, the kids get the message that their parents would like them better if they were better students! The situation is made worse when parents use different teaching methods than the ones being used in the child's classroom. Furthermore, homework can exacerbate the social and economic differences between students, since some parents are more able to give appropriate support for homework assignments than others.

Scenario: Stacy

Stacy was a second grader who brought home hours of homework every night. Her mom had to meet the school bus to physically help Stacy get off, since the pile of books and papers she carried was often higher than her line of vision.

Where did all this homework come from? Stacy had been conditioned by her over-helpful parents that whatever was too hard for her to complete in school should be brought home so they could help. In fact, the parents had created learned helplessness in Stacy. Since she correctly perceived that her parents thought she was incapable of learning without their assistance, she had adopted that attitude as well. What made her situation especially ironic was that Mom was a teacher by profession! Naturally Mom

was frustrated because she knew she was helping her students learn but felt powerless to help her own daughter.

Together Mom, Dad, and Stacy created the same painful scene at the kitchen table every night. Stacy would begin a task, look up with tears streaming down her face, and moan, "I can't do this! The teacher didn't explain it right. He wouldn't answer my questions. I need help!" Minutes turned into hours. Dad walked away in frustration, and Mom continued to help Stacy into total helplessness.

Ways to Make Homework Meaningful and Manageable

- Homework can keep concepts fresh in students' minds and indicate when reteaching is necessary. Use it as a barometer to determine effective pacing and corrective measures.

- Homework assignments should never be very difficult and should only require materials that are generally available in the home. Never expect students to learn new concepts on their own as homework. Instead, use the assignments to reinforce and extend concepts that you have taught at school.

- Tailoring homework assignments to students' learning style strengths can immediately lead to better results. Help parents understand and appreciate their children's learning styles by sharing with them the information in Chapter 4. Offer several product alternatives so students can select something that complements their learning styles; see page 75 for ideas.

- Give parents the help and encouragement they need to support the practice of regular homework. On pages 224–234* you'll find several handouts to copy and send home, include in your classroom newsletter, hand out at conferences, or make available at open houses. Be sure to include at least five copies of the "Homework Contract" (page 228) with the "How to Use the Homework Contract" handout (page 227).

- Never let students believe that homework is assigned just to keep them busy. Preface each assignment by explaining its educational purpose. (*Examples:* "These problems relate to the math skill we learned today." "This story is required reading for your biography project.") If an assignment doesn't have a clear purpose, don't give it!

- Use a consistent system to assign homework, such as the assignment notebook used by all teachers in your school (see page 166). Allow several minutes at the end of each class for students to write down their assignments. Tell parents to expect this assignment

---

* All forms and handouts for this chapter are found at the end of the chapter.

notebook to come home each day, and ask them to sign off each evening to indicate that the student worked for the agreed-upon period of time. Suggest ways for parents to help their children remember to return their notebooks and assignments to school. You might also use the "Monthly Homework and Project Calendar" (page 169) for this purpose.

■ If students move from class to class during the day, work with the other teachers to coordinate your homework schedules so students (and their families) won't have an extra-heavy load at some times and little or nothing at other times.

■ Don't get into the habit of sending notes home to parents explaining the homework a child is expected to do. The only time you might send home a note for a student with learning difficulties is when the child has *no* homework. This implies that homework time should be a regularly scheduled part of the family's routine, and that no-homework-time is the exception.

■ Even after introducing a new concept at school, don't have students practice it at home more than 10–12 times. After that many repetitions, some students have gained complete understanding while others are likely to repeat mistakes many times over.

■ It's more productive to expect students to work for a certain period of time on an assignment than to assign an arbitrary number of problems or activities. Students should get partial credit for attempting the work or for completing some part of the assignment during the expected time period. See "Goal Setting" on pages 65–68 for an explanation of why this works well for struggling students. Then send home the "Homework Goal Chart" weekly. The first time you send the chart home (and any time during the year when you think this is needed or appropriate), include a note to parents explaining the goal-setting method. Encourage them to work with their children to set a consistent homework time each day. **Tip:** Be sure to keep your own expectations realistic—and remember that struggling students should not spend too much time on homework in general.

■ Don't use homework to lower students' grades. Instead, give partial credit for evidence that students have spent a reasonable amount of time on homework and have used the "Homework Goal Chart."

■ Provide appropriate feedback on all homework assignments—written comments, responses to student questions, and/or specific suggestions for improvement. If you don't plan to give feedback, don't give the assignment!

■ Have students end each homework assignment by completing these sentences, perhaps on the back of the paper:

> The part of this assignment I understood well was _____.
>
> The part I didn't understand at all was _____.

■ For long-term assignments, help students create a backwards timeline to break the project into short-term components. Encourage them to take pride in completing each component. **Tip:** The "Monthly Homework and Project Calendar" (page 169) can help some students stay on task during long-term assignments.

■ When students fail to complete a homework assignment, the problem might be that they simply don't understand what they are supposed to do. Homework should never be used as punishment, nor should assignments be made longer to make up for previously missed assignments.

■ At regular intervals, send home folders of the work the students are doing to help parents keep informed of their children's progress. Coach students on how to describe the work to their parent(s), and send along a "Schoolwork Sign-Off Form" (page 225) for parents to sign and return. Remind parents that giving sincere verbal encouragement and celebrating little successes will motivate their children more than monetary or other tangible rewards. If the parents are unavailable, students might discuss their work with other adult caregivers or with older siblings.

Productive Parent-Teacher Meetings

Be sensitive to the likelihood that many parents of struggling students won't expect parent-teacher meetings to be pleasant experiences. Some will have a history of painful conferences, and there are almost certainly bad feelings at home when children are not doing well at school.

■ Some teachers send home a form that helps parents to prepare for conferences. When parents have a chance to think about a conference ahead of time, and when they know that the teacher will want their input and perspective, they may feel less apprehensive. Send home a copy of the "Parent-Teacher Conference Questionnaire" (page 230) several days before a scheduled conference. Refer to it during the conference.

- If a child's parents don't live together, ask if they want to attend conferences separately or together.

- When telling parents about their child's school experience, be as matter-of-fact and objective as you can.

- Avoid creating a triangle between the student, the parents, and you by sending messages through third parties. (*Examples:* Don't ask the child to remind the parent to come to a conference; contact the parent yourself. Don't ask the parent to pass along your suggestions from a parent-teacher conference to the child; give those messages directly to the child. In this way, all communications will be open and clear, and both you and the parent will give the child similar messages.) At best, third-party communication creates confusion; at worst, it puts the student in the position of being able to get you and his parents upset with each other so you spend less time on his problems. When the student sees that you and his parents are in agreement about problems and what to do about them, negative behaviors almost always subside.

You may find it helpful to follow an agenda when meeting with parents, whether in person or by telephone, formally or informally. Naturally you won't need to include *all* of the items listed below in *every* meeting, but a quick read-through in advance will help to ensure that you don't omit anything important. If the purpose of the meeting is to set up a plan to monitor the student's work or behavior, the student should also be present.

1. Always begin by giving examples of the child's positive traits. Share something about the child that you find particularly attractive or engaging. **Tip:** Try to identify a strength that may have been overlooked in the past because it didn't develop in positive ways. For example, many kids who get into trouble are excellent leaders.

2. Ask the parents to tell you about their child's strengths and strong interests. Tell them that you can't possibly know everything about their child, and you see them as partners in helping you understand his personality and needs. Make a written record of this information for future reference. If the parents have completed a "Parent-Teacher Conference Questionnaire" (page 230), you can use that as your written record, with your notes added.

3. Explain your homework policies. *Example:* "I will assign thirty minutes of homework on most school nights. On days when I don't assign any homework, I'll send home a note to let you know. Your child can spend those thirty minutes on another learning task. If she forgets her homework on days when I do assign it, she

should still spend thirty minutes on some type of learning task." Reassure the parents that you won't assign homework that is beyond the child's ability to do independently. Give them one or more of the homework-related handouts on pages 226–234.

4. Share what you know about the child's learning style. Help the parents understand that their child is intelligent and can be a better learner if his learning style strengths are taken into consideration—at home and at school.

5. Share the information you have about the child's progress to date. Parents enjoy seeing documented evidence of what their child is doing in school. Show examples of the child's work; this will help the parents to recognize that he has strengths. Include references to any forms related to schoolwork or homework that the parents have filled out and returned to you. Avoid discussing the child's rank in class—e.g., top, middle, bottom. This would be a good time to share the child's Report Card Chart (page 185) with the parents so they are aware of their child's goals.

6. Identify only one behavior you would like the student to focus on in an effort to improve his or her learning or personal behavior. Be specific. *Examples:* "I would like Howard to work on the computer for twenty minutes each day as part of his writing time." "I would like Melissa to make two positive comments to her classmates every day." Ask parents for suggestions.

7. If you are using a behavior management program with the student, give the parents a progress report. If the student hasn't been observing the conditions of the plan, it's all right to tell the parents, but make it very clear that you don't expect them to impose any consequences at home for work or behavior plans not met at school. *Example:* Some kids really shine during out-of-school experiences (music lessons, membership on a sports team). Those shining moments should not depend on positive results at school.

8. Encourage parents to support their child's interests outside of school. Share what you know about related programs offered by community organizations at nominal or no cost.

9. If you have any articles, books, or other materials you think might be helpful to the parents, offer them in a friendly manner. Consult the "References and Resources" throughout this book for possibilities. Give parents copies of the handouts at the end of this chapter. **Tip:** Be careful not to inundate them with too much information at any one time. And be sure that you are thoroughly familiar with the handouts before you give them to parents, in case they have any questions.

10. Always conclude by thanking the parents for taking the time to come to the meeting. Tell them that their presence shows that they are interested in their child's education. Explain that this is vital in helping their child develop and maintain a positive attitude about learning.

Throughout the meeting, use active and reflective listening. When parents share something about their child, paraphrase it back to them. This shows that you value them as sources of information and that you're willing to see the child from their point of view.

More and more schools are including students in some or all of the parent-teacher conferences. After all, students are the ones who have to make certain changes, and their input into setting up the conditions of those changes is pertinent to the ultimate success of any plan.

Always make notes immediately after each meeting rather than relying on your memory later. If several meetings are scheduled very close together, talk your comments into an audiocassette recorder.

Open Houses

Open house meetings really have two purposes:

1. for children and their families to become familiar with the school, the classroom, the teacher(s), and the administration; and

2. for teachers to communicate their expectations and routines to the parents.

Schools should not try to accomplish both of these objectives in the same evening. If your school wishes to accomplish several objectives through the open house procedure, it's better to hold several open houses during the school year.

The first open house might be held during the first weeks of school. Parents can have the chance to tour the learning environment, say hello to teachers, and become familiar with the school calendar. Children attend, too, and there is no formal presentation by the teacher.

The next open house, held no later than the second month of school, is where teachers introduce their programs, expectations, policies, and teaching styles to parents. (Some schools call this "Meet-the-Teacher Night.") The teachers clearly explain how parents can get in touch with them and encourage parents to initiate contact rather than waiting for formal conferences. Translators should be present to communicate with parents who speak different languages. Since the purpose of this meeting is for teachers to talk directly to parents, children should not attend.

Provide childcare services for families who might not be able to attend otherwise.

A third open house, held near the end of the school year, is the time when students share their portfolios and other schoolwork with their parents and demonstrate the progress they have made during that year.

Questions and Answers

"What can we do about parents who never show up at school, despite our best efforts to include them?"

Send home specific suggestions about how they can support their children's learning at home. If the parents really won't come to you, ask if it's all right for you to visit them at home. Be sensitive to the fact that some parents may feel inadequate about their own abilities. Never give up on a student because the parents can't or won't get involved with the school.

There is no doubt that students do better in school when their parents actively support their learning. Anything you can do to strengthen parents' ability to demonstrate that support will pay off in huge dividends. Perhaps parents need to be told this directly; we may err in assuming all parents know how important their involvement is. There are many programs in place that have had positive results in increasing parent involvement. Ask your librarian to help you do a computer search to locate such programs so you can contact them and emulate some of their successful strategies. For more ideas, see "References and Resources" at the end of this chapter.

"What should I do if parents are overly interested in their child's grades and appear to not understand the importance of goal setting and slow, steady progress?"

Go back to pages 65–68 to read about the function that effective goal setting plays in people's lives. Explain that the most motivated students and adults are those who perceive the direct relationship between efforts and outcomes. Describe your goal of motivating students to learn that hard work pays off in higher grades. Explain the danger of allowing kids to believe that they can get high grades with little effort. When we gift kids with grades they don't deserve, we communicate our perception that they aren't capable of doing really well.

REFERENCES AND RESOURCES

Dorothy Rich's Families and Schools: Teaming for Success (www.ait.net/catalog). Video staff development program by the author of *MegaSkills*. 1-800-457-4509.

RECOMMENDED READINGS FOR PARENTS

Armstrong, Thomas. *The Myth of the A.D.D. Child: 50 Ways to Improve Your Child's Behavior and Attention Span Without Drugs, Labels, or Coercion.* New York: Penguin/Plume, 1997. A must-read for educators as well as parents, to help avoid premature decisions to medicate kids with ADD/ADHD.

Baum, Susan M., and Steve V. Owen. *To Be Gifted and Learning Disabled: Strategies for Helping Bright Students with LD, ADHD, and More.* Mansfield Center, CT: Creative Learning Press, 2004.

Cline, Foster, and Jim Fay. *Parenting with Love and Logic: Teaching Kids Responsibility.* Colorado Springs, CO: Piñon Press, 1990.

Cummings, Rhoda, and Gary Fisher. *The School Survival Guide for Kids with LD (Learning Differences).* Minneapolis: Free Spirit Publishing, 1991. Specific tips and strategies especially for students with LD. For ages 8 and up. Read it with your kids!

Dinkmeyer, Don, Sr., Gary D. McKay, and Don Dinkmeyer Jr. *The Parent's Handbook: Systematic Training for Effective Parenting.* Circle Pines, MN: American Guidance Service, 1997.

Dreikurs, Rudolf, and Vicki Soltz. *Children: The Challenge.* New York: Plume, 1990.

Faber, Adele, and Elaine Mazlish. *How To Talk So Kids Will Listen & Listen So Kids Will Talk.* New York: Avon Books, 1999. 20th anniversary edition. Strategies to enhance communication between adults and youngsters.

Fowler, Mary. *Maybe You Know My Kid: A Parent's Guide to Identifying, Understanding and Helping Your Child with Attention-deficit Hyperactivity Disorder.* 3rd edition. Secaucus, NJ: Carol Publishing Group, 1999.

Freed, Jeffrey, and Laurie Parsons. *Right-Brained Children in a Left-Brained World: Unlocking the Potential of Your ADD Child.* New York: Simon and Schuster, 1998. Freed shares his techniques for teaching compensation learning strategies to children who have trouble learning. The strategies work whether or not the child has ADD.

Galvin, Matthew. *Otto Learns about His Medicine: A Story about Medication for Children with ADHD.* 3rd edition. Washington, DC: Magination Press, 2001.

Hallowell, Edward M. *ADD from A to Z: Understanding the Diagnosis and Treatment of Attention Deficit Disorder in Children and Adults.* New York: Pantheon Books, 1994. A comprehensive guide to understanding and intervening with persons with ADD.

Kelly, Kate, and Peggy Ramundo. *You Mean I'm Not Lazy, Stupid, or Crazy?! A Self-Help Book for Adults with Attention Deficit Disorder.* New York: Scribner, 1995.

Kravetz, Marybeth, and Imy F. Wax. *The K&W Guide to Colleges for Students with Learning Disabilities or Attention Deficit Disorder: A Resource Book for Students, Parents, and Professionals.* 6th edition (check for the latest). Burlington, MA: The Princeton Review, 2003.

Lee, Christopher, and Rosemary F. Jackson. *Faking It: A Look into the Mind of a Creative Learner.* Portsmouth, NH: Heinemann, 1992. Helps those without learning disabilities understand what it feels like to try to perceive the world while experiencing significant learning disabilities.

Lyman, Donald E. *Making the Words Stand Still.* Boston: Houghton Mifflin, 1986. Writing from his own experience, Lyman describes the anguish that kids with LD feel as they try to learn, then describes his own unique teaching methods.

Moss, Deborah. *Shelley the Hyperactive Turtle.* Bethesda, MD: Woodbine House, 1989.

—*Lee, The Rabbit with Epilepsy.* Bethesda, MD: Woodbine House, 1989. Books that help children ages 4–9 understand hyperactivity and epilepsy.

Rich, Dorothy. *MegaSkills: How Families Can Help Children to Succeed in School and Beyond.* New and expanded edition. Boston: Houghton Mifflin, 1998. Teaches the basic skills needed to be competent in life.

Rimm, Sylvia. *How to Parent So Children Will Learn.* New York: Crown Books, 1996.

Schumm, Jeanne Shay. *How to Help Your Child with Homework: The Complete Guide to Encouraging Good Study Habits and Ending the Homework Wars.* Revised and updated edition. Minneapolis: Free Spirit Publishing, 2005. Strategies and techniques for parents of children ages 6–13.

Vail, Priscilla. *Smart Kids with School Problems (Gifted/LD): Things to Know and Ways to Help.* New York: Plume/NAL Dutton, 1989.

RESOURCES FOR PARENTS

A.D.D. WareHouse (addwarehouse.com). Offers the most comprehensive catalog I have found of materials for and about children with attention deficits and other learning problems. Many are designed to be used by kids themselves. 1-800-233-9273.

Brain Gym International (www.braingym.org). Help for kinesthetic learners. The Brain Gym program has been used successfully by parents and teachers to significantly improve learning attitudes and achievement through non-academic means. Visit the Web site to find certified Brain Gym instructors and classes in your area. Brain Gym books and learning materials by Paul E. Dennison and Gail E. Dennison are also available. Organization: 1-800-356-2109. Store: 1-888-388-9898.

Children and Adults with Attention-Deficit/Hyperactivity Disorder (CHADD) (www.chadd.org). Information and support for parents and teachers of children with ADD. 1-800-233-4050. Children and Adults with Attention Deficit Disorder (CHADD).

SOS: Help for Parents (www.sosprograms.com). This program (and book) for parents teaches basic management skills, including how to handle many difficult behaviors and improve the behavior and emotional adjustment of kids ages 2–12. The video is also available in Spanish. 1-800-576-1582.

Homework Goal Chart

NAME: _____ **WEEK OF:** _____

DIRECTIONS: Decide how much time you will spend each day on homework for each subject. Write a fraction in each box you use. The **denominator** (bottom number) is the amount of time you will spend on that subject. The **numerator** (top number) is the number of pages you will read, problems you will work, sentences you will write, and so on in that time period. **EXAMPLE:** If you plan to read 10 pages of a novel in 30 minutes on Monday, write 10/30 in the Reading box for Monday. When the time is up, write your comments in the box at the far right.

$\dfrac{\text{Number}}{\text{Time}}$	Math	Reading	Writing	Other	Comments
Monday					
Tuesday					
Wednesday					
Thursday					
Friday					
Weekend					

Schoolwork Sign-Off Form

Dear Parent or Caregiver:

This form is being sent to you along with a folder of your child's schoolwork. Please complete and sign this form and return it to school by _____ (date). You may keep your child's work at home.

STUDENT'S NAME: _____ **TODAY'S DATE:** _____

Check all statements that are true:

_____ My child explained to me the work he or she brought home.

_____ I noticed something that was done well and complimented my child.

_____ I have questions about my child's schoolwork.

Write your questions here:

If your child had trouble understanding the homework assignment, ask your child to describe the problem here:

Your signature: _____

How to Be a Homework Helper
Tips for Parents and Caregivers

Children who do homework regularly are more likely to succeed in school. This handout describes ways for you to support and encourage your child to accept homework as a fact of life—and get it done!

1. Communicate your belief that homework is an important part of learning. When you show that you're serious about homework, your child will take it more seriously.

2. Make an agreement with your child about how much after-school time he will spend doing homework each day. Guidelines for maximum times:

   - For children in the primary grades (first through third): 15–30 minutes.
   - For children in the upper elementary grades (fourth through sixth): 30–45 minutes.
   - For middle-school students: up to 1 hour.
   - For high-school students: up to 2 hours.

3. Work with your child to establish a homework schedule and do your part to honor it. *Example:* If your child is supposed to do homework from 5:00 to 6:00 each night, don't serve dinner at 5:45.

4. Provide a place where your child can work. It should be comfortable, adequately lit, and free from distractions. Give your child some choices. If she wants to listen to soft instrumental music, sit on the floor, or work in low light, that's okay—as long as she works for the expected amount of time and keeps up with the teacher's expectations. If these conditions are not met, she should do her homework at a table or desk in a quiet place until her work improves. When favorable reports start coming home from the teacher, let your child make choices again about the homework environment.

5. Create a homework kit. Include pencils, rulers, glue, tape, erasers, a dictionary, a thesaurus, etc.—any materials your child needs to do his homework. Keep everything together in a plastic storage bin or tote. Put smaller items in a zippered case.

6. Remember that your child's homework is his responsibility, not yours! You are only responsible for providing a place where he can work and for making sure that he isn't interrupted. Monitor incoming phone calls and don't allow visitors.

7. What if your child forgets her homework? Or what if the teacher doesn't give any homework on a particular day? Your child should use her regularly scheduled homework time to work on some other type of learning activity. *Examples:* looking at a newspaper, reading a book or a magazine, watching a TV program with an educational focus, writing a story, or learning about a topic that interests her.

How to Use the Homework Contract
Guidelines for Parents and Caregivers

The Homework Contract is an effective way to help your child manage homework time. It gives your child immediate positive feedback for accomplishing specific goals. Several copies of a blank contract are included along with this how-to sheet. If you need more copies, just ask!

For the first few contracts, you can sit with your child and make sure he or she understands what to do. After that, the contract is your child's responsibility.

Three Simple Steps

1. The child sets a goal for each time segment. (The blank contract allows for three time segments, but it's okay if your child chooses fewer or more.)

2. Your and your child decide together on rewards he or she will earn after:

  a. working for an entire time segment without complaining, arguing, or procrastinating (5-minute rewards), and

  b. completing all of his or her goals.

3. Whenever the child completes a goal, he or she enjoys a reward.

Recommended Rewards

5-Minute Rewards:

- a healthful treat (juice, fruit, etc.)
- a stretch break
- listening to a favorite song
- a comic book break
- something else your child enjoys doing

All-Goals-Completed Rewards:

- The best reward for children up to adolescence is to spend quality one-on-one-time with you or another parent or caregiver. When this isn't possible, the reward might be to watch a favorite television show or video/DVD.

- For adolescents who don't consider one-on-one time with adults a reward, allow time with friends on the phone or the computer, or time to work on an ongoing project or passionate interest.

> **IMPORTANT:**
> The reward should never be money!

Homework Contract

NAME: _____ **TODAY'S DATE:** _____

How much time I will spend doing homework: _____

My goal for the FIRST time segment: _____

_____

My 5-minute reward for reaching that goal: _____

_____

My goal for the SECOND time segment: _____

_____

My 5-minute reward for reaching that goal: _____

_____

My goal for the THIRD time segment: _____

_____

My 5-minute reward for reaching that goal: _____

_____

My reward if I complete ALL of my goals: _____

_____

STUDENT'S SIGNATURE: _____

How to Handle Homework Problems
Strategies for Parents and Caregivers

PROBLEM: Your child refuses to do his homework.

WHAT TO DO: First, find out if the material is too easy or too difficult for him. If it's too easy, he might be bored and unwilling to work. If it's too hard, it might be impossible for him to do. Ask for a conference with the teacher to request homework that is appropriately challenging without being overwhelming.

PROBLEM: Your child always asks you for help with her homework.

WHAT TO DO: It's okay to spend a small amount of time with your child to clarify the homework directions. But please *don't* tutor or teach your child. You are not responsible for teaching your child what she hasn't learned in school. If your child tries to work on an assignment for a reasonable amount of time but still seems totally perplexed, let her stop working on it. Help her write a note to the teacher explaining the situation and asking for help.

PROBLEM: You know that your child is capable of doing his homework, but he just won't do it.

WHAT TO DO: The best thing you can do is let him experience the consequences of his decision. If he has to stay after school, receive a lower grade, or miss a field trip, that's his problem, not yours. When parents constantly rescue kids from failure, the kids get hooked on their parents' help. Children learn to take responsibility by learning what happens when they avoid responsibility. Help your child by not helping.

PROBLEM: Your child forgets to bring her homework from school.

WHAT TO DO: Once you have established a regular after-school homework time, your child should always use that time to work on *something* related to improving her skills or increasing her learning. Insist that she spend the designated time on some type of learning activity. *Examples:* reading a book; looking over a newspaper; finding examples of parts of speech in books or encyclopedias; making up a shopping list of items from a catalog, given a specific amount of (imaginary) money to spend. CAUTION: Don't make the alternatives to homework too much fun or she might prefer them and keep forgetting her homework—on purpose!

Parent-Teacher
Conference Questionnaire

STUDENT'S NAME: _____

Dear Parent or Caregiver:

Our parent-teacher conference is scheduled for: _____ (date) at _____ (time).
Please take a few moments to answer the following questions and bring the completed questionnaire to
the conference.

1. What are your child's strengths at home? What is he or she really good at doing?

2. What are your child's chores at home?

3. How does your child spend his or her spare time? What are your child's hobbies and interests?

4. What is your child like to live with?

5. What is your child's personality outside of school?

6. What is your child's social life outside of school?

7. How do you and your child handle homework time?

Please list any questions you would like to have answered during our conference:

Please list any concerns you would like to talk over during our conference:

Thank you for taking the time to complete this questionnaire! I look forward to seeing you at
our conference.

TEACHER'S SIGNATURE: _____

Ways to Help Your Child at Home
Tips for Parents and Caregivers

- Try to spend 10–15 minutes of uninterrupted time with your child every day. Give him your complete and undivided attention. Don't talk about school unless he brings it up; instead, talk about things he is interested in. Listen with your ears, your eyes, and your body language, and resist asking questions or giving advice. Use phrases like these to let your child know that you want to know and understand him better:

  "Tell me about . . . ."

  "So, what you are saying is . . . ."

  "It sounds like you are feeling _____ about _____ . . . ."

- If your child has nothing to say during your time together, tell him something positive about your own day.

- If you have a large family, set up a buddy system and encourage children to share information with each other. During dinner, invite everyone to share something positive about their day.

- Monitor your child's TV-watching, computer-using, and video-game-playing time. Restrict or prohibit violent games and programs, including some cartoons. Help your child choose games and programs that educate. Play and watch them together when you can, and ask questions along the way. Encourage kids to ask questions, too. If no one knows the answer to a particular question, the child might be motivated to look it up.

- Help your child develop a skill she is interested in and shows a natural talent for. Excellence in sports, the arts, crafts, volunteer work, or anything else kids feel passionate about can help develop high self-esteem.

- Never imply that your child should somehow be different in order to be a better person or better student. Help him learn how to separate his wonderful self from any problems he may have at school. Praise his positive qualities at every opportunity. *Examples:* What makes your child special? His ability to make people laugh? His singing? His honesty? His talent at drawing? What else can you think of?

- Use words sparingly when giving your child directions. Always demonstrate what you want her to do. Give one direction at a time, never a string of directions all at once. Show what you mean, give an example, and offer positive reinforcement as soon as she completes the task.

- Predictability, consistency, and routines increase children's sense of security. Strive for regular bedtimes and mealtimes. Provide as much structure as possible—chores to do, homework schedules, time spent together.

- Instead of doing things *for* your child, work *with* him on tasks he is learning to do. Coach him to tell you when he no longer needs your help.

How to Help Your Child Become a Better Reader

If your child is very young . . .

- Hold your child in your lap as you look at and read a book she wants to hear. If you don't have books available, use other reading material—greeting cards, catalogs, newspapers, magazines, shopping lists. The more your child sees that print is important, the more likely it is that she will develop a positive attitude about reading.

- Before you read a story to your child, have him look through it and predict what will happen by looking at the pictures and other clues. Stop reading at frequent intervals to ask him to guess or predict what will happen next or what a certain character will do. This helps him to realize that there are many possible ways for stories to end, and that good readers keep guessing as a story progresses.

- Leave off the last word or words of certain phrases or sentences as you read aloud. Your child will learn to anticipate what's coming and supply the missing words. Reinforce this behavior by saying "Isn't reading fun?" or "You are such a good reader!" Even though she isn't really reading, she will feel like a reader and perceive reading as pleasant and positive.

- Right after you finish reading a story, have your child read it to you. Listen eagerly and pay no attention to accuracy! You'll probably notice that your child is mimicking your expression and pacing, and that's exactly what he should be doing. Praise his efforts: "What a good reader you are!" "I love it when you read to me." "I'm so proud of the way you're trying to help yourself learn to read."

For all ages . . .

- Read to and with your child every day. If possible, spend the last 10–15 minutes of each day together sharing a book. It's a great way to get closer and improve your child's reading skills.

- Take regular trips together to the public library. Get your child his own library card. Ask the librarian to show both of you how to use the computers and microfiche machines to find information your child is interested in. You'll both be amazed at how easy it is to find out almost anything once you know where to look.

- Ask your child's teacher to show you how to use whisper reading.

- When your child is reading to you, don't rush in to supply missing words when she hesitates. Give her plenty of time to think of an appropriate word to insert in that spot. It's better for her to guess a word that makes sense than to keep struggling over the right word.

- If your child asks for help while reading, you might say, "Let's look at the picture and see if we can figure out what that word might be." Or "Skip over this word for now and keep on reading until you get to the end of the sentence. Then come back and try to figure it out." Or simply tell him the word. During the early stages of reading development, don't expect your child to sound out every word accurately. This is a struggle and can lead to a negative attitude about reading in general.

How to Help Your Child
Become a Better Writer

- Encourage *all* of your child's writing efforts, accurate or not. Let the teacher worry about the accuracy. Focus on helping him develop a positive attitude about writing.

- Show her how to make her own "Happy Birthday" or "Get Well" cards for relatives. Suggest that she write a few things down in a diary or journal at the end of the day as part of a bedtime routine. Have her keep a "Things-to-Do" or "My Goals" list and update it daily.

- Whenever your child writes something, give it the proper attention. Put it on the refrigerator and praise her efforts: "I'm so proud of you for learning how to write!"

- Call your child's attention to the many times in a day or week when you need writing. *Examples:* sending and receiving communications from family members and people at work; reading and responding to letters and email; making a grocery list; writing out a check.

- Work with your child to write a letter to the editor of your local newspaper. Express your feelings and opinions about an article or event. This demonstrates that writing is a way to communicate thoughts.

- Work with your child to write a letter to a neighbor or relative who would enjoy receiving mail. Ask for a mailed reply addressed to your child.

How to Help Your Child Become Better in Math

- Use playing cards in simple games like War and Go Fish. Show your child how to figure out the value of the cards by counting the spots. Teach her how cards with more spots win over cards with fewer spots. **Tip:** To avoid confusion, remove the picture cards and the aces until she has mastered the cards from 2–10. Then return the other cards to the deck.

- Playing board games is an excellent way to learn about numbers. Have your child count out loud the number of spaces he moves for each turn. Call attention to whose piece is closest to the beginning and end of the game. You might slip in a few addition and subtraction facts while playing.

- Many children can learn math facts more quickly (and remember them longer) when music, rhyme, and rhythm are used to teach them. Make up counting chants together. Set math facts to familiar tunes.

- Encourage your child to notice the numbers in everyday things. *Examples:*

  - Count the items as we put them into the grocery chart.

  - Count the items as you set the table.

  - Count the items as we fold them from the wash.

  - What number comes after 5? Before 4?

  - Count backwards instead of forward from 10 (or 20, etc.).

  - How many wheels are on your toy dump truck? How many are on your bike? Which has more wheels?

  - How old are you? How old is your brother or sister? Who is older? By how many years?

  - How many kids should we invite to your birthday party? How many pieces will we have to cut from the cake? If everyone gets six pieces of candy, how many pieces will we need?

Index

About the Author

Susan Winebrenner has an M.S. in curriculum and instruction and a B.S. in education. A former classroom teacher and gifted-program coordinator, Susan is an internationally recognized leader in the field of gifted education. She is the author of several books and teaching resources, including *Teaching Gifted Kids in Today's Classroom, The Cluster Grouping Handbook,* and *Differentiating Content for Gifted Learners in Grades 6–12.* Through her consulting and workshop business, Education Consulting Service, Susan presents seminars nationally and internationally, helping educators translate education research into classroom practice. She has contributed articles to various educational publications and served at one time on the faculty of New Leaders for New Schools, a national organization dedicated to training and supporting a new generation of outstanding school principals for urban schools. Susan lives in San Marcos, California.

Other Great Books from Free Spirit

The Survival Guide for Kids with ADHD
Updated Edition
by John F. Taylor, Ph.D.
In kid-friendly language and a format that welcomes reluctant and easily distracted readers, this book helps kids know they're not alone and offers practical strategies for taking care of oneself, modifying behavior, enjoying school, having fun, and dealing with doctors, counselors, and medication. For ages 8–12.
128 pp., softcover; 2-color illust., 6" x 9"

The Survival Guide for Kids with LD*
***(Learning Differences)**
Revised & Updated Edition
by Gary Fisher, Ph.D., and Rhoda Cummings, Ed.D.
This edition retains the best of the original: the warmth, affirmation, and solid information kids need to know they're smart and can learn, they just learn differently. It explains what LD means (and doesn't mean); describes the different kinds of LD; talks about what happens in LD programs; helps kids deal with their feelings; suggests ways to get along better in school and at home; and inspires them to set goals and plan for the future. For ages 8 & up.
112 pp.; softcover; illust.; 6" x 9"

The Survival Guide for Kids with Behavior Challenges
How to Make Good Choices and Stay Out of Trouble
Revised & Updated Edition
by Thomas McIntyre, Ph.D. (also known as Dr. Mac)
Kids with behavior challenges find helpful information, practical strategies, and sound advice to help them make smarter choices, make and keep friends, get along with teachers, take responsibility for their actions, work toward positive change, and enjoy the results of better behavior. A special section at the back addresses diagnosed behavior disorders. For ages 9–14.
176 pp.; softcover; illust.; 7" x 9"

How to Talk to an Autistic Kid
by Daniel Stefanski (an autistic kid)
Kids with autism have a hard time communicating, which can be frustrating for autistic kids and for their peers. In this intimate yet practical book, author Daniel Stefanski, a fourteen-year-old boy with autism, helps readers understand why autistic kids act the way they do and offers specific suggestions on how to get along with them. For ages 8 & up.
48 pp.; softcover; 2-color; illust.; 6¾" x 8¼"

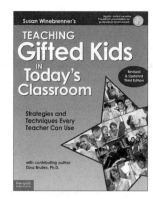

Teaching Gifted Kids in Today's Classroom

Strategies and Techniques Every Teacher Can Use

Revised and Updated Third Edition

by Susan Winebrenner with Dina Brulles

Fully revised and updated for a new generation of educators, this "orange bible" is the definitive guide to meeting the learning needs of gifted students in the mixed-abilities classroom—seamlessly and effectively with minimal preparation time. Included are practical, classroom-tested strategies and step-by-step instructions for how to use them. For teachers, all grades.

256 pp.; softcover; 8½" x 11"; digital content includes reproducible handout masters

Making Differentiation a Habit

How to Ensure Success in Academically Diverse Classrooms

by Diane Heacox, Ed.D.

Framed around critical elements for success in academically diverse environments, this book gives educators specific, user-friendly tools to optimize teaching, learning, and assessment. Following on the heels of Diane Heacox's best-selling teacher resource *Differentiating Instruction in the Regular Classroom*, this book offers new ideas, fresh perspectives, and additional research-based strategies designed to help teachers not only differentiate instruction, but to seamlessly integrate differentiation practices into their daily routines. For teachers and administrators, grades K–12.

192 pp.; softcover; 8½" x 11"; digital content includes reproducible handout masters

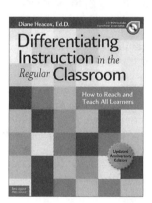

Differentiating Instruction in the Regular Classroom

How to Reach and Teach All Learners

Updated Anniversary Edition

by Diane Heacox, Ed.D.

Differentiation—one of the hottest topics in education today—means changing the pace, level, or kind of instruction in response to learners' needs, styles, and/or interests. In this timely, practical guide, Diane Heacox presents a menu of strategies and tools any teacher can use to differentiate instruction in any curriculum, even a standard or mandated curriculum. Recommended for all teachers committed to reaching and teaching all learners. For teachers, grades K–12.

176 pp.; softcover; 8½" x 11"; digital content includes reproducible handout masters

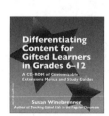

Differentiating Content for Gifted Learners in Grades 6–12 CD-ROM

A CD-ROM of Customizable Extensions Menus and Study Guides

by Susan Winebrenner

More than 140 reproducible forms and templates, plus detailed explanations on how to differentiate instruction for gifted and high-ability learners across a broad range of academic topics: literature, writing, history, social studies, math, science, health, foreign languages, and technology. Unique, timely, and ready to use, this stand-alone CD-ROM is a must-have tool for today's challenging classroom. For teachers, grades 6–12.

CD-ROM; 140+ reproducible handout masters

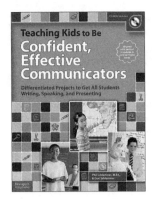

Teaching Kids to Be Confident, Effective Communicators
Differentiated Projects to Get All Students Writing, Speaking, and Presenting
by Phil Schlemmer, M.Ed., and Dori Schlemmer
Build children's proficiency with oral and written communication, promote social and emotional learning (SEL), and allow students to work toward standards while developing critical skills they'll need in later grades. This practical and unique resource presents classroom-tested projects, called "openings," in core curricular areas. Students research topics and present what they have learned to their peers with this kids-teaching-kids approach to differentiated, project-based learning. For teachers, grades K–6.
240 pp.; softcover; 8½" x 11"; digital content includes reproducible handout masters

RTI Success
Proven Tools and Strategies for Schools and Classrooms
by Elizabeth Whitten, Ph.D., Kelli J. Esteves, Ed.D., and Alice Woodrow, Ed.D.
Response to Intervention (RTI) is an innovative instructional method that allows educators to assess and meet the needs of struggling students before they have fallen too far behind. Includes step-by-step guidelines for implementing RTI in schools but goes further; hundreds of pragmatic, research-based instructional strategies allow classroom teachers to target specific skill deficits in their students. Vignettes and school profiles demonstrate RTI techniques in diverse settings, and reproducible forms streamline assessment and documentation procedures. For teachers and administrators, grades K–12.
256 pp.; softcover; 8½" x 11"; digital content includes reproducible handout masters

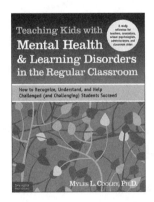

Teaching Kids with Mental Health & Learning Disorders in the Regular Classroom
How to Recognize, Understand, and Help Challenged (and Challenging) Students Succeed
by Myles L. Cooley, Ph.D.
Generalized Anxiety Disorder (GAD). Nonverbal Learning Disability (NVLD). Asperger's Syndrome. Depression. ADHD. How can educators recognize the symptoms, respond appropriately, and meet students' learning needs while preventing or addressing disruptive behaviors? Written by a clinical psychologist, this user-friendly, jargon-free guide describes mental health and learning disorders often observed in school children, explains how each might be exhibited in the classroom, and offers expert suggestions on what to do (and sometimes what not to do). For teachers, special education professionals, school counselors and psychologists, administrators, and teacher aides of all grades.
224 pp., softcover; 8½" x 11"

See It, Be It, Write It
Using Performing Arts to Improve Writing Skills and Test Scores
by Hope Sara Blecher-Sass, Ed.D., and Maryellen Moffitt
Improve students' writing skills and boost their assessment scores with lessons that are aligned to state and Common Core State Standards for English language arts. Students learn how to use acting (early in the year) and visualization (as they progress and when they take tests) as prewriting activities to help them produce lively, personalized responses. Easy-to-use checklists guide students to include specific elements in their writing and to demonstrate skills that are assessed on standardized tests. Add fun while infusing 21st century skills such as critical thinking and problem solving, creativity and innovation, collaboration, and communication. For teachers, grades 3–8.
192 pp., softcover; 8½" x 11"; digital content includes reproducible handout masters

---

Interested in purchasing multiple quantities and receiving volume discounts?
Contact edsales@freespirit.com or call 1.800.735.7323 and ask for Education Sales.

Many Free Spirit authors are available for speaking engagements, workshops, and keynotes.
Contact speakers@freespirit.com or call 1.800.735.7323.

For pricing information, to place an order, or to request a free catalog, contact:

Free Spirit Publishing Inc. • 217 Fifth Avenue North • Suite 200 • Minneapolis, MN 55401-1299
toll-free 800.735.7323 • local 612.338.2068 • fax 612.337.5050 • help4kids@freespirit.com • www.freespirit.com